Wordsworth's PRELUDE

Wordsworth's PRELUDE

A Study of Its Literary Form

By Abbie Findlay Potts

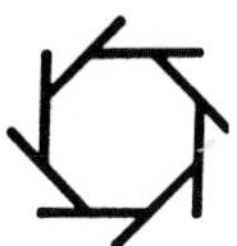

OCTAGON BOOKS

A DIVISION OF FARRAR, STRAUS AND GIROUX

New York 1972

Reprinted 1966
by special arrangement with Cornell University Press

Second Reprinting 1972

OCTAGON BOOKS
A Division of Farrar, Straus & Giroux, Inc.
19 Union Square West
New York, N. Y. 10003

Library of Congress Catalog Card Number: 66-18051

ISBN 0-374-96536-6

Printed in U.S.A. by
NOBLE OFFSET PRINTERS, INC.
New York, N.Y. 10003

This book is inscribed to
the memory of Wordsworth's schoolmaster
William Taylor
1754–1786
Fellow of Emmanuel College, Cambridge
Master of the Free School at Hawkshead

He loved the Poets, and if now alive,
Would have loved me, as one not destitute
Of promise, nor belying the kind hope
That he had form'd, when I at his command,
Began to spin, at first, my toilsome Songs.

The Prelude, MSS AB, X, 511–15

Preface

THIS study has taken form, little by little, during the many years in which Arthur Beatty, Ernest de Selincourt, Helen Darbishire, and Raymond Dexter Havens have notably advanced our knowledge of *The Prelude*. Their interpretation of Wordsworth's doctrine, text, and mind would appear to leave few tasks for others; but there is always fresh occasion for the enjoyment of a poem as part of the fabric of poetry. Belles-lettres are closer to the poet than abstract ideas, even more akin to him than the events of his own life; like Nature they help him to create his 'spots of time.' Were it not too pretentious a title, this book might be called 'The Art of a Poet'; if it reveals anything of Wordsworth's art of poetry, then it should reveal something of the art of every poet.

Among the many instances of good fortune which have come to me of late, I must mention first the kindness of the family of Arthur Beatty, who put his orderly files at my service, and thus permitted me to observe that wise and reverent scholar on his patient way through the philosophy of the eighteenth century. I was the more willing to do this because I was not myself an expert in his field; my book was to be of another kind. I have, however, scrupulously indicated substantial help from him. His bibliographies, which I have shared with Professor Ernest Bernbaum, and his copies of passages from rare books, by shortening my labor, have extended my days.

To Professor Lane Cooper, who suggested in 1918 that I edit Wordsworth's *Ecclesiastical Sonnets*, I have since owed the best of counsel. He has amended some of these chapters in manuscript. For his luminous advice, often followed and rarely disregarded, I here record my thanks. My thanks go as well to Helen Darbishire and George W. Meyer, who have read a major portion of my book with frank and penetrating challenge. This great advantage to my argument in no way implies their approval of my conclusions. Douglas Bush and Northrop Frye have given me valuable notes on Chapters XI and XII. Irene Samuel has helped in the revision of Chapters XII and XIII. The book has been further improved by judicious comment from Edith Batho, Alice Pattee Comparetti, Gilbert T. Dunklin, Frances Eldredge, Katherine Haynes Gatch, Jeremy Ingalls, James Venable Logan, Mary Hatch Marshall, Jane Worthington Smyser, and Ruth Zabriskie Temple. And, in this connection, I am glad also to acknowledge the courtesy, through many years, of Raymond Dexter Havens and Ernest Bernbaum in the field of their own fruitful scholarship.

The leisure to complete this study was made possible by gifts from Ruth Morris Bakwin, from Helen Drew Richardson and others of my colleagues, and from alumnae and students of the centennial year of Rockford College. In the John Hall Sherratt Library at this College I have depended on the hospitality and skill of its librarian, Jean MacNeill Sharpe. An alumna of the College, Janice Chilcott Merson, has put my copy into type.

During the preparation of the text, I have received unfailing consideration from the editors of the Cornell University Press on the campus of my Alma Mater; to them and to Her my grateful acknowledgment. Ruth Morris Bakwin has generously assisted me to bring the book forth; and with her bounty I wish to join in remembrance the courage of my mother, who sat faithfully by me into her ninety-fifth year while the book was written, but could not wait for its publication.

Finally, I must assume that the readers of this book have read

The Prelude of William Wordsworth, and that they will now reread it, preferably in the great edition of Ernest de Selincourt to which my citations refer; and I hope that our common effort to understand the relation between schoolmasters and poets will be of service to our country, which must have more good schoolmasters before it will produce its share of good poets.

ABBIE FINDLAY POTTS

Troy, New York
February, 1953

Contents

Wordsworth's PRELUDE

I

The Prelude: *What Is It?*

Poems, like men and women, seem to us unique when we enjoy them one by one and have no responsibility for them; but when they are brought together they demand attention for what is common in their aspect and behavior. At first we are annoyed. This which we have admired and set apart is only another poem. We also feel an increasing burden of thought upon us; we have come into wearisome relation with all poetry. Scarcely does the common nature of poems make amends to us for their lost singularity until we discover them to be members of a powerful fellowship with a necessary joint purpose. Then, at last, they appear rightly sociable and thus as individuals richer and more delightful. Nor shall we feel perfectly at ease with our one poem in its extended relationships until our own widening knowledge of poems has been likewise organized into an effective and congenial society. Therefore the scholar who interprets poetry must consider its generic attributes, its literary form.

The Prelude of William Wordsworth, a poem on the 'Growth of a Poet's Mind,' is a record of experience through which we all go. Like him we have been youngsters with vacations ahead of us and travel pending. Like him we have toured countries whose soil is still for us, as it was then for him, 'too hot to tread upon.' Like him, chiefly, we have come out of school and college into a world of monstrous war and doubtful peace. In such a world we are also hard put to maintain our imaginative powers unimpaired, or at a loss to restore them after blight and injury. When Wordsworth's record is studied as one of a kind it confirms our own disasters. We begin to trust it. Even the comfort it brings is trustworthy. Within our years of dismay, years in which we recapitulate the old human agony at a cost higher and more insistent with each cycle of years, healing 'spots of time' may yet develop for us, as they did for him.

Again like men and women, poems at their best share their wealth, and provoke new adventure for the common good. That is why we must recapitulate this old art whereby experience is illuminated and transmuted, the art of poetry. Its processes and techniques Wordsworth had revered, investigated, and practiced from his teens into his thirties. He had done this not from the outside and above as pedant and critic, not from below as an amateur aping the fashion, but from within as a lover appropriating what he loved: he memorized poems. In his own poems, and in *The Prelude* above all, poetry is a familiar affair, a common enterprise. If it is to be our affair, too, we cannot ignore the craftsmanship he learned from earlier poets. His mind and art grew very much as theirs had grown; and our minds and art might well grow as his grew.

For these reasons our first question about *The Prelude* concerns its common nature, that something in its matter and form which it shares with other poems: what is *The Prelude?*

When its author called it 'a poem on my own early (earlier) life,' or spoke of the imagination as 'our theme,' [1] he was answer-

[1] *The Early Letters of William and Dorothy Wordsworth*, ed. by Ernest de Selincourt, Oxford, 1935, pp. 370, 386; *The Prelude, or Growth of a Poet's Mind,* by William Wordsworth, edited from the Manuscripts, with Introduction, Textual and Critical Notes, by Ernest de Selincourt, Oxford, 1926, XIII, 185. Unless it is otherwise indicated, I refer to *The Prelude* in the version of 1805–6. This is divided into thirteen books, the tenth of which became the tenth and eleventh of the edition of 1850. Roman numerals are used to designate the Books of *The Prelude* (and of other long poems), e.g., Book XI (XII) means Book XI of MSS AB (1805–6) and Book XII of the edition of 1850.

ing an important question—what is it about?—but he was not answering the question we now ask here. Even when, in the Preface to *The Excursion* (1814), he spoke of his 'preparatory poem' as 'biographical,' as a record in verse of 'the origin and progress of his own powers,' and as an 'ante-chapel' to his unfinished 'gothic church,' *The Recluse*, he was giving us dim suggestions of a poem rather than a clear definition. He left his manuscript for his wife to name; and seemingly he relied on Coleridge and later interpreters to classify it. His gothic church stands without walls, roof, or altar; its nave and transept are a mere human crossroads; but around it and in its ante-chapel we still gather for conversation, discourse, and worship, which is for most of us more 'animating' than classification.

Not that Wordsworth refused to classify poems. In the Preface to the first collected edition of his own poems (1815), he furnished his reader with a very tidy chart of the 'moulds' by which 'the materials of poetry' are cast into 'divers forms':

> First, the Narrative,—including the Epopœia, the Historic Poem, the Tale, the Romance, the Mock-heroic, . . . the metrical Novel.
>
> Secondly, the Dramatic,—consisting of Tragedy, Historic Drama, Comedy, and Masque . . . The Opera may be placed here . . . The characteristic and impassioned Epistle, of which Ovid and Pope have given examples, considered as a species of monodrama, may . . . be placed in this class.
>
> Thirdly, the Lyrical,—containing the Hymn, the Ode, the Elegy, the Song, and the Ballad . . .
>
> Fourthly, the Idyllium,—descriptive chiefly either of the processes and appearances of external nature, as the *Seasons* of Thomson; or of characters, manners, and sentiments, as are Shenstone's *Schoolmistress* [and] *The Cotter's Saturday Night* of Burns . . . or of these in conjunction with the appearances of Nature, as most of the pieces of Theocritus, the *Allegro* and *Penseroso* of Milton, Beattie's *Minstrel*, Goldsmith's *Deserted Village*. The Epitaph, the Inscription, the Sonnet, most of the epistles of poets writing in their own persons, and all loco-descriptive poetry belong to this class.

Fifthly, Didactic,—the principal object of which is direct instruction; as the Poem of Lucretius, the *Georgics* of Virgil, *The Fleece* of Dyer, Mason's *English Garden*, etc.

And, lastly, philosophical Satire, like that of Horace and Juvenal . . .

Out of the three last has been constructed a composite order, of which Young's *Night Thoughts*, and Cowper's *Task*, are excellent examples.

Was *The Prelude* one, several, or all of these? Or was it something new and different? We need not insist on names, on 'moulds,' on external 'forms'; but what was the inner form of *The Prelude*, its quiddity, its essence, its life?

Coleridge, for whom the poem was written and to whom it was first recited in January of 1807, called it a 'Lay,' a 'Lay more than historic,' a 'prophetic Lay,'

> An Orphic song indeed,
> A song divine of high and passionate thoughts
> To their own music chaunted! [2]

This work, says Coleridge, 'makes audible a linkèd lay of Truth,' a 'sweet continuous lay . . . of Truth profound.' In its 'various strain' it is 'a long sustainèd Song.'

No other critic would be so eloquent; and years later when Miss Fenwick mentioned Wordsworth's 'grand autobiographical poem,' [3] she echoed rather the plain speech in the household of which she had become the interpretative member. Her phrase serves most helpfully for succeeding editors and critics. Toward and away from its definite literary classification, the autobiography, Émile Legouis pointed when he referred to *The Prelude*, Wordsworth's 'unique autobiographical poem,' as 'less a narrative than a study of origins, less the history of a man than the

[2] *To William Wordsworth, Composed on the Night after His Recitation of a Poem on the Growth of an Individual Mind.* MS W of Coleridge's poem reads 'An Orphic Tale . . . a Tale divine.'

[3] In a letter of March 28, 1839, cited by de Selincourt, p. xix.

philosophy of a mind.' [4] Arthur Beatty recognized the *Lines . . . on the Wye* as 'the forerunner of *The Prelude*' and called the total writing a 'psychological autobiography.' [5] Herbert Read has observed that in *The Prelude* 'the poet is conceived not merely as William Wordsworth, but as an ideal character progressing towards a state of blessedness.' [6] This view Raymond Dexter Havens modifies as follows: '*The Prelude* is as unprejudiced an account of his development as Wordsworth was able to give.' [7]

Professor Havens' phrase, 'account of . . . development,' denotes the narrative form of the poem not less briefly and simply than Wordsworth's thematic subtitle, 'Growth of a Poet's Mind,' suggests the content of it. Undeniably, the poem written through a period of years records an experience that took place as other narratives do, in time; but this particular 'account' has values other than sequence. To these Professor Havens also directs us, when, calling it 'an autobiography, of a kind,' he distinguishes it from Rousseau's *Confessions* and Wordsworth's own 'Autobiographical Memoranda.' It is 'singularly impersonal'; it exhibits 'a simplification of facts'; it is a 'picture'; it presents 'essential truth'; it has 'an ethical as well as an aesthetic and a biographical purpose.' With Ernest de Selincourt, who detected in the poem 'something of epic structure,' [8] Professor Havens agrees that it has been 'conceived as . . . a kind of philosophic epic'; and in its action of the restless soul seeking and finding rest he discovers a kinship with the ideal action of the *Confessions* of St. Augustine.[9]

Since this recent interpreter of *The Prelude* has fairly stated the case when he says that the poem 'does not follow any one pur-

[4] *La Jeunesse de William Wordsworth*, trans. by J. W. Matthews as *The Early Life of William Wordsworth*, 1897, pp. 11, 14.

[5] *William Wordsworth: His Doctrine and Art in Their Historical Relations*, Madison, 1927, p. 71.

[6] *Wordsworth*, New York, 1931, p. 50.

[7] *The Mind of a Poet*, Baltimore, 1941, p. 286.

[8] *Prelude*, p. xxvii.

[9] *The Mind of a Poet*, pp. 270–87, and p. 2.

pose throughout,' let us have recourse to the early manuscripts themselves, and there, hidden along the generic changes of Wordsworth's 'autobiography, of a kind,' let us seek for its very life.

MS JJ, written at Goslar in 1798–9, is an apostrophe to Nature's 'beings,' an invocation to the 'Soul of things' or 'Eternal Spirit,' and in one instance an address to a 'dearest Maiden.' It has an 'argument,' yet it is a painting, and it is a 'song'; it is an affirmation of belief, a credo; it is a series of memories or 'recollected hours'; and it is a series of episodes in a 'discipline,' a record of the teaching or 'ministry' of 'genii' in a 'school.' [10]

Before MS JJ by a few months only, the poem written near Tintern Abbey on July 13, 1798, exhibits these same generic traits. That, too, is an apostrophe, but to the Wye rather than the Derwent. Although Wordsworth does not yet invoke the joyful 'presence' and the impelling 'spirit,' but addresses himself rather to 'my dear, dear Friend,' or 'my dear, dear Sister,' he has recognized Nature as the important influence in his 'heart' and 'mind.' Further, he is 'painting' and making a 'prayer,' consciously adorning his argument with idyllic and lyric beauty, uttering an impassioned 'belief,' giving outer form to a simple creed. Already, he has taken to good advantage the retrospective attitude that in MS JJ will furnish a series of recollected hours. More important, he is already acknowledging a discipline and thanking a teacher. Most important, he is accepting a 'service,' and as a 'worshipper' he is partaking of a ritual. This mere hint of liturgical quality in his metaphors of 1798 we must not forget as we acknowledge the kinship of the *Lines . . . on the Wye* and MS JJ, the yet

[10] At this point I wish to acknowledge the work done by Deolice Miller, under the direction of Professor David Bishop, and the labors of the late Arthur Beatty and his students in reconstituting early manuscripts of this poem from the edition of 1926 by de Selincourt and de Selincourt's report of MS JJ to the *London Times Literary Supplement* for November 12, 1931. Thanks to the kind offices of both Miss Helen Darbishire and Mr. D. M. Davin of The Clarendon Press, I have permission to quote from the de Selincourt edition of *The Prelude* and *Wordsworth's Poetical Works,* edited by E. de Selincourt and Helen Darbishire.

anomalous 'description of [his] boyish pleasures,' Dorothy's name for the new poem.[11]

MS V, written in 1799 at Sockburn after the return from Goslar, collects these 'boyish pleasures' into a ritual year, through which the poet pursues his theme. The episodes have taken on spiritual significance as 'spots of time'; and they are further adorned with 'fair scenes' and associated with 'walks' or perambulations. The lyrical quality of MS JJ is in MS V enhanced by certain beatitudes: 'Blest be the Babe,' and 'many are the joys of youth,' and 'Oh, what happiness!' Thematic organization is clearer in the forthright statement: 'I have endeavour'd to display the means whereby . . .' The organization in psychological time is emphasized; MS V is both a 'history' of feelings and a 'record' of activities. The various forms of apostrophe, invocation, and address are subordinated to the one valedictory passage for Samuel Taylor Coleridge, the 'Friend.' Yet, over and above the enlargement of the scope of the poem and the widening of its horizons, the main accomplishment of MS V has been the ordering of its inner wealth, those forms

> That yet exist with independent life
> And like their archetypes know no decay.

MS W, the most doctrinal of the early manuscripts of *The Prelude*, was composed in February and March of 1804. The poet's 'wanderings' and 'pleasures' are still seen as 'spots of time'; but these spots of time become illustrations of an educational theory in which they serve as a conscious 'retrospect,' with a 'register' of debts to books and a 'record' of reading. A sketch of the badly educated child confronts a sketch of the maid who 'conversed with things in higher style,' and to these are affixed approving or disapproving comments. Wordsworth does not forget that his poem is still 'a song,' but, like many of his predecessors, he will now enter upon 'abstruser argument'; the history of feelings has become a 'meditative history.' Its 'pleasing argument' will be em-

[11] *Early Letters*, p. 208.

bodied in 'living pictures,' taken from books about Columbus, Sir Humphrey Gilbert, Mungo Park, and William Dampier; yet these bookish *exempla* will later be discarded to make way for the eulogy of great books, 'shrines' before which he himself when a novice has 'made a league and covenant' and for a time 'religiously' preserved a 'vow.'

The pattern of the nature ritual is scrupulously maintained in MS W, and all the seasons of the year have now their illustrative adventures: for instance, to MS V's winter experiences of skating on Esthwaite and the 'expected steeds' at Christmastime Wordsworth adds an account of summer on Snowdon in moonlight, another of autumn at Coniston with storm and rainbow, not used in the final script. Although he includes a dedication, he does not yet amplify it in terms of the 'returning Spring' of his first college vacation at Hawkshead. This, however, must be an almost contemporary passage, and it will finally take its place as Book IV of MSS AB.

The main formal advance in MS W is its 'analogy between the mind of man and nature'; the restorative 'power' of nature as exhibited in the rainbow over the hills and lake of Coniston or the moon above 'the top of Snowdon' resembles a certain 'power' or 'faculty' or 'agency' in the mind of man. Nature indeed calls on Man 'to give new grandeur to her ministry, man suffering or enjoying.' Incidents in the life of the poet are selected and arranged to illustrate, in a cycle of their own, a 'malady' and its 'cure,' an 'impairment' or 'abasement' in his mind and a 'restoration.' Although the language and assumptions of the moralist are still awkwardly present, the poet struggles on toward an imaginative equivalent for natural and moral power. By the ingenious isthmus of diction he crosses from the ethical continent to a kind of aesthetic peninsula. Instead of 'Soul' we now have the 'Imagination of the Whole'; instead of vice, 'the perversion of the [imaginative] power misplaced and misemployed'; instead of wickedness, 'the barren dream of use and habit'; instead of pride, aesthetic 'presumption'; instead of sin, 'malady'; instead of penitence, 'restoration'; instead of virtue, we have 'delight' and 'love.'

Such a linking of virtue and happiness would of course be no new association of ideas to a classical student; [12] but it is characteristic of Wordsworth that the Nature who earlier served him as a schoolmistress appears more and more frequently in his 'argument' as his beloved. Nor is the fruitful relation of the Poet and Nature out of keeping with the mythic fertility of legendary hero and heroine, Sun or Moon in their relation to Earth. What would otherwise be a somewhat arid sermon is changed into the best of sermons, a parable or myth. In all these ways MS W is a kind of metamorphosis, and we are not surprised to have it end with a particular transformation: Wordsworth throws off 'the barren dream of use and habit entirely and forever' and stands again 'in Nature's presence . . . a meditative and creative soul.'

For part of what is now Book V and for almost all of what is now Book VI we have no early manuscripts. The allegory of the shell and the stone, Poetry and geometric Truth, is in keeping with the 'living pictures' of MS W, and with its pattern of 'simply fashion'd tale[s].' The 'pleasures' of MS V are also kept in mind as Wordsworth plans 'a more ambitious strain to tell of later pleasures, link'd to these,' of the 'conscious pleasure' of 'words themselves.' He seems to have dallied with the maze of life as a theater, and himself as a theatergoer; and in the early months of 1804 he has developed the generic pattern of song-idyl-history into a somewhat wider spectacular or monodramatic form. We see him looking at poetry as at 'a never-ending show,' and the 'Visionary Power' in literature is made to appear like the producer of a spectacle, a 'mystery' of 'forms and substances . . . recogniz'd in flashes.' [13] In April of 1804, at the age of thirty-four, he wrote of the ash tree beneath the frosty moon of his sophomore year

[12] Wordsworth's knowledge of Stoic ethics has been ably set forth in *Wordsworth's Reading of Roman Prose,* by Jane Worthington, New Haven, 1946, chap. iii, pp. 43 ff.

[13] *Prelude* V, 177, 558–9, 573–5, 606–7, 619–29.

at Cambridge as a Spenserian 'vision'; the 'clear Synthesis' of geometric abstractions had a delight for him like 'a plaything, or a toy embodied to the sense.' 'Through some window's open space' or 'on the Turret's head' of the monastic Castle of Emont with Dorothy, William 'look'd abroad' or 'lay listening' in 1788; not much later Coleridge, the 'liveried Schoolboy' of Christ's, lay on its 'leaded Roof' to 'gaze upon the clouds moving in Heaven': both were spectators at a show, not novices in a discipline. Although a late revision of Book VI speaks of Jones and Wordsworth in 1790 as slighting 'academic cares . . . near the close of [their] Novitiate,' their pilgrimage to France, Italy, and Switzerland is represented rather as a panorama than as a worship: 'enchanting show.' 'Evening Meal' and dancing in a ring are yet more important than 'Monastery Bells,' 'Spire,' and the 'Convent of Chartreuse.' At present the poet has been 'seduce[d]' into 'a record of wanderings.' [14] What the 'two brother Pilgrims' see is portrayed as if read in a book, until, with the crossing of the Alps, it receives in Wordsworth's mind the form of an authentic apocalyptic vision, and

> the light of sense
> Goes out in flashes that have shewn to us
> The invisible world.

Yet this, too, is a kind of show.

Whether or not he was helped out of this merely spectacular pattern by the images of the Chartreuse and the religious significance of Alpine scenery, Wordsworth did not long put off a reconsideration of the disciplinary and liturgical possibilities attempted in MSS JJ, V, and W;

> on the front
> Of this whole Song is written that my heart
> Must in such temple needs have offer'd up
> A different worship.[15]

[14] *Ibid.* VI, 104–9, 135–87, 229–31, 276–80, 387, 402, 415, 659–60; and pp. 188, 194–8.

[15] *Ibid.*, 534–6, 669–72.

MSS W, X, and Y are written in notebooks said by de Selincourt to be 'similar.' Whether MS X was composed before MS Y, at the same time, or afterward, it sets forth, in passages later to become Book VII of *The Prelude* and parts of *The Excursion*, the idea of the city as a particularly difficult center of poetic or redemptive effort. While we listen to a 'homely tale' of rustic life told by one who inhabited a 'little cell' or 'little sanctuary' in a 'lonely dale,' and learn of the rescue of a 'homeless Pensioner,' we are unexpectedly presented with an apocalyptic spectacle; on mists and storm clouds appears a 'mighty City,' 'the revealed abode of Spirits in beatitude,' one of those sights 'such as by Hebrew Prophets were beheld in vision.' [16] This apocalypse toward the beginning of the manuscript and the antimasque of blank confusion at its end in St. Bartholomew's Fair enclose a description of London in which two metaphors compete for the poet's attention. Shall he present city life as a pageant or show, or shall he defer to the pattern of ritual and liturgy already important to MSS V and W and present it as a religious ordeal?

At first, and on the one hand, all aspects of London—possibly we might say all the different Londons now to be read of in Book VII—constitute a pageant in the mind of the poet: fancied 'sights and shows, processions, equipages'; 'pageant fireworks' at Vauxhall and Ranelagh; 'the real scene'; all the dramatis personae who traverse it; the 'Spectacles within doors' and 'mimic sights' of the 'Painter' and 'mechanic Artist'; 'exhibitions . . . of wider scope' at Sadler's Wells,

where living men,
Music, and shifting pantomimic scenes,
Together join'd their multifarious aid
To heighten the allurement.

In 'dramas of living Men' and Shakespearean revivals Wordsworth discovers new significance only when, through their 'gross realities,' he recognizes the 'real grandeur' of 'the poet's beauteous

[16] Now to be read in *Excursion* II, 741 ff., especially 831–76.

world.' Passing 'from entertainments that are such' to the Court drama of lawyers, and 'that great Stage' of Parliament 'where Senators . . . perform,' he goes on to 'other public shows . . . of a kind more light, and where but in the holy Church?'

And hence we must also review MS X for its liturgical implications. In a hidden metaphor he has 'threaded' his 'string of figures . . . an Indian toy of many coloured beads'—beads which we, too, have told as the processions and pageants came and went. Standing in the gutter with him we contemplate the figure of the prostitute, that 'Human Form' divorced from 'humanity.' This schism is our dilemma, too, nor can we disregard it as text for an *exemplum* or homily:

> that in society . . .
> There are no gaps, that whatsoever shape
> It may put on, a breathing object is
> No statue and doth momently send forth
> Her respirations to be blown about
> At random by the universal air.

Look! here, like a Madonna, comes Mary the Maid of Buttermere with her Babe, and shadowing them, like devils in an old Hell's Mouth, their counterparts, the 'painted' Mother and her 'lovely Boy . . . among the wretched and the falsely gay, . . . begirt . . . with dissolute men and shameless women.' 'The face of every one that passes by' us is 'a mystery' in a 'second-sight procession'; and there 'unmoving' amid 'the moving pageant'—*Ecce homo!*—we have seen the shape of a blind beggar,

> who, with upright face,
> Stood propp'd against a Wall, upon his Chest
> Wearing a written paper, to explain
> The story of the Man, and who he was.

What, then, is the literary meaning and value of MS X? Is it not that again we find ourselves at the crossroads of the old medieval town? Out from the ecclesiastical or industrial center of that town comes the great procession on its pageant cars, bearing the story of mankind in its noblest mythic form. Although the cycle is now burdened with crude properties and grotesque personae, we note that Lucifer has again fallen, and that Eve, the tempted woman, and Mary, the unmarried mother, face each other again. Before Wordsworth's inner eye, and ours, the prophets make their way, describe their visions; the shepherds watch over or neglect their sheep; the magi—lawyers, statesmen, and men of God in eighteenth-century England—work their wisdom or their magic; innocents are slaughtered; and finally, gaping at our own enormous martyrdom, we join the townsfolk of the eighteenth century in the place 'where Martyrs suffer'd in past time, and named of St. Bartholomew.'

Although it is presented as a story, not represented as a miracle or saint's play, within itself MS X carries the pattern of the mystery cycle of the late middle ages, partly ecclesiastical, partly processional, wholly mythic. Like the mystery cycle it leads us away from the historical Church only to remind us of the Church Universal.

We are not surprised, therefore, to learn that the nearly contemporary manuscript, MS Y, begins as a series of functional and representative *characters*,[17] whose personae are 'Fellow-beings' conceived as taking part in a human 'service' not unlike the ritual year of the historical Church. The Patriot, Beaupuy, serves as in 'a religious Order'; Wordsworth is summoned back to his poetic task by a glowworm shining like 'a Hermit's taper,' and by the minstrelsy of 'a Quire of Redbreasts.' The 'Minstrel' or 'obscure Itinerant' of MS Y associates with baronial or royal courtiers, is 'cheered with gifts munificent,' meets now an 'armed knight' and now a 'pilgrim,'

> beneath an abbey's roof
> One evening sumptuously lodged; the next,
> Humbly in a religious hospital;

[17] This word, in italics, will be used throughout to indicate descriptions, particular or general, of a person or group of persons.

Or with some merry outlaws of the wood;
Or haply shrouded in a hermit's cell.

Wordsworth himself is such a minstrel. And Raisley Calvert is such a hospitaler, who,

in his last decay
From his own Family withdrawing part
Of no redundant Patrimony,

by his bequest enabled the poet 'to pause for choice, and walk at large and unrestrain'd.' The chivalric and quasi-religious *characters* of Beaupuy and Calvert, however, lead to the supreme redemptive *character* of the shepherd. Of him is told a tale of rescue, which does not appear in the edition of 1850.[18] His pastoral office, situation, and appearance set him

Above all height! like an aerial Cross,
As it is stationed on some spiry Rock
Of the Chartreuse, for worship.

The long description in MS Y of the Child, a novice learning a way of life as if he were a 'sequester'd . . . monk or priest' bound to the 'altar' of Nature, deserves a paragraph by itself. It never became part of *The Prelude* and can now be read only in de Selincourt's notes.[19] Throughout, it represents natural appearances, both familiar and alien, in the guise of religious symbols, 'ponder'd as a miracle.' Words

By frequent repetition take the place
Of theories, repeated till faith grows
Through acquiescence, and the name of God
Stands fixed a keystone of the mighty arch.

Then, in 'the season of his second birth,' the novice makes 'a redemption of himself.' Not only does he appropriate 'the vast universe . . . by right of spiritual sovereignty,' but in other sym-

[18] 'The Matron's Tale,' copied in from MS J, 1800, contemporary with *Michael*, and like that poem related to Biblical and Miltonic situations of similar redemptive kind.

[19] Pp. 550–9.

bols (path, taper, smoke, sunbeam, garden, churchyard, church bell, roaring ocean, and waste wilderness) he comes to revere 'the mild humanities' of social life, those which have nourished in his heart 'its tender sympathies,' and which constitute 'one [human] service.'

Behind the various interpretations of pastoral life in MS Y and behind this account of the probationer, we recognize an age-old literary species associated with all traditions of the holy life: the *regula* or rule. Moreover, although the poem remains as hitherto a 'story,' a 'biographic Verse,' its episodes have become more and more strongly tinged with the communal metaphors of the Universal Church; the 'deformities' of life pursue us 'into the Temple and the Temple's heart.' Once there, we partake of a communion indeed: 'Tillers of the Soil,' 'Ploughman,' 'Men and Boys . . . with the rake,' 'Old Men and Ruddy Maids, and Little Ones,' Quarryman, Fishermen, and Miner. About us we observe certain representative figures: like Dame Poverty the 'hunger-bitten Girl,' and the 'Artificer' with the ailing Child upon his knees, like a Wordsworthian *pietà*.

We attend to the service, the very working of the poetic faculty. In it we note the perils that accompany the poetic or image-making process: its 'fictions,' its possible sentimentality, its 'wild obliquities,' its 'wilful fancy,' the 'adulterate power' and 'vagaries' into which poetry is sometimes betrayed. When rightly viewed, Wordsworth tells us, this creative process should be a sacrament, an association with 'Godhead,' a 'union or communion,' a rest 'with God.' Thus considered, MS Y is not only a *regula;* it celebrates that experience whereby the poetic life is constantly renewed, and therefore as one mode of human participation in divine life it shares the generic nature of the Eucharist.

But the strongly personal quality of Wordsworth's imagination weighs against a completely liturgical metaphor; he is nostalgic for 'Pathways,' 'lonely Roads,' 'strange fields and groves,' the 'public road,' the 'Mariner,' the 'strolling Bedlamites.' He must set forth a more catholic kind of worship; the 'unity of man' must

be illustrated in his 'great city' and in his 'rural neighborhood' as well as in the 'Temple.' Therefore the poet reconceives the communicants as 'men within themselves,' man as a 'mountain-Chapel,' and human contemplations, however mute, as a 'high service . . . perform'd within.' Of these he will sing a 'Song' which shall teach, inspire, enrapture. Its theme shall be 'the very heart of man.' Not a 'dream,' this, but 'things oracular'!

Anon I rose
As if on wings, and saw beneath me stretch'd
Vast prospect of the world which I had been
And was; and hence this Song, which like a lark
I have protracted, in the unwearied Heavens
Singing, and often with more plaintive voice
Attempered to the sorrows of the earth;
Yet centring all in love, and in the end
All gratulant if rightly understood.

This recessional passage of MS Y is an organic part of the liturgical pattern; it ends a poem that has maintained its generic homogeneity from 'boyish pleasures' to manly worship. For the most part it is now to be read in Book VIII of *The Prelude*, 'Love of Nature Leading to Love of Mankind'; but from Book VIII the initial liturgical or religious constituents have been omitted, or, when scattered and reorganized, have disseminated their power elsewhere. By the early autumn of 1804, however, Wordsworth's poem had taken on its ultimate philosophical and imaginative form. In MS Y he had interpreted human life as itself universal and, when rightly lived, poetic. Through worshipful love it appears to him susceptible of the highest kind of beauty, well-nigh divine. This is a *religio poetae*.

MSS AB, to be read with revisions in the 1805–6 text of *The Prelude*, edited by the late Ernest de Selincourt, maintains most of these generic associations, but they are less in focus now than formerly. 'The holy life of music and of verse,' the allusions to 'prophecy,' to 'priestly robe,' to 'holy services' dimly recall the

attempted and discarded ecclesiasticism of MS Y. 'Aeolian visitations' and the poet's soul as a 'harp' intensify the lyric quality of Book I; but the search for a 'noble theme' has been at last successful. The forms of 'Tale' and 'story' apparently have prevailed over more elaborate patterns of ritual and liturgy; this autobiography has epic possibilities. The various devices of address and description are not discarded; and the course of the poem often veers into byways of idyl and beatitude; but reading Book II currently we discover that the poet is preparing for an action. Book III is a 'dream' or 'vision' of education through which, nevertheless, we still hear of a 'heroic argument,' and see a 'novel show,' and are spectators of an 'opening act.' Book IV, the spring episode of the ritual year, with its 'swellings of the spirit,' its dedication, and its human blessing, points ahead to other than a nature cycle. Book V, containing the myth or parable of the stone and the shell, reminds us of themes and devices of Plato and of Jesus, and hence of wider philosophic relationships and more heroic actions; its record of books is one of the freshest of those lists of things, and people, and events of which literature itself is only a complicated form. Book VI, in part a 'progress,' or 'travel,' in the mode of Goldsmith, also furnishes us, in the mode of Young, with a new kind of visionary delight, an aesthetic apocalypse at the crossing of the Alps, to be followed by other stirring revelations in the developing action.

But right here at the center of his poem, in Books VII and VIII, Wordsworth faces one crux of his imaginative and literary life: will he reside or will he go on? Is he to be the poet of quiet 'spots of time,' or of events in the active world of time and space? The titles 'Residence at Cambridge,' 'Residence in London,' 'Residence in France,' all suggest the operation of a mind happily settling itself on the countryside of poetry; Book VII, 'Residence in London,' adds one very successful new item to the long list of English loco-descriptive poems, like some of them actual, like others of them visionary or Utopian; and Book VIII, based for the most part on MS Y, and entitled 'Retrospect,' places our poet on the

familiar old specular mount and in the familiar old gothic cathedral. Were it not for some great impetus given to his latent love of wandering and adventure, we should have lacked what became Books IX, X, and XI. As it is, under the misleading title, 'Residence in France,' we may include for the crown of our generic list the inner form of an epic poem or monodrama. Postponing any discussion of the reasons for this, let us set forth these three books as an action, and let us then estimate some of its constituents.

In the 'argument' that awaits him, the preservation of himself as a poet amid the personal and civic turmoil of a revolution, he had passed

> Into a theatre, of which the stage
> Was busy with an action far advanced.

Although the French Revolution is not his action, he is seen entangled in it, becomes a 'Patriot'; little by little his fancy, filled with 'fair forms' from 'the Historian's Tale,' his thought and moral feelings 'tutor'd' by Nature, are focused upon and receive direction from Michel Beaupuy.

Now Beaupuy, who becomes as it were the second agent of Wordsworth's monodramatic action, is the poet of affairs, a kind of happy warrior in blank verse,

> One devoted, one whom circumstance
> Hath call'd upon to embody his deep sense
> In action, give it outwardly a shape,
> And that of benediction to the world.

Their 'earnest dialogues' and 'heart-bracing colloquies' are interrupted by nostalgic memories of a literary past: Angelica and Erminia and Pastorella; the 'matin Bell,' 'the evening Taper,' and 'the Cross.' But these symbols of the 'chivalric' and ecclesiastical tradition lose their power before the sight of 'a hunger-bitten girl' (transferred from MS X). ' 'Tis against *that* which we are fighting,' says Beaupuy 'in agitation.' And Wordsworth, 'youthful Patriot,' shares his friend's civic fervor and noble purpose, and for the time agrees with his revolutionary procedure.

Then he confronts the *character* of Beaupuy with the 'tragic tale' of Vaudracour and Julia. Although Vaudracour is not an agent in Wordsworth's action as Poet, he illustrates the merely romantic hero, absorbed in personal concerns exclusively, deaf to 'the voice of Freedom,' unable to rise out of his own errors and disasters. The liabilities of any noble 'Youth' similarly involved with others in a mistaken course of domestic action—witness Wordsworth himself—are more than casually portrayed.

Between these two examples of partial and ineffective dealing, the revolutionary and the romantic, Wordsworth seems to place his Poet. What part can the Poet play to alleviate domestic distress and resist civic tyranny?

Somewhat awkwardly, to be sure, and under several different metaphors, Wordsworth conducts for his Poet an ordeal similar to that in Book III of *Paradise Regained.* As hero in the epic of the imagination the Poet is tempted to renounce his career for a political entanglement. Or—and this is the other horn of his poetic dilemma—will he be unfitted for 'public hope' and waste his days, as did Vaudracour, in a predicament arising out of his personal errors and disasters? Without prejudice to the ties of either patriot or lover, we observe that, again like Milton's hero, Wordsworth chooses a way of life including both devotion to country and love of home. The Poet has a deed to do beyond personal disaster or triumph, beyond civic disaster or triumph. This action is for him more real than either, and obligates him more profoundly.

And what, then, is the poetic action proper, as distinguished from, but not disjoined from, the civic and domestic actions? Discovering anew in Book X that

> Year follows year, the tide returns again,
> Day follows day, all things have second birth,

he realizes that no expedient or temporizing solution is called for. Occasional reference to the Old and New Testaments indicates that the personal crisis in the mind of Wordsworth's Poet as well as the political crisis in France are both now thought of in terms of the action Milton adapted from the Bible, even of that cycle of religious events celebrated by the Universal Church as the necessary ordeal of Mankind Itself.

This religious action is at the center of both medieval liturgy and modern drama. How will Wordsworth deal with it in his narrative blank verse?

Briefly, he places at the center of the plot of Books IX, X (XI), and XI (XII) the choices of the main agent. Like the indecision of good men when Louvet denounced Robespierre, his own indecision is emphasized: revolutionary or poet? His ordeal must be no slight intellectual matter; he has been 'moved,' has 'felt most deeply,' has been 'greatly agitated.' At high cost he first chooses to return to England and continue poet. Whether or not we agree with this particular decision, let us not misunderstand his dilemma.

Then comes the Aristotelian change of fortune, the Wordsworthian 'change and subversion.' His 'beloved country' declares war on the French Republic. His ordeal is now intensified; in this dilemma shall he turn vengeful partisan or remain loving poet? He turns vengeful partisan. The 'ill requiem' of the sunset cannon for the British Fleet near the Isle of Wight is heard with 'spirit overcast'; 'unhappy counsel' in England and 'atrocities' in France bring him in his dreams before 'unjust Tribunals,' and he is made to acknowledge 'treachery and desertion' in his 'own soul.' Since the action is the preservation of Wordsworth as a poet, the despair, hatred, and hope of vengeance he has been indulging betoken an unpoetic choice.

Book X, indeed, is a kind of Jeremiad, pointing out the 'strange reverse' from the 'blameless spectacle' of 1790 when Jones and Wordsworth, 'youthful pilgrims,' partook of 'the glad time' of early revolution in the Town of Arras, birthplace of an infamous son, Maximilian Robespierre; but Book X has also a second and happier 'change.' The 'fulgent spectacle' over 'the smooth Sands of Leven's ample Aestuary' at the news that Robespierre is dead reminds Wordsworth that he has been born and bred a poet—whence his elegiac tribute to William Taylor, who taught him to love the poets. Nor is the reference to the Masses said in ancient times at the 'Romish Chapel' on the rocky island above the sands and ebbing tide and variegated crowd a mere descriptive item; it is a literary device to remind us, as it did Wordsworth, of the life above time and of the long human ordeal that has accompanied the spiritual struggle. Appropriately, this episode ends with a hymn; but it is a hymn still too much tinged with 'joy in vengeance' and accidental 'triumph.' The ordeal is not yet concluded; the Poet still confounds this fortuitous victory in the realm of events with one 'far higher and more difficult,' 'triumphs of unambitious peace at home and noiseless fortitude.'

The next change of fortune follows upon an ironic bit of special pleading, what students of Aristotle would recognize as *dianoia*, an attempt to magnify or minify some aspect of the persuasive argument. English 'shepherds' are blamed in part for Wordsworth's errors; but the 'ascent' and 'fall' of man in his own soul is still not understood. The Poet is 'lodged only at the Sanctuary's door, not safe within its bosom,' and he must return yet again to his 'own history.' In his 'noviciate' his 'paradise' has been only a paradise of dreams; now his 'Utopia' has indeed become 'the very world.' Many of his previous discoveries are seen to be false, though unintentional fallacies, Aristotle's fifth form of discovery. Events do not, it now appears, always prove assumed principles; the French have 'become oppressors in their turn.'

Not yet completely aware that he himself has been the 'false Prophet,' he makes another bad choice, attempting to 'accomplish' his 'transition' into a 'higher nature' 'by such means as [do] not lie in nature,' by 'a work of false imagination.' Seeking the 'ground,' and the 'rule,' and the 'sanction' of 'moral obligation,' he turns aside 'from Nature'; he demands '*proof*.' [20] And as a last bad choice he abandons 'moral questions' for 'mathematics.' Mathe-

[20] Wordsworth's italics.

maticians and logicians will agree that this is not a bad choice in itself; but Wordsworth's was a poetical, not a mathematical or logical, action.

Three other agents, Coleridge, Dorothy, and Nature's Self, then enter the action as redeemers. The 'feelings of [his] earlier life' are 'revived,' and the Poet's renewed 'strength and knowledge full of peace' uphold him through the Napoleonic 'catastrophe.' He reminds himself that

> there is
> One great Society alone on earth,
> The noble Living and the noble Dead,

and ends Book X with an invocation for Coleridge lingering by Arethuse:

> Oh! wrap him in your Shades, ye Giant Woods
> On Etna's side, and thou, O flowery Vale
> Of Enna! is there not some nook of thine,
> From the first playtime of the infant earth
> Kept sacred to restorative delight?

Although the shift from Christian to pagan imagery is unexpected, it makes way for the return of the poem to the nature ritual characteristic of the earlier books. *The Prelude* began as a 'Song'; it will end as a 'Song.' 'Spring returns.' *The Prelude* began as a series of 'recollected hours'; it ends as a history of 'intellectual power . . . advancing, hand in hand with love and joy.' The Poet now recognizes those 'mysteries of Passion' which make

> One brotherhood of all the human race
> Through all the habitations of past years
> And those to come.

He turns toward

> the laws of things which lie
> Beyond the reach of human will or power;
> The life of nature, by the God of love
> Inspired, celestial presence ever pure.

He renounces all idolatrous fancies for true poetry. This is the reversal.

Like the 'one greater man' of *Paradise Regained*, the 'Poet' of *The Prelude* has faced a constantly more subtle series of temptations. Unlike Milton's hero he must depend somewhat on others to resist and overcome them; yet he himself has endured the ordeal necessary for his restoration. Thus, in his representative nature as Poet he has illustrated for all men the perils threatening the poetic or imaginative life. After the 'test of such a trial' he is 'moderated' and 'composed.' His 'meditations,' here contrasted with false and arrogant persuasions, which have deceived him, are now humbled to a communion with 'lowly men.'

Although he disentangles himself slowly from this epic or monodramatic action with its exacting ordeal, Wordsworth's 'Record of myself,' his 'history' of a poet's mind, is primarily and ultimately a less rigorous matter. In the final beatitude Coleridge and Wordsworth, 'joint-labourers in a work . . . of redemption,' are 'Prophets of Nature' rather than protagonists in revolution. They are to 'be bless'd with true happiness' because they can 'love' and 'teach.'

What Is It Like?

Of the various questions asked about literature, the one least frequently answered by scholars is the one most frequently raised by the Poet: what is it like? Not the quiddity of a poem or its quality, not its matter or its manner, not even the circumstances of its genesis or its avowed aim, is more fruitful knowledge for the prospective writer than its similitude and dissimilitude. Metaphor is the very habit of the poetic mind: *this* is like *that;* or, *this* is *not* like *that*. Once aware of correspondences, the young poet needs no longer think of his poem as a lonely fact or of other poems as outworn stereotypes; nor will he try so hard to be different. There is a kinship among poems; they have all one face *sub specie aeternitatis*. Recognizing this, the novice will acknowledge his poetic kindred gladly, and with their help he will gratefully accomplish his own identity, his unique imaginative life: a *nova progenies.*

So was it in the growth of a poet's mind when that poet was William Wordsworth. Along with the principle of association in the early manuscripts of *The Prelude* [21] there are references to 'first-born affinities' and 'feelings . . . analogous' to other feelings. *These* are like *those*, he seems often to say. There is a

> sense of dim similitude which links
> Our mortal feelings with external forms.
> . . . Nor should this, perchance,
> Pass unrecorded, that I still had lov'd
> The exercise and produce of a toil
> Than analytic industry to me
> More pleasing, and whose character I deem
> Is more poetic as resembling more
> Creative agency. I mean to speak
> Of that interminable building rear'd
> By observation of affinities
> In objects where no brotherhood exists
> To common minds.[22]

To this poet, then, from his seventeenth year onward, and in his study of books as well as of nature and man, the question here posed would not have seemed an alien or impertinent challenge; nor need it seem so to us. Placing *The Prelude* side by side with the poems that Wordsworth studied in school and in college, we, too, may call upon our powers of observation to discover that *this* is like *that*. Similar to other narratives in its action and in its agents, in its codes, compacts, ordeal, discoveries and reversal; comparable with other *characters* in the choices, thought, and diction of its persons; familiar and yet distinct to the ear and eye in its rhythm and imagery: thus matched and harmonized and framed, *The Prelude* will better hold its own among its kin, both in the 'prog-

[21] The interweaving of the passions with high objects (MS JJ), the quaint associations of collateral objects and appearances (MS V), and the collateral attachment of Nature's forms to schemes of holiday delight (MS V).

[22] MS V. Cf. de Selincourt's edition, pp. 564, 60–2.

ress' of English 'poesy,' and at home in the 'interminable building' of poetry itself.

Nor is this a study to prove mere indebtedness or to suggest casual influence. Wordsworth himself has acknowledged his enjoyment of and gratitude for the poetry of Pope, Beattie, Gray, and Collins, of Thomson and Goldsmith, of classical writers, of Edward Young and Mark Akenside and William Cowper, of his four great predecessors in English verse, Chaucer, Spenser, Shakespeare, and Milton, and of a notable group of Elizabethan, Jacobean, and Caroline minor versifiers, prose writers, and preachers. The reiteration of such matters leads nowhere, however, unless we re-examine the creative processes that follow upon the literary gift. Nor shall we profit much from similarity in diction alone, placing side by side phrases indicating superficial association between this poem and that.

With due caution, lest we fall into Polonius's willingness to compare the incomparable cloud with all manner of fantastic shapes, let us, then, say frankly, and illustrate by a somewhat more dynamic investigation of plots and purposes than is usual, that *The Prelude* is very like many markedly different English poems. In its lyric and idyllic quality it is like Beattie's *Minstrel*, Thomson's *Castle of Indolence*, and Gray's *Bard*. More and more, while Wordsworth reshapes it into a nature ritual, it grows to be like Thomson's *Seasons*. When it reaches its apocalyptic episodes, it is akin to Young's *Night Thoughts*. And when its author works out its action, he has help from the *Pilgrim's Progress* of John Bunyan.

More specifically, William Wordsworth, historian of infancy, childhood, and 'boyish pleasures,' in his Books I and II takes over an aesthetic task from the unfinished Book IV of the *Pleasures of the Imagination* of Dr. Mark Akenside, physician, and student of growing bodies and minds. Book III of *The Prelude* is like Pope's *Dunciad*, Book IV; and Book VI of *The Prelude* refers in its itinerary to Goldsmith's *Traveller*. As he grows into and up through his roles of lover, friend, and holy man, William Wordsworth, main character in *The Prelude* as a *character*, is brother to William Habington, lover, friend, and holy man: *The Prelude* is like *Castara*.

In the mature experiences of its poet, too, *The Prelude* may be likened to its greatest English predecessors. It is a spousal verse celebrating the mutual love of Poet and Nature; it recalls the spousal verse of Edmund Spenser, studied for the structure of the *Ode: Intimations of Immortality*.[23] It is also an ethical romance, the ordeal of an eighteenth-century knight of poesy, and as such has been conceived in the temper of Spenser's Red Cross Knight, who was not less painfully deceived by what is unholy—unpoetic. With Milton's *Paradise Lost* and *Paradise Regained* we may compare not only 'Despondency' and 'Despondency Corrected' of Books III and IV of Wordsworth's *Excursion*, but 'Imagination How Impaired and Restored,' Books XI and XII of MSS AB of his *Prelude*. And, notably, those who remember the trumpet call of Milton's sonnets and prose will acknowledge Miltonic echoes in the action of the patriot of Books IX and X of *The Prelude*.

For a prior likeness, however, we must reach still further. Although this poem differs in style from the georgics of Virgil and the eclogues of Theocritus, it, too, celebrates the cultural and pastoral life. It is also an old theory of poetry, substantially in agreement with the discourses written on that subject by Horace, Aristotle, and Plato. It bears little external resemblance to the epics of Virgil and Homer; and yet, as they do, it deals with the professional career of the hero. The warrior has made way for the poet, to be sure; but their mistakes, their wanderings, their conflicts, their arrivals and their victories are in many respects comparable. Like all these classical forerunners *The Prelude* derives from firsthand experience of human fortunes and destiny. In the words of Aristotle οὗτος ἐκεῖνος: Wordsworth's Poet is very man

[23] Cf. Abbie F. Potts, 'The Spenserian and Miltonic Influence in Wordsworth's "Ode" and "Rainbow,"' *Studies in Philology* 29 (October, 1932), 607–16.

himself, presented not explicitly, as in a Horatian epistle or an Aristotelian treatise, but with a persuasive likeness for all men. And, functionally considered, there is nothing quite comparable with Wordsworth's poem until, looking backward, we come upon the *προοίμιον* or 'prelude' described in the Platonic *Laws*, the kind of tuneful discourse that prepares us for obedience to law. Thus it is that *The Prelude* sings itself into the heart.

These are large assertions and we must support them concretely as we take our way through one poet's varied heritage toward his single work of art. What he brought so patiently into order and focus reminds us of other records of the operation of Christian love. Yet Wordsworth saw darkly through the fervent and sanctimonious *Night Thoughts* of Edward Young, and the bland *Sermons* of William Fleetwood,[24] even the schematic progress of Bunyan's Pilgrim. His Poet must grow otherwise; and when, with Chaucer's help, he caught a glimpse of the medieval Church, its intenser holiness, its franker wisdom, its more substantial joy, he recognized the value, for his own 'general and operative' truth, of the Christian premise of universal and inclusive life. Witness the two Chaucerian tales he modernized in 1801. The devout little child of the Prioresse and the impassioned but reckless singer and archer of the Manciple play their part in the poetic character as Wordsworth delineates it for us in *The Prelude*. Chaucer's prosaic Parson, disregarded by many readers of his *Canterbury Tales*, tells a story of sin and penitence comparable with Wordsworth's account of impairment and restoration.

But we may not stop even with the legends and homilies of the medieval Church and their echoes in the art of Chaucer. Students of *The Prelude* are on their way back to the more fruitful life of early Christianity and the more animating parables of Jesus himself. This, I take it, is the consummate likeness of *The Prelude* as of Wordsworth's other pronouncements in the service of poetry.

[24] Cf. Abbie F. Potts, 'Wordsworth and William Fleetwood's "Sermons,"' *Studies in Philology* 26 (October, 1929), 444–56.

The acorn and primrose flower; shepherd's boat and dog and schoolboy's skates; crosses-and-ciphers; loquacious clock; rough terrier of the hills

> and that single Wren
> Which one day sang so sweetly in the Nave
> Of the old Church:

these are in their time as real as farthing and talent and sparrow were real to the contemporaries of Jesus, as real as the salt, the candle, and the bushel were real, as real as leaven was real. Further, they were used by both artists similarly, as properties of real life, not for literary adornment but for poetic use. Wordsworth shared the conviction that the Kingdom of Heaven is at hand. *The Prelude* is a gospel of a sort in the tradition of divine life, poetic life, as it may be lived just where we are, by our very selves.

The Prelude will not suffer from the illustration of its literary origins; in its nature as a frank study of the poetic mind it should afford from the work of many poets the richest possible evidence of the gift of one poet to another. When his early experiments in writing are reviewed with ample detail from the English models which for the most part he has himself acknowledged, we do not imply that his autobiographical poem, even where derivative, is for that reason counterfeit. Quite otherwise: in this study of his predecessors his own unique power was evoked and repeatedly challenged.

This is a long story. In telling it no scholar may disregard Wordsworth's phenomenal memory for words, phrases, patterns of phrase, images, metaphors, and rhythms, all those literary ideas so different from the concepts of the metaphysician or the fancies of the layman. The power of Wordsworth's mind has been freely acknowledged by all; but the wealth of his mind, his learning, will be fruitful only for the scholar or young poet who is willing to accept it. Such readers will discover that what Wordsworth appropriates he does not always transform, but that what he transforms is always authentic, true both to himself and the tradition in which and through which he grew. Lastly, and in chief, humble readers will learn anew the secret of

> that considerate and laborious work,
> That patience which, admitting no neglect,
> By slow creation doth impart to speech
> Outline and substance even, till it has given
> A function kindred to organic power,
> The vital spirit of a perfect form.[25]

[25] A passage written in 1798–1800; see de Selincourt, p. xliii.

II

Wordsworth's First Teacher of English Composition

'The Power of Education'

THE FIRST noun in Wordsworth's published verse is 'Sun,' the first abstract noun is 'Science,' the first abstract phrase is 'the Power of Education'; all are personified, and the Power of Education is a woman. The *Lines* in which they appear were written as a school exercise at Hawkshead in 1784–5, when the poet was fourteen years old.[1] He imagines himself visited by a 'celestial Fair,' who exhorts him to 'snatch the slumbering lyre' and sing a song in praise of Archbishop Sandys, the founder of Hawkshead Grammar School in the year 1585.

She describes for him the flight of Superstition from Britain under the lustrous eye of Religion, and the liberation of the soul under the cheerful ray of enlivening Hope, the shade-dissolving beam of Science, and the guidance of Philosophy. Influenced by 'the finer arts,' the sons of Britain have left 'the listed fields' for 'seats of learning.' 'Hawkshead's happy roof' has been reared.

[1] *Poetical Works*, ed. by E. de Selincourt (and Helen Darbishire for Volumes 3–5), Oxford, 1940–9, Vol. 1, pp. 259–61.

Here William and other young scholars have studied 'the golden precepts of the classic page,' have been led to the 'Elysian plains' of 'immortal Science' and 'sacred Truth,' have been taught

> to search the mystic cause of things,
> And follow Nature to her secret springs;

and, last but not least, 'fluctuating' as youth ever is, they have been guided 'firm in the sacred paths of moral truth.' Thus Wordsworth at the age of fourteen conceived of education. In his boyish view, such was the proper course of study for a grateful poet: the arts, the classics, *prima philosophia*, theology, natural philosophy, and moral philosophy, and all these as a discipline for poetry.

The cultural process that has resulted in the curriculum of Hawkshead he compares, first, to a natural process, sunrise on the ocean after storm and darkness; secondly, to a mental process, light in the soul brought about by the study of science, with freedom from seductive shadowy forms made possible by the study of philosophy, and, at the dismissal of monkish teachers from their gloomy cells, the release of the mind from 'mazy' and perplexing rules.

Wordsworth's understanding of the triple sunrise of nature, personality, and culture is notable in a boy of fourteen. Moreover, the range of his ideas about education and his ability to discriminate between them, his familiarity with the traditional branches of learning and their value for those who study, are not less impressive than the ease with which he has learned and can use phrases to denote intellectual and emotional experience. For instançe, the Power of Education has at her side

> all the powers, design'd
> To curb, exalt, reform the tender mind.

The functions of the Power of Education are 'to show,' 'to lead the mind,' 'to teach . . . to roam,' to teach 'to search,' to teach 'to follow,' 'to guide,' 'to regulate,' 'to quench,' 'to enlarge,' 'to purge.' Her educational program is to be carried on by 'industry

. . . with steady pace' and beaming 'smile'; under their liberal tuition in 'secret grotto' Britain's sons shall 'court majestic truth, or wake the golden lyre.' In other words, they are to study the sciences and the arts.

And last, it is the art of song to which young William is specifically summoned. In good time a prelude on his lyre shall repay Hawkshead for her precepts, precepts that have quelled the strife of his passions, smoothed the rugged walks of his life, pointed him 'forth'

the blissful way
That guides the spirit to eternal day.

Some eleven centuries before the lad in Westmoreland conceived his vision, a Northumbrian cowherd at Whitby was also visited by a celestial messenger who bade him sing: the beginning of created life and the might of the Maker who shaped heaven as a roof for the bairns of men and earth as their middle yard. Caedmon's song is better known than Wordsworth's *Lines;* but the first English lyric and the first poem of Wordsworth are comparable in that both are songs of praise, both are sung in obedience to a heavenly vision, and both celebrate the rearing of roofs for the breeding of the children of a father. After his vision, Caedmon went on to translate and versify Scripture for the students of the Abbess Hild; Wordsworth's masters furnished him rather with the texts of Anacreon, Catullus, Virgil, Horace, and Moschus, parts of which he also turned into English verse. But for our present argument this is a less important distinction; both scholars were remanded to their books, at Whitby or Hawkshead.

Another poet, a ploughman, had been taught by a visionary lady on Malvern Hills four centuries before Wordsworth's Power of Education appeared to him in the Vale of Esthwaite; and still another ploughman, Robert Burns, was indebted to a 'heavenly-seeming Fair' for his *Vision,* Coila of the 'green, slender, leaf-clad holly-boughs.' She, too, that 'tight, outlandish hizzie, braw,' was a teacher. Giving her 'counsels all in one' she warned him to fan his tuneful flame carefully, to 'preserve the dignity of Man,' and to 'trust the Universal Plan.' The 'heavenly-seeming Fair' of Burns fled away in light 'like a passing thought'; Wordsworth's celestial Fair 'smiled like the morn and vanish'd into air.'

Burns acknowledged the 'Scota' of Alexander Ross as the ancestress of his 'Coila,' and dated his 'Coila' long before the publication of the Kilmarnock edition of his poems in 1786.[2] But allegorical ladies are too frequent in ceremonial literature to encourage here the study of their family tree; nor is it likely that either Burns or Wordsworth had Caedmon or *Piers Plowman* consciously in mind. Heavenly messengers have appeared in visions to passionate or lethargic poets not less often than to indolent founders of dynasties. Some of these messengers have been ladies; witness Aeneas' mother and the Philosophia of Boethius. Chaucer's Nature and Fame, Thomson's Liberty, Thomas Newcomb's Oblivion, and Pope's Dullness [3] were all ladies; but like Burns's Coila Wordsworth's Power of Education was not only a lady, she was undeniably a schoolma'am.

In his 'Autobiographical Memoranda' [4] Wordsworth confessed that his verses at fourteen years 'were but a tame imitation of Pope's versification, and a little in his style.' The matter of the poem, however, bears witness that its author, although a docile student, was no mere copyist. Traditional ethics and Popian couplets serve as medium for what, in his many years devoted to letters, came to be known as characteristic of Wordsworth, the imaginative representation of moral beauty.

It is a long shift of view from Wordsworth's *Lines* on the Power of Education to Pope's *Dunciad* on the Power of Dullness, yet a study of the language of the two poems reveals that three-fourths

[2] *The Letters of Robert Burns*, ed. by J. de L. Ferguson, Oxford, 1931, Vol. 1, pp. 69, 205.

[3] Newcomb, a friend of Dr. Young, published in 1712 an anonymous satire, 'Bibliotheca, a Poem occasioned by the sight of a modern Library.' Its goddess may have assisted in the conception of Pope's Dullness, of *The Dunciad* (*Dictionary of National Biography*, Vol. 14, p. 318).

[4] *Memoirs of William Wordsworth*, ed. by Christopher Wordsworth, Vol. 1, pp. 10–11.

of the words used by young William occur in *The Dunciad*. Of the remaining fourth only a dozen or so are not in the common parlance of the *Satires* and *Essays*.[5] Pope's gigantic 'empire of Dullness,' her College in the city with her private Academy for Poets in particular, when set by the side of Wordsworth's little Grammar School at Hawkshead; Pope's satire on Great Britain subjugated to the power of Dullness, who destroys Order and Science, leads captive the Sciences, silences the Muses, when considered as one source of Wordsworth's panegyric on the Power of Education; the action of the *Dunciad*, consummated by the restoration of Night and Chaos, when compared with the ending of the Wordsworthian *Lines* in bright morning and music: this triple comparison of the subject, the manner of its presentation, and the conduct of the action helps us to foresee that, although William has understood what Pope meant and will carry on the fight against the forces of darkness, like another David he is measuring himself, student and artist, against the eighteenth-century Goliath, Alexander Pope. The visionary lady has become another vision to Wordsworth as to Burns; the giants must give over; Dullness will resign to Coila and the Power of Education, to her

who trains the generous British youth
In the bright paths of fair majestic Truth.

Since our argument is schooling, we shall be rewarded for our patient study of the schoolboy's vocabulary in these *Lines* by the disclosure that his own nature is at work on the materials offered him by Pope. The inventory—good English words all—is a sample in little of the great reflective poems of Wordsworth's prime.

[5] The most unusual words in Wordsworth's *Lines* are 'steel' and 'indurated':

Britain's sons
No longer steel their indurated hearts
To the mild influence of the finer arts.

'Steel' as a verb occurs in Pope's *Elegy* 41. From Goldsmith's *Traveller* (1764) Wordsworth doubtless knew the couplet (231–2):

And Love's and Friendship's finely pointed dart
Fall blunted from each indurated heart.

The word goes back to the Vulgate as well as to Ovid: cf. Exodus 7:13, 22, 'induratum est cor Pharaonis'; *Metamorphoses* XI, 1.

Nature, occurring once, is personified: her lineaments, almost always metaphorically employed, are the *sun* with its *ray*, *night* with its *shades*, *day* with its *light; winter snows;* the *main*, its *tides* and *waves;* the *world*, *plains* and *springs*, *isle* and *grove* and *grotto*, *fires* and *flame* and *blaze; things* and *dross; air*, *storm*, *winds*, the *ring* or *vault* of *heaven*, *pole* to *pole*, and the *skies* with their *checquer'd bow*. When the poet is only fourteen, the rainbow must have an epithet to adorn it.

Life is as yet not very concretely represented, but it has its *hour* and *times*, its generic *age* and its specific *youth*. Divine nature as *God* and *Goddess*, and human nature as *Man*, *men*, *boy*, *Sires* and *sons*, take their place in the chain of being. *Warrior*, *guide* and *charge*, *wretch*, *bigot*, and *monks* diversify the conditions of mankind. The *frame* of the body comes within the scope of the student's verse: *eyes*, their *view*, their *lustre*, and their *tears; forehead*, *cheek*, *face* and its *hue; side*, *breast*, and *heart*. *Spirit*, *forms*, *powers*, *beauties*, this particular *vision* and its *sacred train*, denote as terms rather than connote as ideas; *pomp* and *influence* are not at all spiritualized; the *cause* of things and human *defects* have as yet little logical or substantial relationship; and yet the range of the denotation is itself remarkable.

Man-made things noted, typically more than actually, are *paths* and *walks*, *fields* of war and *listed fields*, *cell*, *dome*, *mansions*, *roof; gold*, *dye*, *chariot*, *fetters*, *sword*, *lance*, *ring*, and *lyre; design*, *book*, *page*, and *song*.

In young William's view the *mind* of man is able to conceive *Virtue* and *Vice*, *Fame* and *Shame*, *Reason* and *Passion*, *Truth* and *Superstition; Industry*, *Hope*, *Emulation; Science*, *Philosophy*, *Education*, and *Religion*. Although these are still figures of speech to him, or unsubstantial conceits, there is little doubt that he knows what the terms mean, or that he could properly apply or illustrate them. Also he writes of *arts* and *manners* and *rules* as one aware of their function in social life. He has profited, indeed, by the 'golden *precepts* of the classic page.'

His psychological terms, like his ethical, have come to him in doctrinal wise from his teachers; but again, the range of them and the selection do credit to his understanding and judgment: *sense* may be of *pleasures* or *rigours*, *passions* may be of *joy* or *woe*, of *rapture* or of *rage*, of *terrors*, of *agony; merit*, *gratitude*, *obedience*, and *trust* are states of the *soul; name*, *fame*, *power*, *majesty*, and *law* are ideas to recognize and revere; *thoughts*, *mien*, *smiles*, *accents*, *praise*, *strife* constitute the expressive media of the young student; *steady pace* is already a respected manner of locomotion, and *vision* is his characteristic mode of perception.

Geography to him means *Britain* (*British*) or *Britannia* and *Hawkshead*, whence his literary memory rather than his imagination carries him by way of the *Ocean*, to *Rome*, *Tyre*, and the *Elysian Fields*. History reaches back to Archbishop Sandys, to Francis *Bacon* and *Edward* the First or Third. *Hebe*, the *Siren*, and the sacred allegorical train of the goddess of *Education* make up his womankind.

His critical powers demand the following native adjectives and adverbs for their precise expression, and these bear witness to both sensibility and perspicuity: *fair*, *bright*, *beamy*, *cheerful*, *blissful*, *heavenly; dark*, *shadowy*, *gloomy; soon*, *quick*, *slow; again*, *anew*, *oft*, *first*, *last; more*, *less*, *all*, *every; yon*, *far*, *wide*, *long*, *deep*, *aside*, *mazy; soft* and *rugged*, *mild* and *cold; weary*, *short-lived*, *dead; own*, *darling*, *happy*, *great*.

Epithets from Latin and Greek show a riper judgment, if not a greater sensibility: *close*, *distant; pale*, *pure*, *fine*, *peaceful*, *pensive*, *serene*, *noble*, and *savage*, *gaudy*, *vile; private*, *secret*, *secure*, *silent; tender* and *gentle* and also *firm*, *severe*, and *indignant; rapid*, *splendid*, *rigid; curious*, *generous; honest*, *just*, *moral*, *superior; sacred*, *visionary*, *celestial*, *immortal*, *eternal; lethargic*, *classic*, *majestic*, *mystic*.

Present participles refer primarily to light and movement: *kindling*, *glimmering*, *glittering*, *beaming*, *flaming*, *dazzling; slumbering*, *soothing; pleasing*, *blushing*, *enlivening; trembling*, *panting*, *fluctuating; jarring*, *warring*.

The verbs, including the past participles, are also for the most part native, and suggest Wordsworth's remarkable kinaesthesia at fourteen: *awake, arise, begin, hear, call, seem, see, beam, look up, seek, gaze, scan, behold, deem, learn, think, flush, smile, say, show; rest, sit, leave, go, walk, roam, clap* wings, *fly, flee, flow, roll, toss, throw* back, *run, ride, follow, lead, guide, have, do, rear, break, dare, steel, bid, drive, quell, snatch, spurn, quench, weep, lull, hush, smoothe, soften, love, plight, bless.*

Verbs from the Latin or Greek or Romance languages are proportionately fewer than we should expect in a student of classical literature: *search, brave; stain, purge; move, curb, muse, point forth, join, paint; court, train, throne, reign; advance, appear, array, centre, checquer, confine, design, dictate, disorder, display, dissipate, dissolve, emerge, enlarge, entice, exalt, humour, honour, indurate, inspire, involve, perplex, peruse, pursue, reflect, reform, regulate, rehearse, retire, return, revert, subside, vanish.* Very few of these are unusual, or exclusively bookish.

'Lo!' as young William says twice, 'Lo!' What a lesson! Education in the year 1784 has in certain ways been justified by its pupil. Although history, and science as we know it, are still rudiments in his mind, although the marvel of his experience when out-of-doors and the pictures recorded by it have not here craved utterance, although literature, belles-lettres, has scarcely prepossessed him, his boyish exercise in verse is distinguished for what later he was to call 'the multiplicity and quality of . . . moral relations'; [6] and these matters, it seems, can be taught and encouraged, whether as doctrine and discipline, or as a verbal pattern or web of precepts later to be substantiated by experience or colored by feeling or imagination.

The words of most frequent occurrence in the *Lines* are *wake, rise, teach, inspire; eyes* and *breast; night, shade, day, light, paths, heaven; mind, precepts, Virtue; soul, passions, joy; bright, fair, golden; tender, sacred, heavenly; sons, Britain; Science, Truth.* At the age of fourteen Wordsworth reiterated the words for images

[6] Preface to *Lyrical Ballads,* 1800.

and ideas he was emphasizing at forty. Moreover, in a tradition long given to what Wordsworth's 'celestial Fair' calls 'immortal Science' and 'sacred Truth,' Wordsworth is already at this early age associated not only with Bede's Caedmon, Alfred's Boethius, Langland's Ploughman, but with Pope's satiric attack on all the forces of Night and Chaos. Yet in the imagination of the novice at Hawkshead these have yielded to bright morning; the Power of Education is at work.

And hence out of his early visionary experience, academic as it was, may have come this poet's desire to be considered 'as a Teacher or as nothing.' [7] At least his vision of the Power of Education was to point him all along his novitiate toward his unaccomplished philosophical poem (*The Recluse*), toward his intellectual love for Nature and Mankind (*The Prelude*), toward those exhortations of the Sage and that vision of an enlightened land which we know as *The Excursion*, and, finally, toward his poem on the English Church, a loftier roof than that of Hawkshead Grammar School, yet with a similar discipline from its sacred train of martyrs, saints, and sages. Were its ends likewise not Enlightenment, Truth, and pure Religion? The initial *γράμματα* of the Wordsworthian text, 'Sun' and 'Science' and 'the Power of Education,' were also the final λόγοι of this teacher or 'nothing.'

Pope's *Essay on Criticism* and Wordworth's Critical Essays

Assuming from Wordsworth's acknowledgment of Pope's influence in the *Lines . . . anno aetatis 14* that Pope was the first English poet to teach him English composition, we may well look to the *Essay on Criticism* as the first assignment in the course. Many of its verses must have been among those several thousand lines of Pope he could repeat in his sixties with what he called 'a little previous rummaging' of his memory.[8] Nor did the pupil

[7] *The Letters of William and Dorothy Wordsworth*, ed. by E. de Selincourt: *The Middle Years*, Oxford, 1937, Vol. 1, p. 170.

[8] Havens, *The Mind of a Poet*, pp. 402, 405, quoting Wordsworth's comments on Barron Field's manuscript Memoir.

forget the meaning of the lesson, as is indicated by the lines now to be found at the very front of his *Poetical Works:*

> If thou indeed *derive thy light from Heaven,*
> Then, to the measure of that heaven-born light,
> Shine, Poet! in thy place, and be content.

Pope had written (11–14):

> In Poets as true genius is but rare,
> True Taste as seldom is the Critic's share;
> Both must alike *from Heaven derive their light,*
> These born to judge, as well as those to write.[9]

'The Poet's fire,' that 'spark of . . . celestial fire' which Pope had begged from Homer and Virgil and other 'Bards triumphant' for himself, 'the meanest of [their] sons' (100, 189, 195–6), remained for Wordsworth, too, the chief symbol of poetic power.

The *Essay on Criticism* has three parts: Part I recommends, as the best guide for the critic, Nature, methodized into such rules as are derived from the practice of the ancient poets; Part II sets forth a theory of criticism and the causes hindering a true judgment; Part III supplies us with the *character* of a good critic and the history of criticism. The critical works of Wordsworth which roughly correspond with these three parts of Pope's *Essay* are as follows: with Part I, the Appendix to the Preface (1802), in which Wordsworth traces poetic diction downward from its origin in the natural language of passion to the 'mechanical adoption' of figures of speech; with Part II, the Preface to *Lyrical Ballads* itself (1800), its theory of poetry and its remarks on language; with Part III, the Essay, Supplementary to the Preface (of 1815), Wordsworth's *character* of a good critic and history of English criticism.

Within their analogous discussions let us briefly indicate the principles of poetry and criticism common to Pope and Words-

[9] Pope's lines, except those from *The Dunciad,* are quoted from the edition by George Sherburn, 1929, *The Best of Pope,* The Ronald Press Company. For *The Dunciad* see the Twickenham edition of *The Poems of Alexander Pope,* Vol. 5 edited by James Sutherland, New York, 1943, Methuen and Co. Ltd. and Yale University Press.

worth. Pope's first imperative is 'follow Nature . . . unerring NATURE, . . . one clear, unchanged, and universal light' (68, 70–1). Although the word 'Nature' would mean to Wordsworth something other than to Pope, the notion of Nature as a metaphorical guide was irresistible; and the notion of Nature as a metaphorical light, with vision as the activity of the critic, proved not less congenial. Most suggestive of all to Wordsworth the critic, Pope's 'Nature methodised' (89) reappeared in the Appendix of 1802 somewhat further depreciated as Nature mechanized, which is no longer natural.

Secondly, in Part II of his *Essay on Criticism,* Pope's survey of the 'whole' as the method of the critic evidently impressed and stimulated the selfhood of the young Wordsworth. What Coleridge was to call 'esemplastic power,' and Wordsworth himself, possibly catching a hint from Coleridge's talk of Spinoza and his *amor intellectualis,*[10] would translate as *intellectual love* or imagination, must originally have been felt as a kind of wholeness in the soul of man comparable to the wholeness of the objects he observed, felt, imagined, or judged.

Of the various forms of impairment of genius and taste—the teacher would say, 'short Ideas' or 'a love to parts'—Pope warned Wordsworth against partial attention to 'glitt'ring thoughts,' to 'Language' or 'Style,' or to 'Numbers.' Again, as the master suspected ornaments that hide the 'want of art,' so the pupil disliked the wordiness compared by Pope to leafage, which conceals the the lack of 'fruit of *sense* beneath.' And from Pope he learned that '*diff'rent styles with diff'rent subjects sort*' (287–8, 290, 305–7, 337, 294–6, 309–10, 322). His signal restatement of Pope's doctrine follows:

I have wished to keep the Reader in the company of flesh and blood, . . . to bring my language near to the language of men, . . . to look

[10] Spinoza, *Ethics,* translated by W. Hale White, revised by Amelia Hutchison Stirling, 4th ed., Oxford, 1930, Part V, propositions xxxiii–xxxviii. In his *Strange Seas of Thought,* Duke University Press, Durham, 1945, chap. vi, Newton P. Stallknecht has further illustrated Wordsworth's possible debt to Spinoza.

steadily at my *subject;* . . . and my ideas are expressed *in language fitted to their respective importance.* Something must have been gained by this practice, as it is friendly to one property of all good poetry, namely, good *sense.*[11]

Farther on in the Preface, in a passage not dropped until 1836, he explicitly acknowledged Pope's lesson: 'We see that Pope by the power of verse alone, has contrived to render the plainest common *sense* interesting, and even frequently to invest it with the appearance of passion.' [12]

Furthermore, when Pope advised the critic to 'regard the writer's End,' he furnished his pupil with the main justification for his experiment, *Lyrical Ballads,* those poems distinguished from trivial and mean verses, their author says, by their 'worthy purpose.' He would not be one of Pope's 'poets unskill'd to *trace* the naked *nature* and the living grace'; rather he would illustrate his master's preference for (299–300, 311–17)

Something, whose *truth* convinced at sight we find,
That gives us back *the image of our mind.* . . .
False Eloquence, like the prismatic glass,
Its *gaudy colours* spreads on every place;
The *face of Nature* we no more survey,
All *glares* alike, without distinction gay.
But *true expression,* like th' unchanging Sun,
Clears and improves whate'er it shines upon,
It *gilds all objects, but it alters none.*[13]

In his own words, and with his characteristic emphasis on his own feeling and power, Wordsworth would disavow '*gaudiness* and inane phraseology'; over incidents and situations chosen from com-

[11] *Poetical Works,* Vol. 2, p. 390. Here and hereafter italics in quoted passages are mine unless otherwise indicated.

[12] *Ibid.,* p. 401. It is not my purpose here to direct attention to Pope's sources, classical or French, or to other English critics whom young Wordsworth also knew; rather, I submit to intensive study the one critical poet he likely knew best as a boy. Yet 'infelix operis summa, quia ponere totum nesciet,' Horace, *De arte poetica* 34–5.

[13] Cf. 'image of our mind' with 'perfect image of a mighty Mind,' *Prelude* XIII, 69.

mon life he would throw 'a certain *colouring* of imagination' (not the '*gaudy colours*' of 'false Eloquence'), 'whereby ordinary things should be presented to the *mind* in an unusual aspect' (cf. Pope's 'something . . . that gives us back the image of our mind' cleared and improved by the sunshine); and he would 'make these incidents and situations interesting by *tracing* in them *truly* . . . the *primary laws of our nature*.' To this obvious restatement of Pope's doctrine he adds a phrase now connected with Hartley: 'chiefly, as far as regards the manner in which we associate ideas in a state of excitement.' [14]

Thirdly, the heavenly origin of both poetical 'genius' and critical 'taste,' the prime lesson he had learned in his teens from Pope's *Essay on Criticism*, he reiterated and amplified at the age of forty-five in his own Essay, Supplementary. Using the history of English criticism as Pope in Part III had used the critical tradition from Aristotle to Lord Roscommon, Wordsworth gave to the term 'taste' that dignity which he had given to 'imagination' in *The Prelude*. He acknowledged that both words had been 'forced to extend [their] services far beyond the point to which philosophy would have confined them'; but his effort to reconceive 'taste' as an intellectual act and operation and to make the creation of the taste by which he is enjoyed 'the ultimate test of a truly original poet' is as creditable to his genius as to the indoctrination of Pope.

Even while condemning Pope for faithlessness to his own doctrine, in this later essay Wordsworth returned to the metaphorical light and color which had pleased him as a schoolboy: 'An eye accustomed to the *glaring* hues of diction . . . will for the most part be rather repelled than attracted by an original Work, the *colouring* of which is disposed according to a pure and refined scheme of harmony.' [15] As Pope, too, grew older, he had amplified his metaphor to ennoble the poet or critic as well as nature itself, a strong hint for his pupil. His mature argument shines in its most colorful radiance in the first epistle of *Moral Essays* (31–6):

[14] *Poetical Works*, Vol. 2, p. 386.
[15] *Ibid.*, p. 411.

The difference is as great between
The optics seeing, as the object seen,
All Manners take a tincture from our own;
Or come discolour'd through our Passions shown.
Or Fancy's beam enlarges, multiplies,
Contracts, inverts, and gives ten thousand dyes.

Pope's figurative language is intensified by his pupil in that passage of *The Prelude* considered eminently 'Wordsworthian'; but, like so much else Wordsworth wrote, it is the gift to him from his elder poets. He is in the tradition when he says:

An auxiliar light
Came from my mind which on the setting sun
Bestow'd new splendour; . . . and the midnight storm
Grew darker in the presence of my eye.

Such a contribution from the optics seeing to the objects seen would be the first exercise of Fancy; but Fancy would go on to contribute an emotional tincture, color, or dye from the heart feeling to the object felt. Just so, Wordsworth tells us, he 'transferr'd' his own enjoyment to 'unorganic natures.' From this second exercise of Fancy to 'the glorious faculty which higher minds bear with them as their own' is only one degree; in the third exercise—of Imagination—these higher minds, as does Nature herself,

from their native selves can send abroad
Like transformations, for themselves create
A like existence.[16]

The wedding of the Mind of Man with Nature is not far off. The pattern of creative influence, through poetry or criticism, is the same; the bestowal has become a transference, and the transference has become a 'transformation.'

Most memorably in *The Prelude* we hear valid echoes of Pope's survey of the 'whole.' Throughout Book VI, 'Cambridge and the Alps,' and Book VII, 'Residence in London,' we detect still at

[16] *Prelude* II, 387–93, 405–11; XIII, 89–95.

work the Alpine lesson in the *Essay on Criticism* and the contiguous lesson on the architectural wonders of Rome, a resistless challenge to the pupil from his master's instructive pen (219–32, 243–52):

> *Fired* at first sight with what the Muse imparts,
> In fearless youth we tempt the *heights* of Arts,
> While from the bounded level *of our mind*
> Short views we take, nor see the *lengths* behind;
> But more advanced, behold *with strange surprise*
> New distant scenes of endless science rise!
> So pleased at first the tow'ring Alps we try,
> Mount o'er the vales and seem to tread the sky,
> Th' eternal snows appear already past,
> And the first clouds and mountains seem the last;
> But, those attained, we tremble to survey
> The *growing labours* of the *lengthened way,*
> *Th' increasing prospect tires our wand'ring eyes,*
> Hills peep o'er hills, and Alps on Alps arise! . . .
>
> In wit, as nature, what *affects our hearts*
> Is not th' exactness of *peculiar parts;*
> 'T is *not a lip, or eye,* we beauty call,
> But the *joint force* and full result of all.
> Thus when we view some well-proportioned dome,
> (The world's just wonder, and even thine, O *Rome!*)
> No *single parts* unequally *surprise,*
> All comes *united to th' admiring eyes;*
> No *monstrous height,* or *breadth,* or *length* appear;
> The *Whole* at once is bold, and regular.

Wordsworth's Alpine climb '*with eagerness,* though *not at length without surprise,*' and his 'dejection' and 'sadness' felt when he had crossed this ridge of the world, recall the 'strange surprise' of Pope's 'fearless youth' on their 'lengthened way' to the 'heights of Arts,' and their weariness at the 'increasing prospect' of 'endless science.' Contrariwise, Wordsworth's triumphant recognition of the glory of his own soul and, when 'the light of sense' goes out, the might of his own imagination in the face of endlessness or infinitude, give him the main revelation, the apocalypse, of his autobiography:

> Our destiny, our nature, and our home
> Is with infinitude, and only there;
> With hope it is, hope that can never die,
> Effort, and expectation, and desire,
> And something evermore about to be.

Taking Pope's beauty of lip or eye irrevocably out-of-doors, he enumerates with fresh descriptive energy the peculiar features of the Alpine face and then indeed gives them their joint force and full result. 'The *immeasurable height* of woods,' 'the stationary blasts of water-falls,' 'winds thwarting winds,' 'torrents,' 'rock,' 'crags,' 'raving stream,' 'unfetter'd clouds,' 'darkness and . . . light,'

> Were all like *workings of one mind*, the *features*
> *Of the same face*, blossoms upon one tree,
> Characters of the great Apocalypse,
> The types and symbols of Eternity,
> Of first and last, and midst, and without end.[17]

Wordsworth surveyed not only the 'whole' of the Alps, but the 'whole' of London as well. In his arrangement of the book on city life to follow the book on mountain travel, he articulated his plot in the pattern of his early lesson: from Popian hills to Popian domes, from Alps to Rome. Indeed, like Pope, he explicitly summons aid from the hills; and the habitual influence of the mountain's outline and steady form, and the forms perennial of the ancient hills, help him to find order and relation in London, the '*monstrous* ant-hill on the plain,' even in Bartholomew Fair, that 'Parliament of *monsters*,' and

> type not false
> Of what the mighty City is itself . . .
> To the *whole* Swarm of its inhabitants. . . .

17 *Ibid.* VI, 508–9, 491–2, 534–5, 538–42, 556–72.

But though *the picture weary out the eye,*
By nature an unmanageable sight,
It is not *wholly* so to him who looks
In steadiness, who hath among least things
An under-sense of greatest; sees the *parts*
As parts, but with a *feeling of the whole.*[18]

Dunciad IV and *Prelude* III and V

The names of two pre-Wordsworthian giants in literature in the century of his birth are linked by the dedication of *The Dunciad* of Alexander Pope to Doctor Jonathan Swift. The services of these writers were the ones demanded of genius and taste in any age: the persistent effort to penetrate darkness, set chaos in order, rebuke villainy and folly, improve and refine the activities of men—responsibilities Wordsworth and Ruskin would undertake in the nineteenth century. However strange it may seem to compare *The Dunciad* with *The Prelude,* if we disregard their difference in mode (Pope's, bitterly satirical; Wordsworth's, mildly censorious), both poems are concerned with the impairment of the wit or imagination, and in their characteristic ways with its restoration. Pope reminds us that his presiding goddess, Dullness,

> is not to be taken contractedly for mere stupidity, but in the enlarged sense of the word, for all slowness of apprehension, shortness of sight, or imperfect sense of things. It includes . . . labour, industry, and some degree of activity and boldness; a ruling principle not inert, but turning topsy-turvy the understanding and inducing an anarchy or confused state of mind.

There are such mischievous influences in Wordsworth's first school, too, the school of Nature in *The Prelude;* but from the industrious theft of woodcocks and the laborious sequestration of the rowboat in childhood, he goes on to his collegiate and post-graduate misfortunes, the sleepiness of imagination in youth and

[18] *Ibid.* VII, 721–2, 725–9, 691, 695–8, 707–12. Note the verbal echo: whole, wholly, whole.

the false philosophy, shortsighted study, anarchic despair of his young manhood in France.

Behind the autobiographical data of Books V and III of Wordsworth's poem there are two sets of contrasting portraits or *characters* of a more general and operative nature: the badly educated child versus the well-educated child; and the foolish college versus the wise college. Wordsworth's hapless pupil who is 'no Child, but a dwarf Man,' a 'prodigy' whose soul is 'Vanity,' who is pounded within 'the pin-fold of his own conceit,' [19] should be compared with Pope's 'dauntless infant' and other vain and arrogant sons of Dullness in the fourth book of *The Dunciad*, youths perverted because confined to 'words only,' kept 'out of the way of real knowledge,' according to a system which 'establishes self-love for the sole principle of action.' [20] The cup passed around at the court of Dullness is the cup of self-love; and among the self-lovers are found not only Aristarchus, the pedant, and Paridel, the loafer or loiterer, but also those myopic enthusiasts who 'see Nature in some partial narrow shape'—nest, toad, fungus, flower, or butterfly; those misers who forget 'the author of the whole' for coin or mummy; and, most foolish of all, those gloomy clerks who take the

> high Priori Road
> And reason downward, till [they] doubt of God: . . .
> Find Virtue local, all Relation scorn,
> See all in *Self*, and but for self be born:
> Of naught so certain as our *Reason* still,
> Of naught so doubtful as of *Soul* and *Will*.[21]

This is the very disease of Wordsworth's vain Stripling, to whom, direct from Pope's 'young Aeneas,' had come the bad habit of partial and superficial study with 'telescopes, and crucibles, and maps,' whose knowledge of astronomy, navigation, geology, geography, and politics had divorced him from sky, ocean, wood-

[19] *Ibid.* V, 294–5, 320, 361–2.
[20] *Dunciad* IV, 501, and the note of Pope and Warburton on it.
[21] *Ibid.* IV, 398, 400, 436, 455–6, 471–2, 479–82. Italics in Pope's text.

land and riverside, from meadows and flowers and man, whose brain was overgrown with propositions, whose path was choked with grammars, who knew and remembered everything, but could not forget himself (V, 350–54):

> Now this is hollow, 't is a life of lies
> From the beginning, and in lies must end.
> Forth bring him to the air of common sense,
> And, fresh and shewy as it is, the Corpse
> Slips from us into powder.

From this life of his dwarf man Wordsworth bids us turn our eyes toward the real children educated by Nature. 'There was a Boy' among the 'Cliffs and Islands of Winander' for whom a wiser spirit was at work, and for whose successors in the rural school at Hawkshead the poet wishes (V, 445–9):

> Simplicity in habit, truth in speech. . . .
> May books and nature be their early joy!
> And knowledge, rightly honor'd with that name,
> Knowledge not purchas'd with the loss of power!

Whereas the students of Dullness in *The Dunciad* appear 'conglobed' like 'buzzing Bees about their dusky Queen,' Wordsworth's more fortunate youngsters are the 'Brood' of a 'Parent Hen.' No comparison of Popian satire with Wordsworthian sentiment is more revealing than that which observes Wordsworth's mother doing for her little brood what the allegorical queen bee could only undo for her many drones.

The officers, faculty, and students of the Alma Mater of *The Dunciad*, Book IV, Pope's satire on letters and education, resemble masqueraders in a pageant or procession; indeed they constitute a spectacle so like a college commencement that we find them as droll as did Wordsworth. At the footstool of Dullness, Science is in chains, Wit dreads exile, and the Muses are in tenfold bonds and watched by Envy and Flattery; Sophistry has gagged and bound rebellious Logic, Billingsgate wears the robes of languishing Rhetoric, Chicane in furs and Casuistry in lawn draw strait the cord about expiring Morality; and mad Mathesis,

> Too mad for mere material chains to bind,
> Now to pure Space lifts her ecstatic stare,
> Now running round the Circle finds it square.

Before the conferring of degrees, Dullness grants the members of the graduating class the aid of firm Impudence, mild Stupefaction, kind Self-conceit, Interest, and the Syren Sisters—but not before the Spectre with the dreadful wand in his index-hand has threatened the English schoolboy with a memorable beating.

Surely it is by no accident, but the result of Pope's excellent teaching of English literature, that Wordsworth has personified the 'old Humourists' of Cambridge as members of an academic pageant: bald Government, murmuring Submission; Hope and Idleness; simple Pleasure foraging for Death; misguided Shame and Witless Fear; Honour misplaced and Dignity astray; Feuds, Factions, Flatteries, Enmity, and Guile; Decency and Custom starving Truth; Emptiness; and—again with special significance for English schoolboys—blind Authority beating with his staff the child that might have led him.

In the monstrous graduation exercises of *The Dunciad*, Pope's caricatures rustle before us with timeless warning: the dunce, hypocrite, fop, pedant, staunch polemic, fierce logician, rakish traveler, ever-listless loiterer, numismatologists, antiquaries; then, 'thick as locusts,' the naturalists. On bended knees all draw near for the conferring of degrees. They bring their gems, coins, toads, fungi, flowers under glass, and dead butterflies to the museum (567–70); but at the last the most accomplished son of Dullness turns 'Air, the Echo of a Sound,' and the Saturnian commencement ends in a universal yawn (16, 282, 322, 605–18).

His own Alma Mater, Cambridge University, Wordsworth compares first to a puppet show, pageant, or spectacle, and secondly to 'a Cabinet or wide Museum (throng'd with fishes, gems, birds, crocodiles, shells)'; hints for both similes are inescapable in *The Dunciad*. Although he was not one of what he calls the 'honest dunces' at St. John's, he confesses that he was a 'Dreamer.' Soon, in Pope's metaphor of somnolence, Wordsworth's 'Imagination slept,' 'the memory languidly revolv'd, the heart repos'd in noontide rest'; 'hush'd . . . was the undersoul, lock'd up in such a calm, that not a leaf of the great nature stirr'd'—Wordsworthian parlance for the Popian 'All nature nods.' He was no Aristarchus, no young Aeneas, no Annius or Mummius, no Silenus, save for his one fall from grace in Milton's lodgings; but he was a Paridel of sorts. Like Pope's 'loiterer,' borrowed from Spenser, Wordsworth was, in Pope's words, 'stretch'd on the rack of a too easy chair,' and his 'everlasting yawn' is heard to 'confess the Pains and Penalties of Idleness.' In his own words, his heart 'was social and loved idleness and joy'; he traveled 'with the shoal of more unthinking Natures, easy Minds and pillowy.' And he interrupts his account of his academic career with Pope's very word: 'I play the loiterer.' [22]

Yet he tried to be fair to his University. From her olden repute in those ages when, at that 'Seat of Arts,' Doctors studied and Princes prized 'spare diet, patient labour, and plain weeds,' he draws a more agreeable picture of what she had been and, in spite of the later impairment of her genius and taste, might be again:

> the image of a Place
> Which with its aspect should have bent me down
> To instantaneous service, should at once
> Have made me pay to science and to arts
> And written lore, acknowledg'd my liege Lord,
> A homage, frankly offer'd up, like that
> Which I had paid to Nature.

Here 'dignity within' would correspond to 'stately groves' and 'majestic edifices'; 'works of high attempt' would be performed with 'love'; 'toil and pains' would 'spread from heart to heart';

[22] *Dunciad* IV, 337–9, 341–4; *Prelude* III, 652–4, 64, 28, 260, 336–8, 539–41, 518–20, 614.

the 'joy' in 'knowledge' would arise from the sincerity with which it is sought 'for its own sake';

> and over all
> Should be a healthy, sound simplicity,
> A seemly plainness, name it what you will,
> Republican or pious.[23]

The initial and most revealing episode of Book V of *The Prelude* is a visionary deluge from which a phantom Arab maniac bears to safety a shell and a stone, symbolizing poetry and geometric truth. 'This Semi-Quixote,' as Wordsworth calls him, 'the very Knight whose Tale Cervantes tells, yet not the Knight,' may be half-Popian; witness Pope's Knight of La Mancha, from *Don Quixote* II, who carried an Aristotle with him in Part II of the *Essay on Criticism.* What is even more probable, the deluge which threatens human culture looks like a Wordsworthian version of Pope's deluge of dullness and darkness which 'drown'd . . . Sense, and Shame, and Right, and Wrong,' in *The Dunciad.*[24]

And the final passage of Wordsworth's Book V, 'Books,' is an appropriate adaptation of the finale of *The Dunciad;* Pope's 'Universal Darkness' has been transformed into the 'light divine' of Wordsworth's 'great Nature that exists in works of mighty Poets.'

> Visionary *Power*
> Attends upon the motions of the winds
> Embodied in the *mystery of words.*
> There *darkness* makes abode, and *all the host*
> *Of shadowy things do work their changes there,*
> As in a mansion like their proper home;
> Even forms and substances are circumfused
> By that *transparent veil* with *light divine;*
> And through the turnings intricate of Verse,
> Present themselves as objects *recognis'd,*
> *In flashes,* and with a glory scarce their own.

[23] *Prelude* III, 471, 460–2, 467–70, 381–7, 389–407.

[24] *Criticism* 267–83; *Dunciad* IV, 625; *Prelude* V, 49–161.

This beneficent revelation is better understood, however, when we set it side by side with the dark 'Pow'r' of Pope's Dullness, before which

> Fancy's *gilded clouds* decay,
> And all its varying Rain-bows die away.
> Wit *shoots* in vain *its momentary fires*,
> The meteor drops and in a *flash* expires. . . .
> Thus at her felt approach, and secret might,
> Art after Art goes out, and all is Night.
> See skulking Truth to her old Cavern fled,
> Mountains of Casuistry heap'd o'er her head!
> Philosophy, that lean'd on Heaven before,
> Shrinks to her second cause, and is no more.
> Physic of Metaphysic begs defence,
> And Metaphysic calls for aid on Sense!
> See *Mystery* to Mathematics fly!
> In vain! they gaze, turn giddy, rave, and die.
> Religion, blushing, *veils her sacred fires*,
> And unawares Morality expires.
> Nor *public Flame*, nor *private*, dares to shine;
> Nor *human Spark* is left, nor *Glimpse divine!*
> Lo, thy dread Empire, CHAOS! is restor'd;
> *Light* dies before thy uncreating *word:*
> Thy hand, great Anarch! lets the curtain fall;
> And Universal *Darkness* buries All.

Power, *mystery*, *darkness*, *word*(*s*), occur in both passages; but the transparent *veil* of Wordsworth is more hopeful than the veil with which Pope's Religion, *blushing*, *veils her sacred fires; the objects recognis'd in flashes* are more gratefully perceived by the later poet than wit's vain meteor expiring in a *flash* was conceived by the earlier; Wordsworth's shadowy things working their changes are more real than the metamorphoses of Pope: disappearing Arts, skulking Truth, shrunken Philosophy, defensive Physic, sensual Metaphysic, mysterious Mathematics, and expiring Morality.

The 'Restoration' of Night and Chaos, set forth by the argument to the last book of the poem on dunces, seems to have been Pope's challenge to his young pupil, a challenge finally and successfully met when Imagination and Taste were 'restored' in *The Prelude* by the work of those 'Prophets of Nature,' Coleridge and Wordsworth. Then, says Wordsworth (XIII, 433–41),

> Though men return to servitude as fast
> *As the tide ebbs*, to ignominy and shame
> By Nations *sink together*, we shall still
> Find solace in the knowledge which we have,
> Bless'd with true happiness if we may be
> United helpers forward of a day
> Of firmer trust, joint-labourers in a work . . .
> Of their redemption, surely yet to come.

The deluge may return in all the forms of Night and Chaos; but Light and Order are the poetic means of redemption, as of course Pope intended his pupils to learn, young William Wordsworth among them.[25]

The Prelude as an Epistle

In the contagion of *character* writing, that form of the *idyllium* which underlies epistolary art, Pope had illustrated for Wordsworth a method more helpful to an autobiographer than all the generalized portraits from the pilgrims of Chaucer to the pilgrim of John Bunyan. Pope's *characters*, whether of men and women, as in the *Moral Essays*, or the Cibber and Fermor of his mock-

[25] Other echoes of *The Dunciad* in *The Prelude:* Pope's Smithfield Muses (I, 2) and Wordsworth's Bartholomew Fair; Pope's London pageants (I, 85 ff.) and Wordsworth's Book VII; Pope's review of poets laureate (I, 98 ff.) and Wordsworth's catalogue of poets in III and V; the address to Dullness (I, 163 ff.) and the addresses to Nature; the initial discouragement of the poet in both poems; the dedication of the poet, with mystic words and sacred opium in *The Dunciad* (I, 287–8), in *The Prelude* with 'the sweetness of a common dawn, dews, vapours, and the melody of birds, and labourers going forth into the fields'; the public games and sports (in Book II of both poems); the pranks of Fancy in the visionary experience of both Cibber and Wordsworth, and the specular mount from which each saw his vision; and in both poems the references to Newton's genius and Milton's flame, and to the London theaters.

heroics, have real people lurking behind the mask. Such objective validity encouraged in the greatest English autobiography of the nineteenth century a frankness which was to exclude from *The Prelude* no individual form of delight, neither 'autumnal crocus' (cf. Pope's 'bright crocus' of the spring pastoral) nor Belisarius crying 'an obol give!' (cf. Pope's 'Belisarius, old and blind' from *Lines* for Mr. Dennis's benefit in 1733). As Settle and Cibber reside behind Pope's satiric *character* of a dull poet, so William Wordsworth and Samuel Taylor Coleridge are in the frame of *The Prelude*, the *character* of a loving poet and his beloved friend.

The outer form of Pope's art, however, is not the *character*, but the epistle; and on March 25, 1736, he sketched for Swift his unfinished 'epistle in verse,' a design shadowing forth the exchange of large prospective views such as those later shared by the friends Wordsworth and Coleridge. Pope had in mind the following discussions:

1. Of the Extent and Limits of Human Reason and Science.
2. A View of the useful and therefore attainable, and of the un-useful and therefore unattainable, Arts.
3. Of the Nature, Ends, Application, and Use of different Capacities.
4. Of the Use of Learning, of the Science of the World, and of Wit.

Never quite satisfied with the *Essay on Man*, where Man is studied in his relation to the universe and society not less than in his relation to himself and his own happiness, Pope continued to reach for the whole of scientific, ethical, social, and metaphysical lore as a theme for poetry, a possible essay on education. Coleridge's later effort to arrange these vast matters in cosmic form was to remain a prospectus; and Wordsworth's great philosophical poem never was finished. Yet the intellectual correspondence between a Swift and a Pope, or a St. John and a Pope, would not end with its own limitations if it set the pattern for that somewhat warmer, though not less noble, address from Wordsworth to Coleridge in *The Prelude*. In so far as the epistolary essay is a unilateral dialogue, it is in the tradition of profound matters written by friend to friend; and to this tradition *The Prelude* contributes its own beauty.

Then what would Wordsworth learn from his third lesson in English letters, the epistles from Pope to his friend St. John?

While intending the *Essay on Man*, Pope wrote to Swift September 15, 1725: 'Your Travels I hear much of; my own, I promise you shall never more be in a strange land, but a diligent, I hope useful, investigation of my own territories. I mean no more translations, but something domestic, fit for my own country and for my own time.' [26] The arresting command of the *Essay on Man* is the Socratic 'know thyself'; *The Prelude*, an autobiography, is Wordsworth's answer.

In their 'own territories' Pope and St. John would 'expatiate free o'er all this scene of Man'—a maze, a wild or garden, an ample field with open and covert, latent tracts and giddy heights (I, 5–11). Was Wordsworth not expatiating over the same scene when he called the Mind of Man his 'haunt' and 'the main region of [his] song'? [27] In the *Prelude*, however, the scene is to be a particular mind. It will have its own 'rock' planted with 'flowers' and hung with 'shrubs'; its 'caverns,' its 'river,' its 'suburbs,' its 'prospect,' its 'storm' and 'sunshine,' its 'horizon' are all highly personal.[28] Wordsworth is not studying men in the abstract, as did Pope in the first epistle to St. John; his concern is

> A more judicious knowledge of what makes
> The dignity of individual Man,
> Of Man, no composition of the thought,
> Abstraction, shadow, image.

Again and again he emphasizes this point: he knows and will attest 'what there is best in individual Man'; he craves 'truths of individual sympathy'; in learning the habit of intellectual love Man must keep 'his individual state.' [29] This is strongly reminiscent

[26] *Dunciad*, ed. by Sutherland, p. ix.
[27] *Recluse* I, 1, 41, 793–4.
[28] *Prelude* XIII, 231–6; II, 214, 371; III, 246; VII, 506; X, 104–5; XII, 56.
[29] *Ibid.* X, 667; XII, 82–5, 118; XIII, 190.

of the shift from Pope's first epistle, 'Man in the Abstract,' to his second, 'Man with respect to himself as an Individual.' Yet Wordsworth would carry the individualization still further. The stock reference to the intellectual hero, Newton (*Man* II, 34), he changes to an individual experience with a particular statue of Newton; Pope's 'blind beggar' and 'cripple' (II, 267), types, reappear as individuals in Wordsworth's autobiography. The autobiographer is Wordsworth studying Wordsworth instead of a Man studying Mankind.

From his teacher of English letters Wordsworth might learn not only his metaphor for the human mind as a natural scene, but also his most vivid image of those feelings which he would restore to their proper place in the mind of man. The chain of being [30] was for Pope (III, 7–26) a

chain of Love
Combining all below and all above.
See *plastic Nature working* to this end,
The single atoms each to other tend,
Attract, attracted to, the next in place
Formed and impelled its neighbor to embrace.
See Matter next, with various life endued,
Press to one centre still, the gen'ral Good.
See dying vegetables life sustain,
See life dissolving vegetate again:
All forms that perish *other forms* supply,
(By turns we catch the vital breath, and die,)
Like bubbles on *the sea* of Matter born,
They rise, they break, and to that sea return.
Nothing is foreign; Parts relate to whole;
One all-extending, all-preserving Soul
Connects each being, greatest with the least;
Made Beast in aid of Man, and Man of Beast;
All served, all serving: nothing stands alone;
The chain holds on, and where it ends, unknown.

[30] *The Great Chain of Being,* by Arthur O. Lovejoy, Cambridge, 1936, is the signal discussion of the history of this image and related images and concepts.

It is easy to understand that while a collegian, and fresh from his reading of Pope, Wordsworth, too, thought of the chain of being as binding him in the chain of love (III, 124–67):

> To *every natural form*, rock, fruit or flower,
> Even the loose stones that cover the high-way,
> I gave a moral life, I saw them feel,
> Or *link'd* them to some feeling: . . . I had an eye
> Which in *my strongest workings*, evermore
> Was looking for the shades of difference
> As they lie hid in *all* exterior *forms*,
> Near or remote, minute or vast, an eye
> Which from a stone, a tree, a wither'd leaf,
> To *the broad ocean* and the azure heavens,
> Spangled with kindred multitudes of stars,
> Could find no surface where its power might sleep[;]
> Which spake perpetual logic to my soul,
> And by an unrelenting agency
> *Did bind my feelings, even as in a chain.*

Nevertheless, we are enlightened when we observe that Pope's 'plastic Nature working' becomes with Wordsworth 'my strongest workings.' Wordsworth's 'eye . . . eye' has been stimulated by Pope's imperative 'see . . . see'; but the 'power' of that eye has its own 'perpetual logic,' its own 'unrelenting agency' to bind the feelings. The 'all-preserving Soul' of the eighteenth-century writer has become a 'quickening soul' for the young collegian (III, 128); as a vital part of it he will himself give 'a moral life' to Pope's 'forms' and 'beings,' see them feel or link them to some feeling.

In his analysis of Man, Pope told Wordsworth that there were two principles in operation 'to move or govern' all: 'Self-love, to urge, and Reason, to restrain' (*Man* II, 53–6, 59–92). These Wordsworth recalled when, in his Books on the impairment and restoration of Imagination and Taste, he wrote of the 'two attributes' or 'sister horns' of Nature, her 'twofold influence': 'energy' of mind and 'stillness' of mind. Both are gifts of Nature to the Genius of the poet, 'which exists by interchange of peace and excitation.' From Nature's gifts—and may we also say somewhat from Pope's teaching?—he has learned

> To seek in Man, and in the frame of life
> Social and individual, what there is
> Desirable, affecting, good or fair
> Of kindred permanence.

What he finds constitutes an important discovery of *The Prelude:*

> Once more in Man an object of delight,
> Of pure imagination, and of love.[31]

Through this action of *The Prelude* there are two villains working against the delightful revelation and the magnanimous reversal: wrong Reason and the tyrant Eye. From the Popian phrase, '*Nature* that *Tyrant* [Man] checks' came a hint for his own phrase 'the means which *Nature* . . . employs to thwart . . . *tyranny*.'[32] And wrong Reason was Pope's chief villain too: 'In Pride, in reas'ning Pride, our error lies'; 'from pride, from pride, our very reasoning springs.' When Reason does not 'keep to Nature's road,' it gives 'edge and power' to 'the Mind's *disease*, its RULING PASSION.'

> Yes, Nature's road must ever be preferred;
> Reason is here no *guide*, but still a guard.

In the books Wordsworth studied as a very young man there is no clearer statement of his own poetic flaw as chief agent of the action of *The Prelude:*

> There comes a time when Reason, not the grand
> And simple Reason, but that humbler power
> Which carries on its no inglorious work
> By logic and minute analysis
> Is of all Idols that which pleases most
> The growing mind. . . . Suffice it here

[31] *Prelude* XII, 1–14, 39–43, 54–5.
[32] *Man* III, 51; *Prelude* XI, 178–80.

To hint that danger cannot but attend
Upon a Function rather *proud* to be
The enemy of falsehood, than the friend
Of truth, to sit in judgment than to feel.

Service to this Idol had betrayed Wordsworth by 'reasonings false from the beginning . . . drawn out of a heart . . . *turn'd aside from Nature* by external accidents, and . . . thus . . . *misguiding* and *misguided*.' At last 'sick, wearied out with contrarieties,' he has 'yielded up moral questions in despair.' This is 'the crisis of that strong *disease*.' [33]

According to Pope's cure for this disease of the mind, this catastrophe of mankind, the Passions are composed by Reason, but Reason must follow Nature and God (II, 115–19):

Love, Hope, and *Joy*, fair pleasure's smiling train;
Hate, *Fear*, and Grief, the family of *pain;*
These mixed with art, and to due bounds confined,
Make and maintain the balance of the mind.

Here Wordsworth obtained one prescription for his own cure, recorded in the last book of his history (XIII, 143–7):

To *fear* and *love*,
To love as first and chief, for there fear ends,
Be this ascribed; to early intercourse,
In presence of sublime and lovely forms,
With the adverse principles of *pain* and *joy*.

Like Pope, Wordsworth goes on up the ladder from 'self-love' to 'social' to 'divine.' Pope's is a little stairway of eighteenth-century Love based on that eighteenth-century Virtue which alone is eighteenth-century Happiness; Wordsworth's love is pervading and 'diffusive,' reward of a mountain climb at least; but both master and disciple operate under that greater first epistle of Paul to the Corinthians, XIII. Witness, first, Pope (IV, 327–74):

[33] *Man* I, 123, 161; II, 115, 138, 147, 161–2. *Prelude* XI, 121–8, 133–7; X, 801–89, 900–01; (1850) XI, 306.

See the sole *bliss* Heaven could on all bestow!
Which who but feels can taste, but thinks can know: . . .
Slave to no sect, who takes no private road,
But looks through Nature up to Nature's God;
Pursues that Chain which links the immense design.
Joins heaven and earth, and mortal and divine;
Sees, that *no Being any bliss can know*,
But touches some above, and some below;
Learns, from this union of the rising Whole,
The first, last purpose of the human soul;
And knows where Faith, Law, Morals, *all began*,
All end, in LOVE OF GOD, and LOVE OF MAN. . . .
Self-love thus pushed to social, to divine,
Gives thee to make thy neighbour's blessing thine. . . .
Happier as kinder, in whate'er degree,
And *height of Bliss* but height of Charity. . . .
The *centre* moved, a circle straight succeeds,
Another still, and still another spreads; . . .
Earth smiles around, with boundless bounty blest,
And Heaven beholds its image in his breast.
Come then, my Friend! my Genius! come along;
Oh master of the poet, and the *song!*

Noting that this passage precedes Pope's ultimate address to his friend, St. John, Wordsworth has studied it fruitfully; in the final passages of his song about intellectual love, he, too, ascends from the love of Nature and the love of Man to the love of God:

and hence *the highest bliss*
That can be known is theirs, the consciousness
Of whom they are habitually infused
Through every image, and through every thought,
And all impressions. . . . By love, for here
Do we *begin* and *end*, *all* grandeur comes,
All truth and beauty, from pervading love. . . .
And so the deep enthusiastic joy,
The rapture of the Hallelujah sent
From all that breathes and is, was chasten'd, stemm'd

And balanced by a Reason which indeed
Is reason; duty and pathetic truth;
And *God* and *Man* divided, as they ought,
Between them the great system of the world
Where Man is sphered, and which God animates.
. . . And hence this *Song!* which like a lark
I have protracted, in the unwearied Heavens
Singing, and often with more plaintive voice
Attempered to the sorrows of the earth;
Yet *centring* all in *love*, and in the *end*
All gratulant if rightly understood.[34]

This epistolary song, or lyric epistle, like Pope's addressed to his friend, ends in an address to Coleridge, that 'most loving Soul':

what we have loved
Others will love; and we may teach them how;
Instruct them how the mind of man becomes
A thousand times more beautiful than the earth
On which he dwells, above this Frame of things . . .
In beauty exalted, as it is itself
Of substance and of fabric more divine.

Wordsworth's reading of Pope at an early age would yield him more than his theme, his action with its reversals and discoveries, and his precepts. The generic form of Pope's writing, as distinguished from its metrical form, so prevailed upon his own mode of expression that never for long did he abandon the habit of personal address. Whether in the utterance of feeling, the delineation of character or manners, or the telling of a tale, the words are said or written to another, a man is speaking to another man, to a woman or child, to other men, or, in more inspired moments, to all men. Thus, even a mind so different from the mind of Pope, so much more aware of its own nature and adventures, thanks to the traditional economy of English poetry works its way out of mawkish effusions, nocturnal meditations, and other invertebrate musing into the considerate and logical presentation, the

[34] *Prelude* XIII, 107–11, 149–51, 261–8, 380–5.

clear parlance of the hearth, the parlor, the Court, the market place, the forum. The essays and epistles of Pope, it would seem, had a share in the predetermination of *The Prelude*. In that poetical essay on important concerns in the education of one poet, Wordsworth writes to Coleridge as Pope wrote to Granville, to St. John, to Dr. Arbuthnot, and ultimately to the fine intelligence of Jonathan Swift. Without this early discipline in the social responsibilities of literature, Wordsworth might have been content to hear himself talk, or surrender the severe duty of interpretation in favor of the profound subjectivity of the aesthete or metaphysician. Instead, he emerged from the bog of self and the tangle of jargon; his message and speech are those of a man to men.[35]

[35] *Wordsworth and Pope*, The Warton lecture on English poetry given before the British Academy in 1944 by J. R. Sutherland, contains explicit references to Pope by Wordsworth in his later years. Possibly what seems in that lecture an undue eagerness to emphasize differences between Pope and Wordsworth may be modified by the argument and evidence I have given here.

III

Minstrel and Bard

Beattie's Edwin and Young William Wordsworth

In truth he was a strange and wayward wight,
Fond of each gentle, and each dreadful scene.

THESE lines describing Edwin in James Beattie's *Minstrel* [1] reminded Dorothy Wordsworth of her brother William, as she wrote in a letter to her friend, Jane Pollard, on June 16, 1788: 'indeed the whole character of Edwin resembles much what William was when I first knew him after my leaving Halifax.' [2] William alias Edwin in the summer of 1787 deserves more careful study than he has yet received, although Henry A. Beers in 1898 and Kurt Lienemann in 1908 both noted the likeness between *The Minstrel* and *The Prelude:* that is, between 'The Progress of Genius' and the 'Growth of a Poet's Mind.' [3]

[1] *The Minstrel; or, The Progress of Genius:* with Other Poems, . . . by James Beattie, LL. D. To which are prefixed, Memoirs of the Life of the Author, by Alexander Chalmers, F.S.A. London: 1811. *The Minstrel,* Book I, was first published in 1771 anonymously; Book II appeared in 1774.

[2] *Early Letters,* pp. 97–8.

[3] Henry A. Beers, *A History of Romanticism in the Eighteenth Century,* 1898, first edition, p. 304: 'The subject of [*The Minstrel*], indeed, is properly the education of nature; and in a way it anticipates Wordsworth's *Prelude,* as [the]

Since 1940 we have had at hand the remnants of William's youthful minstrelsy, especially *The Vale of Esthwaite*, written by the year 1787, with its quotation from the end of *The Minstrel* (II, lxii):

> Adieu, ye lays, that Fancy's flowers adorn,
> The soft amusement of the vacant mind!

And hence to de Selincourt's mention of several echoes in it from Beattie's poem,[4] we may add others, not only of phrase, but of persons and things and adventures—what might be called the agents, properties, and action of minstrelsy at Hawkshead.

Beattie's Spenserian stanza is yet too difficult for the seventeen-year-old; William chooses Milton's octosyllabics instead. But Beattie's 'shepherd-boy' (II, xxvi) with the 'wild harp' (I, lvii) and his 'ancient man' whose 'harp lay him beside' (II, xxv) are the prototypes of William's shepherd boy (23), his minstrel with hollow-groaning, shrill-shrieking 'harp' (61), and his 'tall, thin Spectre' (328) with 'poet's harp of yore' (335). 'The lamentable strain' (II, xxix) of Beattie's old minstrel is comparable with the 'dismal song' (357) of William's old minstrel; and the 'gothic dome' (II, xvii) and 'shuddering [a]isles' (I, xxxii) of Beattie have suggested William's 'Gothic mansion' (47) and 'aisles that shuddered as we pass'd' (254).

Nor have Beattie's warnings escaped William's attention (I, lvi):

> Is there a heart that music cannot melt? . . .
> The sophist's rope of cobweb he shall twine;
> Mope o'er the schoolman's peevish page; or mourn,
> And delve for life in Mammon's dirty mine.

---

hoary sage does the "solitary" of *The Excursion*.' Kurt Lienemann, *Die Belesenheit von William Wordsworth*, 1908, pp. 92–3. The phrasal echoes of Beattie's poem in *An Evening Walk* and *Descriptive Sketches*, where not acknowledged by Wordsworth himself, have been pointed out by Lienemann, in 1896 by Émile Legouis (*La Jeunesse de William Wordsworth*, translated by J. W. Matthews, 1897, pp. 155–6), and by Ernest de Selincourt (*Poetical Works*, Vol. I, pp. 320, 323, 328).

[4] *Poetical Works*, Vol. 1, pp. 368–9.

The rebuke to sophist and schoolman will constitute an important part of *The Prelude;* at present the minstrel of Hawkshead fears these dangers less than that he must resign his minstrelsy 'to delve in Mammon's joyless mine' (559). When William changes the adjective here from 'dirty' to 'joyless' he is driving his own roots deep into Beattie's soil.

It is not by Beattie's agents and properties, however, that William is most fruitfully stirred; to help him with whatever rudimentary action is now discernible in manuscripts A, B, and C of his *Vale of Esthwaite* he has borrowed from Beattie the idea of subordinating fancy little by little to truth, as follows:

At first Beattie expresses sympathy with the ardor of his 'visionary boy' Edwin, who chases the rainbow in the rear of the summer rain (I, xxxi):

> Perish the lore that deadens young desire;
> Pursue, poor imp, th' imaginary charm,
> Indulge gay hope, and fancy's pleasing fire:
> Fancy and hope too soon shall of themselves expire.

Except for one reference to 'fond sickly Fancy's idle toys' (269), William agrees (296–7):

> Compared with fancy what is truth?
> And Reason, what art thou to Youth?

In an almost identical evening adventure Edwin and William 'pursue . . . th' imaginary charm' with comparable results. 'Young Edwin, lighted by the evening star' (I, xxxii), and young William, 'while lighted by the star of eve' (302) have started off as it were together. For Edwin 'the setting Moon . . . [hangs] o'er the dark and melancholy deep' (I, xxxiii); for William the moon has 'retired,' air is 'blacken'd round.' Then each has a vision. In wild wind Edwin sees the 'vault of night' 'illumed' by 'tapers bright,' and 'a portal's blazon'd arch'; and in tempest under 'the wide vault dark and blind' William imagines the hall of a Baron. Within the portal 'right venerably old' minstrels wake the warbling wire for Edwin; 'on one branded arm' a tall thin 'Spectre' with eyes like 'two wan wither'd leaves' bears for William 'the poet's harp of yore.' These are not merely fancied adventures; they present fancy as the essential form of minstrelsy; or, in our contemporary language, they imply an aesthetic theory of poetry.

But chanticleer, who wakes us all up into the light of common day, interrupts Edwin's vision also; and the 'visionary boy' must then descry in the scenes of morn the actual lineaments of nature: wild brook, lowing herd, simple bell of sheepfold and pipe of early shepherd, clamorous horn and hum of bees and linnet's lay of love, cottage curs and tripping milkmaid, whistling ploughman, ponderous wagon and astonished hare, village clock, whirring partridge, mournful turtledove, and shrill lark. These have become a fanciful convention for us; for Edwin and William such sights and sounds were true. And when William breaks away from his somewhat more horrid tale—which is complicated by his reading of Gray's *Bard*, as we hope to show later—he, too, returns to images of actual life: the 'little horse' to bear him home, the 'dear hills' about Coniston, and the 'darling tide' of Winander. Should we not thank Beattie for this?

There is a further dilemma awaiting the young minstrel. When he overhears the lamentable strain of the old sage, and is dismayed at the ugly transcripts of history, he wishes to turn his back on earthly cares and, again in retreat, to follow 'where Love and Fancy lead.' But he is told that 'Fancy enervates . . . the heart and . . . wounds the mental sight.' The alternative is philosophy and science; and then 'how sweet the words of Truth, breath'd from the lips of Love.' Edwin is converted and proceeds to explore 'the path of Science.' Meditating 'new arts on Nature's plan,'

> From Nature's beauties variously compar'd
> And variously combin'd, he learns to frame
> Those forms of bright perfection,* which the bard,
> While boundless hopes and boundless views inflame,
> Enamour'd consecrates to never-dying fame.[5]

[5] II, xxxix, xl–xli, liii, lvi–lviii. Beattie's asterisk refers us to Aristotle's *Poetics* and the *Discourses* of Sir Joshua Reynolds for such 'general ideas of excellence, the immediate archetypes of sublime imitation, both in painting and in poetry.'

At this point, upon the death of his friend and teacher, John Gregory, Beattie bids adieu to fancy and gives over his account of the education of Edwin.

Young Wordsworth, however, will carry on. He copies into his poem at the beginning of MS B the two valedictory lines of Beattie and continues from there:

> What though my griefs must never flow
> For scenes of visionary woe?
> I trust the Bard can never part
> With Pity . . .

and Charity and Hope, and Sentiments of Affection for inanimate Nature. As Beattie has hinted, in the second stanza of his second book, at the importance of feeling and human relationship—

> But spare, O Time, whate'er of mental grace,
> Of candour, love, or sympathy divine,
> Whate'er of fancy's ray, or friendship's flame is mine—

William writes his own touching lines:

> While bounteous heaven shall Fleming leave,
> Of Friendship what can me bereave?
> Till then shall live the holy flame,
> Friendship and Fleming are the same.

The end of the action is clear for both Edwin and William: fancy has been disciplined not only by truth, but by the truth which is breathed from the lips of love. Even more definitely in *The Vale of Esthwaite* than in *The Minstrel* the reconciliatory progress of genius is foreshadowed by the youngster whose chief doctrinal position as a mature poet will be the need of sweet counsels between the head and the heart. William not only leads his young minstrel 'astray' (55) into a superstitious frightening world where 'fancy, like the lightning gleam, [shoots] from wondrous dream to dream' (65–6); he comforts him by restoring him to friendship and sisterhood from the

> forms of Fear that float
> Wild on the shipwreck of the thought,

While fancy in a Demon's form
Rides through the clouds and swells the storm.

These echoes of Beattie's *Minstrel* in Wordsworth's Juvenilia would be themselves casual or insignificant, were we not sure that Dorothy and William had pondered the likeness of Edwin and William, and that even at the age of seventeen William was dealing with those tensions in the mind of the poet which concerned him throughout his life. Beattie's presentation in Edwin of a minstrel on the search for the right relation between fancy and truth he would modify and enrich; but he could not forget it.

The Progress of Genius and Manuscripts of *The Prelude*

And thus we are brought to the action of *The Prelude*, the minstrelsy of that grown-up minstrel, the thirty-five-year-old William Wordsworth, who through a score of years had persisted in his difficult attempt to say words of truth from the lips of love. When, thanks to Nature, he came home at last to sisterhood and friendship out of the shipwreck of his thought and the aberrations of his demonic fancy, he was repeating in clearer and richer terms his experience of *The Vale of Esthwaite*.

First to be noted in any discussion of *The Prelude* as derived from his early study of Beattie's minstrelsy are several echoes of Beattie's design for his poem, 'to trace the progress of a poetical genius, born in a rude age, from the first dawning of fancy and reason, till that period at which he may be supposed capable of appearing in the world as a Minstrel, that is, as an itinerant poet and musician.' This reminds us not only of Wordsworth's phrase 'very dawn of infancy' in MS V and of 'the Minstrel . . . this obscure Itinerant' of MS Y, but chiefly of the explicit statement about his 'biographical poem,' which 'conducts the history of the Author's mind to the point when he was emboldened to hope that his faculties were sufficiently matured for entering upon the arduous labour which he had proposed to himself,' *The Recluse*.

Because Beattie's design was interrupted by the death of his friend and teacher, the record of Edwin's progress ended before his hero had begun the study of Virgil, Homer, and professional minstrelsy; likewise William's progress in poetry was interrupted by the death of his friend and teacher, William Taylor, near the end of his Hawkshead days. This may be one reason why the first two books of *The Prelude*, which roughly parallel the two books of *The Minstrel*, remained so long unfinished (MSS JJ and V). The hero of *The Minstrel* did not, as it were, get to college; and for a while it looked as though the hero of *The Prelude* would not get to college either, in Book III, 'Residence at Cambridge.'

What was Wordsworth doing when he was not finishing *The Prelude?* He was studying Chaucer, Spenser, and Milton, just as Edwin planned to study Virgil and Homer; and in *Lyrical Ballads* he was trying his hand at minstrelsy of a less demanding kind, something more like the legends, heroic ditties, and tales of rural life told Edwin by his beldame; and in the Preface to *Lyrical Ballads*, which mentioned the story of *The Children in the Wood* (told to the boy Edwin also), he was meditating on the principles of poetry and the poetic life; and he was writing elegies about his dead friend and teacher, the so-called Matthew poems. But principally he was wrestling with 'the hoary sage' long intertwined in his memory with his *alter ego*, Edwin.

Minstrel disciplined by Sage: this was to be the main crux of Wordsworth's literary career. The Sage, that ancient man of whom Beattie thought so well, would contribute his pious sentiments and his misanthropical plaints respectively to the Pedlar of *The Ruined Cottage* and the Solitary of *The Excursion;* and his address to 'sacred Polity' and 'sacred Freedom' would help to furnish the political sonnets of 1802–3, written under the more immediate spur of Milton's sonnets. We need not be surprised that Wordsworth's loyal but frustrate attempt to compose a philosophical poem according to the prescription of another sage, Samuel Taylor Coleridge, interrupted the account of his own youthful minstrelsy until in 1804 Coleridge set out for London and Malta. Coleridge's influence is one fact in Wordsworth's literary biography. Another fact, less often regarded, is young William's early identification of himself with the little Edwin whose 'celestial art' had been so heavily controlled by 'the hermit's strain.' Beattie's unaccomplished *Minstrel* echoes in the emptiness of Wordsworth's unfinished *Recluse*.

Therefore it is to be expected that the arguments of Beattie's hoary sage had to be met and resolved in the later Books of *The Prelude:* 'Imagination, How Impaired and Restored.' For instance, the remorse and grief of one now in retreat from humankind had unsettled Edwin's delight in nature and man, that disaster which the study of history, moral philosophy, and science was intended to repair. Whatever the final effect of these lessons on the minstrel, at first the study of history dismayed him; similarly for the yet unrestored Poet of *The Prelude* 'an emptiness fell on the Historian's Page.' Thenceforth both apprentices in minstrelsy turned from history to philosophy and science; but for Wordsworth, at least, abstract philosophy and pure mathematics were lifeless substitutes for—what?

The answer to this question, and the beginnings of Wordsworth's attempt to think of his progress as a 'meditative history' are found in passages written in February-March of 1804. MS W opens with the seductive and perplexing influence of gauds and feast and dance, and public revelry. Whereas Edwin always avoided the 'sprightly dance' and 'rude gambol' of the village youth, William was on his way home from a 'promiscuous rout' of maids and youths, old men and matrons, where he had 'passed the night in dancing, gaiety, and mirth.' Then his dedication took place, and he started to recover 'that religious dignity of mind, that is the very faculty of truth.'

To illustrate Nature's part in this redemption Wordsworth gathers together in MS W three episodes that echo the three adventures of Edwin, in stanzas directly preceding and following the one Dorothy quoted to characterize William. These Wordsworthian episodes are: (1) dedication at dawn after his night of dancing in a festal company two miles from Hawkshead; (2) the revelation on Snowdon above the mist in the moonlight; and (3), found only in MS W, the fierce autumn storm over Coniston ending in the rainbow 'lovelier than day.'

First, Edwin had

> traced the uplands, to survey,
> When o'er the *sky* advanced the *kindling dawn*,
> *The crimson cloud*, *blue main*, and *mountain grey*,
> And lake, dim-gleaming on the smoky *lawn:*
> *Far* to the west the long long vale *withdrawn*,
> Where twilight loves to linger for a while;
> And now he faintly kens the bounding fawn,
> *And villager abroad at early toil.*
> But lo! the Sun appears! and heaven, earth, *ocean*, *smile.*

William writes in MS W:

> the *sky* was *bright with day*. . . .
> *The Sea was laughing at a distance;* all
> The *solid Mountains* were as *bright as clouds*,
> *Grain-tinctured*, drench'd in empyrean light;
> And, in the meadows and the lower grounds,
> Was all the sweetness of a common *dawn*,
> Dews, vapours, and the melody of birds,
> *And Labourers going forth into the fields.*

The second instance of William's kinship with Edwin in their debt to Nature is as follows:

> And oft the craggy cliff he [Edwin] loved to climb,
> When all in *mist* the world below was lost.
> What dreadful pleasure! There *to stand* sublime,
> Like shipwreck'd mariner *on desert coast*,
> And view th' enormous waste of *vapour*, tost

In billows, lengthening to th' horizon round,
Now scoop'd in gulfs, with *mountains* now *emboss'd!*
And hear *the voice of* mirth and song rebound,
Flocks, herds, and *waterfalls*, along the hoar profound.

Edwin's sea of mist is in tumult; but, when in 1791 William had panted up Snowdon to find himself on the shore of a similar 'huge sea of mist,' it was 'meek and silent':

A hundred *hills* their dusky backs *upheaved*
All over this still Ocean, and beyond,
Far, far beyond, the *vapours* shot themselves,
In headlands, tongues, and promontory shapes,
Into the Sea, the real Sea, that seem'd
To dwindle, and give up its majesty,
Usurp'd upon as far as sight could reach.
. . . *We stood*, the *mist*
Touching our very feet; and from the shore
Not distant more perchance than half a mile
Was a blue chasm; a fracture in the mist,
A deep and gloomy breathing-place through which
Mounted the *roar of waters*, torrents, streams
Inseparable, roaring with *one voice*. . . .
. . . In that breach
Through which the homeless *voice of waters* rose,
That dark deep thorough-fare had Nature lodg'd
The Soul, the Imagination of the whole.

The third instance of kinship between Edwin and William is their delighted response to what Beattie called the 'sad vicissitude' of Nature. Edwin's autumn, when 'the storm howls mournful' and 'the dead foliage flies in many a shapeless flake,' may be contrasted with William's autumn, 'fierce with storm,' with its 'roaring wind, mist, and bewilder'd showers,' and the 'green leaves . . . rent in handfuls from the trees.' William's autumn storm, moreover, has 'a large unmutilated rainbow'

With stride colossal bridging the whole vale,
The substance thin as dreams, lovelier than day.

This is 'immoveable in heaven . . . as if it were pinn'd down by adamant,' and we have more confidence in it than in Edwin's rainbow, which follows a storm of summer rain, and has 'fled afar' from the vain chase of the fond fool that deems 'the streaming glory nigh.'

These three episodes not only articulate spring, summer, and autumn in a ritual year suggested also by Thomson's *The Seasons;* they make vertebrate the progress of genius itself in a triple ceremony of dedication, inner vision or discovery, and the kind of reversal that comes with the rainbow after great struggle. Only the hoary sage with his wintry message can cut short such an imaginative action.

At this point in MS W Wordsworth tentatively sketches episodes and doctrines to illustrate or explain the 'faculty' that, with Nature's help, he must restore before he can get on with his poetic action. As did Beattie (I, iv, vii, viii, xxvii, xli), he mourns the unremitting warfare waged upon the imagination by petty duties and degrading cares, labor and penury, disease and grief. Beattie's phrase is 'penury, disease, and storm' (II, liv). As did Beattie's Sage (II, xxxi, xliii), he approves the 'great ends of Liberty and Power.' But where Beattie gives credit ultimately to Art, Industry, and Science, Wordsworth cannot forget Beattie's earlier hymn of gratitude to Nature and books (I, xl):

> O Nature, how in every charm supreme!
> Whose votaries feast on raptures ever new!
> O for the voice and fire of seraphim,
> To sing thy glories with devotion due!
> Blest be the day I 'scap'd the wrangling crew,
> From Pyrrho's maze, and Epicurus' sty;
> And held high converse with the godlike few,
> Who to th' enraptur'd heart, and ear, and eye,
> Teach beauty, virtue, truth, and love, and melody.

He ends MS W with a nostalgic hymn to the soul of Nature, excellent and fair, the cry of one who

> had received
> Impressions far too early and too strong
> For this to last: I threw the habit off [6]
> Entirely and for ever, and again
> In Nature's presence stood, as I do now,
> A meditative and creative soul.

Out of Beattie's negation of fancy, sophistry, pedantry, and cupidity Wordsworth would make an affirmation, almost as if he were Edwin grown up. And even the 'hoary sage' was to become a wise old Wanderer, too, and would continue to preach a doctrine which William learned first from Beattie, that 'virtue is the child of liberty, and happiness of virtue' (II, xxxi).

Moreover, in this imaginative action, this progress of genius which will come to be a progress of poesy, there is necessarily counterpoint—if we may, as did Wordsworth, mix a musical metaphor with the growth of a poet's mind, a mind 'fashioned and built up even as a strain of music' (MS V). Both Edwin and William delighted in scenes both gentle and dreadful; and we watch with particular interest through Wordsworth's MS V and MS Y until, in its most memorable presentation at the beginning of Book XII of MSS AB, we reach the extending diapason and amplifying volume of that common trait of the two little minstrels. The contrast between 'grandeur and tumult' and the 'tranquil scenes' of MS V becomes in MS Y 'two feelings . . . of grandeur and of tenderness'; and, more elaborately stated in MSS AB, these are the 'two attributes' of Nature, her 'twofold influence,' 'the sun and shower of all her bounties.' From her come both 'emotion' and 'moods of calmness.' Again an important principle of the poetic life allies the adventures of Edwin and William Wordsworth.

And there is something more in the progress of a minstrel, more than fancy or feeling, more than philosophy or science, more even than nature, or books, or truth. It is the art of poetry. From

[6] Of presumption, idolatrous worship of logic and minute analysis, despotism of the eye (XI, 126–7, 174).

the first William must have been aware of the fine harmonies, the careful workmanship, and the poetical wisdom which later he praised in Beattie. Like Edwin he was himself learning to frame forms of bright perfection. The 'archetypes' of Beattie's footnote and his reference to the 'transcripts' of history (II, xxxv) combine to furnish an arresting doctrinal passage in MS Y of Wordsworth's education of a minstrel:

> And in this season of his second birth . . .
> He feels that, be his mind however great
> In aspiration, the universe in which
> He lives is equal to his mind, that each
> Is worthy of the other; . . . 'tis not here
> Record of what hath been, is now no more,
> No secondary work of mimic skill,
> *Transcripts* that do but mock their *archetypes;*
> But primary and independent life.

This is part of an extended passage of MS W which does not appear in MSS AB or in the edition of 1850. I suggest that when Wordsworth was planning a summary, now Book VIII, for his 'Love of Nature Leading to Love of Mankind,' he sketched a 'progress of genius' which combined his own memories with the experience of Edwin: his peacock's fan with Beattie's peacock's plumes; his rainbow, skylark, little rill, river, flower, snow, rain, lightning, thunder, moon, enormous snake, comparable with Beattie's as participants in the various experiences of babyhood and childhood. His magic 'attestations' from the universe of fable and romance ('trees that bear gems for fruit') recall Beattie's Chilian mountains glowing 'with gold and gems,' his forests blazing 'with . . . rays . . . of gems.' Most impressive, the 'Galileo's glass' of Wordsworth and his 'optic tube of thought' are extended from Beattie's 'microscope of metaphysic lore.' Finding this sketch too deferential or dependent, he set it aside. It repays study, and at present can be read in de Selincourt's notes on *The Prelude* (pp. 551–9).

Minstrelsy is a great profession, Beattie would have us believe.

Beattie wrote no Book III and Edwin did not get to college; but although Edwin's father was a humble swain 'of the north countrie' (I, xi), Scotia or thereabouts, he came of a distinguished ancestry dwelling in Fairyland, in Sicilian groves, and in the vales of Arcady. This traditional minstrelsy is carefully differentiated from the shepherd minstrelsy of Wordsworth's *Prelude* in a brilliant passage of MS Y; but the kinship and friendship which bind Edwin and William are not without value for minstrels of our own day.

In spite of Beattie's confidence in good teaching, 'converse with the godlike few,' and his belief in nature, art, industry, science, philosophy, truth, *The Minstrel* breaks off in heart-consuming grief, bitter tears, unavailing woe, and anguish over the loss of his friend John Gregory. Such literary behavior is not characteristic of Wordsworth, even in the loss of his brother John. And hence, when he renounces his poetic errors at the beginning of Book XI of *The Prelude* and resumes his minstrelsy as a minstrel with minstrels, he makes good in the action of *The Prelude* what Beattie has failed to accomplish in *The Minstrel.*

Long time hath Man's unhappiness and guilt
Detained us; with what dismal sights beset
For the outward view, and inwardly oppress'd
With sorrow, disappointment, vexing thoughts,
Confusion of opinion, zeal decay'd,
And lastly, utter loss of hope itself,
And things to hope for. Not with these began
Our Song, and not with these our Song must end.

Whenever he speaks of *The Prelude* as a song, Wordsworth seems to be remembering Edwin, the minstrel of the unfinished song.

The Progress of Poesy: Gray's Bard and Wordsworth's Poet

The arrangement of items in what the young poet considers the objective world, the not-self, is an early literary problem; proceeding from a mere list of those items, each bearing its epithet, the better to attest the writer's observant or critical power, he will advance to an ordering of the items in space or time. Order in space appears to be easier than order in time; witness the advantageous ratio of pleasant scenes and interesting persons over good plots. Soon, however, from his pseudo-Homeric catalogue of ships or his pseudo-Miltonic atlas of places, the novice goes on to erect contiguous or continuous items into the structure of climax or anticlimax, or to follow them along a path upwards or downwards to fit his idea of improvement or its contrary. Thus Homer, thus Virgil, thus Dante. For those at the center of the world the path will lead inwards, to them; for those at the rim of the world the path will lead outwards, to them. Whether the path itself go up or down, in or out, let us call the literary form recording it by its old name, 'progress.'

An anticlimactic progress, or such a tour of wasteland, catacombs, or western isles as amounts to non-arrival or retrogression, has suited the temper of certain ages and certain writers. But in Thomson's *Liberty* and Gray's *Progress of Poesy*, to name two more triumphant albeit still cautious literary progresses over a fixed geographical chart, eighteenth-century man traces his departures, aberrations, and arrivals more tidily and happily, not assuming any frank responsibility for the progress, but secretly glad that a wiser spirit is at work than his. Most important for him —and for us, we may now say—Liberty and Poesy travel from Greece to Britain.

Akin to such progresses in literary space are progresses in literary time, bequests from one generation to another of the functions, perquisites, and insignia of an order, patriarchal or hierarchal: for instance, Lamech begat Noah 'and Noah begat Shem, Ham, and Japheth'; instance, also, Spenser's great Welsh genealogy in Book II of *The Faerie Queene*. Joining an order, in literature as in life, asks deference to the laying on of hands, confidence in howsoever narrow or brief a tradition we may inherit or adopt.

The more comprehensive and representative a tradition, the more complimentary it is to its novices. Episcopal function aside, none is more dignified than the prophetic or bardic. Somewhere in any progress of poesy—and in this sense *The Prelude* is one such —the poet will defer to his forbears. As a collegian he will laugh with Chaucer, call Spenser 'Brother, Englishman, and Friend,' will even pour out libations to Milton's memory. Recalling his college days, he will be less homesick for his contemporaries than for the scholarship of Bucer, Erasmus, or Melancthon. Dissatisfied with his own reading, he will pay his respects to 'all books which lay their sure foundations in the heart of Man.'

One of these progresses of poesy in one of these books is that of Thomas Gray, whose Pindaric apostrophe to the Aeolian lyre traces the 'power of harmony'—the poetic genius—from the springs of Helicon over Thracia's hills and Idalia's velvet green, in wide circuit through the ice-built mountains of the North and the boundless forests of Chili, back to its main path from Delphi's woods, the Aegean Isles, the fields of Ilissus and the waves of Meander, via Latian plains, to Albion's sea-encircled coast. But, alas, there is now in Albion no Aeolian spirit who can match the odes of Pindar. What a challenge, this, to the youthful poet reading Gray's humble and plaintive finale.

Editor de Selincourt has noted two contributions of Gray's *Progress of Poesy* to Wordsworth's *Descriptive Sketches*,[7] and others might be pointed out in the later poems. For instance, the 'key' with which Shakespeare is supposed to unlock his heart in Wordsworth's 'Scorn not the sonnet' (1827) Gray had given to the Bard of Avon in 1757. A more important contribution, and especially for the motivation of *The Prelude* of 1805–6, is implied in Wordsworth's answer to Gray's challenges (*Prelude* XII, 298–312):

Dearest Friend,
Forgive me if I say that I, who long
Had harbour'd reverentially a thought
That Poets, even as Prophets, each with each
Connected in a mighty scheme of truth,

[7] *Poetical Works,* Vol. 1, pp. 327, 328.

Have each for his peculiar dower, a sense
By which he is enabled to perceive
Something unseen before; forgive me, Friend,
If I, the meanest of this Band, had hope
That unto me had also been vouchsafed
An influx, that in some sort I possess'd
A privilege, and that a work of mine,
Proceeding from the depth of untaught things,
Enduring and creative, might become
A power like one of Nature's.

The progress of poesy was not to end with the contemporaries of Thomas Gray.

Granted that Wordsworth's autobiographical poem is a less obvious progress of poesy than if written by his predecessors in the 'mighty scheme of truth,' it is fully as substantial. It is true to type geographically and historically in that it brings its proud relationships all the way from Theocritus in Sicily to James Thomson in Scotland and Thomas Gray in England. Plato and Euclid help to guide it; the Bible serves and exalts it; Virgilian and Horatian vistas open out of it. Its positions are not charted without reference to schoolmen and doctors and monks. Its fair weather comes from Ariosto, Tasso, and Spenser, and from Philip and Mary Sidney at work on the *Arcadia.* Its brooding storms have the authority of Shakespeare's *Romeo and Juliet* and *Lear.* In its dusks and dawns we recognize the *Arabian Nights* and the matins of *Don Quixote.* Most mysterious of its adventures on its most distant horizons are the shadowy exploits of Jack the Giant Killer, and Robin Hood and St. George. Its primal theory of poetry is set forth in a reverie of Stonehenge. Its ultimate poetic association is with the Druids. And in its literary progress westward its outposts are the sands of Leven, the plain of Sarum, and the top of Snowdon.

'In yonder grave a Druid lies'; listening at Hawkshead while his death-marked schoolmaster, William Taylor, uttered Collins' elegiac lines on Thomson, or himself conning the chant of Thomson's Druid to the captives of *The Castle of Indolence*, young William was unforgettably impressed by the druidical character. Those gentle lines of his own written at nineteen in remembrance of Collins, as Collins had remembered Thomson, were not ready; instead, in 1786 the boy learning to love the poets craved for his poetic ideal a more intense, a sadder, and a fiercer strain. When the schoolmaster turned from the recitation of Gray's *Elegy* to the chanting of Gray's *Bard*, William was pleased; for his *Vale of Esthwaite* he could at first hand absorb 'poesy' as the real Druid understood it, the Druid of Druids, the last of the Druids. To that wild Welshman he was more akin than to any plaintive rural swain; for he also haunted 'the giddy steep that hung loose trembling o'er the deep.' Reliving Gray's account of the toilsome march of Edward the First, English butcher of Welsh poets, down the steeps of Snowdon's shaggy side, he heard in his heart and would not forget the echoes of the Cambrian bard cursing the English tyrant. Someday he, too, would stand on Snowdon; someday he, too, would lash with his words the stupidity and cruelty of the rulers of men.

Let us listen to William Taylor and William Wordsworth as they study Gray's *Bard*.

> On a *rock*, whose haughty brow
> *Frowns* o'er old Conway's foaming flood,
> *Robed* in the *sable* garb of woe
> With *haggard* eyes the Poet stood; . . .
> And with a Master's hand, and *Prophet's* fire,
> *Struck* the deep sorrows of his *lyre*.

Hoel, Llewellyn, Cadwallo, Urien, Modred? Where are they now?

> 'On dreary Arvon's shore they lie,
> Smear'd with *gore*, and ghastly pale;

but they do not sleep, these

'Dear last companions of [the] tuneful art. . . .
On yonder cliffs, a *griesly* band,
I see them sit, they linger yet,
Avengers of their native land.

In dreadful harmony they chant prophetic curses on the murderers to come in Edward's line, on Isabel the she-wolf of France and Richard the bristled Boar. Only with their prophecy of a Welsh Tudor for the British throne do they tie up the web of the woes of the race of Edward. Then, leaving the last of their number to die alone,

'In yon bright track, that fires the western skies,
They *melt*, they vanish from my eyes.
But oh! what solemn scenes on Snowdon's height
Descending slow their glitt'ring skirts unroll? . . .
No more our long-lost Arthur we bewail.
All-hail, ye genuine kings! Britannia's Issue, hail!

Of the genuine kings the crowning figure is the 'form divine' of Elizabeth; and to carry on the genuine bardic tradition Spenser, Shakespeare, Milton, not yet, but yet to be, are invoked by the solitary Welsh bard.

'And distant warblings lessen on my ear,
That lost in long futurity expire. . . .
To triumph, and to die, are mine.'
He spoke, and *headlong* from the mountain's height
Deep in the *roaring tide* he plung'd to endless night.[8]

[8] Along with the *Progress of Poesy*, *The Bard* made its appearance as the first volume issued from Horace Walpole's Press at Strawberry Hill, August 8, 1757. I quote from the *Poetical Works of Gray and Collins*, edited by Austin Lane Poole, Oxford, 1926, pp. 44, 54. de Selincourt, *Poetical Works*, Vol. 1, p. 369, refers the 'haggard eyes' and 'giddy steep' of *The Vale of Esthwaite* to Collins' *Ode to Fear* ('haggard eye' and 'ridgy steep' 7, 14–15) and quotes Mr. Frederick Page, who also believes that the Gothic passages of William's poem echo Collins. But Gray's *Bard* gives not only phrases but a complete situation to be copied by his youthful disciple at Hawkshead. Wordsworth owned Gray's *Poems* with Memoir . . . by W. Mason, 1776 (*Transactions of the Wordsworth Society*, No. 6, p. 246).

What did William make of this? He did not then know that his own vision above the 'roar of waters' on Snowdon's height, now to be read at the beginning of the last book of *The Prelude*, would conclude another notable illustration of the druidical or bardic character, or that he would pen for the third book of that poem an ideal *character* of the college freshman as

> A youthful Druid taught in shady groves
> Primaeval mysteries, a bard elect
> To celebrate in sympathetic verse
> Magnanimous exploits, nor unprepared,
> If high occasion called, to act or suffer
> As from the invisible shrine within the breast
> Nature might urge, or antient story taught, . . .
> . . . the young Initiate who had seen
> Thrice sacred mysteries mid Druid groves
> Or where grey Temples stood on native Hills.

But at once, still a schoolboy, in his *Vale of Esthwaite* he started to mimic Gray.

> Hark! the ringing harp I hear
> And lo! her [Superstition's] druid sons appear.
> Why roll on me your glaring eyes?
> Why fix on me for sacrifice?

He, too, becomes a Druid, looking upon

> A dark and dreary vale below,
> And through it a river [strong?]
> In sleepy horror heav'd along,
> And many a high *rock* black and steep
> Hung *brooding* on the darksome deep,
> And on each *sable* rock was seen
> A Form of wild terrific mien. . . .
> While *ghosts of Murtherers* mounted fast
> And grimly glar'd upon the blast.
> While the dark whirlwind *rob'd*, unseen,
> With black arm rear'd the clouds between;
> In anger Heaven's terrific Sire

Prophetic struck the mighty Lyre
Of Nature; with Hell-rouzing sound
Now shriek'd the quivering strings around;
At each drear pause a hollow breath
Was heard—that song of pain and Death,
While, her dark cheek all ghastly bright,
Like a chain'd *Madman* laugh'd the Night.
Again! the deep tones strike mine ear,
My soul will *melt* away with fear,
Or swell'd to *madness* bid me leap
Down, *headlong* down, the hideous steep.

Gray's Welsh Bard served William not only for the 'grisly guide' of his Juvenilia. 'Peace to the brawling din,' says the Hawkshead schoolboy. The 'solemn scenes' and 'distant warblings' of *The Bard*, which furnished a quiet and hopeful peripety for *The Vale of Esthwaite*, foreshadowed also the end of *The Prelude.* The reversal of Books IX-XIII from French tyranny and woe and British misrule to the happy and fruitful life at Racedown with Dorothy, the 'beloved woman,' has taken form in the likeness of Gray's 'deep sorrows' turned into 'bright Rapture.' Also in geographical particulars Wordsworth chooses the Welsh or old British scene to illustrate his new 'progress of poesy.' From the Leven to Sarum to Snowdon, and in this order, goes the author of the 'Growth of a Poet's Mind'; and the poet's experiences in the West of Britain are organized into a sort of Welsh triad, a parable of the art of poetry. The first poem is a hymn of triumph; the second, a reverie; the third, an apocalyptic vision.

The first, the hymn, was sung on the sands of Leven when Wordsworth received news of Robespierre's death: 'Come now ye golden times!'

They who with clumsy desperation brought
Rivers of *Blood*, and preached that nothing else
Could cleanse the Augean Stable, by the might
Of their own helper have been swept away;
Their *madness* is declared and visible,

Elsewhere will safety now be sought, and Earth
March firmly towards righteousness and peace.

Gray's bardic prophecy of Tudor glory has become Wordsworth's Georgian hope; and the Welshman's last words of triumph re-echo from the lips of a greater bard after a disaster which, we still hope, is but the black night before the dawn of righteousness and peace. Nor may we forget that Bard Wordsworth's hymn at a vision of better times was breathed forth on the very day he had visited the grave of his schoolmaster, William Taylor, whose stone bore as epitaph lines from the *Elegy* of Thomas Gray.

The second, the reverie, occurs at the end of Book XII. Ranging over Salisbury Plain amid the monumental ruins of Stonehenge, Wordsworth 'saw the past,' the 'sacrificial Altar, fed with living men' and

the bearded Teachers with white wands
Uplifted, pointing to the starry sky
Alternately, and Plain below, while breath
Of music seem'd to guide them, and the Waste
Was chear'd with stillness and a pleasant sound.

This passage was a final reworking of the druidical frame of reference which had supported not only *The Vale of Esthwaite*, but MS 1 of the poem *A Night on Salisbury Plain*, written in the summer of 1793. There, too, Wordsworth had drawn on Gray's *Bard* for his pictures of druidical horror and his compensatory images of beneficent starlight and moonlight. One word in MS 1 prefigured the title of the autobiographical poem which was to be.

Not thus, when clear moon[s] spread their pleasing light
Long-bearded forms with wands uplifted shew
To vast assemblies, while each breeze of night
Is hushed, the living fires that bright and slow
Rounding th' etherial field in order go.
Then as they trace with awe their various files
All figured on the mystic plain below,

Still PRELUDE of sweet sounds, the moon beguiles[,]
And charmed for many a league the hoary desart smiles.[9]

Then, third, the apocalypse on Snowdon owes its setting and implications to Gray as well as to personal adventure. Four years after he haunted the Vale of Esthwaite, but two years before he wandered over the Plains of Sarum, in 1791 Wordsworth climbed the Welsh mountain. Standing where the last of the Druids had stood, eager to bear his part in the 'distant warblings' of a 'long futurity,' he must have had clear memories of Gray's odes and shadowy intimations of the bardic character as it would always be conceived. Resistance to tyranny was part of that character; ire against treachery and brutality; faith in poetry and love of country; 'solemn scenes on Snowdon's height . . . visions of glory'; confidence that the 'orb of day' would outshine the 'sanguine cloud.' These were the gifts of Gray's Bard to his successor, William Wordsworth.

[9] *Poetical Works,* Vol. 1, pp. 100–5, 334–41.

IV

Shepherd Swain

'The Landskip's Various Treasure'

ONLY a ruthless gardener would disentangle *The Vale of Esthwaite* and its much stronger offshoot, *An Evening Walk*, from the thick shrubbery around Milton's *Il Penseroso* and Thomson's *Summer*. There they should remain, along with the poems of many another swain or wight of the hence-hither school, those who rise with sun and moon both and seem rarely to sleep in their beds. Mirthful or melancholy invocations, with descriptions of the daily or yearly course of earth and the heavens, are the earliest sprouting of poetry; and the mind of every young poet, rooted in the same rich loam of deciduous time, blossoms toward the same everlasting sky overhead. With patience, however, it is possible to detect in the tangle of literary life out of which *The Prelude* itself grew strong a certain Miltonic and Thomsonian morphological strain. But avaunt, vain deluding joys of metaphor, even though we talk of the 'growth' of a poet's mind.

And hail, old experience. There is a common poem, a daily poem, a yearly poem. *The Vale of Esthwaite* was Wordsworth's first attempt to write it; *An Evening Walk* was his second attempt; in *The Prelude*, and in similarly conceived passages of *The Excursion*, he wrote it, better than any other English poet before or after him. Through his boyhood adventures and study and his mature life and art *The Prelude* became the record of man's 'imaginative' day and year; as such it invites comparison with the Book of Hours and the holy year of canonical Christianity.

The ritual pursuits of boyhood—its hours of tit-tat-toe, loo, and whist, and its calendar of bathing, roving, climbing, boating, fishing, bowling, walking, riding, kite-flying, nutting, and skating, not to speak of solitary poaching and responsive hooting—have naught to do with explicit theological statement; but in them exist all the energies, efforts, ordeals, and aspirations which, when disciplined, make possible the arts and religion. Nor should we forget that theological doctrine and religious ceremonial were more familiar to the eighteenth-century schoolboy than to many a twentieth-century schoolmaster. Philosophy herself was an inmate of the schoolroom; and even before the young poet was acquainted with associationist psychology, he would have learned the outlines of Baconian systematic thought and recognized the Platonic assumptions in the hymns of Spenser. Nor would he need more than a hint from his schoolmaster, William Taylor, to discover the cosmology behind Spenser's pseudo-Aristotelian romance, or in the mighty action Shakespeare had conducted from *Midsummer Night's Dream* to *Winter's Tale* and the superlunary *Tempest.* Virgil—and possibly Lucretius [1]—was his staple at school. For a schoolboy who intended poetry, not philosophy, 'the dial's moral round' was set in 'fair scenes' amid 'sweet sounds'; his days went by in Miltonic rhythms and Thomsonian images. Most important of all, the secret *de rerum natura* was in himself.

The octosyllabic couplet is best for a novice who knows *L'Allegro* and *Il Penseroso* by heart; if it had sufficed Milton for the dismissal of Melancholy and the welcome of Mirth, or to banish the brood of folly and summon the sage and holy goddess, it was good enough for the poet of *The Vale of Esthwaite.*

[1] 'Loca pastorum deserta atque otia dia' he quotes in 1793 for his *Descriptive Sketches.* Cf. also *The Theocritean Element in the Works of William Wordsworth,* by Leslie Nathan Broughton, Halle, 1920.

[?] avaunt! with tenfold pleasure
I [?] the landskip's various treasure. . . .
And see, the mist, as warms the day,
From the green vale steals away.

What was young William banishing? Night? Darkness? Dismay? The manuscript of 1786–7 does not say; but we who have read *The Prelude* remember his vain perplexity in beginning that poem, too; how he was mocked with a sky that did not ripen into a steady morning until he had reoriented himself; and how, when the literary mists had cleared away, Books I and II of his autobiographical poem recorded his infancy as 'a visible scene on which the sun is shining.'

Let us not get too far ahead of our story. In the boyish octosyllabics written at Hawkshead the first foot of the first verse of the first couplet remains undetermined; then, like Milton, his disciple speaks out with explosive vigor; where Milton wrote 'Hence!' William writes 'Avaunt!'

After that his words come easily, faint copies of Milton's phrases, but his own nevertheless. With sunrise he can see 'the landskip's various treasure'; so Milton's eye in *L'Allegro*

hath caught new pleasures
Whilst the Lantskip round it measures.

Reserving the Miltonic cock, hounds and horn, and milkmaid for later embellishment, he gazes through Milton's eyes upon the 'civil-suited Morn' of *Il Penseroso*, 'Cherchef't in a comly Cloud.' He will use that device himself; his morning mist shall be thrown on the 'lovely bosom' of the lake like a 'silver zone.' Nature is already a lady.

Meanwhile the shadow on the dial has crept to noon. Where is the pensive man at noon? When the 'Sun begins to fling his flaring beams,' he hides from 'Day's garish eie' in 'twilight groves' or seeks out the 'dimm religious light' of the cloister; at 'noon' Wordsworth also makes his way into 'gloomy glades, religious woods, and midnight shades.' There, however, instead of Milton's pensive nun with her 'sable stole' he will find 'brooding Superstition' weaving 'a stole of sable thread,' and the 'druid sons' of Superstition will roll on him their 'glaring eyes.' It is the 'horrid shapes, and shrieks, and sights unholy' of Milton's 'Stygian Cave forlorn' that justify the so-called gothic horrors of *The Vale of Esthwaite*. In it Milton's

> Daemons that are found
> In fire, air, flood, or under ground

become 'Demons of the storm,' or 'strange forms . . . white and tall . . . against the coal-black wall' of

> castle moated round
> In black damp dungeon underground.

At Hawkshead Wordsworth's 'strange forms' were frightful or grotesque; at Cambridge they would become 'appearances,' but undeniably natural; only when he was grown and had given himself to retrospection or introspection did they become spiritual or ideal. In one guise or another they inhabit all his significant poems. Thus, even while enjoying his haunted castle, his iron coffer marked with blood, his wan and ashy female, his icy chain, his specters and ghosts, the schoolboy warns us against them; they are 'fond sickly Fancy's idle toys.' When next he describes them, in *An Evening Walk*, although 'strange apparitions,' they will be 'a gorgeous show' of shadows. In Goslar, thinking back to his boyhood and the stolen boat at Patterdale, he will say (MS JJ, 188–97):

> For many days my brain
> Work'd with a dim and undetermin'd sense
> Of unknown modes of being; in my thoughts
> There was a darkness, call it vacancy,
> Or blank desertion, no familiar shapes
> Of hourly objects, images of trees,
> Of sea or sky, no colours of green fields;
> But huge and mighty Forms that do not live

Like living men mov'd slowly through my mind
By day and were the trouble of my dreams.

Only in that passage of *The Prelude* where he suggests the somewhat more than gothic horrors of the French Revolution have Milton's 'horrid shapes' grown into the very substance of Wordsworth's art; and here, although still under the influence of Milton's holy goddess Melancholy, they are introduced by a simple adjective (X, 369–77):

Most melancholy at that time, O Friend!
Were my day-thoughts, my dreams were miserable;
Through months, through years, long after the last beat
Of those atrocities . . .
I scarcely had one night of quiet sleep
Such ghastly visions had I of despair
And tyranny, and implements of death.

This time it is an unendurable social and civic glare from which the young Englishman retreats into the shadows of perilous abstraction, into the central gloom of despair, away from the wholesome affairs and affections of the countryside.

Can *The Prelude* be to some extent a diurnal action, its personal dawn, morning, noon, evening, and night another and ampler presentation of the life of a poet made in the image of Milton's pensive hero? If so, the peaceful hermitage at the end of *Il Penseroso* may have helped toward the 'hermitage' of *Prelude* I, 115, and the Recluse of Wordsworth's projected philosophical poem.[2] That daily round which became a literary pattern for *The Vale of Esthwaite* and *An Evening Walk* holds good for the imagery of the autobiographical poem, too. The dispersal of night's shadows, the vision of morning, the retreat at noon are more than a personal experience or a literary device; they resemble events in the old nature myth which underlies all poetry, art,

[2] Into his Esthwaite meanderings William copies a few phrases from *Paradise Lost*, as de Selincourt points out (*Poetical Works*, Vol. 1, pp. 368–9): for *Vale of Esthwaite* 83–7, cf. *Paradise Lost* IV, 588–620 and VII, 371. From *Il Penseroso* de Selincourt has noted only the echo of lines 75–6 in *Vale of Esthwaite* 161–2.

and religion. To complete the diurnal cycle may we expect in *The Prelude* a reversal at twilight and the ultimate lunar discovery?

For his boyish verses, at least, Wordsworth was following the pattern; the cure for the erring and disillusioned soul is the flight of the young minstrel away from

> Spirits yelling from their pains
> And lashes loud, and clanking chains,

back into 'Twilight' and a vision of 'sweet Pity' and 'Hope.'

> Adieu, ye forms of Fear that float
> Wild on the shipwreck of the thought.

'Philomela' singing for William as for Milton's pensive man, Twilight's 'Elfins' like Milton's 'Cherub Contemplation,' and 'Holy Melancholy' herself make for the poet of Esthwaite a characteristically Miltonic evening: its 'tender twilight' softly steals 'o'er the heart'; and with it comes a 'still repose,' to be repeated in the dominant mood of *An Evening Walk*, and to be again repeated in those passages of *The Prelude* where the mature poet represents himself as 'moderated' and 'composed.'

Then, at night, the 'wandering Moon,' likened by Milton to

> one that had bin led astray
> Through the Heav'n's wide pathles way,

returns as the 'pale-faced child of Night . . . wandering through the pathless skies' above Esthwaite. But the moon is not only a wanderer; the moon is a symbol of Hope, 'emerging fair on the dark night of sad despair.' In *An Evening Walk*, the moon is still Hope. And now, without surprise, we recall the lunar vision over Snowdon which closed Wordsworth's poetic day in Book XIII (XIV) of *The Prelude*.

And what is the nature of that mature vision?

Possibly the most revealing phrase in *The Vale of Esthwaite* is 'the moonlight of the poet's mind.' Also in *Beauty and Moonlight*, an ode in octosyllabic couplets, written about Mary Hutchinson, whom he left behind him in Penrith on his return to Hawkshead in 1786, moonlight is compared to the operation of the poet's mind. Mary's forehead, played on by William's wakeful fancy, gleams through her sable hair as the rock on Windermere's shore gleams through the pendent boughs of tressy yew when played upon by the moonbeam. Nature was a lady even then when her name was Mary; and moonlight was the illustration of the lover's creative or poetic power. Small wonder, then, that in *The Prelude* moonlight over Snowdon, dominant 'upon the outward face of things,' is chosen to represent the imaginative power of higher minds, which are thus placed in beneficent relation 'with all the objects of the universe': a 'universal spectacle . . . shaped for admiration' (D), 'framed . . . for delight' (A^2), and 'with magnificence impregnated' (D).

We have seen that MS A of *The Vale of Esthwaite* is a rough exercise on *Il Penseroso* and, less notably, on *L'Allegro;* in the missing pages of this manuscript, we may surmise, and in MSS B and C there were more independent efforts to transcend or apply Milton's lines. As John Milton pledged himself, under certain poetic conditions, to live with Mirth, or Melancholy, so William Wordsworth was early betrothed to Nature. At present, however, in 1786–7, it is a very young poet who writes:

> Long wandering oft by Esthwaite's stream
> My soul has felt the mystic dream.

Had not Milton referred to

> Such sights as youthfull Poets dream
> On Summer eeves by haunted stream?

And what happened to lines on the seven pages cut out of MS A of the poem? In accord with a suggestion of de Selincourt [3] that their matter and imagery were absorbed into *An Evening Walk,* I further suggest that they encountered the unrhymed pentameter

[3] *Poetical Works,* Vol. 1, p. 319.

of James Thomson's *The Seasons,* were able to maintain only their rhyme, and came forth as decasyllabic couplets.[4]

Already, in MSS B and C of *The Vale of Esthwaite,* William had referred to the seasonal nature of the poetic life (italics mine):

> I trust the Bard can never part
> With Pity, *Autumn* of the heart!
> She comes and o'er the soul we feel
> Soft tender tints of Sorrow steal;
> Each flaunting thought of glowing dye,
> The offspring of a brighter sky
> That late in *Summer* colours drest
> The laughing landscape of the breast,
> Is dead, or, ting'd with darkened shades
> In sickly sorrow droops and fades.
> But, Charity, thy treasures show
> A warmer tint and riper glow,
> And richly teem with smiling store
> For the long *Winter* of the poor.

The seasons have an analogy in the feelings; there is a necessary sequence in laughter, sorrow, pity, and charity.

For an apprentice, however, the annual cycle is too difficult; until he is more skilful he must keep to his daily round; his thoughts are still for the most part twilight thoughts and the 'landscape of [his] breast' is still a summer scene. Nevertheless, into his poem reflecting those Miltonic 'summer eeves by haunted stream' he will convey Thomson's—imagery?—no, he will insist on his own images. Thomson's diction?—no, he will leave out all those livid, tepid, humid, turbid, torpid, gelid, sordid, limpid, fetid, lurid adjectives, all except 'lucid.' Thomson's experiences? —no, his own are already powerful enough for him. What, then, will he convey from Thomson? What, indeed, but the sense of

[4] For evidence from Thomson's *Poetical Works* refer to the edition by J. Logie Robertson, Oxford University Press, 1908. Wordsworth owned the first collected edition of *The Seasons,* 1730 (*Transactions of the Wordsworth Society,* No. 6, p. 255).

a very close literary relationship between nature and the life of man.

He opens his copy of *The Seasons* to *Summer* (1379 ff.).

> Now the soft hour
> Of walking comes for him who lonely loves
> To seek the distant hills, and there converse
> With nature, there to harmonize his heart,
> And in pathetic song to breathe around
> The harmony to others. Social friends,
> Attuned to happy unison of soul . . .
> Now called abroad, enjoy the falling day.

Although William's new poem will not be carefully shaped until his freshman and sophomore years in college, nor published, as *An Evening Walk*, until 1793 on his return from France, it is in process at Hawkshead. He conserves for it from *The Vale of Esthwaite* the Miltonic dismissal of Melancholy and the Miltonic summons to Mirth, the Druids, the fanciful forms and actual scenes of his boyhood, and the appearances of sunset and moonrise. To these, possibly encouraged by Thomson, he adds the human activities of the countryside; and he insists on maintaining his own selfhood in the midst of nature and men, as Thomson did not. His transformation of all of this into a unified whole is exciting to watch, and may not be disregarded by a student of *The Prelude*.

> Say, will my friend, with soft affection's ear,
> The history of a poet's evening hear?

What used to be 'the landskip's various treasure' has now, in deference to Thomson's sophisticated verse, become

> Fair scenes! with other eyes, than once, I gaze
> The ever-varying charm your round displays. . . .
> Then did no ebb of chearfulness demand
> Sad tides of joy from Melancholy's hand. . . .
> Return Delights! with whom my road begun, . . .
> When link'd with thoughtless Mirth I cours'd the plain,
> And hope itself was all I knew of pain.

Whereas his friend of Esthwaite had been John Fleming, the absent friend of his evening walk becomes Dorothy. Had not Thomson said to Amanda, 'which way, Amanda, shall we bend our course?' [5] Shall we climb Shene, go to Highgate, Hampstead, view Augusta (London), Harrow, Windsor? Shall we turn to the silver Thames and its matchless vale with Twit'nam, Hampton, Clermont, Esher, the Mole? asked Thomson. What more might be demanded of an evening walk? Wordsworth had his answer ready: 'hoary Derwent,' 'high Lodore,' 'Rydale's mere,' 'Grasmere's lonely island,' the 'clust'ring isles' of 'shy Winander,' and the 'twilight glens of Esthwaite.'

He would not—indeed, he could not—omit the sights shared by himself and his predecessor; England is their common vision. Thomson's 'dark-brown water' (*Spring* 383) flows into Wordsworth's 'dark-brown bason,' past Thomson's 'shaggy rocks' (*Summer* 600) and under Wordsworth's 'half-shagged bridge.' 'The inverted landscape' (*Summer* 1247) seen in 'the well-known pool' looks very much like those similarly 'inverted shrubs' in the gardens of Rydale. And the visto! In the 1727 edition of *Summer* Thomson had rested his eye

> Where in long visto the soft-murmuring main
> Darts a green lustre trembling through the trees;

the young poet liked that word 'visto,' and he would try it out:

> Beyond, along the visto of the brook . . .
> The eye reposes on a secret bridge.

From cascade to cliff for Thomson; from 'small cascade' to 'midway cliff' goes the imagination of Wordsworth, too. Thomson's 'mountains big with mines' (646) justify in *An Evening Walk* the inclusion of the thunders of the 'blasted quarry.' Nor can its author resist a picture of 'the shorten'd herds amid the tide,'

[5] Note the echo of this in lines 29–32 of Book I of *The Prelude:*

> Whither shall I turn
> By road or pathway or through open field,
> Or shall a twig or any floating thing
> Upon the river, point me out my course?

sketched in with original power from Thomson's 'various group' of 'herds and flocks' (485–8):

> Rural confusion! On the grassy bank
> Some ruminating lie, while others stand
> Half in the flood.

The 'spiry' head of the beacon in the later poem has been translated from the 'spiry towns' of Thomson's *Spring* (955); the 'tremulous cliffs of high Lodore' profit by the 'effulgence tremulous' of Thomson's sweet Venus (*Summer* 1699); the Wordsworthian 'idle tale of Man' is simplified from Thomson's 'idle summer life' of 'luxurious men' (346–7); and the account of the sinking of the daystar has by Wordsworth himself been acknowledged as from Thomson.

It is everybody's sunset and moonrise; but from Thomson's line (1620), 'Low walks the sun, and broadens by degrees,' Wordsworth makes his phrase, 'broad'ning sun.' At sunset Thomson's valleys that 'float with golden waves' (1448–9) give thoroughfare to Wordsworthian 'babbling brooks' of 'liquid gold'; and at moonrise, Thomson's 'silver-streaming threads' (first edition, 1727; passage excised, at line 607, for edition of 1744) are akin to what Wordsworth puts in quotes as ' "faint silvery threads." ' There is a pictorial likeness between Thomson's 'illumined mountain' (*Spring* 193) and Wordsworth's 'purple steep,' or Thomson's 'central depth of blackening woods' (*Summer* 719) lending its adjective to Wordsworth's 'central gloom.'

Moreover, from Thomson the novice has learned how to modify the particulars of his idyl in order to ingratiate them. The 'thistly lawn' (1658) of the earlier poet makes way for the 'thistle's beard' of the later; ashes 'wild' for Thomson (471) become 'bat-haunted' for Wordsworth; and Thomson's phrase, 'sympathetic glooms' (*Spring* 1026), seems to justify the pathetic fallacy for his pupil, whose 'tender vacant gloom' and 'sympathetic twilight' better the instruction.

The value of animals for idyllic effect Thomson had amply recognized. His 'evanescent insects' (*Summer* 303) antedate Wordsworth's 'insects like dust'; his 'timid hare scared from the corn' (*Autumn* 401–2) and his 'fearful hare' who 'limps awkward . . . from the bladed field' (*Summer* 57–8) are as contributive to the 'feeding hare thro rustling corn' of *An Evening Walk*, as are his greyhound and house dog (232–5) to its 'lonely hound' and 'mill-dog'—the same literary canines in spite of their different professional experience. Noting the use Thomson has made of Milton's cock, Wordsworth embellishes it from his memory of Rossuet's cock and reinstates it into his pastoral script along with modifications of the Thomsonian swan and glowworm. The graphic devices of the two poets are almost identical.

The area of similarity between Thomson and Wordsworth is more extensive for sights than for sounds; but Thomson's phrase 'distant bleatings of the hills' (*Spring* 200) is echoed in Wordsworth's 'bleating of the fold'; and the boy who 'plunges' into the Thomsonian 'blue profound' (*Summer* 1248) takes on audibility when Wordsworth associates 'the faint uproar' of boys that 'bathe remote' with the 'plunge profound' of the anchor of 'the talking boat.' The bathing in both poems precedes the sunset, which in both poems is followed by the widow and her babes. For emotional effect in *Summer* the great thunderstorm is the prime device (798–9, 1134–45). Its 'deluge of sonorous hail' may have lowered the temperature and deepened the 'roar' of the 'torrent gale' when the widow and her 'cold' and 'frozen' orphans 'perish heart to heart' in *An Evening Walk*. Yet the range of 'sweet sounds' in the later poem is more distinguished than that in any comparable passage of *Summer*.

Most important, not only for *An Evening Walk* but for the autobiographical poem which is to be, are the human activities of *Summer*.[6] Thomson's episodic descriptions of haymaking, sheepshearing, bathing, walking, and the like, are imitated, al-

[6] In his compendious volume, *Topographical Poetry in XVIII-Century England*, New York, 1936, Robert A. Aubin calls such poetical devices 'genre sketches' or 'genre pictures' and points out their frequent occurrence in topographical poems.

though as a device not quite appropriated, in *An Evening Walk*, where these activities are merely decorative; but finally in MSS JJ and V of *The Prelude* they become a kind of ceremony whose gerunds are combined into a disciplinary action. Out of bathing, poaching, rowing, birding, nutting, skating, riding, rather than out of 'views,' spring those 'spots of time' which constitute the successive discoveries not only of the growing boy of 1784–7 but of the literary craftsman of 1798–9. This, it seems to me, is an important lesson in both pedagogy and poetics.

Thomson's *Seasons* and MSS JJ, V, W, Y, and *Prelude* IV

A second lesson, and this time in the method of composition, may be learned when we notice how Wordsworth uses an archetype, how he follows or deviates from the oldest literary pattern of all, the nature myth. *The Seasons* is the conspicuous forerunner of *The Prelude* as a pastoral; with Thomson's scheme in mind we may now discover a likely order for the accretions of Wordsworth's less tidy poem; also we may distinguish the original gift of the later poet in a comparison of his manuscripts with the myth as he inherited it. If our findings are corroborated by facts already known, the process of his literary growth may be further revealed. What Thomson called 'the glories of the circling year' (*Summer* 14), and the seasonal interests of man, have long been the necessary frame of reference for personal growth. It would seem that, after exploiting *Summer* for his youthful *Evening Walk*, Wordsworth was destined to consider the availability of *Autumn*, *Winter*, and *Spring*.

Let us look first at MS JJ, the earliest extant of any considerable part of the poem on the growth of his own mind; and then we may advance to the study of MS V, the amplified version.

In MS JJ, written at Goslar, 1798–9, along with the metaphors of night and day—for instance, 'the dawn of being' and 'our infancy a visible scene on which the sun is shining' and noonday 'darkness'—there are beginnings of another and more inclusive scheme, the course of the year: 'in springtime,' the roving in high places above the raven's nest; on 'a summer's day,' one long bathing; in autumn, woodcock-snaring; and for 'the frosty season,' the skating scene, sent in a letter to Coleridge, December-January 1798–9, contemporary with MS JJ. If to these we add *Nutting*, also composed at Goslar, and the theft of the shepherd's boat when the fields were green, we have reason to believe that Wordsworth is trying himself out on the seasonal plan.

Even as he acknowledged the seasonal aspect of human life, Thomson had asked (*Spring* 468–70):

> But who can paint
> Like Nature? Can imagination boast,
> Amid its gay creation, hues like hers?

In a manuscript note said by de Selincourt (pp. 508–9) to be contemporary with or prior to MS JJ, Wordsworth replies to Thomson's question in the same metaphor. The poet, too, can paint; and God Himself is a Painter:

> Nor . . . *while* . . . *I* . . . *paint*
> How nature by collateral interest
> And by extrinsic passion peopled first
> My mind with beauteous objects, may I well
> Forget what might demand a loftier song.
> For oft the Eternal Spirit, He that has
> His life in *unimaginable* things,
> And he who *painting* what He is in all
> The visible *imagery* of all the World
> Is yet apparent chiefly as the Soul
> Of our first sympathies—O bounteous power.

In general Wordsworth is not theologically explicit; he is experimenting with new terms. Shall he write 'Eternal Spirit,' 'bounteous power,' 'soul of things,' 'eternal beauty'? How well we all know that effort to say something old in a novel way, to imply new values merely because we tamper with an old idiom. In MS JJ, however, the poet makes valid distinctions between Nature and God and the imagination of the Poet, and he puts himself in right relation to both; and when in MS V, later, he relieves these lines of their theological verbiage, he is still able to say simply that he has lived 'with God and Nature communing.'

Along with the images of the painter the rhythms of the musician lend the poet help with his metaphors. In 1798–9 the time interval is his most obvious poetic device; for instance, in the *Lines . . . on the Wye* about his past, present, and future visits near Tintern Abbey: 'again I hear . . . once again do I behold . . . again repose . . . once again I see; and now . . . the picture of the mind revives again.' This periodicity gives to experience its pulsating and emotional constituent, its rhythm.

Leaving for later study in another connection (pp. 253–67) the psychological affinity of the *Lines . . . on the Wye* and MSS JJ and V of *The Prelude*, here we must substantiate from MS JJ Wordsworth's continuing preoccupation with temporal rhythm. From the time of 'unrememberable being' (18) to 'rememberable days' (108) the 'naked feelings' (110) are 'renewed'; 'primordial feelings' (145) are disciplined by the repeated visitations of Nature, gentle or severe, into a 'communion' (246); and the disciplinary rhythm leads to the recognition of grandeur 'in the beatings of the heart' (56–7). As with the pulse of our bodies, and the waves of the sea, the surface of the universal earth is made to 'work' with feelings. It is in pulsation, rather than in 'views,' that the love story of Nature and the Poet begins.

Among these natural rhythms he accomplishes a kind of superfeeling, an intensification, sublimation, or transformation of feelings. Familiar as he was with the 'visionary hour' of the eighteenth century, witness Thomson in *Summer* (556), he wins from his 'recollected hours' (JJ 257) the charm of 'visionary things' (258). He says this in many ways: it was the 'steady cadence' of Derwent which composed his thoughts (10–11); 'amid the swell of human passion' his 'primordial feelings' were serene and calm (145–7); and he imagines these moments of vision, composure, and serenity to be 'islands in the unnavigable depth of our departed time' (259–60). Whatever literary or actual islands are at the back of his mind, he seems to be living over again, as a poet may, that sudden moment of consciousness after the ebb and flow of prenatal or subconscious welter. In MS JJ, where for the most part the heart has been beating hard, and the mild creative breeze has become a tempest with rushing power and mountings of the mind, where even the hills are in 'fluctuation' (287–306), he accomplishes the clearest illustration of what he is to call his 'spots of time.' Thomson's 'visionary hour' and Wordsworth's 'spots of time'—and in our day Whitehead's 'drops of experience'—have much in common.

And when the Wordsworthian 'communion' calls for invocation or address, he can scarcely avoid Thomson's apostrophes. In *Spring*, *Summer*, and *The Hymn*,[7] we hear prophetically the apostrophes of MSS JJ and V: 'ye beings of the hills,' 'ye powers of earth, ye spirits of the springs,' 'ye . . . clouds,' 'ye . . . lakes and standing pools,' 'ye visions of the mountains,' 'ye Souls of lonely places,' 'ye rocks and islands of Winander and ye green peninsulas of Esthwaite.' We note, however, Wordsworth's addition of the words *beings*, *powers*, *spirits*, *visions*, *souls*. His mind is at work modifying Thomson's form of address in the direction of spiritual value.

Although in MS JJ the fashioning of the soul of the lover of Nature is set forth as a rhythm, 'a strain of music,' the poet is verging toward quietude in his representation of Nature herself, toward idyllic or graphic poetry. This is more noticeable in the next record of his growing poem, MS V, which gains help from systematic pastorals. Also, like Thomson and others who thought of their poems as themes and arguments, Wordsworth now calls

[7] 'Ye fostering breezes' (*Spring* 49), 'ye softening dews' (50), 'ye tender showers' (50), 'thou world-revolving sun' (51); 'ye shades . . . ye bowery thickets' (*Summer* 469), 'ye lofty pines! ye venerable oaks!' (470), 'ye ashes wild' (471); and of *The Hymn:* 'ye vocal gales' (40), 'ye brooks, . . . ye trembling rills' (48), 'ye headlong torrents' (50), 'ye softer floods' (51), 'thou, majestic main' (52), 'ye forests . . . ye harvests' (59), 'ye constellations' (64), 'great source of day' (66), 'ye hills' (72), 'ye mossy rocks' (72), 'ye valleys' (74), 'ye woodlands' (76). Cf. what Basil Willey calls the 'sermon-panegyric' of Shaftesbury's Theocles in *The Moralists: A Philosophical Rhapsody* (*The Eighteenth Century Background,* New York, 1950, pp. 62–3).

the story of his life a 'theme' and 'argument.' His summaries are more definite and inclusive; and the argument is followed

> Through snow and sunshine, through the sparkling plains
> Of moonlight frost and in the stormy day.

He speaks of his task more artfully:

> I might pursue this theme through every change
> Of exercise and play, to which the year
> Did summon us in its delightful round.

He vigorously enriches his blank verse with particular activities added on the seasonal plan: fishing in summer; nutting in autumn; for winter, games indoors by the warm peat fire; and a long wait for horses by the whistling hawthorn 'one Christmas-time'; kite-flying on gusty days; the ride with James when the turf was green; and the April episode of the man drowned while bathing in Esthwaite. Thomson's tapestry of flowers in *Spring* (530 ff.), where primrose, crocus, and snowdrop grow together, now shares its snowdrop. In MS JJ we had vernal primrose and autumnal crocus properly distributed; now in MS V Wordsworth has been busy 'ere the birth of spring planting my snowdrops among winter snows.'

The pictorial effect of MS V is enhanced at some cost. The skating episode has been matched with Thomson's skating scene in *Winter* to Wordsworth's great advantage; [8] but adjectives sought for their own sake distract us from the powerful rhythmic suggestions already accomplished in MS JJ; witness the 'oaks' *umbrageous* covert' of the isle on Windermere in summer, Furness Abbey with its '*shuddering* ivy,' and the '*horizontal* boughs' overhead on Coniston. The eye and ear are caught at every turn, and they steal from the pulse somewhat of its commanding power. Thoughts are more distinct; in his fourteenth summer, boating on Coniston, he was

[8] Legouis mentions in this connection the skating scene from the *Confidences* of Lamartine (Bk. V, 5).

> Then first beginning in my thoughts to mark
> That sense of dim similitude which links
> Our mortal feelings with external forms;

at strawberry time on Windermere, while bowling, singing, flute-playing, he could better objectify his experience. Now he is aware of his control over his perceptive life.

> Thus day by day my sympathies increas'd
> And thus the common range of visible things
> Grew dear to me.

The domestication of Nature and the Poet in this fruitful exchange of their delightful knowledge excites him almost as much as the earlier more capricious exchange of feeling between Himself and Nature, and he exclaims:

> Oh! what happiness to live
> When every hour brings palpable access
> Of knowledge, when all knowledge is delight,
> And sorrow is not there. The seasons came,
> And every season brought a countless store
> Of modes and temporary qualities
> Which, but for this most watchful power of love
> Had been neglected, left a register
> Of permanent relations, else unknown.

The annual pattern is never disregarded; 'we ran a boisterous race; the year span round with giddy motion' (MS U); ' 't were long to tell' (MS V)

> What spring and autumn, what the winter snows,
> And what the summer shade, what day and night,
> The evening and the morning, what my dreams
> And what my waking thoughts supplied, to nurse
> That spirit of religious love in which
> I walked with Nature.

To enhance this 'spirit of religious love' in appropriate literary form, his idyl now and again breaks into lyric; he celebrates the sun and moon in the temper of Thomson's 'Hymn to the Sun' in *Summer*. Recalling the 'holy calm' (*Summer* 550) of Thomson's creatures who sing of 'Nature . . . and Nature's God,' he likewise approves the 'holy calm' of 'tranquil scenes.' In traditional parlance he refers to his communion 'with God and Nature'; and Thomson's hymn to the 'Almighty Father . . . the varied God'—

> The rolling year
> Is full of Thee. . . .
> And every sense, and every heart, is joy. . . .
> Nature, attend! join, every living soul
> Beneath the spacious temple of the sky,
> In adoration join; and ardent raise
> One general song!—

resounds in Wordsworth's familiar passage with overtones beyond the art of Thomson:

> In all things now
> I saw one life, and felt that it was joy.
> One song they sang, and it was audible,
> More audible then when the fleshly ear,
> O'ercome by grosser prelude of that strain,
> Forgot its functions, and slept undisturbed.

Indeed, when Wordsworth finishes MS V, he has accomplished the record of a new imaginative service based on the old nature ritual; it is amply indebted to Thomson, but it is very much his own.

MS V is a fairly unified poem concerned with the activities of childhood and schooltime. If the story of growth is to be continued, the ritual year must be extended. Let childhood, then, connote spring; and boyhood and early youth, summer. For a poem 'in five books' Wordsworth will need to add only a book devoted to the activities of autumn; a book for winter; and a book for spring resurgent after winter.

Our next problem, therefore, is to relate Book III with this seasonal plan. What autumnal suggestions for 'Residence at Cambridge' might he find in Thomson's *Seasons?* Thomson's heavy drunken scene of *Autumn* (530 ff.), with the reverend 'doctor' outdrinking all his 'flock,' is a humorous antecedent for Wordsworth's breathless arrival at chapel after the festive libation to Milton. The *character* of the patriot, Argyle, in *Autumn* is a prototype of the *character* of Beaupuy, to be copied into MS Y from an earlier script. And, as Oswald Doughty has remarked, Wordsworth's comparison of himself to 'a shepherd on a promontory' may well be read on the background of Thomson's shepherd in *Autumn:*

> Indistinct on earth,
> Seen through the turbid air, beyond the life
> Objects appear, and, wildered, o'er the waste
> The Shepherd *stalks gigantic*. . . .

Later, in MS Y, he was to make a more exact replica of the Thomsonian shepherd, 'in size a *giant, stalking* through the fog,' whose task it is 'to wait upon the storms . . . the winter long.' Above all, he would not forget Thomson's lists of patriots, philosophers, and poets in *Summer*. For Thomson it is 'wild' Shakespeare, 'sublime' Milton, 'gentle' Spenser, 'laughing' Chaucer; for Wordsworth it will be 'I laughed with Chaucer,' and 'that gentle Bard . . . sweet Spenser.' Thomson's Milton, 'as the bloom of blowing Eden fair,' may have contributed to Wordsworth's Milton 'with his rosy cheeks angelical.' The English poets will go into Book III.

But Book III has no room for such as Thomson's indoor meditations, his 'high converse with the mighty dead' (*Winter* 430–3). Something more must be said about that 'society divine' of Bards: Homer, Virgil, and 'the British Muse.' Wordsworth will need another book, a book on 'Books.' In the late winter of 1804 he starts what we know as MS W.

MS W must have been preceded by his account of the return to Hawkshead, for its first line assumes him to be there for his 'dedication.' But where we should expect its mood to be spring-like, disquiet enters as he sets forth an 'inner weakness,' an 'abasement in my mind,' a 'malady' of college life prior to his Alpine tour in 1790. He pays homage to books, to be sure, those 'adamantine holds of quiet thought or passionate where Bards and Sages dwell'; he composes a Popian satire on the badly educated child to match his lines 'There was a boy'; he transfers the episode of the drowned man from MS V in recognition of what fairy stories and romances do to hallow ghastly sights; yet this argument on books and education, an autumn or winter theme, is in temper gusty and threatening, far different from 'rural nature's milder minstrelsies.' How will he bring again into harmony these disturbing elements in what he now calls his 'meditative history'?

He writes '5th book' and begins it by copying into his new script the summer vision of the moon and mist seen from Snowdon, written—so scholars believe—at Goslar; but then he writes an autumn scene:

It was a day
Upon the edge of Autumn, fierce with storm;
The wind blew through the hills of Coniston
Compress'd as in a tunnel, from the lake
Bodies of foam took flight, and the whole vale
Was wrought into commotion high and low—
A roaring wind, mist, and bewilder'd showers,
Ten thousand thousand waves, mountains and crags,
And darkness, and the sun's tumultuous light.
Green leaves were rent in handfuls from the trees,
All distant things seem'd silent, din so near
Block'd up the listener's ear, the clouds [?]
The horse and rider stagger'd in the blast,
And he who look'd upon the stormy lake
Had fear for boat or vessel where none was.
Meanwhile, by what strange chance I cannot tell,
What combination of the wind and clouds,
A large unmutilated rainbow stood
Immoveable in heav'n, kept standing there

With stride colossal bridging the whole vale,
The substance thin as dreams, lovelier than day,—
Amid the deafening uproar stood unmov'd,
Sustain'd itself through many minutes space;
As if it were pinn'd down by adamant.

In this stormy scene the rainbow plays the same part as does the moonlight above the breach in the fog over Snowdon; it illustrates the imaginative faculty. The seasons are to be transcended. With these passages Wordsworth has by now dedicated himself to an 'abstruser argument'; like Thomson during 'the winter glooms' he, too, will 'scan the moral world.' Thus MS W, on books and on the 'meditative and creative soul' of the young collegian, must speak chiefly of indoor sports, the studies of the dedicated poet, as Thomson had done in *Autumn* and *Winter*.

We have noted that the first lines of MS W imply that they follow a passage, now Book IV, lines 1–268, in which the freshman returns to Hawkshead after 'his laboring time of Autumn, Winter, Spring' at St. John's College. During this first summer vacation his boyhood 'walks did now, like a returning Spring, come back on [him] again' (126–7); now, too, he perceived 'a freshness . . . in human Life' (181–2) 'even as a garden in the heat of Spring, after an eight-days' absence' (186–7). He uses phrases familiar in the language of resurgence and resurrection: he had 'something of another eye' (200, 205); he looked 'with new delight' (207), with 'something of a subtler sense' (ed. 1850). He had 'a new-born feeling' (233), and 'new employments of the mind' (269). When these lines were written we do not know; but they share in the traits of the 'gentler spring' of Book XIII of *The Prelude*. Although Thomson's 'prelusive drops' (*Spring* 175) might have served as baptism for Wordsworth's prelusive poem, the spring of Wordsworth begins another literary year. No longer is the 'grand ethereal bow' (204) an 'amusive arch' (216); it is a simple rainbow. The listed flowers of *Spring* taken altogether do not create, nor do all Thomson's birds, as springlike a feeling as the flowers and shrubs and little birds of that 'gentler spring' Dorothy shared with, even made for, her brother, when (XIII, 241 ff.)

> every day brought with it some new sense
> Of exquisite regard for common things,
> And all the earth was budding with these gifts
> Of more refined humanity.

Writing 'gentler spring' Wordsworth would scarcely forget the invocation of Thomson, 'Come, gentle spring'; but his earth had budded with another kind of life.

We must also note that in Thomson's *Spring* there had been a foreshadowing of serious reversal, from the 'golden age' to 'iron times,' from the 'concord of harmonious powers . . . which forms the soul of happiness' to 'the distempered mind,' where 'all is off the poise within,' until (305–8)

> At last, extinct each social feeling, fell
> And joyless inhumanity pervades
> And petrifies the heart. Nature disturbed
> Is deemed, vindictive, to have changed her course.

Then in Thomson's verse, came the 'deluge' (315–16),

> Till, from the centre to the steaming clouds,
> A shoreless ocean tumbled round the globe.

Since he knew the deluge to be implicit in the literary myth, in MS V Wordsworth had represented himself as made ready by Nature for 'times of fear,' the 'melancholy waste of hopes o'erthrown,' 'indifference,' 'apathy,' 'sneers,' 'dereliction and dismay.' He must have 'a more than Roman confidence.' Later, when he should write about the 'reservoir of guilt and ignorance' that 'burst and spread in deluge through the Land' of France, he, too, would acquit Nature of the blame (X, 426–40):

> If from the affliction somewhere do not grow
> Honour which could not else have been, a faith,
> An elevation, and a sanctity,

> If new strength be not given, or old restored
> The blame is ours not Nature's.

And, after his brother John's death by drowning, February 5, 1805, when the deluge haunted his poem even more intimately, he must still deal with his own deviations from joy. The metaphor occurs several times in the later books of *The Prelude*, written in the spring of 1805 or revised from earlier scripts. Spells forbade him to land on the shore, his 'business was upon the barren sea,' the future would see man to come parted from him who had been, 'as by a gulph.' The sea had 'small islands in the midst of stormy waves'; but

> I could see
> How Babel-like the employment was of those
> Who, by the recent deluge stupefied,
> With their whole souls went culling from the day
> Its petty promises to build a tower
> For their own safety.

For both Thomson and Wordsworth joyless inhumanity is the depth of wintry gloom; for Wordsworth a more refined humanity is the gentler spring, the budding of *The Prelude*.

Moreover, Thomson's lovers 'whom gentler stars unite,' Celadon and Amelia, or Lyttleton and Lucinda, are related to the lovers and the concluding love songs of *The Prelude* at the time of Wordsworth's 'gentler spring,' 'for nought but love can answer love, and render bliss secure' (*Spring* 1124–5). This resembles Wordsworth's (MS Y)

> one dear state of bliss, vouchsafed
> Alas! to few in this untoward world,
> The bliss of walking daily in Life's prime
> Through field or forest with the Maid we love,
> While yet our hearts are young, while yet we breathe
> Nothing but happiness, living in some place,
> Deep Vale, or anywhere, the home of both,
> From which it would be misery to stir.

And, finally, for every 'gentler spring' there is a 'higher love' (MSS AB amplified from MS W),

> a love that comes into the heart
> With awe and a diffusive sentiment;
> Thy love is human merely; this proceeds
> More from the brooding Soul, and is divine.

With all these echoes of Thomson's *Seasons* in mind, may we assume that in the spring of 1804, when Wordsworth was planning a poem in five books, his design ran somewhat as follows: I 'Childhood,' spring; II 'Schooltime,' summer; III 'Residence at Cambridge,' autumn; a fourth book on 'Books' (to become Book V), winter; and a fifth book (now parts of Books IV, XI, XIII) for a gentler spring with poetic dedication and rededication, the spiritual interpretation of the natural cycle? Wordsworth had indeed modified his archetype.

The first part of MS W was assimilated into Books IV and V of *The Prelude*, and the second part of MS W, following what had been intended for the final book ('5th book'), was set aside. Why?

Thomson's seasonal nadir, 'joyless inhumanity,' and the obligation Wordsworth shared with Milton and Thomson 'to scan the moral world,' encouraged in *The Prelude* what Beattie and Thomson would have called the 'historic muse,' and we note that the poem on the growth of his own mind is henceforth thought of less as a song and more as a story or history. Even his avowed aim in MS W, his 'meditative history'—

> to contemplate . . .
> The diverse manner in which Nature works
> . . . upon the outward face of things,
> As if with an imaginative power . . .
> A Brother of the very faculty
> Which higher minds bear with them as their own—

even this 'pleasing argument' and the 'living pictures' in which he embodies it as yet constitute a mere digression, 'which will conduct in season due back to the tale which we have left behind.'

That tale will carry him to France, Italy, and Switzerland with Jones in 1790, to Cambridge, to London, to Wales, to London, to France again, to London—what could he say about France? At least he must finish the college story and look at *Descriptive Sketches* with a view to borrowing from it for Book VI. As the spring of 1804 goes by, it is a comfort to follow Coleridge's route to Malta and Sicily, keep him safe in their common imagination. He will address him in Book VI, regret that they were not contemporaries at Cambridge. Well, what of his sophomore and junior autumns at St. John's, and those 'two winters' of reading? He might tell of the many books 'devour'd, tasted or skimm'd, or studiously perus'd,' books which helped him from his indolent life as 'a lodger in the house of letters' into a 'fellowship' with 'mighty names.' Thomson? Thomson's *Summer* had been a valuable help in the preliminary writing of *An Evening Walk;* Thomson's *Castle of Indolence* had opened his eyes to the poetic meaning of his freshman year, and given an inner form to Book III (see pp. 120–31); his winters as a collegian at St. John's might have somewhat further in common with Thomson's *Winter.*

April of 1804 is upon him and it is his thirty-fourth birthday (VI, 61–4). Why do we suggest that Thomson's *Winter* is in his mind on this gladsome spring day? Well, the word 'winter' occurs again and again in Book VI of *The Prelude:* 'All winter long . . . at night' he frequented the groves and tributary walks. The 'single tree,' an ash, 'trimm'd out by Winter for himself' had gathered upon it the collegian's powers of observation and imagination as he stood 'on winter nights' 'beneath a frosty moon,' 'footbound,' 'uplooking at this lovely tree.' He was another such as Thomson's happy man (*Autumn* 1327–32):

> Even Winter wild to him is full of bliss.
> . . . At night the skies

Disclosed and kindled by refining frost,
Pour every lustre on the exalted eye.

'Uplooking' will be better than Thomson's 'exalted eye.' Here he closes his mind to echoes of Thomson's text; he is impatient to be on his way across the straits of Dover, with Jones and the adventures of 1790, with Coleridge and the present hopes and fears of 1804:

The employments of three winters when I wore
A student's gown have been already told.

These lines, excised from the final script of the poem, remind us again of the seasonal emphasis on Cambridge as an autumn or winter experience. Among the Alps, however, he will again meet 'Winter like a tamed Lion.'

Then, Book VI done, and his continental memories reawakened, how much of the French Revolution as he saw it will be pertinent for the poem? We do not know; indeed he seems not to have known. He had given over; his 'assurances' had 'failed.' Was it 'voluntary holiday' or 'outward indolence,' he asks. And we may add: was it too difficult to write himself free of his revolutionary entanglements? Or did the confines of his seasonal plan forbid him to begin an epic passage before he had finished his idyl of the imagination? How can he escape from his association with the old myth? Will memories of Thomson help or hinder?

How does MS Y fit into the changing purposes and tentative energies of the year 1804?

After the summer 'rest' he returns to his script and, may we suggest, to Thomson's *Winter,* this time more patiently and humbly. He rereads it. There is 'the vapoury turbulence in heaven'; 'low waves the rooted forest'; 'Ocean . . . with . . . blind commotion heaves' (56, 148–9, 181). These outer literary storms match his inner poetic turmoil. His favorite grove this morning, 'tossing its dark boughs in sun and wind,' is spreading through him 'a commotion like its own'—not the 'blind commotion' of

Thomson's ocean, but 'something that fits me for the Poet's task.'

A little farther on in *Winter* enter 'the fowls of heaven.' Not only Thomson's rooks, owl, cormorant, seafowl, but Thomson's robin (246–50):

> The redbreast, sacred to the household gods,
> Wisely regardful of the embroiling sky,
> In joyless fields and thorny thickets leaves
> His shivering mates, and pays to trusted man
> His annual visit.

This last night Wordsworth himself has received such an annual visit from the robins. He, too, will versify them in what seems to start as an amplified winter idyl, MS Y.

> A Quire of Redbreasts gather'd somewhere near
> My threshold, Minstrels from the distant woods
> And dells, sent in by Winter to bespeak
> For the Old Man a welcome, to announce,
> With preparation artful and benign,
> Yea the most gentle music of the year,
> That their rough Lord had left the surly North
> And hath begun his journey. . . .
> 'Ye heartsome Choristers, ye and I will be
> Brethren, and in the hearing of bleak winds
> Will chaunt together.'

With such echoes of Thomson's *Winter* we are introduced to what we know as Book VII of *The Prelude.*

MS Y is also the parent of Book VIII. Wordsworth will make some final representation of his love for Nature as leading to a new theme, his love for Mankind.[9] The first substantial passage in it is a copy, from an earlier script, of the *character* of Beaupuy. Now this will stand at the head of a series of sketches of men at work, in professional communion as it were, but without undue deference to religious tradition. When Wordsworth has called the

[9] Cf. the suggestion of de Selincourt that MS Y may have been intended to complete the poem, *Prelude,* p. xxiv.

robins 'Choristers,' and the glowworm a 'Hermit's taper,' his 'Plato' and 'Dion' as representatives of a Thomsonian 'Antiquity' give way in his new quasi-liturgical design to communicants in a Christian service. In MS Y his redemptive figure will be the pastoral shepherd,

> glorified
> By the deep radiance of the setting sun,
> A solitary object and sublime,
> Above all height! like an aerial Cross,
> As it is stationed on some spiry Rock
> Of the Chartreuse, for worship.

What more fitting for a ritual poem raised to its highest religious value—except that the religious spirit shall ultimately be known as the poetic power in every individual man?

How much of this worshipful quality can be found in Thomson's *Winter?* How much help has Wordsworth taken from his archetype?

Once the two poets share the annual visit of the redbreast, Wordsworth's good memory serves him well. Thomson's address to the shepherds with the bitter death of the disastered swain in the snow has its counterpart in Wordsworth's 'Matron's tale,' a story of the redemption by the father of his son lost in the snow while the boy himself is trying to redeem the lost lamb of the flock—a very simple tale, but Wordsworth has added the redemptive character and the redemptive action. What a difference between the typical shepherd of Thomson and the individual but representative shepherd of Wordsworth!

Thomson's next passages express pity for the grief-stricken, the wretched, the poor, the starving, and the imprisoned; he calls on 'sons of mercy' to wrench from tyrant hand oppression's iron rod. So Wordsworth's patriot Beaupuy is agitated by the 'hunger-bitten girl.'

Next come the Thomsonian 'wolves in raging troops,' used in Wordsworth's Book I; witness the sound of the splitting ice on

Esthwaite, 'like the noise of wolves when they are howling round the Bothnic Main.' And the 'happy Grisons': yes, he had used them for his gypsy in *Descriptive Sketches*. Enough of Alpine winters; come to Thomson's 'rural, sheltered, solitary scene' and 'the mighty dead.' He has already copied Beaupuy into the script: was he not comparable to Thomson's Socrates, Lycurgus, Leonidas, Aristides, Cimon, Timolian, Pelopidas, Epaminondes, Phocion, Agis, Aratus, and others? It is better to concentrate on one beloved patriot than to dissipate the feelings among a list of names; Beaupuy will be remembered when most of the others are forgotten. The poets? He has set them forth in Book III and Book V. 'The sage historic muse'

> Should next conduct us through the deeps of time,
> Show us how empire grew, declined, and fell
> In scattered states;

that will justify him in his efforts to shape fitting passages for the action of which Beaupuy and himself were a part, the yet unwritten books on France; that is, if he should decide to tell that story.

Meanwhile he will now set down his imaginative adventures in the city, as Thomson does. 'The city swarms intense'; at this point in Thomson's *Winter* Wordsworth's Book VII may have started its independent life. Along with Thomson, Wordsworth goes to the theater: Thomson to see *Hamlet*, *Othello*, *The Orphan*, and *Venice Preserved;* Wordsworth to see—shall we say *Cymbeline* and *As You Like It?* If Wordsworth needed further literary justification for enlarging on his own experience in London, here he found it, replete with 'sons of riot' (Wordsworth will say 'dissolute men and shameless women'), 'loose stream of false enchanted joy' (Wordsworth will say 'endless stream' or 'quick dance of colours, lights, and forms'). Next Thomson has added (in 1744) complimentary lines to Chesterfield; Wordsworth will add complimentary lines to Burke (not in MS Y, or in MS X, not even in MSS AB, but as a revision of MS A).

He meditates a moment on Thomson's beloved skating scene;

he goes with Thomson's Laplanders to the 'Finland fairs.' Why not a fair on Helvellyn for the country passages of his idyl? And if he should, like Thomson, enlarge his city passages, why not a Bartholomew Fair? And from Thomson's summary of the ritual of the seasons with its moral epilogue he might take an enabling pattern for what is now planned as his final book, the argument of which would likewise lead from love of Nature to love of Mankind.

> Virtue sole survives . . . And see!
> 'Tis come, the glorious morn! *the second birth*
> Of heaven and earth! . . . The great eternal scheme,
> Involving all, and in a perfect whole
> Uniting, as the prospect wider spreads,
> To reason's eye refined clears up apace.
> Ye vainly wise! ye blind presumptuous! now,
> Confounded in the dust, adore that Power
> And Wisdom . . . Ye good distressed!
> Ye noble few! . . .
> The storms of wintry time will quickly pass,
> And one unbounded Spring encircle all.

He will repeat the phrase 'second birth' in MS Y (168) and use the word 'uniting' and images equivalent to 'reason's eye' and 'glorious morn' in summarizing his own human ritual, his own new kind of communion (VIII, 823–35):

> Among the multitudes
> Of that great City, oftentimes was seen
> Affectingly set forth, more than elsewhere
> Is possible, the unity of man,
> One spirit over ignorance and vice
> Predominant, in good and evil hearts
> One sense for moral judgements, as one eye
> For the sun's light. When strongly breath'd upon
> By this sensation, whencesoe'er it comes
> Of union or communion doth the soul
> Rejoice as in her highest joy: for there,

There chiefly, hath she feeling whence she is,
And, passing through all Nature rests with God.

Moreover, the Paradise of Wordsworth's new script, the beauteous domain where first his heart was opened to the sense of beauty, must be disentangled from all other Paradises. And here Thomson's *Summer* would help him to exclude the fabulous palaces, domes of pleasure, dells for Eastern Monasteries, sunny mounds with Temples crested, and all fabulous beasts and birds, snake and cataract, fountains, and gardens.[10] Instead he will sketch Westmoreland scenes and 'the elements and seasons in their change,' a path, a taper, cottage smoke, a sunbeam in a sunny shed, a garden, a churchyard, a church bell, ocean and wilderness.

Familiar things and awful, the minute
And grand, are destined here to meet, are all
Subservient to one end, near or remote;
One serv[ice] have in which they all [partake].

Next he will substitute the shepherds of Westmoreland for Arcadian, Shakespearean, Spenserian, Theocritean, Virgilian, or Hercynian pastoral life. This he is at pains to say and to say exquisitely and memorably.

Finally, the worshipper himself is conducted through the service. Here, too, Thomson's chief winter sport, contemplation, has rung true in Wordsworth's religious ceremony. And here we must regret that the long passage excised from MS Y, and now to be found only in de Selincourt's notes,[11] was not itself redeemed for the final *Prelude*. When

That great Magician, the unresting year,
Hath play'd his changes off, till less and less
They excite in us a passionate regard,

the child favored by constitution and circumstances has a 'second birth,' makes 'a redemption of himself.' The poetic conversion,

[10] With these compare *Summer* 663 ff.
[11] Pp. 550–8.

this, to match in the moral world the resurgent spring of the physical universe.

Wordsworth is now in full career.

Then rose
Man inwardly contemplated, and present
In my own being, to a loftier height;
As of all visible natures crown; and first
In capability of feeling what
Was to be felt; in being rapt away
By the divine effect of power and love,
As more than anything we know instinct
With Godhead, and by reason and by will
Acknowledging dependency sublime.

And it will be the poet's task—note that he is still assuming the end of MS Y to be the end of his revised poem—

to teach,
Inspire, through unadulterated ears
Pour rapture, tenderness, and hope, my theme
No other than the very heart of man
As found among the best of those who live
Not unexalted by religious hope,
Nor uninformed by books, good books though few,
In Nature's presence.

A winter's tale, indeed, and far beyond the seasonal pattern of Thomson; but Thomson's postlude, the *Hymn on the Seasons*, is a reminder that Wordsworth's idyl of himself growing under the care of Nature and coming to his second birth in the communion of Mankind is still a love song. He will make that clear in the last lines of the poem we know as MS Y.

Anon I rose
As if on wings, and saw beneath me stretch'd
Vast prospect of the world which I had been
And was; and hence this Song, which like a lark
I have protracted, in the unwearied Heavens

> Singing, and often with more plaintive voice
> Attempered to the sorrows of the earth;
> Yet centring all in love, and in the end
> All gratulant if rightly understood.

Shall we give Thomson the last word?

> When even at last the solemn hour shall come,
> And wing my mystic flight to future worlds,
> I cheerful will obey; there, with new powers,
> Will rising wonders sing: I cannot go
> Where universal love not smiles around.

V

Loiterer and Pedestrian Traveller

William Rereads *The Castle of Indolence*

WHEN Wordsworth drew the final outline of what he called 'a map of my Collegiate life' (VI, 199–203), he confessed to

> a multitude of hours
> Pilfer'd away by what the Bard who sang
> Of the Enchanter Indolence hath called
> 'Good-natured lounging.'

As a place Cambridge reminded him of the Castle of Indolence. Had he not been sucked into it through the old Castle of Cambridge, like one of Thomson's 'pilgrims . . . from all the roads of earth' drawn 'ever and anon more nigh' and finally 'constrained to enter in'? 'Fast by a river's side'—Cam itself?—stretched the lazy realm of Thomson;

> A pleasing land of drowsyhed it was:
> Of dreams that wave before the half-shut eye.

William Wordsworth was such a dreamer, and his freshman year at St. John's College was such a dream.[1]

While the freshman of 1787 reread Thomson's 'allegorical poem' in the manner of Spenser, he was appropriating many phrases and images newly come alive in terms of his own recent experience as an academic novice. For instance, that master-porter of the Castle of Indolence who displayed for the initiates 'great store of caps, of slippers, and of gowns,' and the deep thirsty ritual draughts of that rare fountain of Nepenthe, and the 'high-flavoured' wines, the 'rich viands': to match them he thought of his own tailors, his powdered hair, his silken hose, his 'lordly Dressing-gown'; of his brain reeling after the libations to Milton; of the 'invitations, suppers, wine, and fruit.' And Thomson's 'endless pillows' reminded him of the 'pillowy' minds of many of his classmates. Their 'unprofitable talk at morning hours' was very like the 'social glee' at the Castle, 'turning the night to day and day to night'; well, his own heart, too, 'was social, and lov'd idleness and joy.' In the stanza about 'good-natured lounging' he would certainly underline the warning against 'interest, envy, pride, and strife'; this was the very way he felt about examinations.

Such had been 'the opening act' of his college life, the tenor of it at least. But that was not quite all; whenever he left his comrades—'compeers' Thomson called them, and he, William Wordsworth, would one day write 'compeers'—there was a kind of spell on him. Thomson's 'noontide shades, . . . where purls the brook with sleep-inviting sound' (I, lviii, 1–2), were an invitation to his own heart to repose 'in noontide rest.' Reading of the 'tender musings' on the Harp of Aeolus in the Castle gardens, he had recently felt more confidence in what he might call his own 'independent

[1] In Book III Wordsworth explicitly calls himself a dreamer in a dream (28); and many inferences from the text accord with dreamlike experience: 'as if by word of magic or some Fairy's power' (33–4); 'a strangeness in my mind, a feeling that I was not for that hour, nor for that place' (79–81); 'how my sight was dazzled' (202–3); 'spells seem'd on me' (232); 'imagination slept' (260); 'the memory languidly revolv'd' (336); 'the inner pulse of contemplation almost fail'd to beat' (337–8); 'delight . . . lull'd asleep' (648–9).

musings.' He slipped his copy of *The Castle of Indolence* into his pocket and started out for the hawthorn shade near Trompington.

Here he read and dozed the noon away, turning his mind in upon itself, poring, watching, expecting, listening, spreading his thoughts wider and wider. The great mass of which he felt himself a part 'lay bedded' (thus he might translate Thomson's 'full-swelling bed') 'in a quickening soul.' He chanted his favorite stanza (I, xvi):

> What, what is virtue but repose of mind?
> A pure ethereal calm that knows no storm,
> Above the reach of wild ambition's wind,
> Above those passions that this world deform,
> And torture man, a proud malignant worm!
> But here, instead, *soft gales of passion play*,
> And *gently stir the heart* thereby to form
> A *quicker sense of joy;* as *breezes* stray
> Across the *enlivened skies*, and make them still more gay.

He was glad to be away from the imprisoning confines of the courts of St. John's, those three gloomy courts. 'But here, instead' —he repeated the last four lines of Thomson's sixteenth stanza with emphasis on the phrases he specially liked.

A little farther on, Thomson referred to the 'roseate smile on nature's face.' The freshman reminded himself that Thomson was always writing of Nature's face as if Nature were a woman. And now he forgot that he was in Cambridge. He seemed for a moment to be back at Hawkshead, walking around Esthwaite. Well, whatever look, terror, love, or beauty, 'Nature's daily face put on from transitory passion,' he would be as wakeful to it as—well, as 'waters to the sky's motion'; as obedient to it as Thomson's Aeolian harp or—'a lute that waits upon the touches of the wind.'

And he would remember Thomson's gentle breezes from the enlivened skies, breezes that stir the heart and form a quicker sense of joy. What a good way to begin a poem of his own:

Oh, there is—blessing—in this gentle breeze
That blows from—the green fields and from the clouds—
And from the sky: it beats against—my cheek—
And seems—half-conscious—of the joy it gives.

He shook himself awake and made his way back again into prison, over the level fields to the populous plain; but what he would call 'the blue concave of the sky' was still over his head, and it seemed somehow alive, quickened—'enlivened,' Thomson would say.

That night he was more than usually wakeful, and Trinity's clock was more than usually disturbing. He would go on with his reading. Thomson's comparisons of the Castle to the 'luxurious state' of the Caliphs of Bagdad he did not fancy; he himself had been bred up 'amid Nature's luxuries.' The tales of Arcadia and Sicily in the tapestries of Indolence, however, reminded him of the Castle of Emont near Penrith, where, so it was said, Sidney had penned some snatches of the *Arcadia;* a few months hence he would be free to climb that Castle with Dorothy. But would he ever get to Sicily? That must be still, might always be, a dream.

He had reached the second canto of Thomson's poem. How much of it could he say by heart? [2]

I care not, fortune, what you me deny:
You cannot rob me of free nature's grace;
You cannot shut the windows of the sky,
Through which Aurora shows her brightening face:
You cannot bar my constant feet to trace
The woods and lawns by living stream at eve . . .

He also was 'ill-tutor'd for captivity.' He was a 'Freeman'; in the purest sense he was free, as free as Thomson to trace the woods and lawns by living stream at eve. Should he try to turn his *Vale of Esthwaite* into some kind of *Evening Walk?* Thomson would approve:

[2] He quoted the third stanza in a letter to Sir George Beaumont, August 28, 1811 (*Middle Years,* Vol. 2, p. 469).

Come, then, my muse, and raise a bolder song:
Come, lig [lie] no more upon the bed of sloth,
Dragging the lazy languid line along,
Fond to begin, but still to finish loth,
Thy half-writ scrolls all eaten by the moth.

His own memory had, indeed, been revolving 'languidly.' He had been playing 'the loiterer.' He must get back to work on those half-written sheets of *The Vale of Esthwaite*. He would make *his* verse, too, deal boldly with substantial things, things he knew, things around Hawkshead.

That glistening wet rock visible in the distance through the open door of Dame Tyson's cottage: it was like the burnished shield—no, 'the burnished mail,' to be exact—of Thomson's Knight of Arts and Industry when he set out to overthrow the Wizard Indolence. He, William Wordsworth, was not unlike that Knight, 'active,' 'vigorous.'

For him no tender parents troubled were;
He of the forest seemed to be the son.

Minerva and the Muses had nurtured the Knight of Industry

In every science and in every art . . .
That can or use, or joy, or grace impart,
Disclosing all the powers of head and heart.

Like this Knight, who was 'full of great aims and bent on bold emprise,' he had himself come to college endowed with 'holy powers and faculties, whether to work or feel.'

He thought back to those times, those homely days, when the Knight had called the Muses westward

Where Isis many a famous nourseling breeds,
Or where old Cam soft paces o'er the lea. . . .
But now, alas! we live too late in time.

He found himself repeating Thomson's ejaculation: 'Alas! Alas!' and dreaming of the image of a place which should at once have made him pay homage to science and to arts as his liege Lord—

a place not unlike the Castle of Indolence, but different. He would hold in mind Thomson's word 'nourseling.'

Down the page he saw the lines

> Unbroken spirits, cheer! still, still remains
> The eternal patron, Liberty!

And what did the Knight of Arts and Industry do to the Wizard Indolence? He called on Philomelus the bard, that 'little Druid wight . . . in russet brown bedight.' 'Come,' quoth the Knight; . . . come, Philomelus.'

> 'There must,' he cried, 'amid so vast a shoal,
> Be some who are not tainted at the heart,
> Not poisoned quite by this same villain's bowl.' . . .
>
> The bard obeyed; and, taking from his side,
> Where it in seemly sort depending hung,
> His British harp, its speaking strings he tried,
> The which with skilful touch he deftly strung,
> Till tinkling in clear symphony they rung.
> Then, as he felt the muses come along,
> Light o'er the chords his raptured hand he flung,
> And played a prelude to his rising song.

A prelude? The Prelude. A good name for a poem, some day.

William had always liked Philomelus. Should he himself live and die a poet, he would summon the little Druid wight of the keen, sweet eye to draw near his grave, to sing again, ardently, as now to the victims of indolence:

> What is the adored Supreme perfection? say!
> What, but eternal never-resting soul,
> Almighty power, and all-directing day,
> By whom each atom stirs, the planets roll;
> Who fills, surrounds, informs, and agitates the whole? [3]

He himself had felt such 'incumbencies,' such 'visitings of the Up-

[3] Cf. Thomson of God (*Spring* 852–5): 'boundless spirit . . . and unremitting energy,' who 'pervades, adjusts, sustains, and agitates the whole.'

holder of his . . . soul.' 'How awful is the might of souls!' Would this not be, in truth, 'an heroic argument'? 'How the immortal soul with God-like power informs, creates'—no, Thomson says 'informs and agitates the whole.' Philomelus had touched it with a strong hand, but he, William, not yet. The 'rising song' of Philomelus must wait, with Hydropsy, Hypochondria, Tertian, Gout, Apoplexy, and Intemperance at the end of canto i, and Beggary and Scorn at the end of canto ii. They reminded him of certain old humorists on the faculty of St. John's College. He was tired of school and books. 'Great Homer's song, . . . sweet Maro's muse, . . . our Milton's Eden, . . . my master Spenser . . .' Thomson was too fond of making lists of great men, here and in *The Seasons*. He flipped a few pages. In those eloquent verses to the memory of Sir Isaac Newton there were some good phrases, 'intellectual eye,' for instance, and that bit about his stemming alone 'the noiseless tide of time, all bearing down to vast eternity's unbounded sea.' Trinity's loquacious clock struck two, struck two again. He put *The Castle of Indolence* under his pillow, under his 'pillowy' mind. Snuffing his candle, he looked through the moonlight into the Antechapel of Trinity a few yards off. There stood the statue of Newton with his prism and his silent face. William lay down and closed his 'intellectual eye.'

Soon he was dreaming of stately groves, majestic edifices—domain for quiet things to wander in—by the shy rivers—the heron upon the cypress spire—in lonely thought—the pelican—alas!—alas!

We who thus feebly attempt to read *The Castle of Indolence* through the eyes of a homesick freshman in 1787, but who have also read Books III and VI of *The Prelude*, may now with eyes no longer arrogantly dream-laden recognize in the mature, retrospective account of the residence at Cambridge certain traits of the literary dream-allegory which hitherto have escaped general notice. The conflict between indolence and industry, the meditative sorrow for what has been and no longer is, or for what is not but might be, are characteristic of this kind of writing. The seeming lack of connectivity, the digressions and retrogressions, the alternation of moods, the interpolated comment, all of which would impair the quality of Book III as a narrative, are discovered proper for the poet's conception of his college life. The strangeness in his mind, the feeling that he was not for that hour, nor for that place, constitute actual experience, as all of us graduates know; but they are now seen to be fitting in a literary sense as well. The tapestry of famous figures, the allegorical persons of the educational pageant, are less satirically treated by Wordsworth than in Pope's *Dunciad;* as in Thomson's *Castle of Indolence* they have the mildly disturbing effect of guilt manifestations in a nightmare, not yet the profoundly terrifying impact of disasters seen by Michael and Adam from the specular mount of *Paradise Lost.* Alas! Alas! But no, Wordsworth seems to say; they are not real—merely a puppet show, phantoms, a mock fight, a pageant, a cabinet or museum, a gaudy congress.

Thomson was read in the family circle at Dove Cottage on November 15, 1801; and on December 26 Wordsworth set to work again on his 'poem to Coleridge,' possibly on this very freshman dream of Book III.[4] A few months later he reached again for his pocket copy of *The Castle of Indolence*, and in it he wrote, May 9 and 11, 1802, eight Spenserian stanzas about himself and his later 'compeer,' Samuel Taylor Coleridge.

> He would entice that other Man to hear
> His music, and to view his imagery:
> And, sooth, these two did love each other dear:
> As far as love in such a place could be:
> There did they dwell—from earthly labour free.

'From earthly labour free': again the poetic nostalgia, and again at hand the poem which so ably sets forth its symptoms and its

[4] *Journals*, Vol. 1, pp. 80, 96. The reference in the entry for December 27 to 'the third part' is applied by Miss Darbishire to *The Ruined Cottage* instead of *The Prelude* (*Poetical Works*, Vol. 5, p. 409); but the immediate prior reference is to *The Prelude*.

cure. Wizard of Indolence or Knight of Arts and Industry? Which? [5]

At what exact point in the composition of *The Prelude* Wordsworth decided to write a book on London we do not know; but its origin lies partly in *The Castle of Indolence*, entangled with his own indolent career at Cambridge. One of the amusements of Thomson's 'fatal valley' was (I, xlix)

> In a huge crystal magic globe to spy,
> Still as you turned it, *all things that do pass*
> Upon this *ant-hill* earth; where constantly
> Of *idle-busy men* the restless fry
> Run bustling to and fro with *foolish* haste
> In search of *pleasures* vain, that from them fly,
> Or which, obtained, the caitiffs dare not taste.

And hence, when Wordsworth spoke his own incantation to London (1850):

> Rise up, thou monstrous *ant-hill* on the plain
> Of a too *busy* world! Before me flow,
> Thou endless stream of *men* and *moving things!*

we infer that from Thomson's crystal magic globe came help necessary to make Book VII of *The Prelude* possibly its most unified.

Just what was that help? What had Thomson spied in his globe? The 'muckworm' father of 'a gaudy spendthrift heir'; 'pimps, lawyers, stewards, harlots, flatterers'; 'the race of learned men, still at their books'; writers 'in a Thespian rage';

> Then would a splendid city rise to view,
> With carts, and cars, and coaches roaring all.

'The puzzling sons of party . . . in dark cabals and nightly juntos met' and set 'the nations all on fire.' 'Kings' went by, and 'gypsies brown,' with 'nameless numbers moe.'

[5] See *Poetical Works*, Vol. 2, pp. 25–7, 470–1.

Wordsworth writes of his 'fond imaginations' of London as surrendering to the objective truth of 'the real scene'; he asks

Shall I give way,
Copying the impression of the memory,
Though things unnumber'd *idly* do half seem
The work of fancy, shall I, as the mood
Inclines me, here describe, for pastime's sake
Some portion of that *motley* imagery,
A vivid *pleasure* of my Youth, and now
Among the lonely places that I love
A frequent day-dream for my riper mind?

But no, this passage about London as a 'day-dream' is to be cut out of the revised *Prelude;* he will substitute for it the incantation to the monstrous anthill on the plain. Thomson's device of day-dreaming has been renounced for Thomson's vision in the magic globe.

This vision will include the splendid city; all specimens of Man through all the colors the sun bestows; an itinerant vehicle; samples as of ancient comedy and Thespian times; harlots; the brawls of lawyers in their courts before the ermined judge; senators, kings; a compassionate father and his sickly babe (1850); and outbreaks of 'passion, vengeance, rage, or fear,' with executions, fires, mobs, riots, rejoicings; and one annual festival, St. Bartholomew's Fair. O blank confusion!

The fair as a literary device comes rather from *The Seasons* than from *The Castle of Indolence;* but the form of Wordsworth's urban myth does not much vary from the magic vision of Thomson. Details are added, subtracted, modified, revived, or brought up to date; even Wordsworth's roving Indian and sunburnt Arab (1850) recall Thomson's 'gypsies brown.' And we may henceforth think of Book VII and the urban passages of Book VIII as something 'like a magician's airy pageant,' as Wordsworth himself tells us in Book VIII,

embodying everywhere some pressure
Or image, recogniz'd or new, some type

Or picture of the world; forests and lakes,
Ships, Rivers, Towers, the Warrior clad in Mail,
The prancing Steed, the Pilgrim with his Staff,
The mitred Bishop and the throned King,
A Spectacle to which there is no end.

Wordsworth omitted the 'magician' and his 'Spectacle' in the final version of *The Prelude;* for the story of the growth of his mind, however, we must generously acknowledge his debt to Thomson.

In the passages referring to his London experiences in Book IX, indeed, William Wordsworth has become a veritable Knight of Arts, if not of Industry. Like Thomson's hero, who 'passed his youthly morning, void of care, wild as the colts that through the commons run,' so the hero of *The Prelude:*

Free as a colt at pasture on the hill
I ranged at large, through the Metropolis
Month after month.

Wordsworth's delay in entering professional life would have been encouraged by Thomson's belief in the arts, which are 'the quintessence of all, the growth of labouring time, and slow increast.' The Knight himself, before his victory over Indolence, had escaped 'the toilsome scene' for 'a farm in Deva's vale.' Thus Wordsworth left London for Wales, and, in time, for France. Like Philomelus, the Druid poet who assisted the Knight of Arts and Industry, he must serve as a poet serves; and, in a passage later excised from Book III, he wrote himself down 'a youthful Druid.'

If canto i of *The Castle of Indolence* furnished a point of departure for Books III, VI, and VII of *The Prelude*, canto ii may have given a hint for the relation between the Knight Beaupuy and the Bard Wordsworth in Book IX. Beaupuy's devotion to the mean, obscure, and lowly, and the withdrawal of both Knight Beaupuy and Bard Wordsworth from the routs, card tables, and societies of privilege in Orleans accords with the origin, tastes, and behavior of Knight and Bard in Thomson's Spenserian poem. This, Wordsworth would seem to acknowledge when he represented Beaupuy wandering through the deformities of his time 'as through a Book, an old Romance or Tale of Fairy.' The Knight's cheeks glowed, 'indignant,' and his eye full spoke 'his ardent soul'; about Beaupuy when he was bent on works of love or freedom there was 'a kind of radiant joy.' And surely the Knight and the Bard on steed and milk-white palfrey respectively are, with their Spenserian ancestors, the literary progenitors of Beaupuy and Wordsworth strolling along the banks of the Loire. Thomson's pair 'moralized' and

> talked of virtue, and of human bliss.
> What else so fit for man to settle well?
> And still their long researches met in this,
> This truth of truths, which nothing can refel:—
> From virtue's fount the purest joys outwell.

So Beaupuy and Wordsworth discoursed, somewhat more elaborately,

> about the end
> Of civil government, and its wisest forms.
> Of ancient prejudice, and chartered rights,
> Allegiance, faith, and law by time matured,
> Custom and habit, novelty and change,
> Of self-respect, and virtue in the Few.

These echoes of Thomson's two cantos in *The Prelude* do not prove *The Castle of Indolence* to be an efficient cause of the later poem; but they suggest that, knowing the earlier poem so well, Wordsworth recognized in it the universal quality of many of his own adventures and relationships; and, even more, that he now understood their availability for poetic treatment in a literary medium. The vehicular phrases of Thomson had become part of his own diction; this was his good fortune.

In Oliver Goldsmith's Footsteps

Both Oliver Goldsmith and William Wordsworth had been compared by their sisters with Edwin of Beattie's *Minstrel.* Like

Oliver, whose father, dying, left him to the care of an uncle contributing to his support and anxious to prepare him for holy orders, William, too, was dependent upon uncles who expected him to enter the Church. Both young men were by nature wanderers. However much of this Wordsworth knew, he and Dorothy had long been readers of Goldsmith's poetry.[6]

In the long vacation of 1790, preceding his graduation as Bachelor of Arts in 1791, William refreshed his memory of literary topography from Dr. Goldsmith's *Traveller*, and with Robert Jones, a fellow student, journeyed from Calais through France, by way of the Saône River toward the Grande Chartreuse, and by way of the Rhone past Mont Blanc and across the Simplon to Lakes Maggiore and Como; from Italy to Switzerland and the high Alps they went homeward by way of the Rhine. Reminding ourselves that *Descriptive Sketches* was written in 1792 on the banks of that same Loire celebrated by Goldsmith—

> How often have I led thy sportive choir
> With tuneless pipe, beside the murmuring Loire!—

let us review the debt of Wordsworth the 'pedestrian traveller' of 1790 and 1793 and the 'poet' of 1804 to that one of his predecessors who, whether abroad in Helvetia, or homesick for 'sweet Auburn,' had always, as must his successor, made his own felicity. Wordsworth's 'pensive road' (*Descriptive Sketches* 30) and Goldsmith's 'pensive hour' (*Traveller* 32) are akin; it is in Goldsmith's literary footsteps that Wordsworth will make his way across eighteenth-century Europe.

Although in *The Traveller* Goldsmith concedes (81–2) that

> Nature, a mother kind alike to all,
> Still grants her bliss at Labour's earnest call,

he sorrows 'to see the hoard of human bliss so small' (58); he wishes (59–64)

[6] Lienemann, *Die Belesenheit von William Wordsworth*, p. 86. Cf. *Early Letters*, pp. 8, 84, 402.

amidst the scene to find
Some spot to real happiness consign'd,
Where my worn soul, each wand'ring hope at rest,
May gather bliss to see my fellows blest.
But where to find that happiest *spot below*
Who can direct, when all pretend to know?

Wordsworth begins his poem in well-nigh the same words, but more reassuringly:

Were there, *below*, a *spot* of holy ground,
By Pain and her sad family unfound,
Sure, Nature's GOD that spot to man had giv'n,
Where murmuring rivers . . .

A young poet must defer to the literary convention of a melancholy hero, of course; but with greater confidence in Nature, a young poet can improve on the inconclusive melancholy of Goldsmith's Traveller.

Of Italy, the first nation to undergo his ambivalent judgment, Goldsmith says (*Traveller* 111–12, 123–4, 157–61):

Could Nature's bounty satisfy the breast,
The sons of Italy were surely blest. . . .
But small the bliss that sense alone bestows,
And sensual bliss is all the nation knows. . . .
While low delights, succeeding fast behind,
In happier meanness occupy the mind;
As in those domes where Caesars once bore sway,
Defac'd by time, and tottering in decay,
There in the ruin, *heedless* of the dead,
The shelter-seeking peasant builds his shed.

Wordsworth varies these images in the service of the same idea (*Descriptive Sketches* 116–19, 156–7):

Heedless how Pliny, musing here, survey'd
Old Roman boats and figures thro[ugh] the shade,
Pale Passion, overpower'd, retires and woos
The thicket, where th' unlisten'd stock-dove coos. . . .

[The] fragrant gales and lute-resounding streams,
Breathe o'er the failing soul voluptuous dreams.

Yet Wordsworth does not leave Como until he has sketched for us the compensatory picture of the 'hermit—with his family around' (156–75).

From Italy both Goldsmith and Wordsworth go to Switzerland, the former chanting (*Traveller* 165–70):

My soul . . . turn we to survey
Where rougher climes a nobler race display;
Where the bleak Swiss their stormy mansions tread,
And force a churlish soil for scanty bread;
No product here the barren hills afford
But man and steel, the soldier and his sword; . . .
No zephyr fondly sues the mountain's breast,
But meteors glare, and stormy glooms invest.

In similar words the later traveller urges himself on (*Descriptive Sketches* 283): 'from such romantic dreams my soul awake!' He goes from Urseren's 'open vale serene' to savage Uri; but as if recalling Goldsmith's line, 'Yet still, e'en here content can spread a charm,' he writes (323): 'Ev'n here Content has fix'd her smiling reign.' Goldsmith's comparison of the 'sterner virtues' of the Swiss to 'falcons cow'ring on the nest' may have suggested Wordsworth's more energetic phrase, 'fire-clad eagle's wheeling form'; Goldsmith's 'churlish soil' becomes Wordsworth's 'churlish gales'; that soldier and his sword which are for Goldsmith the main product of the barren hills of Switzerland (*Traveller* 169–70) encourage Wordsworth to a fine passage (*Descriptive Sketches* 324–6):

Exulting mid the winter of the skies,
Shy as the jealous chamois, Freedom flies,
And often grasps her sword.

Goldsmith's 'patriot passion' will be the theme for Wordsworth's final prayer for Freedom. Goldsmith's two domestic couplets on the pastoral Swiss (195–8):

While his lov'd partner, boastful of her hoard,
Displays her cleanly platter on the board;
And haply too some pilgrim, thither led,
With many a tale repays the nightly bed,

echo in the same rhyme from Wordsworth's picture of the happier domestic scene under Freedom (*Descriptive Sketches* 736–9):

By clearer taper lit a cleanlier board
Receives at supper hour her tempting hoard,
The chamber hearth with fresher boughs is spread,
And whiter is the hospitable bed.

Again with Switzerland, as earlier with Italy, Wordsworth tempers the darker side of Goldsmith's picture; against Goldsmith's sneer at the '*vulgar* breast' of the Swiss in their annual debauch,' he remonstrates (*Descriptive Sketches* 510–17):

Think not, suspended from the cliff on high[,]
He looks below with undelighted eye.
—No *vulgar* joy is his, at even tide
Stretch'd on the scented mountain's purple side.
For as the pleasures of his simple day
Beyond his native valley hardly stray,
Nought round its darling precincts can he find
But brings some past enjoyment to his mind.

From Switzerland Goldsmith turned to France; and although in fact Wordsworth and Jones had visited France before going to Italy and Switzerland, Wordsworth follows the descriptive sequence of *The Traveller*. He travels from Switzerland toward the French Alps in yet unemancipated Savoy and toward France herself:

Last let us turn to where Chamouny shields,
Bosom'd in gloomy woods, her golden fields . . .
A scene more fair than what the Grecian feigns
Of purple lights and ever-vernal plains.

Mont Blanc dallying with the Sun; 'glad Day-light' laughing upon its snowy top although below all is black; the sun-gilt groves along the Loire (*Descriptive Sketches* 680–5, 773): these are not only personal memories, they are also literary reflections from that luminous couplet of *The Traveller* (239–40):

> To kinder skies, where gentler manners reign,
> I turn; and France displays her bright domain.

But in 1791–3 the author of *Descriptive Sketches* is too near France to resolve her social and political dilemma; nor is he yet able to accomplish more than a shrill finale for the travels he has taken in Goldsmith's footsteps. With help from the myth of a golden age he has written a well-integrated *character* of the pastoral Swiss, but his treatment of the French people is unassociated with any authoritative tradition or sure personal conviction. His poem ends in a spate of frothy personifications: Liberty, Pride, Love, Truth, Justice, Consumption, Freedom, Conquest, Avarice, Pride again, Death, Famine, Oppression, Machination, Persecution, Ambition, Discord, Power, Fire, Sword, Gladness. His pen drops wearily (*Descriptive Sketches* 810–13):

> To-night, my friend, within this humble cot
> Be the dead load of mortal ills forgot,
> Renewing, when the rosy summits glow
> At morn, our various journey, sad and slow.

That particular literary journey was not renewed, nor the pen resharpened, until the spring of 1804, a decade or so later. When, at Dove Cottage, he began the revision of his European memories to illustrate a poetical rather than ethical or political theory, he would not abandon the inheritance from Goldsmith's poem which he had emphasized in Book III: 'A Traveller I am, and all my Tale is of myself.' Not only Goldsmith's title, but also his sententious finale must then have been in mind; and now it is Goldsmith's 'bright domain' of France which shines from the many facets of Wordsworth's mature interpretation of her: 'France standing on the top of golden hours,' the 'bright' faces in Calais. Goldsmith's mention of pipe and dance, even, is written anew in Wordsworth's 'blithe company' dancing 'round and round the Board' and in the 'spirit-stirring sound' of the 'fife of War.'

Moreover, during the spring of 1804 Wordsworth's 'tones of learned Art and Nature mix'd' reveal a fresh literary quality in the poem on his 'own earlier life.' Metaphors derived from the nature cycle or from married life have yielded to less concrete forms in a more abstract frame of reference. Witness in Book VI the up-and-down imagery and statement, with resulting freedom of treatment; witness also the references to Spenser's 'human Forms with super-human Powers,' to 'pleasure . . . from the elements of geometric science,' to the 'Laws of Nature,' to 'pure Intelligence,' and to Coleridge's 'platonic forms of wild ideal pageantry.' [7] In short, Wordsworth has become newly interested in Form for its own sake.

Such an inference is further borne out in the correspondence with and about Sir George and Lady Beaumont, who opened to the Wordsworths a hitherto unstudied realm of pictorial art during those months of 1804 when the author of *The Prelude* was 'advancing' with his work: (March 6) William longed for Sir George to enjoy with him a scene in which may be found 'whatever Salvator might desire'; (July 20, August 31, and December 25) William discussed with Sir George the Discourses of Sir Joshua Reynolds, recently read with care.[8] Somewhat of the painter's zeal for the composition of the whole picture—rather than the aggregation of picturesque details, sentimental items, traits of character, anecdotes, or spots of time—is apparent in the writing of Book VI, especially in the revised account of the pedestrian tour of 1790, which had been published in 1793 as *Descriptive Sketches*.[9] He must gain perspective. If Goldsmith had supposed

[7] VI, 604, 107, 136–7, 146, 187, 309–10.

[8] *Early Letters*, pp. 365, 401–2, 409–10, 423.

[9] For discussions of the two versions of this tour, cf. George M. Harper, *William Wordsworth*, Vol. 2, pp. 89 ff. (1916); H. W. Garrod's chapter on the *Descriptive Sketches* in *Wordsworth* (1923); articles in *Proceedings of the Modern Language Association* 44 (December, 1929), 1144–58, and 45 (June, 1930), 619–

himself seated on an imaginary mountain in Helvetia to aid his reflections in the fields of morality and sociology, Wordsworth might suppose himself crossing the imaginary Alps to assist his meditations in the field of poetics.[10]

For the severe economy of this literary enterprise now coming into focus he would of course have been indebted to others than Goldsmith: Young, for instance, in important ways soon to be set forth (pp. 178–92), and Milton of the 'abyss' and 'specular mount'; and possibly Gray, that nice artist whose travels took him also to the Grande Chartreuse, and whose Latin poem on that subject his friend Isola had doubtless recommended when he tutored Wordsworth at Cambridge.[11] Although the prose written on aesthetics during the century had illustrated artistic effect by formal and informal sketches of nature, and although the ruins of many an architectural treasure had supplied cross reference galore for theorists in all fields, Wordsworth's mountain ranges with their green recesses and valleys, his chasms and falls of a

---

23, by Janette Harrington and E. N. Hooker, respectively; by R. D. Havens in *English Literary History* I (September, 1934), 122–5, and in *The Mind of a Poet* (1941), pp. 406 ff. In his notes to *The Prelude* (1926), pp. 538–42, E. de Selincourt suggests Shakespearean and Miltonic reminiscences; and E. N. Hooker points to the 'innumerable antecedents in English literature throughout the 18th century' of expressions of primitivism and the golden age, and to the 'humanitarianism in vogue in English poetry about 1790'; Wordsworth himself, and after him Legouis, generously annotated the text of 1793 with its English and French literary associations.

[10] From Legouis (*La Jeunesse de William Wordsworth*) comes the hint I propose to follow more in detail (*Early Life*, p. 150): 'The only one of [Wordsworth's] fellow-countrymen to touch upon the subject in verse had been Goldsmith, who supposes himself seated on an imaginary mountain in Helvetia, and thence indulges in some mild moral reflexions concerning the various European countries which he pictures as stretched beneath him.'

[11] Cf. the text in the edition of Gray's *Works* edited by Edmund Gosse (1912), Vol. I, p. 182, where the only similarities I can detect are in certain phrases: *Oh Tu, severi Religio loci* becomes in *Descriptive Sketches* (55) 'Power whose frown severe'; *veteresque sylvas*—(75) 'old woods'; *sonantes Inter aquas*—(67) 'groaning torrent'; *placidam . . . quietem*—(57) 'deathlike peace.' Cf. Gray's *clivosque praeruptos* and in *The Prelude* Wordsworth's 'shining cliffs'; *invias rupes, fera per iuga*, and 'spiry rock'; more particularly, *lege silentii* and 'law of silence.' Gray's Alcaic Ode was written in the album of the Grande Chartreuse, August 1741, a half-century before the visit of Wordsworth.

great river, his moon shining clear above the fog-hidden floods, or laying a dull red image on the sullen water, and his Grande Chartreuse as a myth or 'embodied dream' would differ from the more explicit structures of eighteenth-century prose and poetry, somewhat as a painting differs from an etching.

Toward this increasingly colorful effect, Wordsworth had been helped by Goldsmith's ambivalent scrutiny of Italy, Switzerland, and France, with the illustration in light and shade of those opposed or varying emotional and ethical states which give human life its significant instead of superficial form: its 'alternate passions,' as Goldsmith calls them, [contesting] 'powers,' 'good [begetting] peculiar pain,' 'contrasted faults.' [12]

Life's fairer side, represented by Goldsmith's Village Preacher of *The Deserted Village*, had been mirrored in Wordsworth's Wanderer of *The Ruined Cottage* and would reappear in his Pastor of *The Excursion.* Its less fair side, represented by Goldsmith's Broken Soldier of *The Deserted Village*, was shadowed as Wordsworth's Discharged Soldier of the Alfoxden Notebook, 1798, and Book IV of *The Prelude*, and as his Solitary of *The Excursion;* and that Old Cumberland Beggar whom Wordsworth was delineating in 1795–8 also repeated the outline of the 'long-remembered beggar' of *The Deserted Village*, 'whose beard descending swept his aged breast.' As years went by and brought to the author of the *Ode: Intimations of Immortality* the 'philosophic mind'—another phrase from Goldsmith's *Traveller*—he would not forget both sides of whatsoever picture.

Yet he was to add to this old device of contrasts something of his own. Where Goldsmith was content with presenting the disparate traits of nature, man, and society, Wordsworth would win the literary battle; hope, joy, and freedom must have the victory. From initial dejection to terminal prayer for Freedom, the *Descriptive Sketches* was an ethical if not a poetical improvement

[12] *Traveller* 55, 89, 98, 127. In the words of the Vagabond of *The Vicar of Wakefield,* Wordsworth, too, 'fought [his] way towards England; walked from city to city, examined mankind more nearly, and . . . saw both sides of the picture.'

on Goldsmith's *Traveller;* Wordsworth's *Ruined Cottage* had brought the comfort lacking in Goldsmith's *Deserted Village;*[13] and similarly Book VI of *The Prelude* must elicit from 'tumult and peace,' 'darkness and light,' an apocalyptic vision of 'one mind.'

Goldsmith had given him the right clue in the last passage of *The Traveller:*

> Vain, very vain, my weary search to find
> That bliss which only centres in the mind: . . .
> Still to ourselves in every place consign'd,
> Our own felicity we make or find.

This we recognize as a translation into memorable couplets of an old Stoic assumption which would have come to Wordsworth from many a classical text construed in his boyhood; but it is worth noting that Goldsmith's axiom is echoed and re-echoed in final and summary passages of *The Prelude* (XII, 223–5; XIII, 188–97):

> Here might I pause, and bend in reverence
> To Nature, and the power of human minds,
> To men as they are men within themselves. . . .
> . . . Here must thou be, O Man!
> Strength to thyself; no Helper hast thou here;
> Here keepest thou thy individual state: . . .
> The prime and vital principle is thine
> In the recesses of thy nature, far
> From any reach of outward fellowship,
> Else is not thine at all.

Such is the psychological solution of the dilemma of human life. It furnishes the doctrine of intellectual love, those 'sweet counsels between the head and heart' of which *The Prelude* is an eminent illustration. But we have now to consider an artistic or poetic matter. What is the formal equivalent of 'imagination'? How does the

[13] There are only about thirty rhymes in Wordsworth's *Evening Walk* not to be found in *The Traveller;* and only about fifty rhymes in *Descriptive Sketches* not to be found in *The Traveller* and *The Deserted Village.*

artist or poet bring into one, by this exercise of his esemplastic power, the literary contraries of which Goldsmith's *Traveller* is a scarcely accomplished, and *The Prelude* a highly accomplished instance? If 'Imagination' be the only cure for the mind 'perplex'd' with 'moral questions,' sick with a two-sided ethic of 'contrarieties,' what is the cure for literary perplexity and artistic two-sidedness? Goldsmith's ambivalent view of society, his antithetical expression of what he saw, was a strong challenge not only to Wordsworth's imagination, but also to his craftsmanship.

Goldsmith's first lesson in the art of poetry, the importance of an antithetical interpretation of national as of personal character, was applied by Wordsworth in the following instances: the contrasting characters of Beaupuy and Vaudracour in Book IX; the 'strange reverse' of Arras, birthplace and victim of Robespierre in Book X; and in the same book the two kinds of victory, the violent triumph over Robespierre and the Invaders as contrasted with triumphs of 'unambitious peace at home and noiseless fortitude.' Witness, also, throughout the later books of *The Prelude* the handling of British duplicity and French apostasy; and witness finally his recognition of a double quality in himself as the literary hero of his poem (X, 869–77):

> Having two natures in me, joy the one
> The other melancholy, and withal
> A happy man, and therefore bold to look
> On painful things, . . . I took the knife in hand . . .
> Endeavoured with my best of skill to probe
> The living body of society
> Even to the heart.

Analysis, however, was not the cure for the French dilemma nor for Wordsworth's dilemma. In 1804 he sets forth these various 'contrarieties' with full knowledge not only of their literary ancestry but with full assurance of the imaginative mode in which they are to be reconciled. In Nature there is a 'counterpoise.'

For that 'twofold Frame of body and of mind' 'in which the eye [is] master of the heart' Nature has means to thwart what is tyrannical, makes all the senses and their objects 'subservient in their turn to the great ends of Liberty and Power.' Moreover, the two attributes of Nature herself, her two gifts, emotion and calm, her 'twofold influence,' compared to 'sun and shower,' are 'in origin and end alike benignant.' Here Wordsworth reconciles two pairs of natural opposites by reference to creation and creative purpose. As Nature thus 'lifts the Being into magnanimity,' so 'gifts divine' are unified in 'the pervading grace that hath been, is, and shall be.'

Yet this colorful 'magnanimity,' this luminous 'grace,' will, in its turn, gain literary effect when given a shadow. As if he must make some use of that yet unappropriated passage of *The Traveller* where Goldsmith deals with the main liability of Holland, her avid pursuit of wealth, he insists on 'the utter hollowness of what we name the wealth of Nations.' Now in *The Traveller* Goldsmith had gone from wealth-producing Holland back to Britain. It is in the pattern of a continental journey, then, that Wordsworth should follow his diatribe against a 'false philosophy' of economics with a challenge to his own countrymen and a resort to the 'path-ways' and 'lonely roads' of his native land. Again he becomes the Traveller; and it is as a reformed traveller that daily he will peer into the depth of human souls, convinced that the genius of the Poet (XII, 144, 294–6) 'may boldly take his way among mankind wherever Nature leads.'

The second lesson he might have reviewed in Goldsmith's poetry, even had he learned it first from Goldsmith's teachers, was the formal value of a lofty position for a reconciliation of the twofold aspect of human life. This device, the *state super vias* of Jeremiah, which Chaucer prefixed to his *Parson's Tale*, a device which Milton used for his specular mount, had by Goldsmith's time been freed somewhat from its association with sin and sorrow and penitence. What would Wordsworth do with it?

There had been no actual or poetical mountaintop in *The Borderers* with its contrasting natures of Marmaduke and Oswald, no balance from Oswald's 'two columns, one for passion, one for proof.' The verbal magic which changes Spinoza's two words 'intellectualis' and 'amor' into one word 'imagination,' akin to the Pauline 'caritas' and the 'holiness' of the Saxon saint, is inadequate to work the miracle of fusion as the literary craftsman regards it. How to deal with what in Book VI of *The Prelude* he calls a 'wide circuit'?

How, indeed, but by a series of revelations of altitude and depth? Whereas the landscape of Wordsworth's poetry, whatever its spiritual hills and valleys, had hitherto been predominantly horizontal,[14] now in 1804, either from his observation of Michael and Adam, renewed thought about Edward Young's Christian mountaintop, some memory of Snowdon and the Alps in association with Bunyan's Delectable Mountains, or the growing awareness of pictorial beauty and terror in the hills about him and the scenic ups and downs of the Scotch tour of 1803, there comes increasingly into his handling of myth and into his metaphorical idiom what might be called a vertical correlative. Witness in Book VI himself 'foot-bound, uplooking' at the ash green with ivy 'almost to the top'; in the elements of geometric science he found 'enough to exalt, to chear me and compose'; the peace that awaited upon his study was 'transcendent,' the pleasure 'calm and deeper,' and this 'paramount' endowment of the human mind gave him an image of the one 'surpassing Life . . . out of space and time.' John Newton's story of diagrams drawn upon the sand of his desert isle Wordsworth tells again to introduce his own delight in geometry as a 'clear Synthesis built up aloft'; two formal processes are here combined in one activity. The presence of Dorothy on his holiday in 1788, between his 'sundry wanderings,' seemed to him 'a joy above all joys,' 'another morn risen on mid noon'; and from their rambles he chooses the dangerous climb up to the

[14] What some critics, referring to content, call matter-of-factness.

turret's head of the Castle of Emont to signalize their reunion. The indestructible friendship of those 'Twins almost in genius and in mind,' Coleridge and Wordsworth,

> Predestin'd, if two Beings ever were,
> To seek the same delights, and have one health,
> One happiness,

is enhanced by the memory of Coleridge 'on the leaded Roof' of Christ's Hospital, where he was used 'to lie and gaze upon the clouds moving in Heaven,' [15] and thus superlatively twinned with the boy at Hawkshead.

In that part of Book VI where he reviews his tour of 1790 this access of vertical images and patterns is still more notable. The thought of Coleridge wandering in Sicily, brings memories of his own wanderings in France;

> But 'twas a time when Europe was rejoiced,
> France standing on the top of golden hours,
> And human nature seeming born again.

It is 'beneath the Evening Star' that William and Robert see 'those dances of Liberty.' The Rhone is swift between 'lofty rocks,' and the vales they spy in passing are 'deep and stately.' William and Robert are guests welcome 'almost as the Angels were to Abraham of old.' [16] And in order that the Biblical reference may be associated with an ecclesiastical equivalent of later times, Wordsworth makes an early addition to MS A of a revised account of his visit in 1790 to the Convent of the Grande Chartreuse. Issuing from Vallombre's groves, where the travellers fed the soul with darkness, they beheld

> with uplifted eyes . . .
> In every quarter of the bending sky
> The cross of Jesus stand erect, as if
> By angels planted on the aerial rock.

[15] VI, 93, 101, 141, 150–7, 182, 211–13, 218–32, 263–80.
[16] VI, 352–4, 380, 385–7, 391, 401–4.

The Convent itself is a 'transcendent frame of social Being.' To Wordsworth 'a radiant cloud'—this time not an angel—descends 'through the still bosom of the azure sky.' He is abstracted from his 'trance,'

> but as the sea prolongs
> Her agitation though the wind which first
> Call'd up the surges from the peaceful deep
> Be spent or intermitted, so my mind
> Continued still to heave within herself.

This, indeed, is another 'spot of time,' and it is used like the simpler ones of his childhood and boyhood for mythic effect. Noting that below St. Bruno's wood with its 'piny top' 'murmured the sister streams of Life and Death,' we discover the formal device of height again used to reconcile mighty opposites. What is more, he places Nature on her Alpine throne, which she may be considered to have usurped from Dr. Goldsmith, to reconcile with her wise words the civic contrarieties of Revolutionary France:

> 'Honour to the patriot's zeal,
> Glory and pride to new born Liberty,
> Hail to the mighty passions of the time,
> The vengeance and the transport and the hope,
> The gay or stern delight of this big hour!'

If past and future, another pair of opposites, be wings 'harmoniously conjoined' to support 'the great Spirit of human knowledge,' these courts of Mystery must be spared. 'Peasant' and 'King' alike are initiated by 'one holy thought, a single holy thought.' [17] 'Heaven-imparted truth' and 'the imaginative impulse sent from . . . majestic floods . . . shining cliffs,' and enduring forests—

[17] The reconciliation of formal opposites from a higher point is made even clearer in the edition of 1850: 'to equalize in God's pure sight monarch and peasant.'

so Nature says in still another pair of opposites—will redeem the house and its blameless priesthood, as long as man looks upward from 'the blank abyss' for consolation.

The physical height and spiritual exaltation of this lofty 'temple' in contrast to the abyss of bodily existence are only less important to Wordsworth's formal craftsmanship than the loftiness of the mountains and the depth of the valleys. This is not a journey 'step by step,' but 'from vale to vale, from hill to hill'; earthly images in their swift changes are compared to the swift changes of clouds in Heaven; the travellers are likened to birds of prey, a ship on the stretch in a fair wind. And Wordsworth's heart, which in 1802 leaped up at the sight of a rainbow, 'leaps up' when he 'looks down' on the deep aboriginal vale. The summit of Mont Blanc and the Vale of Chamouny are next 'reconciled' as realities in the mind of the traveller; soaring eagle and descending lion, haycock and mountain are sketched in to adorn this further instance of contrasting values. The 'truth of Young and Old' is 'the universal reason of mankind'; it is read by Robert and William in many a lesson of 'sound tenderness' as they pace 'side by side,' taking up 'dejection for pleasure's sake'; yet contrasted with this pleasurable dejection William acknowledges 'a far different dejection,' 'a deep and genuine sadness,' a kind of 'under-thirst of vigour' (VI, 426–90).

These sensitive particulars, amplified out of a very simple device, are crowned by the often-quoted crossing of the Alps, itself a delicate tissue of contrasts in space. Robert and William, 'upturning with a Band of Travellers,' 'descending . . . to a rivulet's edge,' started to climb 'up a lofty Mountain,' but 'must descend'; 'thenceforward all [their] course was downwards.' As Wordsworth penned this anticlimax in 1804, however, Imagination 'lifting up itself' came athwart him. In the crisis of a limited 'sense' experience the glory of the 'Soul' must be recognized; 'infinitude,' not 'up' and 'down,' is our destiny. Finally, that other pair of opposites, Time and Eternity, must be reconciled; 'tumult and peace,' 'darkness and light' (VI, 494–572),

Were all like workings of one mind, the features
Of the same face, blossoms upon one tree,
Characters of the great Apocalypse,
The types and symbols of Eternity,
Of first and last, and midst, and without end.

We next observe the vertical presentation, in a way to delight the pictorial artist, of Wordsworth's memories of Como. These are now set forth not as a barren opposition of sensual bliss versus voluptuous and shameless slavery, but as light and shadow seen by one who had passed 'like a breeze or sunbeam' over that 'treasure'

by the earth
Kept to itself, a darling bosom'd up
In Abyssinian privacy.

What had been in *Descriptive Sketches*, as in Goldsmith's *Traveller*, a mere delineation of contrasts becomes in Book VI of *The Prelude* a richly emotional chiaroscuro. First, for the fair side, Como's beauty is 'an impassion'd sight of colours and of forms.' Then, secondly, for the darker side, the lake puts on 'a sterner character.' The voice of the Italian clock is 'unintelligible'; 'unknown birds' and 'the noise of streams' and 'rustling motions nigh at hand' arouse personal fear. 'The withdrawing Moon' which has thrown on the 'sullen water' 'a dull red image' changing its form 'like an uneasy snake' brings out the shadows in a companion piece without which the imaginative picture of the poet would lack its twofold beauty.

Under the mythic guise of Temple or of Mountain and Valley Wordsworth has suggested to us the formal truth about his art. In *The Prelude* the eighteenth-century Traveller has been made to scale heights and plumb depths Goldsmith could scarcely see from his Helvetian mountaintop.

'But here I must break off,' says Wordsworth; and like him we, too, may reconcile this long antithesis as follows (VI, 661–705):

Let this alone
Be mention'd as a parting word, that not
In hollow exultation, dealing forth
Hyperboles of praise comparative,
Not rich one moment to be poor for ever,
Not prostrate, overborn, as if the mind
Itself were nothing, a mean pensioner
On outward forms, did we in presence stand
Of that magnificent region. . . . Whate'er
I saw, or heard, or felt, was but a stream
That flow'd into a kindred stream, a gale
That help'd me forwards, did administer
To grandeur and to tenderness.

VI

Exile Returned

Cymbeline and *The Borderers*

THANKS to his father, William Wordsworth while yet a boy learned the plays of Shakespeare. Among them the very British *Lear* and *Cymbeline* caught his fancy because they peopled the western hills for him and located on the map of his own country that original Britain wherein 'Lud's town' would else be only a name. From *Lear* for *The Vale of Esthwaite* he drew a reference to Edmund:

> I saw the ghosts and heard the yell
> Of every Briton [   ] who fell
> When Edmund . . .

From the octosyllabic dirge in *Cymbeline*, as well as from Collins' *Dirge in Cymbeline* and Chatterton's *My love is dedde*, he adapted at Hawkshead his own octosyllabic *Dirge Sung by a Minstrel.*

There are two versions of this *Dirge* in a manuscript not published until 1940: [1] the first is a dirge for a boy, and the second, much shortened, is a dirge for a maiden. In this uncertain sorrow we recognize the dead boy revised to be a dead maiden as a copy

[1] By de Selincourt, who refers only to Chatterton and Collins in this connection (*Poetical Works,* Vol. 1, pp. 267–9, 367).

of Shakespeare's Fidele (Imogen), whose pains gave such anxiety to the brothers Guiderius and Arviragus, and whose assumed death was musically announced by the 'ingenious instrument' of Belarius, and mourned with such exquisite devotion. Guiderius and Arviragus supposed the stranger, Fidele, to be a boy; Wordsworth, having read *Cymbeline*, knew that she was a maiden and their sister. Which should he lament?

List! the bell-Sprite stuns my ears
Deeply howling for a boy;
[*Revision:* Slowly calling for a maid;]
List! each worm with trembling hears
And stops his dreadful trade for joy. . . .
[*Revision:* And stops for joy his dreadful trade.] . . .

By frequent feet the grass around
His grave shall all be worn away,
Yet never human foot be found
On the green turf-hill o'er his clay.

That turf by soft Fays only trod
Whose foot ne'er burst a drop of dew,
That grave that heaves its [ ] sod
As some green island sweet to view. . . .

And should some boy wild in the race
On thy green grave unweeting start,
Strange fear shall flie across his face
And home he goes with haunted heart. . . .

Dumb is the ploughman's whistle shrill,
The milkmaid at her pail is dumb,
The schoolboy's laughing game is still,
And *mute* all evening's mingled hum. . . .

Guiderius had said of Fidele (Imogen), 'With female fairies will his tomb be haunted.' Collins borrowed from Shakespeare to read 'The female fays shall haunt the green.' Chatterton refers to 'elfin fairies.' Wordsworth adapts as follows: 'That turf by soft Fays only trod.' Flowers and fairies are common to the lament of Shakespeare, Collins, Chatterton, and Wordsworth. Shakespeare's Fidele (Imogen), however, had two distinctive traits: he (she) could sing 'angel-like'; and he (she) could smile, even in assumed death was 'smiling, . . . his [her] right cheek reposing as on a cushion.' So also with Wordsworth's boy-maiden:

Her lips with sweeter fragrance glow'd
And livelier tenants did enclose
And from them sweeter music flow'd
Than may-morn hedgerow ever knows. . . .

I saw him in his grave-cloaths drest,
His chearful cheek did smile as sweet
As when he hied in sabbath vest
At morning [knell?] his God to meet.[2]

Collins omits the worm, the song, and the smile; Chatterton omits the worm and the smile; Shakespeare and Wordsworth include all three. Thus, it seems likely that one source of Wordsworth's *Dirge* is the dirge in *Cymbeline*, with the pertinent blank verse preceding it, written by Shakespeare for Guiderius and Arviragus at the grave made ready for Fidele (Imogen).

From *Cymbeline*, too, for his address to Dorothy and his friend Fleming in *The Vale of Esthwaite*, Wordsworth may have adapted the brother-sister-lover-friend association of the sons of Cymbeline with Fidele (Imogen), their sister disguised as a boy. In a similarly passionate vein he wrote (528–35, 542–45):

Sister, for whom I feel a love
Which warms a Brother far above,
On you, as sad she marks the scene,
Why does my heart so fondly lean?
Why but because in you is given
All, all my soul would wish from Heaven?
Why but because I fondly view
All, all Heav'n has claimed, in you? . . .

[2] Here we remember Belarius's insistence that his young charges arise early in the morning to cry 'Hail, heaven!'

While bounteous heaven shall Fleming leave
Of Friendship what can me bereave?
Till then shall live the holy flame,
Friendship and Fleming are the same.

Editor de Selincourt suggests that verses 528–35 of this passage must have been added after William left Hawkshead, because while there at school 'he had not seen Dorothy for nine years.' [3] May it not be that the sister of *The Vale of Esthwaite* is a poetical sketch for which the dimly remembered Dorothy has coalesced in her brother's mind with the vividly imagined Fidele (Imogen)? We know from *The Prelude* that at Hawkshead young William 'passionately loved' John Fleming, the companion of his 'morning walks' around Esthwaite. Consoling each other in the absence of family ties, reminding themselves that Dorothy had long been a stranger to them, as Fidele (Imogen) to Guiderius and Arviragus, they would quote Shakespeare's lines with fresh interest. And as they looked down on the grave of that William Raincock who was so good at mimic hootings, or that John Vickars who died in July, 1782, they might well recall Fidele, in whose loss the stripling Guiderius could not sing because of grief, and for whose grave the stripling Arviragus promised flowers 'whilst summer lasts and I live here.'

A decade or so later, in 1798, Wordsworth wrote lines deriving from his schoolboy *Dirge:* 'There was a boy.' Now to be found in Book V of *The Prelude*, these lines bring a faint literary fragrance from the flowers of Arviragus and echo in a silence like the silence of Guiderius:

This Boy was taken from his Mates, and died
In childhood, ere he was full ten years old.
—Fair are the woods, and beauteous is the spot,
The Vale where he was born; the Churchyard hangs
Upon a slope above the Village School,
And there, along that bank, when I have pass'd
At evening, I believe that oftentimes

[3] *Poetical Works,* Vol. 1, p. 369.

A full half-hour together I have stood
Mute—looking at the Grave in which he lies.

In *The Prelude* Wordsworth also acknowledges his debt to 'adventures endless' spun by the 'dismantled Warrior in old age,' as witness Belarius. He is grateful for romances which hallowed for him all sights of terror, even the ghastly face of the man drowned in Esthwaite; and here we remember Shakespeare's skilful handling of the beheaded Cloten. But for the central relationship of the autobiographical poem, its inner strength and restorative agency, the bond between the two brothers and the sister of *Cymbeline* would serve most notably. The British power, restored when the children of Cymbeline at last came back from exile, was illustrated anew at Alfoxden in the joint energies and restored happiness of William, Dorothy, and Coleridge. Again literary truth transforms or illuminates biographical fact.

Although Guiderius, Arviragus, and Imogen remain safely united in the dramatic art of Shakespeare, there looms a new kind of sorrow for the Wordsworths and Coleridge when the curtain is lowered on *The Prelude*. Separation more bitter than death, grief and dismay of alienated brothers and forlorn sister, shadowing many passages of *The Prelude* itself, foreshadow an ordeal of which Wordsworth says nothing outright. Yet his poem has one dirgelike passage for the brother well-nigh lost. Not even in the grateful words for Raisley Calvert or the 'memorial Verse' for the Maid of Buttermere and her dead infant is there such intensity of feeling, such religious grief for what has not been, is not, or is not to be, as in the regret over Coleridge the schoolboy, exiled from his native stream, Coleridge the collegian, 'debarr'd from Nature's living images,' and Coleridge the yet unknown, absent from the reunion of William and Dorothy at Penrith in 1788. This retrospective sorrow does indeed discover the inmost soul of brotherhood and friendship (VI, 246–69):

O Friend! we had not seen thee at that time;
And yet a power is on me and a strong

Confusion, and I seem to plant Thee there.
Far art Thou wander'd now in search of health,
And milder breezes, melancholy lot!
But Thou art with us, with us in the past,
The present, with us in the times to come:
There is no grief, no sorrow, no despair,
No languor, no dejection, no dismay,
No absence scarcely can there be for those
Who love as we do.

Fruitful as was the grief in *Cymbeline* for the chief personal lament of *The Prelude*, we should go on to consider the actions, agents, and circumstances of Shakespeare's play. Granted some widely acknowledged help from *Hamlet*, *Othello*, and *Lear*, it now becomes clear that the dramatic framework of *Cymbeline* served Wordsworth for the plot of *The Borderers*, and may be further detected in the action of *The Prelude*.

Had Wordsworth seen a performance of *Cymbeline?* From his account of theatergoing in London during his exile there after graduation, this appears likely. Among the 'living Figures on the Stage' he remembered (VII, 445–54) that

some beauteous Dame
Advanced in radiance through a deep recess
Of thick-entangled forest, *like the Moon*
Opening the clouds; or sovereign King, announced
With flourishing Trumpets, came in full-blown State . . .
Of Courtiers, Banners, and a length of Guards;
Or *Captive led in abject weeds, and jingling*
His slender manacles.

The beauteous dame is Imogen, already linked in his mind with Dorothy or Mary Hutchinson and the moonlight over Windermere and that moon over Snowdon which was to usher in the last Book of *The Prelude*. The sovereign King might be any one of many, but may stand for the ostentatious Cymbeline. And surely the captive led in abject weeds, jingling his slender manacles, is

Posthumus disguised 'in a silly habit,' brought in to Cymbeline and by him handed over to the jailer with other Roman 'captives.' Was it not Posthumus who made light of his 'fettr'd . . . shanks and wrists' and was 'merrier to die' than his jailer to live? And with a word used only once by Wordsworth in all his poetry, and by Shakespeare only seven times, twice in *Cymbeline*, was it not for Posthumus that the Messenger brought an order to 'knock off his *manacles*'?

Wordsworth's pleasure at the theater, he tells us (VII, 480–5),

> had been handed down from times
> When, at a Country-Playhouse, having caught,
> In summer, through the fractur'd wall, a glimpse
> Of daylight, at the thought of where I was
> I gladden'd more than if I had beheld
> Before me some bright cavern of Romance.

While he prepared MS X, in which this passage first occurs, he must have revived his memory of the cave of Belarius, the British striplings, and Fidele (Imogen) their 'angel-like' guest, for when he revised MS D, many years later, his thought again acknowledged this literary adventure of his boyhood and youth, and he added an explicit reference to 'the mighty Shakespeare's page.' Although his playhouse experiences are 'humble and low,' he reminds us (VII, 491–5) that they are

> not to be despis'd
> By those who have observ'd the curious props
> By which the perishable hours of life
> Rest on each other, and the world of thought
> Exists and is sustain'd.

There is much in *Cymbeline* to attract a schoolboy: noble outlaws in a savage western country distant from Rome; a beautiful motherless heroine separated by her old father from her lover, the hero, with whom she has been playfellow since childhood; the hero outlawed, and deceived by a villain, who plots the ruin of hero and heroine without adequate motive; the villain hiding in a trunk, on the outlook for evidence and tokens of infidelity; the cruel treatment of the innocent heroine by the suspicious hero on this false evidence; a stepmother interested in flowers distilled into perfumes, and herbs for poisonous drugs; a monster hating the hero and in love with the heroine; a bloody handkerchief and a faithful but frightened servant; the heroine, fugitive, guided to a mountaintop above a haven, then deserted, wandering alone, meeting with the noble outlaws, one of whom knew her father; the monster disguised in the hero's clothes foiled in his attempt to violate the heroine, and slain by an outlaw; a sleeping drug substituted for poison; a bell to announce a death; a Roman invasion of Britain to claim lawful tribute; a battle won by the outlaws under a white-bearded old exile and the exiled hero in disguise, restoring the old father to his throne; the villain defeated in hand-to-hand encounter with the hero; identification of father and son by birthmark; property and position restored to the outlaws; fervent embrace of the remorseful hero by the heroine on their reunion; confession of the villain and his pardon by the hero, who shares his guilt; an apparition of the father, mother, and brother of the hero; a crystal window through which Jupiter peeps out of his marble mansion; Jupiter himself arriving with his thunderbolts, *deus ex machina,* to save the hero, on whose bosom is left an inscription which only the audience and a soothsayer can interpret; and, most notably, before the theatrical happy ending, a terrible ordeal in the mind of the remorseful hero, who has been guilty of a foolish and cruel mistake.

Such was the *Cymbeline* Wordsworth read as a boy and possibly saw as a youth. And such is the play he wrote, *The Borderers:* a band of outlaws in a savage western country distant from Palestine; a beautiful motherless heroine (Idonea) separated by her old father (Herbert) from the hero (Marmaduke), her lover, with whom she has been playfellow since childhood; the hero, and leader of the outlaws, deceived by a villain (Oswald), who plots the ruin of hero and heroine seemingly without adequate motive; the villain continually lurking in ambush, continually falsifying evidence; the cruel treatment of the innocent heroine by the suspicious hero on this false evidence; a Beggar, wickedly alleged to be the heroine's mother, who helps to poison the mind of the hero; a monster (Clifford) hating the hero and allegedly in love with the heroine, in disguise and allegedly plotting to violate her; an ineffective servant to the hero (Wilfred); a well-meaning but frightened peasant (Eldred) involved with blood-stained clothes; the heroine guided by a peasant to a white hawthorn above a hostel in the dell, later wandering alone and meeting with a band of pilgrims, one of whom knew her father; the monster foiled in his alleged attempt to violate the heroine; interest in 'the wild rose and the poppy and the nightshade'—perfume and soporific and poison—displayed by the villain, who (in MS B) carries 'a phial' of drug for toothache 'that will compose . . . to a childlike sleep,' while the hero cries 'Poison! Poison!'; a chapel bell to announce death; Henry III of England and his Sheriffs advancing to the borderland to reinstate rightful claimants in their properties; the Band 'self-stationed' to see justice done, especially the greybeard Wallace and the young hero Marmaduke, who must protect the innocent; the villain defeated by the hero in fierce ethical encounter; identification by facial resemblance of father and daughter; property and position to be restored to father and daughter; fervent embrace of the remorseful hero by the heroine at their reunion; the confession of the villain and his pardon by the hero, who shares his guilt; the story of Idonea's parents and brother at Antioch; a star twinkling through a crevice in a dungeon to summon the hero back to himself and 'the living God'; the thunderstorm as he contemplates his violent deed; the inscription on Herbert's staff with the Lord himself to interpret it—' "*I am eyes to the blind,*" *saith the Lord.* "*He that puts his trust in me shall not fail*" '—and Marmaduke's story to be recorded on the monument comparable to the tablet which disentangles the plot of *Cymbeline;* and, finally and most notably, the ordeal of painful and thoughtful life for the remorseful hero, who has been guilty of a foolish and cruel mistake.

At this point we may ask with Marmaduke, 'What fiend could prompt this action?' (1879–80). That there are two plays instead of one articulated out of this long list of identical or parallel matters is the wonder. Not merely the difference between Shakespeare and Wordsworth or the difference between Elizabethan and Georgian England or the difference between Seneca and Godwin is in question, but the difference between two kinds of literary truth, arising out of two ways of life, the active and the contemplative.

Yet the plot of *Cymbeline* invigorated Wordsworth's dramaturgy in *The Borderers;* and the dramatic circumstances and situations in *Cymbeline* are closer to Wordsworth's play than are those of *Hamlet*, *Othello*, and *Lear*. Posthumus, Hamlet, and Marmaduke are all separated by paternal decree from the woman they love, they are all involved in civic disturbances, all try to think their problems out by discourse of reason, in contrast to Othello's passion. There is in Herbert somewhat of both Lear and Gloucester as well as of Brabantio and Cymbeline. Idonea resembles Imogen more than Cordelia, and Cordelia more than Desdemona. Wordsworth tells us in his prefatory essay that Oswald is like Iago, though we notice in Oswald pitiable revelations of discomfort more like the disquietude of Iachimo than the callous wickedness of Iago. All these similitudes and dissimilitudes, however, do not account for the unique characterization of Marmaduke or reveal the inner form or action of *The Borderers*. That is because Shakespeare's agents, even Ulysses and Prospero, are pledged to an active life. Although the finale of *Cymbeline* is arbitrated by the poet, the exile, Posthumus, has recognized the innocence of Imogen, atoned for his violence by his suffering, and worked himself out of his mistakes by his defense of his fatherland. This is a reversal in the Aristotelian sense; the plot is involved, and the action that Shakespeare intended is performed. Imogen and Posthumus are reunited, the British royal family is restored, and Britain is saved from her inner and outer enemies by the courage of her four patriots, Belarius, Guiderius, Arviragus, and Posthumus.

Legouis, a profound student of the literature and philosophy of Wordsworth's own times, believed that the main purpose of *The Borderers* was the delineation of the philosophical murderer.[4] That would make of the poem a *character*, and in it Oswald would be the chief person, a mischief-maker but scarcely an agent in an action. In the Fenwick Note to the poem, Wordsworth himself acknowledged that his care 'was almost exclusively given to the passions and the characters, and the position in which the persons in the Drama stood relatively to each other, that the reader . . . might be moved, and to a degree instructed, by lights penetrating somewhat into the depths of our nature.' The words 'moved' and 'instructed' indicate Wordsworth's agreement with two of the three important purposes of the dramatic poet according to the Aristotelian doctrine of *catharsis;* he does not, however, imply that the emotions are to be relieved, and thus bungles Aristotle's *mimesis*. As a result, whatever degree of growth or development the agents exhibit will be revelatory but not dramatic: they seem to do deeds, but they fail to do the obvious deed-to-be-done; they act, but their acts do not constitute an action, the Aristotelian *praxis*.

So much for Wordsworth's seeming lack of skill; with Posthumus always in mind let us next investigate his accomplishment. The penalty of Shakespeare's hero was mental suffering to its ultimate degree, after which he was saved by Pisanio, Jupiter, and Shakespeare. Wordsworth's hero must save himself.

From what? There are clear indications in both dramas that the deformity or flaw in the hero is *hubris*, presumption. In spite of frequent allegation that Godwinian truth or fallacy is to blame, it is not excessive passion, compassion, or abstract reason [5] which constitutes the perfidy in *Cymbeline* and *The Borderers*, but credulous folly on the part of Posthumus and Marmaduke and mad pride on the part of Iachimo and Oswald. The barren oppositions

[4] Legouis, *La Jeunesse de William Wordsworth*, tr. by Matthews, p. 270; 309, n.

[5] Cf. the able discussion of *The Borderers* by George W. Meyer in *Wordsworth's Formative Years*, 1943, pp. 154 ff., as modifying earlier exclusively philosophical interpretations of the play.

of Oswald are not between passion and reason, but between passion and proof. Marmaduke makes a wrong choice not because he feels too keenly or reasons too bleakly, but because he has been misinformed. Thus, on the evidence of its Shakespearean antecedents, we are justified in diminishing the importance of the old Godwinian debate among biographers of Wordsworth and critics of his one play; we may substitute the more pertinent question of its dramaturgy.

Like *Lear*, *Othello*, and *Cymbeline* it is a play of false evidence and rash deeds; but its inner or dramatic action is the refusal or postponement of an ill-considered deed, or even the substitution of fruitful suffering for harmful activity. Witness Wordsworth's quotation of a signal passage from *The Borderers* (1539–44) for the later *White Doe of Rylstone*, whose inner action also is fruitful suffering. Outer

> Action is transitory—a step, a blow,
> The motion of a muscle—this way or that—
> 'Tis done, and in the after-vacancy
> We wonder at ourselves like men betrayed:
> Suffering is permanent, obscure and dark,
> And shares the nature of infinity.

Says Marmaduke, 'Truth—and I feel it.' And this, it seems, is the belief of William Wordsworth; witness again his lines in that monodramatic poem, *The Prelude* (VI, 538–42):

> Our destiny, our nature, and our home
> Is with infinitude, and only there;
> With hope it is, hope that can never die,
> Effort, and expectation, and desire,
> And something evermore about to be.

Emotional tinge aside, the recanting military leader of *The Borderers* and the Poet of *The Prelude* articulate the main experience of Wordsworth's life. His poetic career moves from outer toward inner action.

According to the dramatic practice of Shakespeare, Marmaduke's renunciation of Idonea, resignation from the leadership of the Band, and self-exile seem to be a great refusal of the familiar obligations of husband and citizen. If, however, we note the successive positions taken by Oswald in the plot, we find the dilemma more fundamental. Oswald rationalizes, as we now say. Needing activity to dull the remorse that comes with thought, he argues that 'every possible shape of action might lead to good.' Has he himself not mounted 'from action up to action' (1780–81, 1788–9)? The first dark deed to which his jealous pride drove him still inflates his words: 'What must be done?' 'The deed is done—if you will have it so.' 'Great actions move our admiration.' One's 'own act and deed' hushes one's 'foolish fears . . . to sleep' (15–16, 593, 641). For him the issue is speciously clear; between 'thoughts and feelings,' on the one hand, and, on the other, a deed 'which Memory may touch,' he chooses the deed. But whereas through Acts I, II, and III Oswald was successful in driving Marmaduke to an unjustified act, he did *not* accomplish what he intended in Acts IV and V, the supposed enlargement of man's intellectual empire by the destruction of remorse. Marmaduke himself succeeded in doing his deed-to-be-done, action in the literary sense: henceforth he was 'a Man by pain [feeling] and thought compelled to live.' Granting that Wordsworth permits him no clear recognition of the ultimate satisfaction in such a life, we must acknowledge that Marmaduke and not Oswald is the hero of *The Borderers*.

The issue as between thought-and-feeling and violent actions is further illuminated when we watch what happens to a bit of stage property, Marmaduke's sword. He warns Lacy against the sword. At the dungeon he flings away his sword, but Oswald brings it back to him. He uses no 'stroke of arm' when he leaves Herbert to the judgment of God. And he finally renounces the sword as the instrument of justice when he resigns from the Band and sets aside the 'less patient' way of falling on his own 'sword's point.'

There was a plot,
A hideous plot, against the soul of man:
It took effect—and yet I baffled it
In *some* degree.[6]

Marmaduke is 'no coward,' but his 'destiny' is 'to endure.' His dedication to suffering, the Greek *pathemata* rather than *praxis*, has been authorized by Shakespeare's Posthumus in his penultimate woe (Act V, scene 1, lines 22–33, and scene 4, lines 4–29):

I'll disrobe me
Of these Italian weeds and suit myself
As does a Britain peasant; . . . so I'll die
For thee, O Imogen, even for whom my life
Is every breath a death; and thus, unknown,
Pitied nor hated, to the face of peril
Myself I'll dedicate. . . .
To shame the guise o'th'world, I will begin
The fashion: less without and more within. . . .

Most welcome, bondage! for thou art a way
I think, to liberty; . . . Death . . . is the key
T'unbar these locks. My conscience, thou art fettr'd
More than my shanks and wrists. You good gods, give me
The penitent instrument to pick that bolt;
Then, free for ever! . . . and so, great powers,
If you will take this audit, take this life,
And cancel these cold bonds. O Imogen!
I'll speak to thee in silence.

In these passages *Cymbeline* ended for Wordsworth; he would end his play thus, too, disregarding the cheap claptrap of the Elizabethan final act for a new 'fashion: less without and more within.'

In silence hear my doom:
. . . a wanderer *must I*[7] go, . . .
No human ear shall ever hear me speak;

[6] Wordsworth's italics. Cf. *The Borderers* 1029–36, 2142–4, 2343.
[7] Wordsworth's italics.

No human dwelling ever give me food,
Or sleep, or rest: but over waste and wild,
In search of nothing that this earth can give,
But expiation, will I wander on—
A Man by pain and thought compelled to live,
Yet loathing life—till anger is appeased
In Heaven, and Mercy gives me leave to die.

Posthumus and the Poet of *The Prelude*

The substitution of mental suffering for physical violence, and expiation for melodramatic amnesty, is the distinctive accomplishment of the young writer; it does not make a good old-time plot, but it points the way to a new method of characterization and a new kind of story. There are other blessings than marriage, other effective actions than war and statesmanship. When we see William Wordsworth trying to match himself with William Shakespeare, unable to free himself from the grotesque circumstances of the tragicomedy and uncomfortably aware that they were not pertinent to his own age, forcing them into the service of an ordeal that was his own, but even more the ordeal of his generation and ours and of all coming generations, we must allow that he was writing, haltingly and awkwardly, the tragic insufficiency of the active life. The main reversal of *The Borderers* is Marmaduke's renunciation of the outer deeds of the civic leader for the inner deed of the man of feeling and thought. This solution, so unfamiliar in heroic and romantic literature, derives from the Passion Play in which Jesus is the representative hero, himself burdened by the guilt of mankind. Again, *anno domini* 1795–6, the scene has shifted from the outskirts of Rome to the environs of Palestine; and where Shakespeare's Britons make peace with Rome, Wordsworth's Borderers lose their Captain into a Christian land of forgiveness and expiation. Wordsworth has modified, we might almost say he has wrecked, the heroic tradition. Henceforth his poetry will for the most part be the outer form of the contemplative rather than the active life. The border between

Scotland and England has become that other border between pagan and modern literature; patience has become his theme; the thinker and poet will become his hero. When next we find him engaged in serious composition he will be shaping the Wanderer and the Recluse, and after a mere breathing space the Poet.

As a child Wordsworth had watched the Derwent flow into the same sea upon which Posthumus Leonatus embarked at Milford Haven. As a young college graduate traveling through the Welsh countryside above Belarius's cave in 1791 he would call to mind the fugitive Imogen, so like his own sister Dorothy, unhappy in the home of ill-natured kindred, separated from her brothers, possibly one day to be reunited with them. Or, in the same year, shone upon by the moon when he had climbed above the mist to the top of Mount Snowdon, and finding in what he saw and heard the perfect image of a mighty mind, he could not well forget these words of Belarius: 'O thou Goddess, thou divine Nature!'

Very soon Wordsworth, like Posthumus, had gone to the continent; like Posthumus he had become entangled in alien ways and situations. When he returned to Stonehenge in 1793 he could even better sympathize with Posthumus, burdened, distraught, and remorseful. As did Shakespeare's hero, he turned his steps westward, to Wales. On such a Welsh lane as that where the little band of outlaws in Shakespeare's *Cymbeline*—the white-bearded Belarius and the striplings Guiderius and Arviragus—had saved Britain with the help of the returned exile, Posthumus Leonatus, he would think of himself, too, as an exile. Had he not been cut off from Annette and Caroline in France and from Dorothy in England? Had he not been frustrated in his attempt to join the French patriots, to fight his way back to Orleans, even to secure his patrimony from his uncles?

And did he then conceive in some inchoate form the poem later known as *Vaudracour and Julia*, which would make part of the

1805–6 version of *The Prelude*, only to be excised from the version of 1850? Generally regarded as a dim presentation of the personal truth about Wordsworth and Annette Vallon, this episode frequently recalls the adventures of Posthumus and Imogen. The hero and heroine had been playmates and were separated by parental decree because of a difference in social status; the hero had been exiled on threat of a mandate of the state, had committed a deed of violence, was imprisoned, wore the fetters of a criminal, and gained his liberty with the help of a friend at court. Nevertheless, as also in *The Borderers*, Wordsworth changes the Shakespearean reversal by parting the lovers for ever; and this time the hero suffers a breakdown of 'heart and mind' under his 'compunction for the past.'

From such a nadir the despairing Poet of *The Prelude* must be rescued. The final books of the autobiographical poem will set forth the joy of a life lived under the compulsion of feeling and thought. As Imogen embraced again the exiled Posthumus, so Dorothy welcomes William home from his wanderings. On the background of his Shakespearean model, then, Wordsworth's Poet is an 'Exile Returned.'

His literary adventures in 1793 and 1794 belong to another chapter, but stepping westward was the enterprise not only of his boyhood and youth. Again in 1795 he pushed west, as near to the Severn as Racedown; and in 1797 as near to the Wye as Alfoxden. At Racedown and Tintern *Cymbeline* still ran in his head; and when on July 13, 1798, he stood once more on the banks of the Wye, he had been reunited with Dorothy and (like Posthumus Leonatus) could give thanks 'that neither evil tongues' (like the tongue of Iachimo) nor 'rash judgments' (like the judgment of Posthumus himself) nor 'the sneers of selfish men' (like the sneers of Cloten)

> Shall e'er prevail against us, or disturb
> Our cheerful faith, that all which we behold
> Is full of blessings.

Remembering that Imogen's heart was as 'the innocent mansion' of her love, he hoped that Dorothy's mind would be 'a mansion for all lovely forms.' Recalling an Imogen of the London theater as she

> Advanced in radiance through a deep recess
> Of thick entangled forest, like the Moon
> Opening the clouds,

he prayed for Dorothy such delight and wonder as he had found on a Welsh mountaintop:

> Let the moon
> Shine on thee in thy solitary walk;
> And let the misty mountain-winds be free
> To blow against thee.

The *Lines . . . on the Wye* are an epilogue after exile.

It would be many years before he could get back to Snowdon, but meanwhile he would put into verse for Dorothy and Coleridge what he had seen there in 1791, the moon above the mist. In so doing he would give himself to hope, as in *The Vale of Esthwaite* when he was a schoolboy:

> Hope, like this moon, emerging fair
> On the dark night of sad despair,
> Till higher mounted cannot chear
> The sable mountains frowning near
> Yet does she still all fondly play
> On scenes remote with smiling ray.

VII

Philanthropist

The *Recluse-Prelude-Excursion* and *Night Thoughts*

As WITH many another work of exegesis or art, the 'Nights' of Edward Young's *Night Thoughts* are nine. About the time when Blake was busy with his designs for this poem (1796) and with his own poem *Vala, or The Death and Judgement of the Ancient Man, A Dream of Nine Nights* (1797), Wordsworth early in 1798 announced his hope to expand 1300 lines, already written, into a philosophical poem whose title would be *The Recluse; or views of Nature, Man, and Society.*[1] Thereafter, and with revisions of matter and form into *The Ruined Cottage*, *The Pedlar*, the poem on his own life to be called *The Prelude*, Book I of *The Recluse*, and *The Excursion*, this enterprise prepossessed him. Sometime between March 6 and Christmas Day of 1804 the plan for a 'moral and philosophical Poem [on] whatever I find most interesting in Nature, Man, and Society' was significantly reworded as the expression in verse of 'my most interesting feelings concerning Man, Nature, and Society.' [2] Little by little, sketches, episodes, reflections, had been and were to be added to the 'views' or sub-

[1] *Early Letters*, pp. 188, 190, under date of March 6 and 11, 1798.
[2] *Ibid.*, pp. 370, 424.

tracted from them until, in 1814, when the remaining body of his blank verse took shape as *The Excursion*, this poem, too, had nine books.

The prototype of *Vala* and *The Excursion*, Young's *Night Thoughts* had dealt with 'immortal man,' not Popian man in the abstract; this was an obvious step toward the imaginative man of Blake and Wordsworth. In eight 'Complaints' and one 'Consolation,' Young presented the whole cycle of man's mystical or religious experience: in the first three 'Nights,' respectively, 'Life, Death, and Immortality'; 'Time, Death, and Friendship'; and under the title 'Narcissa' the relation between virtue, death, and joy. In 'Night the Fourth' he described 'The Christian Triumph'; in 'Night the Fifth,' 'The Relapse,' he studied the uses of grief; in the sixth and seventh 'Nights,' two parts, he showed 'The Infidel Reclaimed'; in 'Night the Eighth,' 'Virtue's Apology,' he debated worldly versus celestial wisdom; and in 'Night the Ninth' and last he took his observant readers Blake and Wordsworth—and takes those of us who still read him—on 'a moral survey of the nocturnal heavens' with an 'address' to 'the Deity.' More boldly stated, his action is twofold, personal and philanthropic. It goes first from loss of loved ones to personal victory over the sorrows of this world, and then attempts to win the low-lived and skeptical Lorenzo, and whatsoever other mourner, skeptic, or infidel comes within the ordeal of his arguments, to a life of virtue, philosophy, and religion.

This latter, or philanthropic action, is the inner form of Wordsworth's *Excursion*, whose bereaved Cottager in her ruined cottage and skeptical Solitary in his mountain cell are instances of despondency to be corrected by the influence and arguments of the Wanderer, who is much indebted to Dr. Young. Through the graveyard we go to the parsonage for pastoral consolation and then on a Wordsworthian picnic, where we join in an 'address,' like that of Young, to the 'Supreme Being,' Wordsworth's term for Young's 'Deity.'

Moreover, and for our present study highly important, Wordsworth's personal action in *The Prelude*, the dedication of the Poet and the impairment and restoration of his imaginative power, has much in common with Young's consecrated hour, and the Christian triumph, relapse, and consolation. Reserving for later discussion the circumstances under which *The Prelude* detached itself from *The Recluse*, let us here note that in demonstrably traditional figures of speech Wordsworth escapes from tedium on the sea to a dwelling on the shore, from captivity in a house of bondage in the city to freedom in the open fields, from winter frost to vernal promises, from the burden of an unnatural self to miraculous joy, from weary days to peaceful months. The harbor, the hermitage, the priestly robe and the prophetic numbers of the holy life of music and of verse, the sabbath and the consolation and the work of glory are poetry, arising no doubt from one or more authentic experiences, but not intended to record merely a certain actual escape from a particular city in a particular year. We do not know when he first uttered the initial lines of *The Prelude:*

> Oh there is *blessing* in this *gentle* breeze. . . .
> A *captive* greets thee, coming from a house
> Of bondage, from yon City's walls set free,
> A *prison* where he hath been long immured. . . .
> What dwelling shall receive me? In what Vale
> Shall be my *harbour?* . . . what sweet stream
> Shall with its murmur lull me to my *rest?* . . .
> Trances of thought and *mountings* of the mind
> Come fast upon me: it is *shaken off*,
> As by miraculous gift 't is *shaken off*,
> That burthen of my own unnatural self. . . .
> Enough that I am free; . . .
> May quit the tiresome *sea* and dwell on *shore*.[3]

[3] Referred by H. W. Garrod and E. de Selincourt and, more recently in his book, *The Mind of a Poet*, pp. 290–1, by R. D. Havens to September, 1795. Readers primarily interested in the biographical truth of these lines will find the argument well documented in a debate between David H. Bishop and R. D. Havens in *Studies in Philology* 32 (July, 1935), 483–507, 33 (January, 1936), 55–6, and 48 (July, 1941), 494–520. See also *The Early History of 'The Prelude'* by

In that utterance, however, he was recapitulating as part of his own imaginative experience what Young, among others, had written of religious ecstasy (*Night Thoughts* IV, 80–6):

> *Blest* be that hand divine, which *gently* laid
> My heart at *rest*, beneath *this humble shed.*
> The world's a stately bark, on dang'rous *seas;* . . .
> Here, on a single plank, thrown safe *ashore,*
> I hear the tumult of the distant throng
> As that of *seas* remote or dying storms.

Also for any subsequent lapse in faith Young had furnished a memorable image (*Night Thoughts* V, 235–41):

> I, who late,
> *Emerging from the shadows of the grave,*
> Where grief detain'd me *pris'ner, mounting* high,
> Threw wide the gates of *everlasting day,*
> *And call'd mankind to glory, shook off* pain,
> Mortality *shook off,* in *Ether pure,*
> And struck the stars; *now* feel my spirits fail.

This is one prototype of Wordsworth's account in *The Prelude* I, 55–271, of his escape from prison and the ensuing rise and fall of his poetic energies. The 'work of *glory*' to be 'begun, perhaps . . . performed' in his 'hermitage,' was more difficult than he had foreseen:

> Gleams of light
> Flash often from the East, then disappear
> And mock me with a sky that ripens not
> *Into a steady morning.* . . .
> And *now* it would content me to yield up
> Those lofty hopes. . . .
> . . . I recoil and droop . . .
> Unprofitably *traveling towards the grave.*

George W. Meyer, Tulane Studies in English, Vol. 1 (1949), pp. 119–56; and *The Poet Wordsworth* by Helen Darbishire, Oxford, 1950, *passim.*

Characteristically, just as he would add a lakeland picnic to the traditional religious consolation for the finale of his *Excursion*, so for the beginning of his *Prelude* he substituted the 'sweet breath of Heaven' in pastoral England for the 'Ether pure' of the mystic's 'everlasting day.' Whereas Young 'shook off' pain and 'shook off' mortality—notice the repetition—Wordsworth's burden of his 'own unnatural self' is 'shaken off, as by miraculous gift 't is shaken off.' Like Young he repeats the climax. Like Young he cannot resist an anticlimax.

This initial triumph of both poets, reiterated in the telling, this relapse felt by each, are so closely akin that we shall not be surprised to find frequent analogies between the instances of visionary restoration in *The Prelude* and the restorative and consolatory passages of the *Night Thoughts*. Indeed, the echoes of this theme in mystical and imaginative lore are numerous, and will be noted by students of cult and religion as well as by those who interpret English literature. But wherever else Wordsworth found corroboration for the major episode of his young manhood—in Milton's epics, for instance—his reading of Young's poem made it impossible for him to disregard the rationally presented argument of the *Night Thoughts*. He needed a reasonable vocabulary for his imaginative experience; not, this time, a lesson in genius and taste to indoctrinate him, a song or idyl or fable to delight him; but to challenge his moral muse, he needed a work of art in the same kind, a philosophical, or better, a philanthropical poem.

Especially would he prove susceptible to Young's idea of God, capitalized in the text of *Night Thoughts* as 'great PHILANTHROPIST! Father of angels! but the friend of man'; witness the title as Wordsworth suggested it to William Mathews in 1794 for their projected miscellany, *The Philanthropist*.[4] Nor would Young's advice come amiss to a self-conscious young writer: 'Follow nature still, but look it be thine own.' Young's probable contribution to Wordsworth's account of the growth of his own mind, moreover,

[4] *Early Letters*, p. 121.

need not be limited to the main action, and to a phrase here and there. From those nocturnal reveries so little read now, but a century or more ago flourishing on both sides of the Atlantic,[5] Wordsworth learned traditional wisdom, wisdom strong and vertebrate, stronger because vertebrate. No other single work, I believe, had more to do with the early conception of *The Recluse* and its prelusive song.

In his 'Consolation' Young exclaims (1059–71):

How great,
How glorious, then, appears the Mind of man,
When in it all the stars, and planets, roll!
And what it seems, it is: Great objects make
Great minds, enlarging as their views enlarge;
Those still more Godlike, as These more divine. . . .
I meet the Deity in ev'ry view,
And tremble at my nakedness before him.

This passage was fruitful both for the 'views' of Wordsworth in 1798 and for the autobiographical poem that would record his poetic unveiling a decade earlier, in 1788: 'As a face we love is sweetest'

if the heart
Have fulness in itself, even so with me
It fared that evening. Gently did my soul
Put off her *veil*, and, self-transmuted, stood
Naked as in the presence of her God.

Deftly this Book IV of *The Prelude* gathers together and refers to the summer vacation of 1788 many other symptoms of dedication. The '*consummate* happiness' of the eighteen-year-old mystic; the

Strength . . . where weakness was not known to be,
At least not felt; and restoration came,

[5] The edition from which I quote is *The Works of the Author of the Night Thoughts*, in four volumes. Revised and Corrected by Himself. A New Edition, London, MDCCLXII.

> Like an intruder, knocking at the door
> Of unacknowledg'd weariness;

'the swellings of the spirit,' the 'glimmering views,'

> How Life pervades the undecaying mind,
> How the immortal Soul with God-like power
> Informs, creates, and thaws the deepest sleep
> That time can lay upon her;

the spread of his 'new-born feeling' to the *trees, mountains, brooks,* and stars of Heaven, whereby 'shadings of mortality' give way to 'love *enthusiastic*'; the 'deeper joy' of 'the dark *blue vault*, and universe of stars,' and then 'the morning' of dedication, 'more glorious' than he ever had beheld; the 'conformity'

> To the end and written spirit of God's works,
> Whether held forth in Nature or in Man: [6]

much of this Young had said before him with similar words in the last two 'Nights,' describing the

> stream
> *Of glory on the consecrated hour*
> Of man, *in audience with the Deity*. . . .
> Heaven's King! whose *face unveil'd consummates bliss*. . . .
> Something, like magic, strikes from this *blue vault;*
> With just attention is it view'd? We feel
> *A sudden succour, unimplor'd, unthought;*
> Nature herself does half the work of Man.
> Seas, *rivers, mountains, forests,* desarts, rocks,
> The promontory's height, the depth profound
> Of subterranean, excavated grots, . . .
> Ev'n These an aggrandizing impulse give;
> Of solemn thought *enthusiastic* heights
> Ev'n These infuse. . . .
> In a bright mirror His own hands have made,
> Here we see something like *the face* of God.[7]

[6] *Prelude* IV, 136–58, 233–5, 240–6, 331–2, 357–9, 384.
[7] *Night Thoughts* VIII, 721–3; IX, 578, 902–35.

That it would be hard to avoid this most ubiquitous human action and the thoughts and images associated with it may be freely granted; but there is one other notable parallel between Young and Wordsworth as poetic autobiographers. Young's reference to a close circle of kin and friends (not Adam and Eve, not Raphael and Michael, but Philander dead, Lysander drowned, Lorenzo errant, Lucia dead, Aspasia dead, Narcissa buried in the alien soil of France) might well suggest the use of even simpler names: Calvert dead and Beaupuy slain; Coleridge wandering; Lucy dead, Matthew dead, Emma dead; and Julia sequestered in a French convent, lost to her cryptic Words*worth*ian *Vaudra*cour as surely as was Narcissa to Edward Young.

Finally, the metrical style and the language of Young must have hastened Wordsworth's abandonment of Popian couplet and Spenserian stanza. Blank verse served Thomson well for outdoors, and Cowper well for indoors, but for the great matters of philosophy Young had amply, if not greatly, proved that Milton's epic line was possible in a humbler poem dealing with less mighty heavens and hells. And Young's frank treatment of religion and theology as personal matters had opened the way for Wordsworth's self-study of 'intellectual' and 'higher' love.

Although many traits of the redemptive process are necessarily common to the *Night Thoughts* and the content of *Recluse*, *Prelude*, and *Excursion*, there are also particular forms of thought and expression relating Young and Wordsworth in spite of their differences in genius and taste. These will be presented to associate the two not as master and pupil in the way of Pope and Wordsworth, not as crony and crony, not even as fellow travelers through the fair places of literature and life, but rather as brother and brother in the unavoidable ordeal of both literature and life, its pleasant but deceptive circuit, its painful ascent, and its survey or prospect from the top of the specular mount. The 'Doctor Young' whom Wordsworth heard quoted when he went to church in London in 1791 and whom later he spoke of as

> the Bard
> Whose genius spangled o'er a gloomy theme
> With fancies thick as his inspiring stars,

was as familiar to him in his apprenticeship as in 1805, when, after his brother John's death, to comfort himself he reached for the *Night Thoughts*, and quoted from the poem at length in a letter to Sir George Beaumont.[8]

And why not? Young was a churchman; and his effort to make faith reasonable and worship joyful, to spiritualize sorrow at death and loss, and to set man forth as the sublime instance of divine agency, gave his poem special value for a young collegian intended by his guardians for the service of the church. In the years directly following Wordsworth's graduation from Cambridge he, too, lived through many of the temporal and mortal woes with which Young had been oppressed: anxiety about income, separation from loved ones, entanglement in France, hours at the bedside of a dying friend, and always the young man's struggle with regret and disillusionment, with confusion and emptiness, at times with despair.

Although the *Night Thoughts* is written in a style distasteful to some recent students of Wordsworth, we must not quibble about forms or be misled by the idiom of either poet. Behind the change in language whereby Wordsworth transmuted the meaning of Young into his own values, there is a precious residuum of traditional beauty. Indeed, what has been considered infelicitous in Wordsworth's last revision of *The Prelude* may arise from his good subconscious memory, which, throughout his life, reminded him of the books and frame of reference of the century of his youth. If the wide and deep fellowship between the meditations of Young and the imagination of Wordsworth be allowed, we shall see more clearly what intellectual love has in common with the spiritual love of the Christian Church, and we may then ask what views of Nature, Man, and Society would be possible

[8] *Early Letters*, p. 461.

without historical Christianity. These associations, I believe, the evidence will richly illustrate.

And closer examination of the evidence will permit us to read the story of *The Prelude* as lived in the decade before 1798 rather than as written in the decade after 1798. The genesis of Wordsworth's autobiographical poem is not primarily in his first conscious effort to shape a particular work of art. It took place in the years when the experience of life and the pattern of literature were all one. Without prejudice toward the more intense poetic struggle of 1799 and 1800 and of 1804 and 1805, when renewed study of Thomson, Akenside, Bunyan, Milton, and Cowper would exercise the poet in the forms and devices of literary craftsmanship, let us in this chapter observe him, as it were, assimilated into the common lot of poets and men.

The Prelude as a 'Christian Triumph'

When twenty-three years old, Wordsworth acknowledged a debt to Young in the 1793 Quarto of *An Evening Walk,* his loco-descriptive poem begun in the Vale of Esthwaite while he was at school, and revised and enlarged during his first two college vacations. Just when before 1793 he wrote line 361 ('So vanish those fair Shadows, human joys'), which comes from Young's 'Relapse,' line 1042 ('So break those glitt'ring shadows, human joys'), it would now be impossible to prove. As a schoolboy and collegian reading the *Night Thoughts,* he would be more infected by its emotion than convinced by its message, and this line may reflect the literary melancholy of the novice of 1788–90 rather than personal sorrow for good reason on the threshold of manhood.

Nor are we surprised to find in a winsome and lighthearted letter to Dorothy from Switzerland, September 6–16, 1790, a few weeks before he returned to Cambridge for his final months of study, echoes of Young's diction, as in his frequent repetition of Young's favorite adjective 'perpetual': 'My spirits have been kept in a *perpetual* hurry of delight by the almost uninterrupted succession of *sublime* and beautiful *objects* which have passed before my eyes during the course of the last month. . . . I have thought of you *perpetually*. . . . We had also *perpetual* occasion to observe. . . . You are *perpetually* in my thoughts.[9] Young, too, had dreamt of 'joys *perpetual* in *perpetual* change'; for him 'Man, like a stream is in *perpetual* flow'; pleasure is 'a pure, *perpetual*, placid stream'; 'Night . . . weeps *perpetual* dews.' [10]

In his retrospective account of this same Alpine journey, Wordsworth confesses that he and Robert Jones paced along composing 'dreams and fictions' (VI, 477–87),

> Dejection taken up for pleasure's sake,
> And gilded sympathies; the willow wreath,
> Even among those solitudes *sublime*,
> And sober posies of funereal flowers,
> Cull'd from the gardens of the Lady *Sorrow*,
> Did *sweeten* many a meditative hour.

We may assume that they had been quoting Young or other of his melancholy contemporaries. One of Young's fictions (*Night Thoughts* IX, 1976–9):

> How, like a *widow* in her weeds, the *Night*,
> Amid her glimm'ring tapers, silent sits!
> How *sorrowful*, how desolate, she *weeps*
> *Perpetual dews* and *saddens* nature's scene!

is paraphrased by Wordsworth in Book VIII of *The Prelude* (532–40). Here Young's 'Widow' reappears as illustration of efforts made by the youthful 'poetic faculty' to conform itself 'knowingly' to 'the notions and images of books':

> Then, if a *Widow*, staggering with the blow
> Of her distress, was known to have made her way
> To the cold grave in which her Husband slept,
> One *night*, or haply more than one, . . .
> The fact was caught at greedily, and there

[9] *Early Letters*, pp. 31, 34, 35, 37.
[10] Miss Darbishire reminds me that 'perpetual' is a favorite with Milton also.

She was a visitant *the whole year through,*
Wetting the turf with never-ending tears,
And all the storms of Heaven must beat on her.

Moreover, the frugal and enthusiastic collegian, who wrote his sister in 1790 that 'it is the end of travelling by communicating *ideas* to *enlarge* the *mind*,' would find in *Night Thoughts* many arguments to justify his summer vacation:

. . . narrow views betray to misery: . . .
. . . Nature is the glass reflecting God, . . .
. . . boundless Mind affects a boundless Space:
. . . vast surveys, and the *sublime* of things,
The soul assimilate, and make her great: . . .
The more our spirits are inlarg'd on earth,
The deeper draught shall they receive of heaven. . . .
. . . Great *objects* make
Great *minds*, *enlarging* as their views *enlarge*. . . .
How such *ideas* of th' Almighty's Pow'r,
And such *ideas* of th' Almighty's Plan,
(*Ideas* not absurd) distend the thought
Of feeble mortals! [11]

It is unfortunate that William's earlier letter to Dorothy from the Grande Chartreuse has been lost; it may have been absorbed into passages, reminiscent of Young, which occur in the 1793 Quarto of *Descriptive Sketches* and in the Bii, Biii, and A^2 manuscripts of Book VI of *The Prelude*, among them this (pp. 194–8):

Vallombre's groves
Entering, we fed the soul with darkness, thence
Issued, and with uplifted eyes beheld
In every quarter of the bending *sky*
The *cross* of Jesus stand erect, as if
By angels planted on the aerial rock. . . .
'Oh leave in quiet this transcendent frame
Of social Being, this embodied dream[,]

[11] *Night Thoughts* I, 165; V, 712; VIII, 790; IX, 1000–1011, 576–7, 1062–3, 1931–4.

This substance by which mortal men have clothed,
Humanly clothed, the ghostliness of things
In silence visible and *perpetual* calm.
Let this one Temple last; be this one spot
Of earth devoted to Eternity.'

With 'this one Temple,' Wordsworth and Jones, both considering a career in the Anglican Church, would associate the everlasting gates of the spiritual church; and the visual image of the 'cross of Jesus' must have recalled the Cross of 'Christian Triumph' in *Night Thoughts* (IV, 335–8): 'a scale of miracles,'

Its lowest round, high *planted on the skies;*
Its tow'ring summit lost beyond the thought
Of man or *angel!* Oh that I could climb
The wonderful ascent, with equal praise!

Of her brother's visit to the Grande Chartreuse Dorothy wrote to Crabb Robinson on December 21, 1822, 'I do not think that any one spot which he visited during his youthful Travels with Robert Jones made so great an impression on his mind; and, in my young days, he used to talk . . . much of it to me.' [12] That it should make part of his *Prelude*, as well as of his *Descriptive Sketches*, is not strange; nor that other Alpine memories were colored by the meditations, the quasi-religious fervor, the literary sorrow, and the mystical language of Young.

For instance, 'dejection . . . for pleasure's sake' was soon to be superseded by a 'far different dejection . . . a deep and genuine sadness' when Wordsworth was told that they had '*crossed the Alps*' (his italics). 'Halted,' as he says, on the top of this world, he was nevertheless saved for yet unaccomplished ascents in the invisible world by the power he called Imagination (VI, 524–42):

To my Soul I say
I recognize thy *glory;* in such strength

[12] *Prelude*, ed. by de Selincourt, p. 561, which misprints the date 1832. See *Correspondence of Henry Crabb Robinson with the Wordsworth Circle*, ed. by Edith J. Morley, Oxford, 1927, Vol. 1, p. 121.

Of usurpation, in such visitings
Of *awful promise*, when *the light of sense*
Goes out in flashes that have shewn to us
The invisible world, doth Greatness make abode,
There harbours whether we be young or old.
Our destiny, our nature, and our home
Is with *infinitude*, and only there;
With hope it is, hope that can never die,
Effort, and expectation, and desire,
And something evermore about to be.

However much later this record of experience on the Simplon was actually written down, it had meanwhile, and very soon, I believe, associated itself with something already in Wordsworth's mind: Young's account of the release of the spirit for the Christian who has climbed to the Cross (*Night Thoughts* IV, 494–514):

Who looks on That, and sees not in himself
An *awful* stranger, a terrestrial god?
A *glorious* partner with the Deity
In that high attribute, *immortal* life? . . .
I gaze, and, as I gaze, *my mounting soul*
Catches strange *fire, Eternity!* at Thee;
And drops the *world*—or rather, more enjoys:
How chang'd the face of nature! how improv'd!
What seem'd a chaos, shines a *glorious* world,
Or, what a world, an Eden; heighten'd all!
It is *another* scene! *another* self!
And still *another, as time rolls along;*
And that a self far more illustrious still. . . .
How nature opens, and receives my soul
In *boundless walks of raptur'd thought!* . . .
. . . What new births
Of strange adventure, *foreign to the sun!*

Elsewhere (*Night Thoughts* IX, 1090–1), too, Young foreshadows the 'infinitude' so important to Wordsworth: the 'new prospect' of the Christian is 'newest to the man that views it most; for newer still in infinite succeeds.'

From Young's 'great First-Last' of the 'Christian Triumph,' among other poetical transcripts of religious testimony, may also come the 'first and last and midst, and without end' of Wordsworth's apocalyptic vision in the 'Gloomy Pass,' en route from the Simplon to Locarno and Como. Young queries:

> Great *end!* and great beginning! say, Where art thou?
> Art thou in time, or in *eternity?* . . .
> . . . Oh tell me, *mighty Mind!*
> Where art thou? Shall I dive into the deep?
> Call to the *sun,* or ask the *roaring* winds,
> For their Creator? Shall I question loud
> The thunder, if in that th' Almighty dwells?
> Or holds He furious *storms in streighten'd reins,*
> And bids fierce *whirlwinds* wheel his rapid car? [13]

Wordsworth was to answer with a similar list (*Prelude* VI, 557–72): woods, waterfalls, *winds thwarting winds, torrents, muttering* rocks, drizzling crags, raving stream, *unfetter'd clouds, tumult* and peace, darkness and *light.* These

> Were all like workings of one *mind,* the features
> Of the same face, blossoms upon one tree,
> Characters of the great Apocalypse,
> The types and symbols of *Eternity,*
> Of first and last, and midst, and without end.

The passages here quoted from *The Prelude* record feelings recollected in tranquillity some years after the experience that first aroused them; but from the beginning they were feelings associated with memories of the poetry that in 1790 pleased and prepossessed him. From that year until 1793 (when, in the two Quartos then published, over sixty per cent of the adjectives of Latin derivation are found also in *Night Thoughts*) Wordsworth depended somewhat on Young's diction to support his literary enterprises; but Young's meanings and values have not yet become explicit in Wordsworth's *An Evening Walk* and *Descriptive*

[13] *Night Thoughts* IV, 412, 391–7; IX, 290–1.

Sketches. Neither poem is thoughtful. The 'meditative hour' of the summer of 1790 had not yet in 1791 and 1792 borne meditative fruit.

Indeed, there could have been little opportunity for either philosophical or poetic growth during the few months between Wordsworth's return from the Alps and his graduation, as Bachelor of Arts, in January, 1791. Pope, Beattie, Thomson, Collins, Goldsmith, Gray, Young, and some Miltonic recollections, still furnished his Castle of Indolence. The six mild winter weeks spent with Dorothy and his uncle and aunt Cookson permitted only reminiscences of travel on William's part, and reminders from Uncle William that since the Bachelor of Arts had lost his chance for a fellowship at Cambridge, he would do well to study the Oriental languages in preparation for taking orders. When he left Forncett he was still in a dilemma: two years hence, the Church; or tutorial work, permitting travel and some leisure for poetic composition.

What do the records of the year 1791 add to our understanding of this recent Bachelor of Arts?

He went from Forncett Rectory to London, where he spent the late winter and early spring; and late in May from London he arrived to visit Robert Jones at Plas-yn-llan, Wales. On June 17 from Wales he wrote to another college friend, William Mathews, the first extant of a series of letters preoccupied with moral issues. In it he refers as follows to his life in London: 'where my time passed in a strange manner; sometimes *whirled* about by the vortex of its *strenua inertia*, and sometimes thrown by the *eddy* into a corner of the *stream*, where I lay in almost motionless indolence. . . . How very unreasonable are even those among us who are not totally *unphilosophic in wishing* for the end without undergoing the trouble of the means! . . . Miserable weakness!' [14]

The only two English poets listed in the New English Diction-

[14] *Early Letters*, pp. 45–9. Italics for '*strenua inertia*' are Wordsworth's; the others are mine.

ary as using the phrase 'strenuous idleness' are Wordsworth and Young. Young (*Night Thoughts* I, 148–9), too, had grieved over

> A soul immortal, spending all her fires,
> Wasting her strength in *strenuous idleness.*

Young, too, had counseled against wishing (IV, 71–9):

> *Wishing*, of all employments, is the worst;
> *Philosophy's reverse;* and health's decay!
> Were I as plump as stall'd theology,
> *Wishing* would waste me to this shade again.
> Were I as wealthy as a South-Sea dream,
> *Wishing* is an expedient to be poor.
> *Wishing*, that constant hectic of a fool;
> Caught at a court; purg'd off by purer air,
> And simpler diet; gifts of rural life!

Now Young's passage recommending the purer air and simpler diet of rural life for the cure of such as Wordsworth's unreasonable or 'unphilosophic . . . wishing' directly precedes his lines on escape ('Blest be that hand divine'), which earlier we compared with the so-called Preamble of Wordsworth's *Prelude*. Between this Preamble, with its metaphors akin to those of Young, and Wordsworth's letter of 1791 we find other analogies: in the former, the 'harbour,' the quitting of 'the tiresome sea' to 'dwell on shore'; in the latter, the 'whirl,' the 'vortex,' the 'eddy,' and the 'corner of the stream.' Young's strenuously idle soul 'resembles ocean into tempest wrought.' And much as Young's Lorenzo pleads 'the straw-like trifles on life's common stream' when he refuses the '*holy hope of* nobler life to come,' [15] Wordsworth takes as guide on the day of his enfranchisement 'a twig or any floating thing upon the river.' But unlike Young's Lorenzo—and here he may have found a hint of professional orientation—he still looks forward to and rejoices in

> the *hope*
> *Of* active days, of dignity and thought,

[15] *Night Thoughts* I, 152; II, 53, 78.

Of prowess in an honorable field,
Pure passions, virtue, knowledge, and delight,
The *holy* life of music and of verse.

Were his Preamble to be interpreted as matter-of-fact, it would promise a life devoted to liturgical music and verse and traditional service in a recognized field. Is there any reason why he should contemplate, except as a dim figure of speech, the 'holy life,' and —as he was to write retrospectively—the 'prophecy,' the 'priestly robe,' the 'holy services,' the 'work of glory'? Might it be that when he left London for Wales he was indeed thoughtfully reconsidering a career in the Church as soon as he should reach twenty-three years, and that he was joyful at the intervening months of holiday? The reading of MS M of *The Prelude* hints that the enfranchisement is temporary:

Enough that I am free, embrace the day
An uncontroul'd enfranchisement; *for months*
To come may live *a life of chosen tasks*.[16]

We know two facts: that he journeyed from London to Wales in the spring of 1791; and, from his letter to Mathews, that sometime between August 13 and September 23 of that year he was summoned by his father's cousin, Mr. John Robinson, to discuss 'a curacy . . . introductory to the living' of Harwich, a harbor some 67 miles from London.[17]

The first fact fits the metaphorical season of the Preamble, not autumn as he tells us in retrospect, but an exciting day of 'vernal promises' at the 'breaking up [of] a long-continued frost.' And if he already knew, as his letter to Mathews implies, that Mr. Robinson was concerned with placing him in the Church, we might consider that the references to the harbor, the shore, and the holy life were an imaginative equation for a less congenial prospect in actual life, what he would later and more bitterly call 'vegetating on a paltry curacy.'

[16] *Prelude*, ed. by de Selincourt, p. 4.
[17] *Early Letters*, pp. 56–7.

Whether his holiday was temporary or final, and whether he escaped from actual city walls or from the imprisoning city of literary tradition will always, I suppose, be academic questions. His escape from London to Wales in the spring of 1791 is one kind of fact and his 'Dythyrambic fervour' is another. Among the tentative (and unproved) suggestions that he might have been en route from Bristol to Racedown in 1795, from Goslar toward Sockburn in 1799, and from London to Grasmere in 1799, is there room for another: that the Preamble even in 1805–6 owes its ecclesiastical vestments partly to the offer in 1791 of a curacy at Harwich or elsewhere some months later; and that meanwhile young Wordsworth will slip out of London en route to the 'one sweet Vale' of Clwyd.[18]

Not for many years again would his dithyrambs as he uttered them in the Preamble be so free of any tinge of anxiety or sorrow. A vacation at hand and a curacy in the not too immediate future! Meanwhile, he tells us in retrospect, even when his Aeolian visitations had vanished, he drew from the sources of his own voice and the mind's internal echo of it 'a chearful confidence in things to come,' and gave himself up to 'present joy.' Before he should return to whatsoever city (London in the late summer of 1791) or academe (Cambridge in the early fall of 1791) or possible curacy, he would climb Snowdon.[19]

Young had described his Christian Triumph and his ascent to God in a mountain-climbing simile of no mean power, a pattern not only for Wordsworth's account of his distressing experience on the banks of Como near Gravedona, but especially for the excursion from Bethgelert up Snowdon. The passage of Young may be quoted first; and then we shall be prepared for the fresher

[18] Writing to Jane Pollard, August 30, 1793, Dorothy quotes William as saying that the Jones house ' "is quite a cottage, just such an one as would suit us" '; she goes on 'and oh! how sweetly situated in the most delicious of all vales, the vale of Clwyd!' (*Early Letters*, p. 105).

[19] Havens (*The Mind of a Poet*, pp. 607–8) believes that the Snowdon passage in the last book of *The Prelude* describes the trip made in 1791. I agree. To his evidence may be added the statement of Elizabeth Wordsworth, probably echoing the *Memoirs*, in *William Wordsworth*, London, 1891, p. 24.

and more natural imagery of Wordsworth, and his more spiritual interpretation of similar items. Says Young (*Night Thoughts* IV, 563–74):

> As when a wretch, from *thick, polluted air,*
> *Darkness,* and stench, and *suffocating damps,*
> And *dungeon-horrors,* by kind fate discharg'd,
> Climbs some fair eminence, where Ether pure
> Surrounds him, and Elysian prospects rise,
> His heart exults, his spirits cast their load;
> As if new-born, he triumphs in the change;
> So joys the soul, when from inglorious aims,
> And sordid sweets, from feculence and *froth*
> *Of ties terrestrial,* set at large, she mounts
> To *Reason's region, her own element,*
> Breathes hopes immortal, and affects the skies.

At Gravedona the disadvantages to the mountain climbers, Robert Jones and William Wordsworth, had been 'woods immense,' 'sullen water,' 'stings of insects,' '*darkness* visible,' '*breathless* wilderness of clouds'; at Bethgelert, however, Wordsworth's Welsh excursion took him out of the 'dripping mist,' 'the *fog* and *damp*' of 'a close warm night, wan, dull, and glaring,' with 'the barking turbulent' of the shepherd's cur at the hedgehog, up Snowdon until

> The Moon stood naked in the Heavens, . . .
> . . . and on the shore
> I found myself of a huge sea of mist, . . .
> . . . and from the shore
> At distance not the third part of a mile
> Was a blue chasm; a fracture in the vapour,
> A deep and gloomy breathing-place through which
> Mounted the roar of waters, torrents, streams
> Innumerable, roaring with one voice.
> The universal spectacle throughout
> Was shaped for admiration and delight,
> Grand in itself alone, but in that breach

Through which the homeless voice of waters rose,
That dark deep thoroughfare had Nature lodg'd
The Soul, the Imagination of the whole.
A meditation rose in me that night
Upon the lonely Mountain when the scene
Had pass'd away, and it appear'd to me
The perfect image of a mighty Mind,
Of one that feeds upon infinity,
That is exalted by an underpresence,
The sense of God, or whatsoe'er is dim
Or vast in its own being.

The contrast between the indoor dungeon of Young and the outdoor chasm of Wordsworth, between the froth of terrestrial life as Young thought of it and the grandeur of the breach in the mist through which rose the terrestrial 'roar' of Wordsworth's description, reveals much of the personal life and the professional inclination of both poets. Also, when we go from 'Reason's region' of Young to Imagination's lodging of *The Prelude*, or substitute for 'sordid sweets' the food of 'infinity,' we are grateful for Wordsworth's sound sense and pure taste. In both passages, however, the escape and the unburdening and the exultation are structurally identical, possibly because both poets were familiar with *Pilgrim's Progress*, to which we shall return in a later chapter.

Wordsworth's 'mighty Mind,' his 'higher minds,' are human minds, although they be 'from the Deity';

For they are Powers; and hence the *high*est bliss
That can be known is theirs, the *consciousness*
Of whom they are habitually infused
Through every image, and through every thought,
And all impressions.[20]

Young, too, sets forth the 'godlike height' and the 'strange . . . bliss' of 'minds quite *conscious of* their *high* descent.' [21]

It is in the picture of the moonlit heavens that Young found

[20] *Prelude* XIII, 69, 90, 106–11.
[21] *Night Thoughts* VI, 604, 619, 590.

for himself, and helped to validate for Wordsworth on the top of Snowdon, the 'ostentation of creative power.' And hence we are not surprised to learn that Young's 'MIGHTY MIND' is a poetic mind. It is an AUTHOR. It writes books; and Nature is the 'first volume,'

> For Man's perusal; All in CAPITALS!
> In Moon, and Stars (heav'n's golden alphabet!)
> Emblaz'd to seize the sight; who runs, may read;
> Who reads, can understand. . . . Fairly writ,
> In language universal, to MANKIND:
> A language, Lofty to the learn'd; yet Plain
> To those that feed the flock, or guide the plough,
> Or, from his husk, strike out the bounding grain.
> A language, worthy the GREAT MIND, that speaks!
> Preface, and Comment, to the Sacred Page! . . .
> Stupendous book of wisdom, to the wise.[22]

DEITY, moreover, while it transcends, also partakes of other mundane professional responsibilities. First appearing as THOU, or HE, or DREAD SIRE, He is next called great FIRST-LAST. Then, in an effort to conceive Him as a functionary, Young hits upon the name PHILANTHROPIST, which William Wordsworth and William Mathews intended as a title for their monthly miscellany in 1794. God is not only the 'great ante-mundane Father,' ALMIGHTY, OMNIPOTENCE, PROVIDENCE, MAJESTY DIVINE, LOVE, MOST-HIGH, JEHOVAH; as if He were indeed the friend of man, or man among men, He is KING, LORD, JUDGE, ARCHITECT both glorious and stupendous; He is BUILDER, MASTER, GREAT PROPRIETOR; He is great OECONOMIST and GREAT ARTIST, musician and 'mighty *dramatist*'; He is a DIVINE INSTRUCTOR as well as CREATOR; He is the great VINE and also the gardener of the firmament, growing moral fruit for man. All of these textually capitalized functions of DEITY, thus translated into terms of human power, would arrest the eye of whatsoever apprentices in government, law, architecture, the arts, education, business, and agriculture were numbered

[22] *Ibid.* IX, 1658–72.

among the thousands who read *Night Thoughts* when Wordsworth was a youth; but Wordsworth was none of these. For this apprentice in the art of poetry the phrases of Young which connoted divine power most like the power of men were 'invisible, eternal MIND,' GREAT MIND, MIND ALMIGHTY, ILLUSTRIOUS MIND, in chief MIGHTY MIND.

This harmony in emblems arising out of a well-nigh identical experience of Wordsworth in his ascent of Snowdon on his own feet and of Young in his ascent up 'Night's radiant scale' in 'ardent Contemplation's rapid car' [23] prompts us to ask more specifically what each meant by 'mighty mind,' and what characteristics God and man share.

First, what did Young mean? In the '*Temple*' into which 'Night's consecrating shades' turn the '*Universe*' dwells 'a genius,' 'a *Spirit*,' 'BLEST SPIRIT,' 'something *Eternal*.' The moonlit heavens indicate design; '*design* implies *Intelligence* and *Art*.' This 'Spirit' shot '*Motion* . . . through vast masses of enormous weight,' bade 'brute *Matter*'s restive lump assume . . . various forms,' indued matter and motion and form with 'thought, judgment, and genius.' And who else 'gives our hearts with such high thoughts to swell?' [24]

Next, what did Wordsworth mean by the 'mighty Mind'? The answer is not far to seek. The words italicized below show his substantial agreement, even his verbal kinship, with Young:

> Wisdom and *Spirit* of the *Universe!*
> Thou Soul that art *the eternity of thought!*
> That giv'st to *forms* and images a breath
> And everlasting *motion!*

Both poets have sought for synonyms of the words DEITY and GOD; likewise, studying this divine power in its effect, both note that it gives form and motion. Higher minds 'are truly from the Deity,' as Wordsworth acknowledges in Book XIII.

[23] *Ibid.* IX, 1708, 1713.

[24] *Ibid.*, 1347–8, 1355, 1417, 1449, 1461–79, 1560–7. Young's italics.

Finally, it is through the Mind, Spirit, or Soul, whom both poets now and again call Deity, that the relation between Nature and Man is sanctified. According to Young, God is Nature's AUTHOR and also 'Father fond of . . . intellectual beings!' On this idea of the kinship of Nature and Man, Wordsworth would articulate the extension of his love from the one to the other. In the disjunct but important Book VIII of *The Prelude* where his 'Theme'

> Is to retrace the way that led me on
> Through Nature to the love of Human Kind,

his references to God are frequent. Witness the lines which begin MS Y of his autobiographical poem:

> With deep devotion, Nature, did I feel
> In that great City what I owed to thee,
> High thoughts of God and Man, and love of Man. . . .
> There came a time of greater dignity
> Which had been gradually prepar'd, and now
> Rush'd in as if on wings,[25] the time in which
> The pulse of Being everywhere was felt,
> When all the several frames of things, like stars
> Through every magnitude distinguishable,
> Were half confounded in each other's blaze,
> One galaxy of life and joy. Then rose
> Man, inwardly contemplated, and present
> In my own being, to a loftier height;
> As of all visible natures crown; and first
> In capability of feeling what
> Was to be felt; in being rapt away
> By the divine effect of power and love,
> As, more than anything we know instinct
> With Godhead, and by reason and by will
> Acknowledging dependency sublime.[26]

Thus Wordsworth answers Young's question: 'What am I? and from Whence?'

[25] For wings as a method of imaginative locomotion, cf. *Night Thoughts* III, 449; IV, 289–90, 302, 426, 467; VI, 693–5.

[26] Now to be read as *Prelude* VIII, 585–7, 62–4, 623–39.

Young himself, churchman as he was, had given Christian counsel (*Night Thoughts* IV, 442): 'View man, to see the glory of your God!' Seeing man through the truth of redemption, he had cried out (462–3): 'O how is man enlarg'd! . . . How the pigmy tow'rs!' Is this towering pigmy not brother to the Westmoreland Shepherd of Book VIII of *The Prelude* (392–439)?

A Power
Or Genius, under Nature, under God,
Presiding; . . .
In size a giant . . .
A solitary object and sublime,
Above all height! like an aerial Cross
As it is stationed on some spiry Rock
Of the Chartreuse, for worship. . . .
. . . Blessed be the God
Of Nature and of Man that this was so,
That Men did at the first present themselves
Before my untaught eyes thus purified,
Remov'd, and at a distance that was fit.

Asking when this important action took place, we learn from Book VIII that Man was subordinate to Nature in Wordsworth's affections and regards until after his twenty-third summer, the summer of 1792. Only a few weeks later his natural child Caroline was born. If we relate this natural event, which joined Wordsworth inescapably to the world of man—of man, woman, and child—with the sacrament of the Church which Young represented and Wordsworth had expected to enter, we see more clearly why he must rethink the whole problem of Nature and Man. Even in February of 1793 Dorothy, unaware yet of his dependents in France, was looking forward 'with full confidence to the happiness of receiving [Jane Pollard] in my little Parsonage.' [27] May we not assume that a text able to furnish him with a commentary on his Alpine journey of 1790 and his London residence and Welsh jaunt of 1791 would cling to his thoughts dur-

[27] *Early Letters*, p. 84.

ing the anxious years which followed his return to England late in 1792, years of separation from mate and child? At least we know that when in February, 1793, *An Evening Walk* was published in London it acknowledged a debt to Dr. Edward Young.

This is not to say that Wordsworth must read *Night Thoughts* in order to compose parts of Books VI, VIII, IX, and XIII of *The Prelude;* but Young's language, imagery, and ideas were so entangled with the experience of his youth and early manhood that, when he came to write this down, part of the experience itself was such poetry as had helped him to understand and value it. Again, this is of course not to say that Wordsworth learned from Young how or what to feel, or how or what to think and imagine, or how or what to compose; yet, in the recognitive process, years after the actual events, he could not and need not detach Young's 'Moral Survey of the Nocturnal Heavens' from the ideas, images, and language with which he invested his own adventures with Nature and Man, or later with Man and Nature, not forgetting God.

Such an association of imaginative or mystical visions not only in the Alps and in Wales, but also in London, suggests Young's influence at work when the three scenes were actually present to Wordsworth's outer eye: the years 1790–1. That all three places of triumphant vision were set forth in the poetical idiom of his late college and early postgraduate period, reflecting Young's *Night Thoughts* in chief, helps to support our assumption that he grew out of and not into the traditional religious parlance of the English Church.

Wordsworth Manuscripts of 1794–1798 and Young's Poem

Kurt Lienemann traced to line 128 of Young's 'Relapse' ('Revere thyself; and yet thyself despise') [28] a phrase in line 63 of Wordsworth's *Lines Left upon a Seat in a Yew-Tree,* which, the poet told Isabella Fenwick, were 'composed in part at school at

[28] *Die Belesenheit von William Wordsworth,* p. 60.

Hawkshead,' and which in 1815 he dated 1795. Sometime before 1797, when Mary Hutchinson copied down verses of it not yet in their final form, Wordsworth had returned to the yew tree of his schooldays; and the sketch he wrote has echoes of the poetry he had read as a schoolboy. His 'lost Man' of 1787–98 was

> No common soul. In youth by *genius* [1800 *science*] nurs'd
> And *big with lofty views*, he to the world
> Went forth, pure in his heart, against the taint
> Of dissolute tongues, and jealousy, and hate,
> And *scorn*,—against all enemies prepared,
> All but neglect. . . . The man whose eye
> Is ever on himself doth look on one,
> The least of *Nature's works*, one who might move
> The *wise* man to that *scorn* which *wisdom* holds
> Unlawful, ever. O be *wiser*, Thou!
> Instructed that *true knowledge* leads to love,
> True dignity abides with him alone
> Who, in the silent hour of inward thought,
> *Can still suspect, and still revere himself,*
> *In lowliness of heart.*

In his 'Relapse,' Young had also rebuked those 'big in previous thought':

> If *wisdom* is our lesson . . .
> Grief! more proficients in thy school are made,
> Than *genius*, or *proud learning*, e'er cou'd boast. . . .
> [*Genius*] *scorns* to share a blessing with the crowd. . . .
> But *wisdom* smiles, when *humbled* mortals weep. . . .
> Learn well to know how much need not be known,
> And what that *knowledge*, which impairs your sense. . . .
> You *scorn* what lies before you in the *page*
> *Of nature*, and experience, moral truth;
> You . . . dive in *science* for distinguisht names,
> Dishonest fomentation of your *pride*. . . .
> Your learning . . . leaves you *undevout*,
> *Frozen at heart.*[29]

[29] *Night Thoughts* V, 16, 234–5, 251–4, 265–9, 274, 736–9, 743–4, 747–8, 750–2.

Some traits of the lost man under the yew tree appear also in the letters to Mathews from Wales in the summer of 1791, with their clear picture of anxious friendship and their ostentatious moral counsel. We have only one side of the correspondence, but it shows that a letter answered by William Wordsworth on August 13 must have represented Mathews' 'share of happiness . . . small,' his 'time . . . consumed, and . . . spirits worn out, in unproductive labour.' Not that Wordsworth accuses him 'of a splenetic disposition wilfully fostered,' but the 'fatigue' undergone by Mathews disposes him 'to look on the dark side of things.' And on September 23 Wordsworth advises his friend that 'it is much more easy to prevent a *dissatisfaction* like yours from *taking root*, than, when it has taken root, to check its vegetation and stop *the extravagant stretch of its branches, overshadowing and destroying with their baneful influence*, every neighbouring image of cheerfulness and comfort.' He exhorts Mathews to 'hope and industry.' [30]

Over against the picture of the splenetic Mathews sitting under the spreading yew tree of dissatisfaction, we seem to discern the features of a more resolute Wordsworth setting aside vagrant wishes as he returns from Wales to town, to Mr. Robinson, and to thoughts of the curacy which will enable him to 'maintain himself.' This was in 1791, September 23; but, although Dorothy reported him, on October 9, reconciled to the Oriental languages, by November 23 he wrote to Mathews that he had 'no resolution' for the enterprise, that he was 'doomed to be an idler' through his whole life. He approved Mathews' 'resolution,' however; and, possibly for Mathews' benefit, he apologized for his own 'outrageous egotism.' It would seem that both college graduates sat for the portrait of the 'lost man' under the yew tree. Wordsworth's letter from Blois, May 17, 1792, indicates that Mathews was still unhappy: 'Let me entreat you most earnestly to guard against that melancholy which appears to be making daily inroads upon your happiness. Educated as you have been, you ought to be

[30] *Early Letters*, pp. 54–9.

above despair.' But Wordsworth himself has come out into the sun: 'Nothing but resolution is necessary.' [31] In his need to counsel Mathews, he was calling into use arguments with which Edward Young not less than Wordsworth's own guardians dispelled gloom and exhorted to a wiser and humbler life.

Meanwhile, Dorothy had written to her brother Richard a more explicit letter about William's affairs: William had accepted the offer of Uncle William to give him a Title for Orders; Uncle William wondered whether Mr. Robinson would place him at Harwich. 'It would be a charming thing if William could be placed there.' And from William, too, we have the explicit statement to Mathews in the letter of May 17, 1792: 'It is at present my intention to take orders. . . . My uncle the clergyman will furnish me with a title.' This will, he understands, not prevent him from engaging 'in any literary plan.' [32] He had accomplished for himself a triumph—if not a consolation—in the manner of Young.

Yet the birth of his daughter about seven months later was to be the reason not only for a profound moral readjustment, as hitherto indicated, but for serious practical concern and for financial anxiety; and by December 22 William was in London to secure funds and arrange for the publication of *An Evening Walk* and *Descriptive Sketches*, quartos which eight weeks later Dorothy recommended to her friend Jane for their 'many Beauties, Beauties which could only have been created by the Imagination of a *Poet*.' She underlined the word Poet. Not yet did she know that her 'Parsonage' was an empty dream. Not until June 16 would she write to Jane the fear that her scheme 'may prove a shadow, a mere vision of happiness,' [33] and that about William she was 'very anxious.'

Meanwhile William's return to France was blocked. He had been looking for a tutorial engagement, and had secured instead

[31] *Ibid.*, pp. 60–1, 74–6.
[32] *Ibid.*, pp. 69, 70, 75.
[33] *Ibid.*, pp. 82, 87, 89, 92.

the chance to tour western England, with his expenses paid. His wealthy companion was an old schoolmate, William Calvert, to whose generosity he and Dorothy were later to owe the loan of a cottage, not a parsonage, at Windy Brow, Keswick.

When finally the brother and sister sat down together in the Calvert lodgings in the spring of 1794 to mull over his recently published couplets, he must have quarreled with their lack of thought, for in his Quarto of *An Evening Walk* and in a notebook containing initial sketches for *Salisbury Plain*, a story suggested by his recent tour there, he added to the loco-descriptive text meditative passages of script quite in the vein of Young. These passages, first published in the de Selincourt edition of 1940, show him still padding his language with many adjectives of Latin derivation, most of them favorites of Young.[34]

It is tempting to think that nightly strolls under the stars with Dorothy during their reunion in 1793–4 had quickened his memory of Young's poem, possibly refreshed from a Windy Brow copy of *Night Thoughts*. Whereas in the Quarto he had been content with mentioning 'departed pleasures' and 'Melancholy's hand,' with shedding 'an unbidden tear' or two, now, like Young in 'The Relapse' from which he had acknowledged borrowing the verse cited, he returned to symbols of death, the 'mouldering rows of graves' juxtaposed with the playground of noisy children; for, he says,

[34] Adjectives of this sort added in 1794 to the vocabulary of 1793 follow; those occurring in the *Night Thoughts* of Young are italicized: *magic*, *gigantic*, *romantic*, *majestic*, monastic; *mortal*, [im]*memorial*, *universal*, *rural*, *celestial*, *local*, trivial, empyreal, *crystal*, internal, *vernal; sacred*, clear, sober, *vast; obscure*, *pure*, *secure*, *human*, *civil*, *active*, retrospective; *common*, *sublime*, sylvan, oblique, *severe*, proper, sober; *exquisite*, *minuter*, *erect;* vagrant, dulcet, *different*, *patient*, *transparent*, *triumphant*, *redundant*, translucent, *constant*, *frequent*, *incessant*, resplendent, refulgent [*effulgent:* Young]; *sensible*, illimitable, inaudible; *particular*, *momentary; languid* (4 times), *fervid*, *splendid*, humid, morbid, gelid, placid; *virtuous*, *famous*, *loquacious*, *harmonious*, *barbarous*, *delicious*, *cumbrous*, *beauteous*, *devious*, *dangerous*, luminous, *mysterious*. This is in well-nigh the same proportion as with the Quartos of 1793, both *Evening Walk* and *Descriptive Sketches*.

oft those passions of a wider range
That rise in mortal minds from mortal change
To my tamed heart an awful grief inspire
Tempered and cheared by many a big desire;
Chiefly when, guided by *some hand unseen*
Through paths where grey huts thinly intervene,
I seek that footworn spot of level ground
Close by the school within the churchyard bound.

The 'unseen hand' of Wordsworth's manuscript [35] may be the kind hand of Providence stretcht out 'twixt man and vanity' in 'The Relapse.' And when Young's 'dark pencil, Midnight, darker still in melancholy dipt, *embrowns* the whole,' it is the same sort of pencil that helped Wordsworth write, not only 'the brown park,' 'dark-brown bason,' and 'dark-brown mere' of 1793, but the 'brown pool' and 'brown lake' of his 1794 manuscript. He acknowledges nature as sanctifying the soul, pouring balm on morbid passion; and her magic influence carries him into 'worlds beyond the reign of sense.' This is an early phrasing of the Wordsworthian 'serene and blessed mood' and reminiscent of Young's 'pleasant stupor,' which will be discussed later in this chapter.

Also in this manuscript revision of 1794 Wordsworth adds an address to Dorothy so prophetic of that in his *Lines . . . on the Wye,* and so reminiscent of Young's idea of the half-creation by the senses of all they see, and indeed so indicative of a theory of imagination that it deserves special notice.

Yes, thou art blest, my friend, *with mind awake*
To Nature's impulse like this living lake,
Whose mirror makes the landscape's charms its own
With touches soft as those to Memory known; . . .
And are there souls whose languid powers unite
No interest to each rural sound or sight,

[35] First printed by de Selincourt, 1940, in Wordsworth's *Poetical Works,* Vol. 1, pp. 4–37.

To the lone chapel on the ocean coast,
To nameless brook below in ocean lost,
The bridge that spans the brook's small bed half-dry,
And the proud sails in glory sweeping by?
How different with *those favoured* souls who, taught
By active Fancy or *by patient Thought*,
See common forms prolong the endless chain
Of joy and grief, of pleasure and of pain;
But chiefly those to whom the *harmonious* doors
Of Science have unbarred celestial stores,
To whom *a burning energy* has given
That other eye which darts thro' earth and heaven,
Roams through all space and [ ] unconfined,
Explores the illimitable tracts of mind,
And piercing the profound of time can see
Whatever man has been and man can be.[36]

Even so brief a consideration of the 1794 additions to the Quarto of *An Evening Walk* reveals in the author a preoccupation with moral sentiments; and it is easy to assume that the serious, even plaintive tone of Young's 'Relapse' and 'Virtue's Apology' were in keeping with Wordsworth's mood at that time. When on February 17, 1794, he wrote to Mathews: 'What is to become of me I know not. I cannot bow down my mind to take orders,' Young's God the PHILANTHROPIST pointed one way out of the difficulty. The two friends would start a monthly miscellany with that name.

While her brother exchanged theology for philanthropy and poetry Dorothy stood by. Four years before she accompanied him to the banks of the Wye, she was at his side on the banks of the Derwent as they traveled through Cockermouth to Whitehaven.[37] A manuscript sheet written by Wordsworth and now in the Morgan Library, New York City, bears on one side of it attempts at the *Description of a Beggar*, anticipatory of *The Old Cumberland Beggar* of 1797; on the other side is an early sketch

[36] *Poetical Works*, Vol. 1, pp. 12–13.
[37] E. de Selincourt, *Dorothy Wordsworth*, Oxford, 1933, p. 54.

for the main theme, even the main situation—'once again'—of the *Lines . . . on the Wye:*

> Yet once again do I behold the forms
> Of these huge mountains and yet once again
> Standing beneath these elms I hear thy voice
> Beloved Derwent that peculiar voice
> Heard in the stillness of the evening air
> *Half-heard and half-created.*[38]

The phrase 'half-heard and half-created' must, then, anticipate by more than a year's interval the comparable passage written July 13, 1798, near Tintern Abbey; and for this,

> the mighty world
> Of eye and ear, both what they half-create
> And what perceive,

Wordsworth acknowledged his indebtedness to Young.[39] Thus the Derwent and the Wye are both associated with the 'Infidel Reclaimed' of *Night Thoughts.*

Let us now set forth the context of Wordsworth's phrase borrowed from 'Night the Sixth' (413–40): [40]

> Where, thy true treasure? . . . Seek it in thyself,
> Seek in thy naked self, and find it there;
> In being so descended, form'd, endow'd;
> *Sky*-born, *sky-guided, sky*-returning race!
> Erect, immortal, rational, divine!
> In *senses,* which inherit *earth,* and *heav'ns;*
> [Which] Enjoy the various riches nature yields;
> Far nobler! give the riches they *enjoy;*
> Give taste to fruits; and *harmony* to groves; . . .

[38] Quoted with the kind permission of The Pierpont Morgan Library.

[39] *Lyrical Ballads,* 1798, ed. by T. Hutchinson, 3d ed., London, 1920, pp. 129, 253. 'This line has a close resemblance to an admirable line of Young's, the exact expression of which I cannot recollect.' *Poetical Works,* Vol. 2, pp. 262, 518.

[40] At the time this chapter was written I knew of no previous reference to the context of Young's line. Since then, in 1949, before the South Central section of the Modern Language Association, Professor George W. Meyer has discussed the matter.

Take in, at once, the landscape of the world,
At a small inlet, which a grain might close,
And *half* create the wondrous world they see.
Our *senses*, as our reason, are divine. . . .
Objects are but th'occasion; ours th'exploit; . . .
Man makes the matchless image, man admires.
Say then, shall man, his *thoughts* all sent abroad,
Superior wonders in himself forgot,
His admiration waste on *objects* round,
When Heav'n makes him the *soul of all* he sees?

Granted that Young's 'senses . . . divine' are less imaginatively resonant than is Wordsworth's 'sense sublime' of the *Lines . . . on the Wye*, Young's analysis of the mind of man in 'Infidel Reclaimed' has also discovered that the 'sky-born, sky-guided, sky-returning race' carries within itself its 'true treasure.' This 'treasure,' it seems to me, and it may to others who read both Young and Wordsworth, should be compared with Wordsworth's even more universal 'something': 'something' resident in Nature and Man both; 'something'

Whose dwelling is the light of setting suns,
And the round ocean, and the living air,
And the blue *sky*, and in *the mind of man*,
A motion and a spirit, that impels
All thinking things, all objects of all thought,
And rolls through all things.

When Wordsworth recognizes 'in nature and the language of the sense' the 'guide . . . of his heart' and the 'soul . . . of his moral being' he is supporting, or at least echoing the diction of, Young's equally insistent plea for the dignity of the senses.

Seeking other wealth in himself, says Young, Man will find it in 'fancy,' in '*memory's* firm record' (which could 'recall from the dark shadows of o'erwhelming years' whatever is lost to the senses), in 'intellect, in faculties of endless growth,' in 'passions,' in 'liberty to chuse,' in 'pow'r to reach,' and in 'duration to perpetuate—boundless bliss!' From Young's sketch of human wealth,

Wordsworth would take the hint for his remembrance of the lovely forms which have not been 'as is a landscape to a *blind man's eye*.' We are not primarily interested here in a comparison of Young's psychology with that of Wordsworth, but with the likeness in their language and images; both, however, insist on the importance of the senses, both put man into a productive relation with nature, and both give man power to modify sense experience.

Further, Wordsworth may owe to Young among others, to the Wye supremely, 'another gift':

> *that blessed mood,*
> In which the burthen of the mystery,
> In which the heavy and the weary weight
> Of all this unintelligible world,
> Is lightened:—*that serene and blessed mood,*
> In which the *affections* gently lead us on,—
> Until, *the breath of this corporeal frame*
> *And even the motion of our human blood*
> *Almost suspended*, we are laid asleep
> In body, and become a living *soul:*
> While with an *eye* made quiet by the power
> Of *harmony*, and the deep power of *joy*,
> We *see into the life of things.*

Such a mood had been described by Young in 'Night the Ninth,' where Night bribes the poet to be wise, 'with gain and *joy*' (726, 736–9, 741–2, 753, 845–6):

> With pleasing *stupor* first the *soul* is struck
> (*Stupor* ordain'd to make her truly wise!):
> Then into *transport* starting from her *trance*,
> With *love*, and admiration, how she glows! . . .
> This ostentation of creative power!
> This theatre!—what *eye* can take it in? . . .
> My *heart*, at once, it humbles, and exalts. . . .
> How my mind, op'ning at this scene, imbibes
> The *moral emanations of the skies!*

The comparison of Young's 'pleasing stupor' and Wordsworth's 'serene and blessed mood'—even in the repetition of each word by its author—would seem to me to indicate indebtedness more than phrasal, especially because with both poets it leads to vision.

Wordsworth's thorough knowledge of Young clearly antedates the *Lines . . . on the Wye*, even the Pierpont Morgan MS and the manuscript additions of 1794. If so, we should be able to detect also in *Guilt and Sorrow* and in *The Borderers* evidence of Young's influence. Narrative and dramatic as they are, and modified by new social theses foreign to the philanthropy of Young, nevertheless the agents of these actions display personal flaws which Wordsworth, like Young, would call excessive grief and excessive pride. Especially does Oswald share with Lorenzo of *Night Thoughts* the intellectual arrogance whose arguments were familiar to Wordsworth from Young's poem. Nor was Wordsworth untutored as to the traditional answers for these arguments. At some time during his own grievous months in 1793 or 1794, and very likely before the residence at Racedown, he had reviewed Young's meditations with anxious and humble eyes. And in *Night Thoughts*, I suggest, he had found before 1798 encouragement for his own restoration, and for the first dim conception of *The Recluse-Prelude*, and for *The Excursion*. He would soon invigorate Young's sentimental piety with the elegiac outlines of Habington's Holy Man; and in due time he would abandon both modes of treating the moral *peripeteia* for a narrative method learned primarily from the pilgrimage of John Bunyan.

VIII

Holy Man

Wordsworth and Habington as Authors

IN THE *Lines* composed July 13, 1798, on the banks of the Wye above Tintern Abbey, and in the group of poems begun or finished during Wordsworth's residence in Germany, 1798–9, there are many situations, images, maxims, and phrases characteristic also of the elegists and metaphysical poets of the seventeenth century. Wordsworth's knowledge of Vaughan has been assumed, not established; but it has been more frequently discussed than his possible indebtedness to the *Castara* of William Habington, with which collection of poems we are to deal in the present chapter. Habington's *Historie of Edward IV* was in Wordsworth's library,[1] and Habington's Lucy has been compared with Wordsworth's Lucy.[2] Habington, however, is not among those contemporary writers—Herbert, Walton, Suckling, Denham, Waller, Cowley, Marvell—singled out by Wordsworth for critical observation or grateful acknowledgment.

Yet no one of them could furnish him with so concrete an illustration of that cycle of love, friendship, and the holy life on which he was himself engaged in 1798–9 as Habington in his

[1] *Transactions of the Wordsworth Society*, No. 6, p. 203.
[2] Lienemann, *Die Belesenheit von William Wordsworth*, p. 30.

Castara. Even if Habington was not known to Wordsworth—which I find hard to believe—our study of similar passages from their verse will help us to understand Wordsworth's poetic growth in that period. The tentative purposes and uneven quality of his writing between his experiments in balladry and his review of Chaucer, Spenser, and Milton, indicate a new apprenticeship; and where this writing is not successful, does not manifest Wordsworth's own peculiar power, we may the better trace in it the congenial meditative habit and the alien technique of the elegy as Habington wrote it.

Postponing for discussion elsewhere the influence of Habington on Wordsworth's elegies for Lucy and Matthew, here we shall rather place side by side Habington's Author and Holy Man and Wordsworth's Poet. When Wordsworth set down the story of a love refined from 'passion' and 'appetite,' from 'aching joys . . . and dizzy raptures' to 'warmer love . . . far deeper zeal of holier love,' he was consciously transmuting the love poetry of such as Habington into his own terms for that love story of the Poet and Nature renewed on the banks of the Wye near Tintern Abbey. And if the 'holier love' of Nature recorded by the worshipper on July 13, 1798, were to be further deepened and enriched, he might well continue to bring his 'holy powers and faculties' [3] under the influence of the century of Habington, Bunyan, and Milton. Such discipline would be highly significant for his autobiographical poem.

William Habington (1605–45), member of a Roman Catholic family settled at Hindlip, and a man of dignity and sentiment, has left, besides his *Historie of Edward IV*, a tragicomedy, *The Queen of Arragon,* and a collection of occasional poems published in 1634, 1635, and 1640, and finally grouped as 'A Mistress,' 'A Wife,' 'A Friend,' and 'A Holy Man,' under the general title, *Castara.* Each group is accompanied by a *character,* or typical sketch. In 'A Mistress' and 'A Wife' Habington celebrated his

[3] *Prelude* III, 83–8.

love for his mistress and wife, Lucy Herbert, daughter of William, Lord Powys; [4] in 'A Friend' he wrote several elegies on his friend George Talbot; and in 'A Holy Man,' with titles borrowed from the Psalms and the Book of Job, he told of his efforts to 'calcine frail love to piety.'

Before his series Habington had placed an autobiographical essay, a *character* entitled 'The Author,' which reminds us not only of the meditations on the banks of the Wye but also of Wordsworth's projected association of an autobiographical poem with his philosophical poem, the *Recluse*.

First to Habington's 'Author' and to Castara, his 'worthy' 'theame':

Though *my eye* in its survey was satisfi'd, even to curiosity, yet did not my search rest there. The Alabaster, Ivory, Porphyr, Jet, that lent an admirable beauty to *the outward building* entertained me with but a halfe-pleasure, since they stood there only to make sport for ruine. But when *my soule grew acquainted with the owner of that mansion* . . . *wonder* [became] . . . *a lethargie that dulled too much the faculties of the minde.*[5]

[4] Moorman (*Cambridge History of English Literature*, Vol. 7, pp. 28, 19) mentions two other Lucys: Lucy Hay, Countess of Carlisle, to whom both Herrick and Carew wrote verses (cf. Herrick, *Upon a Black Twist, rounding the Arme of the Countesse of Carlile; Carnation*—'Within my Lucia's cheek'; and again, 'Thou seest me Lucia this year droope; . . . some Odes I made of Lucia.'); and Lucy Sacheverell, said to have been Lovelace's Lucasta. Cf. Waller's poems (*Works*, ed. 1729, pp. 33, 34, 37, 38–9) with the Countess of Carlisle as subject; the possible connection of Lucy, Countess of Bedford, with Drayton's 'Idea'; and the Lucinda of *A Divine Love* (*Modern Language Review*, Vol. 20, p. 74). An earlier 'Lucy bright' may be found in Spenser's *Faerie Queene* V, iv, 9, lines 2–4:

To whom but little dowre allotted was;
Her vertue was the dowre that did delight.

For Wordsworth a Castara, Lucasta, Lucia, Lucinda, would be simple Lucy. My study of *Castara* and the Lucy and Matthew poems of Wordsworth awaits publication.

[5] *The Works of the English Poets*, edited by Chalmers, London, 1810, and henceforth cited as *English Poets*. References are given also to Edward Arber's reprint of *Castara*, London, 1870, cited as *A.R.* The latter brings us nearer to the edition of 1640, which would have been the only collected edition accessible to Wordsworth before 1810. In 1948 The University Press of Liverpool published an edition, *The Poems of William Habington*, by Kenneth Allott.

The initial satisfaction of the eye with what is outward, the later discovery by the soul of the life within, and the lethargy of wonder which dulls the faculties of the mind: all this Habington associates with his mistress, Lucy Powys. Wordsworth associates with his mistress, Nature, celebrated in the *Lines . . . on the Wye*, a comparable experience: first, of eye:

> the tall rock,
> The mountain, and the deep and gloomy wood,
> Their *colours and their forms*, were then to me
> An appetite; a feeling and a love,
> That had no need of a remoter charm,
> By thought supplied, *nor any interest*
> *Unborrowed from the eye . . .*

and, second, the sublime experience of the soul with its lethargy of wonder, which becomes in his words

> that serene and blessed mood,
> In which the affections gently lead us on,—
> Until . . . we are laid asleep
> In body, and become a living soul:
> While with an eye made quiet by the power
> Of harmony, and the deep power of joy,
> We see into the life of things.[6]

Again, Habington's metaphor of the owner of a mansion Wordsworth appropriates as 'something . . . whose dwelling is the light of setting suns, and the round ocean and the living air, and the blue sky, and in the mind of man'; and he hopes that Dorothy's mind will be 'a mansion for all lovely forms,' her memory as 'a dwelling-place for all sweet sounds and harmonies.' Although the 'mansion' or 'outward building' of Habington's beloved, Lucy, was a body aggregated from eye, lip, breast, skin, palm, things

[6] *Lines . . . on the Wye* 75–83, 41–9. In *Prelude* II, 367–9, he calls such a lethargy 'a holy calm' overspreading his 'soul,' when 'bodily eyes' are forgotten.

> To which the soule each *vitall motion* gives;
> You are *infus'd* into it, and it lives,[7]

Wordsworth, somewhat as a pantheist might, surely as an artist does, refers to 'something' in his beloved Nature which is 'far more deeply *interfused*' (*Lines* 96, 100–2),

> A *motion* and a spirit, that impels
> All thinking *things*, all objects of all thought,
> And rolls through *all things*.

In 'The Author' of Habington, Wordsworth might also come upon phrases suggestive for his account in *The Prelude* of the difficulties of authorship. The elder poet refers to '*modesty*, so *timorous*, that it represented a besieg'd Citty, *standing watchfully upon her guard*'; under the same figure, of one who withstands or beats off, Wordsworth acknowledges his own '*timorous* capacity, . . . *circumspection*, . . . humility and *modest* awe,' and his 'anxious eye.' Although Habington is modest, his '*Theame* is worthy enough'; if his poems 'are not *strangled with* envie of the present, they may happily *live* in the not dislike of *future times*.' Wordsworth 'would gladly *grapple with* some noble *theme*,' but he doubts his power to people the hearts of men '*now living*, or *to live in future years*' (1850). Whereas Habington's 'rigid friend' may 'question superciliously the setting forth' of his poems, Wordsworth's friend Coleridge is 'prompt in sympathy'; instead of Habington's excuse for the want in his lines of 'that courtship . . . which *insinuates* it selfe into the favour of great men,' and of that satire which wins 'applause with the envious multitude,' Wordsworth speaks to Coleridge 'unapprehensive of contempt, the *insinuated* scoff of coward tongues.'[8]

Habington's renunciation of carnal love, that dull sublunary flame, his distaste for the trivial life of the Court and the cor-

[7] *English Poets*, Vol. 6, p. 461; *A.R.*, p. 69. *Vital* is associated with *motion* also by Spenser (*Faerie Queene* IV, vi, 29, line 4), by Browne, and by Davies in *Nosce Teipsum* (*vital spirits* and the *motion of life*), to mention three of many writers of the sixteenth and seventeenth centuries.

[8] *Prelude* I, 240–9, 139, 175–6, 645–6; II, 470–1.

rupted air of the world, and his resort to the holy shade, the dark, silent grove with the murmuring brooks, are familiar in literary tradition; but there is a peculiar message for Wordsworth in Habington's lines to Sir Ed. P., Knight:

> Enjoy at home what's reall: here the Spring
> By her aeriall quires doth *sing*
> As sweetly to you, as if you were laid
> Under the learn'd Thessalian shade.
> Direct your eye-sight *inward,* and you'le find
> A *thousand regions* in your *mind*
> Yet undiscover'd. Travell them, and be
> Expert in *home* Cosmography. . . .
> Man's a whole world within him selfe.[9]

This is to be Wordsworth's cosmography, the Mind of Man, 'the haunt and main *region* of my *song,*' as he says in his Prospectus; he will contemplate man 'inwardly'; and in the last passage of *The Prelude* he and Coleridge, prophets of nature, will instruct others

> how the mind of man becomes
> *A thousand times more beautiful than the earth*
> On which he dwells, above this Frame of things . . .
> In beauty exalted, as it is itself
> Of substance and of fabric more divine.

Frail Love Calcined to Piety

Both *Castara* and *The Prelude* are songs of love. From the song of 'frail love' Habington goes on to sing the 'chaste chemic art' whereby frail love 'is calcined to piety.' So from the warm love of Nature in the *Lines . . . on the Wye,* Wordsworth would direct us to 'warmer love . . . far deeper zeal of holier love'; later he would call this 'intellectual love,' or imagination, not merely the explicit doctrine of his *Prelude,* but its essential life. Did he hear the term from Coleridge in their talk of Spy-nozy? Its meaning he might have gathered from various metaphysical

[9] *English Poets,* Vol. 6, p. 468; *A.R.,* p. 93.

raptures of the seventeenth century, not least clearly from Habington's *Perfection of Love*, in which another William and his beloved forsake the earth and travel to that pure and glorious sphere where they can 'fix like stars for ever.' [10] Their love is the love of two Angels; their rites in life are only types of the marriage state.

> Our souls on earth contracted be;
> But they in heaven their nuptials *consummate*.

With a similar hallowing of his love for Nature Wordsworth brings to its appointed close his history of 'the discipline and *consummation* of the poet's mind.'

Once our attention is called to the imaginative marriage of the Poet and Nature, that marriage for which *The Prelude* is indeed a prothalamium, we remember as the chief of Wordsworth's many conjugal metaphors the vivid passage from the Prospectus (published 1814) at the end of 'Home at Grasmere':

> For the discerning Intellect of Man,
> When wedded to this goodly universe
> In love and holy passion, shall find these
> [Truth, Grandeur, Beauty, Love, Hope, Faith]
> A simple produce of the common day.
> —I, long before the blissful hour arrives,
> Would chant, in lonely peace, the spousal verse
> Of this great *consummation*:—and . . .
> Would I arouse the sensual from their sleep
> Of Death, and win the vacant and the vain
> To noble raptures; while my voice proclaims
> How exquisitely the individual Mind . . .
> . . . to the external World
> Is fitted;—and how exquisitely, too . . .

[10] For Habington's Holy Man, as well as for the lovers, happiness 'shines a fixt star.' Wordsworth's wish as a recluse is that his song

> With star-like virtue in its place may shine,
> Shedding benignant influence, and secure,
> Itself, from all malevolent effect
> Of those mutations that extend their sway
> Throughout the nether sphere!

> The external World is fitted to the Mind;
> And the creation . . . which they with blended might
> Accomplish:—this is our high argument.

To this end he considers the hearts of mighty poets the metropolitan temple for the sacrament.

From the marriage figure which underlies both *Prelude* and *Recluse* corroborative echoes are as follows: the longing for a home expressed in the early passages of both poems; in *The Prelude* the comparison of the Poet to the Lover; the unconscious intercourse with the eternal Beauty; the 'virgin scene' (in *Nutting*); that more exact and intimate communion which gives its register of permanent relations; the spirit of religious love in which the Poet walks with Nature; the transports; from Nature joy and passion for the uneasy heart; the transitory passions on Nature's daily face; the Poet breeding in Nature's lap and the consummate happiness of his return to her during his first vacation; the moment of the unveiling of his soul, 'naked as in the presence of her God,' and the informing and creative power of that soul; the vow and dedication; the Poet, a wanderer, intimate with living Nature; Nature sovereign in the heart; Nature and the heart of Man fellow laborers; Nature for her own sake a joy, a passion; the Soul passing through all Nature to rest with God; the Poet remembering that in early youth he yielded himself to Nature in strong and holy passion, and finding necessary for his 'second love,' love of humanity, a different ritual; the direct and intimate communion of Youth with Nature and Reason; likings and loves in new channels; human Reason's naked self the object of fervor; the veil lifted and the resultant shock, with the mind let loose and goaded; probing the living body of society even to the heart, pushing without remorse his speculations forward, setting foot on Nature's holiest places; Nature's Self, by human love assisted, reviving the feelings of earlier life; the Poet resorting to Nature, who maintains for him a secret happiness, but his passion has suffered change; the life of Nature by the God of love inspired; Nature and the senses, insatiable delights, thraldom of the sense, appetites; the habit of sense finally shaken off, the Poet standing again in Nature's presence, a sensitive being and a creative soul; Nature's gifts of emotion and calmness, the interchange of peace and excitation; Nature's power to consecrate; in the forms of Nature a passion which intermingles with the works of Man to which she summons him; the Poet following Nature, standing by her side; Nature's domination upon the senses compared to Man's imaginative faculty in creating and catching existence; highest bliss, pervading love.

Whether the holy man calcine his frail love of woman to piety, as did Habington, or the recluse and poet grow from love of nature to love of mankind, as did Wordsworth, in the process they share many figures and phrases; the diction of the holy life lives on in the diction of the poetic life.

The following words do not surprise us from the pen of Habington: pride, ambition, the world, vanities; reason, truth, duty, virtue, eternity; passion, zeal, piety, swell[ings] of the soul [spirit], devotion, awe, glory; Idol, emblem, taper, Oratory, cells, hermit and hermitage, sanctuary, paradise; vows, discipline, blessing, prophecy, miracle; sabbath, priest and priestly, religious, blest, pious, holy, glorious, miraculous, immortal, angelical, God-like; sanctifying, consecrates, consummate, meditative, contemplative. Yet these are key words in the reflective passages of Books I and II of *The Prelude*, and occasionally of Books III and IV.[11] Says Habington: 'Heaven by miracle makes me survive myself.' Says Wordsworth: 'As by miraculous gift 't is shaken off, that burthen of my own unnatural self.' Habington refers to 'celestial music,' to 'the proud miracle of verse'; Wordsworth, to 'the holy life of music and of verse.' The holy life of Habington is one of clear joys, purer fire, purest beauty; Wordsworth acknowledges the never-failing principle of 'joy and purest passion.'

[11] I, 19–23, 40–4, 50–4, 59–63, 85–6, 112, 115, 150–4, 158, 258, 340 (1850), 428–9, 433–4, 439–40; II, 19–21, 65, 114, 367–8, 376, 394; III, 83, 120, 144, 178–80, 291–2, 301, 327, 333, 348, 377–8, 396–8, 440–2, 468–70, 489–91, 599; IV, 52, 130–1, 140–2, 153, 154–8, 226–30, 296–8, 341–5.

In Books V and VII, based for the most part on MSS W and X and composed in 1804, except for occasional words (commerce, frail, quire, hermit's taper) there is little reference to the holy life; in Book VI the visit to Chartreuse, the crossing of the Alps, and the adventures in the gloomy pass and on leaving Gravedona, now and again suggest the pilgrim, the apocalyptic vision, and the temple of eternity; Book VIII shares the traditional reference to the 'fictions' of 'fancy' and the stock contrasts between Nature and the City, between thought and action; but relatively little in these books, and almost nothing in Books IX and X, carries us back to the elegiac temper of 1798–9. Where Thomson and Young are not concerned, the influence of Bunyan and Milton has become evident.

In Books XI (XII), XII (XIII), and XIII (XIV), however, especially in the last, the life of the holy man as Habington had sketched it in *Castara* is almost never forgotten while we read Wordsworth's story of 'Imagination, How Impaired and Restored.' Although the later poet does not root holiness in the forms and formalities of religion, neither does he disregard these as literary metaphors: *the breath of Paradise*, *the bigot to a new idolatry*, the *Idol* reason, *the monk who hath forsworn the world*, *the mysteries of passion*, *the celestial presence*, the *shrine* for *the spirit of the past*, the *pilgrim in quest of highest truth*, the *pervading grace*, the *high service perform'd within*, *mountain-chapel* and *simple worshippers*, *religious hope*, *holy ground*, *Poets* compared to *Prophets*, *the sacrificial Altar*, *angels stopped upon the wing*, *communion with the invisible world* (in 1850 revised to *fit converse with the invisible world*), *Deity*, *solemn temple*, *faith*, *endless occupation for the soul*, and *the rapture of the Hallelujah*. Indeed Wordsworth, too, has *bow'd low to God;* with the *grace* of *Providence* he and his friend Coleridge are to be joint-laborers in *a work of . . . redemption*.[12] Such a collection of phrases from

[12] XI (XII), 2–7, 11, 75–6, 84, 123–8, 222–3, 234–40, 342–3, 374–5, 391–3. XII (XIII), 24 ff., 42–3, 76, 151, 226–30, 242, 266, 275–6, 301, 331. XIII (XIV), 10–84, 103–6, 111–12, 140–5, 149–52, 160–5, 170, 183–8, 261–2, 266–8, 271, 380–4, 431–2, 439–41.

The Prelude is, to say the least, not in the narrow sense Wordsworthian; I believe it to be a record not of imaginative decay but of Wordsworth's apprenticeship to poetry of the seventeenth century.

From this review of diction let us proceed to the study of certain images common to *Castara* and *The Prelude:* the grove, the murmuring stream, the azure sky, the dove, the glowworm; Habington's 'stone of Sisiphus' and Wordsworth's 'burthen of my own unnatural self.' Three figures important toward the beginning of both poems are (1) city life as opposed to the holy shade, (2) the coming to harbor of the weary mariner, and (3) the vision of a cottage. In the early version of *The Prelude* Wordsworth (1) rejoices that he has been freed from city walls; (2) he asks 'In what Vale shall be my harbour?' and compares himself to one who 'may quit the tiresome sea and dwell on shore'—not an autographical fact; and (3) in fancy he sees present before his eyes 'the very house and fields' of his chosen vale, where he shall begin 'some work of glory.' Habington (1) persuades his beloved to seek the silence of a private cell, and his friends to live in the silent shade, to fly the glorious troubles of the Court for the security of the vale, and repair to the pure innocence of the country air; (2) he refers to 'the sad vessell' with 'her Harbour now in ken' and to the vessel moved by 'heavenly love . . . to some blest Port'; and (3) he imagines the 'humble Pilgrim' who 'wondring stands at the great miracle . . . (a view of Christ's cottage . . . by Angel hands transported from sad Bethlehem).' [13]

Further on, in Book II, the 'auxiliar light' which came from the poet's mind and 'on the setting sun bestowed new splendor' should be compared with Habington's 'soul so bright' which must of force 'to her earth contribute light.' Indeed, this figure chiefly, the metaphorical contrast, dear to writers of the seventeenth century, between the sensual and the enfranchised soul as between darkness and light, would have found a genial welcome in Words-

[13] *English Poets,* Vol. 6, pp. 454, 478–9, 446; *A.R., passim* and pp. 44, 60, 18. In the version of 1850 of *The Prelude* Wordsworth also uses 'cottage.'

worth's first conception of *The Recluse-Prelude*. Habington addresses those 'who are earth, and cannot rise above [their] sence.' He has 'wandred . . . [in ways] horrid as night'; but when oppressive 'shadowes . . . begin to cleere,' he sees 'the shape of sinne' to be a guest less welcome than a scorpion; at last he discovers day among 'blind cloudes,' and like Prometheus he steals from heaven fire which is 'endlesse and intire.' [14] In Books VI and XIII (XIV) of *The Prelude* Wordsworth sets forth his experiences 'lost as in a cloud' on the far side of the Alps, or wandering in the darkness near Gravedona, exasperated by 'stings of insects'; again, in the Snowdon passage assumed by de Selincourt to have been written at Goslar, he was 'hemmed round on every side with fog and damp,' his musing interrupted by shepherd's cur and hedgehog. In either instance 'the light of sense' went out in 'flashes' showing 'the invisible world,' or 'light . . . fell like a flash.'

Imagery in the passage of Books III and IV describing college and its vacations is often close to Habington's description of friendship and the enterprise of youth in the arenas of learning and polity. Both poets refer to their predecessors: Habington to Chapman, Spenser, Drayton, Sidney; and Wordsworth to Chaucer, Spenser, Milton. Habington's promise,

> I'le therefore near some murm'ring brook
> That wantons through my meddowes with a booke . . .
> My youth not guilty of ambition spend,

was realized by Wordsworth beside the pleasant mills of Trompington with Chaucer's tales of amorous passion. The poets are alike guilty of convivial moments. Habington, 'who still [sins] for company,' surrenders his brain at a 'glorious supper' party, drinking to 'the health of his good Majestye,' or describing a glass of wine which would impel Prynne to 'a health to Shakespeare's ghost'; [15] Wordsworth drinks until his brain reels in the rooms and to the name of Milton.

[14] *English Poets*, Vol. 6, pp. 456, 479–80; *A.R.*, pp. 51–2, 136–7.
[15] *English Poets*, Vol. 6, pp. 459, 465–6; *A.R.*, pp. 84, 63.

The details of the holier exhilaration, the imaginative, as set forth by Habington in 'Cupio dissolvi':

> The soule which doth with God unite, . . .
> Like sacred Virgin wax, which *shines*
> On Altars or on Martyrs' shrines
> *How* doth she *burne* away;
> *How* violent are her throwes till she
> *From envious earth* delivered be! . . .
> *How* soone she leaves the pride of wealth! [16]

resemble the 'glimmering views' of Wordsworth in his first college vacation:

> *How* Life pervades the undecaying mind,
> *How* the immortal Soul with God-like power
> Informs, creates, and *thaws* the deepest sleep
> That time can lay upon her. *How on earth* . . .

In this connection the scriptural figure of man as dust obsesses Habington: 'My frighted flesh trembles to dust'; 'the just keeps something of his glory in his dust.' Escape from the common destiny is possible only in those souls where God has his altars, and in the fair republic of the mind of the virtuous.[17] Wordsworth, too, in a summary passage of Book XIII (XIV) escapes from the laws of vulgar sense and the universe of death

> by love, for here
> Do we begin and end, all grandeur comes,
> All truth and beauty, from pervading love,
> That gone we are as dust.

These lines bring us back to Dorothy, the beloved. As Castara restores and quickens life (poplar, pine, cedar, and oak 'dance at sight of her'), Dorothy, too, restores life, poetic life; and such charm

> Of sweetness did her presence breathe around
> That all the *trees*, and all the silent hills

[16] *English Poets*, Vol. 6, pp. 481–2; *A.R.*, p. 143.
[17] *English Poets*, Vol. 6, pp. 471–2; *A.R.*, p. 108.

And everything she looked on, should have had
An intimation how she bore herself
Towards them and to all creatures.

Yet when Habington sings to Castara, 'The spring's still with thee,' and Wordsworth says to Dorothy, 'Thy breath, dear Sister, was a kind of gentler spring that went before my steps,' the difference between their styles of thought and diction becomes very clear.

The spiritual action of *Castara* and *The Prelude* is the achievement of holy (imaginative) life. To that end both poets set forth the peril to holiness (the imagination) of merely sensual or merely rational living; secondly, both celebrate the kinship of noble souls as transcending time and illustrating eternity. For instance, Wordsworth's suspicion of 'the human Reason's naked self' is shared by Habington, who reminds us that love is indeed 'something from above shot without reason's guide,' and that the Holy Man's 'impiety is not so bold to bring divinity down to the mistake of reason.' Again and again he refers to weak or fool philosophy, to feeble wit, to bedlam reason, to glorious reason overcome. Secondly, whereas in universal life Wordsworth assumes

One great Society alone on earth,
The noble Living and the noble Dead,

Habington 'piously maintain[s]' with his dead friend, Talbot, of 'noblest birth outshined by nobler vertue, the same commerce [they] held in life.' Such fraternity in spite of death, of absence, Wordsworth conceives as existent between himself and Coleridge. And in expressing that other important idea, eternity, Habington and Wordsworth both speak the language of the holy life.

Aeternity! when I think thee,
(Which never any end must have,
Nor knew'st beginning) . . .

cries Habington, who will expiate his sins 'on some bleak precipice,' amid the disdain of 'neighboring mountains,' under the 'midnight storm,' in winter 'ice,' and 'summer' sun, where the pine rots away and the cedars fall. Such landscape Wordsworth describes in his Alpine journey; in it, however, Habington's aggregate of terrestrial woes comes to a new and joyous life as

> Characters of the great Apocalypse,
> The types and symbols of *Eternity*,
> *Of first and last, and midst, and without end.*

The Recluse as published in 1888, with its first chapter entitled 'Home at Grasmere,' was for the most part composed in 1800 after Dorothy and William settled at Town-end in December, 1799. Except for the spousal image behind the lines which served as Prospectus and were printed in 1814 with *The Excursion*, there is in it not much reminiscence of the elegists of the seventeenth century. To be sure, Dorothy and William come to their vale, like Habington and Castara to Hindlip, that they may 'find in the midst of so much loveliness, love, perfect love; and they who are dwellers in this holy place must needs themselves be hallowed.' Yet references to the forest hermit, and joy at the escape from the city, its crowded streets, and the living and dead wilderness of the thronged world, echo faintly in *The Recluse* of 1800–88 when we compare with it their frequent and emphatic part in the early version of *The Prelude*.

What, then, was the temper of *The Recluse* mentioned in March, 1798? Might it be that rough sketches later to be rewritten into a nucleus for Books XI (XII), XII (XIII), XIII (XIV) of *The Prelude*, would constitute a love song of the reclusive life, consonant with Habington's 'Holy Man,' and not out of key with the *Lines . . . on the Wye?* If so, we may more clearly understand Wordsworth's interest in elegiac sentiments and phrases at Goslar, where he began to record his early communion with the Soul of Nature. But by 1800 the blank verse written at Grasmere reveals fresh study of Milton's epics and Akenside's psychology; and the autobiographical action has taken on the vigor of Bunyan's allegory. Wordsworth has abandoned his elegiac mood; the Poet has succeeded to the Recluse and will soon start on a pilgrimage to be detailed in the following chapter.

IX

Pilgrim

As a discipline and consummation, *The Prelude* belongs to an enormous family of literary texts. Its kin are not only the *Imitatio Christi* and William Law's *Serious Call*, but also the *Plain Man's Pathway to Heaven* and the *Practice of Piety* which started Bunyan on his pilgrimage. The kind of successively more conscious and laborious inwardness that withdrew the medieval novice from this world was not in Wordsworth's experience; nor were Law's reiterated declarations and verbally ingenious *characters* to his taste.[1] Rather, this poet, who loved a public road and the 'disappearing line' which was 'like a guide into eternity,' [2] would turn to the equally populous family of pilgrimages.

Bunyan's dream-allegory is much less an imitation of the holiest of lives than is Wordsworth's autobiographical poem, and Bunyan's Christian never reaches the stature, never displays the refinement of Wordsworth's Poet. Nevertheless there is in the writing of both *Pilgrim's Progress* and *The Prelude* a homeli-

[1] Eugenius, Negotius, Classicus, and Mundanus; Succus, Caecus, and Susurrus; Lepidus and Calidus; Serena and Caelia; Miranda, Lucinda, and Feliciana: all are drawn with a pointed and careful pen. They are disjunct, however, and miss the interest which Bunyan's *personae* gain from a pilgrimage. For Wordsworth's possible indebtedness to Law's ideas, however, see Newton P. Stallknecht, *Strange Seas of Thought*, pp. 69–71.

[2] *Prelude* XII, 145–51.

ness, a forthright quality, which makes for close kinship between these two pilgrims to the life beyond, above, and within this life. John Bunyan, escaping from Bedford jail by way of an imagined pilgrimage, and William Wordsworth, 'captive' in 'a house of bondage . . . a prison where he hath been long immured,' set free on one fine day for his imaginative adventure, are fellows. The one journeys from the City of Destruction to Mount Zion. The other journeys from 'the City'—London? or whatsoever other town of the eighteenth century—into his 'holy life of music and of verse,' and finally to his vision on Mount Snowdon. Their ways will coincide or cross as both trudge ahead over the very same spiritual landscape upon which resides the author of the *Imitatio Christi.*

Doubtless it is in the nature of all pilgrimages to include a City of Destruction, a Slough of Despond and a Wicket Gate of dedication, the discipline of an Interpreter's house, adventures on a Hill of Difficulty, restoration in a Palace Beautiful, the ordeal of the Valley of the Shadow, a perilous Vanity Fair and a disastrous Doubting Castle of the Giant Despair, new vision on the Delectable Mountains, new peril on the Enchanted Ground, new comfort in the Land of Beulah, and a new home on Mount Zion. Once recognized, such a scheme may not be disregarded in any noble action. How Wordsworth adopted or avoided or modified it is another tale that takes some telling, but will prove not entirely fictitious and possibly fruitful; and it may help us to see both the long ancestry and the fresh power of his poem. Moreover, it will yield a new meaning for the first 271 lines of Book I, and new value for Books VI (lines 469–548), VII, VIII, and those parts of V and XI not deriving from MS W. As we make this necessarily brief and sharply focused study of a great and ample theme we shall from time to time review the manuscripts for hints from their date as to Wordsworth's pilgrimage into the poem finally known as *The Prelude*.

The mere enumeration of events in Bunyan's fable sets us to listing analogous items in Wordsworth's true story: his flight from the city, his discipline in Nature's school, and his dedication; the difficulties and humiliation of a poet traveling toward his hermitage; dull and sore experiences in London's Vanity Fair; errors, doubts, and despairs attendant upon life in revolutionary France and reactionary England; a retrospect of the delightful uplands of his youth so different from and superior to the enchanting pastoral traditions of other poets; new vision on the Simplon Pass, new comfort in Dorothy's Land of Beulah, new fellowship with Coleridge, Prophet of Nature; and the ultimate meaning and glory revealed on Mount Snowdon. Such is our brief prospectus.

Bunyan's Christian and Wordsworth's Poet

It is in the initial passage of Book I, lines 1–271, that we come upon the strongest clue to *The Prelude* as a revised pilgrimage. After his escape from the city Wordsworth's Poet, like Christian at the Place of Deliverance, lost his burden:

> As by miraculous gift 'tis shaken off,
> That burthen of my own unnatural self.

'Is there no turnings or windings, by which a Stranger may lose the way?' Christian had asked of Good-will at the Wicket Gate. Wordsworth is similarly interrogative: 'Whither shall I turn by road or pathway?' Yet even on the 'sabbath' of his deliverance the Poet does not forget his 'work of glory'; his 'own voice' (lines 1–54, the so-called Preamble) and 'the mind's internal echo' of it give him 'a chearful confidence in things to come.' Christian, too, hearing the 'pleasant voice' of the visionary choir in the Interpreter's House:

> Come in, Come in;
> Eternal Glory thou shalt win . . .

was encouraged; he 'smiled, and said, I think verily I know the meaning of this.'

For Wordsworth, of course, Nature herself was the Interpreter, and her domain, 'Earth with all her appanage,' was the Interpreter's House. His 'spots of time' and two particular spots of time now in Book XI perform for this pilgrim of the early nineteenth century much the same function as Bunyan's visions of judgment had performed for Christian in the seventeenth century. They bring him a

> Vivifying Virtue . . .
> A virtue by which pleasure is enhanced
> That penetrates, enables us to mount
> When high more high, and lifts us up when fallen.

The first of these two particular 'spots of time' is associated with a 'Murderer . . . hung in iron chains' whose fate so impressed the child Wordsworth when by mischance he was disjoined from 'honest James . . . [his] encourager and guide'; this we may compare with Christian's vision of 'the Man in the Iron Cage.' The second spot of time in Book XI concerns Wordsworth's chastisement by his father's death for his 'feverish . . . impatient' mood when awaiting horses to bear them home at Christmastide ('in the deepest passion I bow'd low to God, who thus corrected my desires'); this reminds us of Christian's vision of 'Passion and Patience.' Both spots of time precede an address to Coleridge,

> for whom
> I travel in these dim uncertain ways[,]
> Thou wilt assist me as a pilgrim gone
> In quest of highest truth . . .

a passage omitted in 1850.

Now after leaving the Interpreter's House, after deliverance from his burden, after the change of raiment and the three leaps for joy, Christian came upon Simple, Sloth, and Presumption, and Formalist and Hypocrisy of the land of Vain-Glory, villainous deterrents in the life of the poet as in the life of the Christian. But he discomfited them all, took a drink from the spring at the foot of the Hill Difficulty, started running—going—clambering—until, midway, 'he sat down to rest him' in 'a pleasant Arbour' where he 'fell into a slumber . . . which detained him in that place until it was almost night.'

In its main outlines this initiation of the Christian work of glory is like the initial experience of Wordsworth, poet. He, too, sat down in 'a green shady place . . . beneath a tree' and there spent the hours preceding sunset in a reverie about 'some work of glory . . . to be begun . . . perhaps perform'd' in the hermitage of the 'one sweet Vale' of his dreams. This is scarcely, he would have us think, a mistake; yet it is a change from the mood in which he fled the city,

> Keen as a Truant or a Fugitive,
> But as a Pilgrim resolute.[3]

When at the top of the Hill of Difficulty Christian searched for his Scroll to confute Mistrust and Timorous, it was gone, dropped in the pleasant Arbour—'O that I had not slept!' He must retrace his steps to find it; and when he had found it, now 'Oh how nimbly . . . did he go up the rest of the Hill!' In like circumstances Wordsworth's soul 'did once again make trial of the strength restored to her afresh,' and two days later (in 1850, three days later) he arrived at the 'hermitage' which in *The Prelude* corresponds to the Palace Beautiful of Bunyan's *Pilgrim's Progress.*

After his daring and safe passage between the lions into the Palace Beautiful, Christian was welcomed and cared for by Discretion, Prudence, Piety, and Charity, to whom he recounted his adventures. At supper 'the Table was furnished with fat things, and with Wine that was well refined'; they laid Christian to rest in a chamber whose name was 'Peace'; and in the morning 'they told him that he should not depart till they had showed him the *rarities* of that place.' But Wordsworth, a century and a half later, spares to speak of the delights of his hermitage,

> of what ensued,
> The admiration and the love, the life
> In common things; the endless store of *things*
> *Rare,* or at least so seeming . . .

[3] Version of 1850.

> The self-congratulation, the complete
> Composure, and the happiness entire.

Whereas on the second and third days Christian had been taken into the Armoury and there 'harnessed . . . with what was of proof,' 'speedily,' says Wordsworth, in a comparable metaphor, 'a longing in me rose *to brace myself* to some determin'd aim.'

Christian found it dangerous going down into the Valley of Humiliation; Prudence had warned him 'to catch no slip by the way,' and he had been furnished with a loaf of Bread, a bottle of Wine, and a cluster of Raisins. Similarly, Wordsworth went into his humble valley through 'impediments from day to day renew'd,' in spite of his effort 'either to lay up new stores, or rescue from decay the old.' Prudence's gifts to Christian of bread and wine and raisins become Wordsworth's 'present gifts of humbler industry.'

Might we also set side by side Wordsworth's 'unruly times,' the 'fits,' the 'unmanageable thoughts,' the 'goadings on' of the Poet when he 'would gladly grapple with some noble theme,' and Bunyan's 'flaming dart,' the 'darts as thick as hail,' the 'yelling' and 'hideous roaring' of the 'foul fiend Apollyon' in his attack upon Christian? On the other hand Bunyan's Dragon-wingèd, Bear-footed, Lion-mouthed Monster in contrast with Wordsworth's 'Mother-Dove' driven as in trouble through the groves illustrates the difference in metaphorical fauna between the grim seventeenth-century pilgrimage and the gentle nineteenth-century discipline.

Conversation in the Palace Beautiful of Bunyan, like meditation in the hermitage of Wordsworth, turned upon what Bunyan called 'Records of the greatest antiquity,' 'the pedigree of the Lord of the Hill,' his Acts and the 'worthy Acts' of his servants, 'how they had subdued Kingdoms, wrought Righteousness, obtained Promises, stopped the mouths of Lions, quenched the violence of Fire, escaped the edge of the Sword; out of weakness were made strong, waxed valiant in fight, and turned to flight the Armies of the Aliens . . . together with Prophecies and Predictions of things that have their certain accomplishment.' And, in particular, the residents of the Palace Beautiful exhibited Moses' Rod, Jael's Hammer and Nail, Gideon's weapons against Midian, Shamgar's Ox's goad, Samson's Jawbone, David's Sling and Stone, and the Sword of the Lord.

This reads like the repertory and properties of the epic poet. Wordsworth's various subjects as he casts about for poetic matter are less amply and inclusively catalogued, but have a comparable scope.

> Time, place, and manners, these I seek and these
> I find in plenteous store; but nowhere such
> As may be singled out with steady choice;
> No little Band of yet remember'd names.

Some British theme unsung by Milton? Some tale of shepherds within the groves of chivalry? Mithridates become Odin? Followers of Sertorius in the Fortunate Isles? 'How some unknown man, *unheard of in the Chronicles of Kings*, suffer'd in silence for the love of truth'? Dominique de Gourges? Gustavus? Wallace? Some philosophic Song of Truth?

But here, possibly, Wordsworth remembered Bunyan's Talkative, who delighted 'to talk of the History or the Mystery of things, . . . Miracles, Wonders, or Signs, . . . things Heavenly, or things Earthly; things Moral, or things Evangelical; things Sacred, or things Prophane; things past, or things to come; things foreign, or things at home; things more Essential, or things Circumstantial.' Christian and Faithful, conversing with Talkative, concluded that 'a work of Grace in the Soul discovereth itself, either to him that hath it, or to standers-by.' Wordsworth's 'vain perplexity' is resolved when he, too, seeks for poetry within.

When were lines 1–271 of Book I written? They are not in the early manuscripts as published; but to these manuscripts we must return for an hypothesis.

Mount Sinai, Valley of the Shadow, and MSS JJ, V, and W

Since both 'spots of time' now to be found in Book XI, 'Murderer . . . in Iron Chains' and 'Impatience at Christmastide,' are parts of MS V, we may first search that manuscript for additional echoes of *Pilgrim's Progress.*

The theft of the skiff within the rocky cave at Patterdale? This is still another instance of Nature's 'severer interventions, ministry more palpable'; and 'the huge Cliff' that rose up between the boy and the stars serves to rebuke William as Mount Sinai rebuked Christian in his attempt to steal ease from his burden, avoiding the 'counsel of the Most High' given him by Evangelist. That hill

> seemed so high, and also that side of it that was next the wayside, did hang so much over, that Christian was afraid to venture further, lest the hill should fall on his head. . . . There came also flashes of fire out of the hill. . . . Here therefore he sweat and did quake for fear. . . . And with that he saw Evangelist coming to meet him; at the sight also of whom he began to blush for shame. So Evangelist drew nearer and nearer; and coming up to him, he looked upon him with a severe and dreadful countenance.

Young Wordsworth suffered further rebuke from 'huge and mighty forms that do not live like living men'; these 'mov'd slowly through [his] mind by day' and were the 'trouble of [his] dreams.'

Bunyan's Valley of the Shadow calls to mind another episode of MS V, now to be found in Book V: the ghastly sight of the drowned man in the Vale of Esthwaite. The Quag and the Ditch when set side by side with the shores and green peninsulas of the Vale of Esthwaite, and the sights of blood, bones, ashes, and mangled bodies of men at the end of Bunyan's valley when compared with 'the spectre shape of terror' seen by Wordsworth the very week of his arrival in his own 'sweet valley' make clear the difference between the imaginative habit of the two authors.

After the episode of the drowned man, MS V goes on with the 'Murderer . . . in Iron Chains':

Moulder'd was the gibbet mast,
The bones were gone, the iron and the wood,
Only a long green ridge of turf remain'd
Whose shape was like a grave.

These appearances gave what he calls a 'visionary dreariness' to his succeeding journey up the 'bare slope' to the 'naked Pool' and the 'Beacon.' In like circumstance, Christian coming out of the Valley of the Shadow had found the Sun rising. Then said he, *His candle shineth on my head and by his light I go through darkness.*' Later, in MS W, Wordsworth developed the episode in the direction of holy light, as follows:

When in the blessed time of early love,
Long afterwards, I roam'd about
In daily presence of this very scene,
Upon the naked pool and dreary crags,
And the melancholy Beacon, fell
The spirit of pleasure and youth's golden gleam;
And think ye not with *radiance more divine*
From these remembrances, and from the power
They left behind?

The third episode of MS V in which the imagination of the Poet struggles with the experience of death is 'Impatience at Christmastide' and the loss of his father.

Was Wordsworth at any other time in Christian's Valley of the Shadow? Yes, and that fourth episode, not in MS V, carries us back still farther, to MS JJ, for the passage 'There was a Boy.' This and the Stolen Boat constitute in that Goslar manuscript faint echoes of Bunyan's pilgrimage through the shadowy vale. Again the underlying theme is death; but this time the customary solitude and silence are prefaced by 'hootings,' 'tremulous sobs,' 'long halloos,' 'screams,' 'echoes loud redoubled and redoubled.' Might this be a substitution, beneficent and natural, of owls for the 'Hobgoblins, Satyrs, and Dragons of the Pit' in the Valley of the Shadow where Christian heard 'a continual howling and yelling

. . . the doleful voices . . . and dreadful noises' of that 'company of Fiends'? Moreover, in MS JJ, while woodcock-snaring 'among the Cliffs and the smooth Hollows,' William heard 'low breathings coming after [him], . . . steps almost as silent as the turf they trod'; when he was birding 'on the perilous ridge,' 'shouldering the naked crag,' 'with what strange utterance did the loud dry wind blow through [his] ears!' It was also part of the discipline of Christian in the Valley of the Shadow to undergo the attack of one who 'stept up softly to him, and whisperingly suggested many grievous blasphemies to him, which he verily thought had proceeded from his own mind.'

The strange voices in MS JJ are accompanied by reference to what gives them schematic unity, the discipline of the young William by genii, Spirits whose interventions are severe, whose ministry is palpable, beings of the hills . . . woods . . . heaths . . . earth . . . springs . . . clouds . . . lakes . . . standing pools, more to his taste, and to ours, than allegorical figures. Most impressive among the disciplinary factors of MS JJ is the 'Eternal Spirit,'

He that has
His Life in unimaginable things
And he who painting what He is in all
The visible imagery of all the World
Is yet apparent chiefly as the Soul
Of our first sympathies.

Such a painting, such 'visible imagery,' setting forth Wordsworth's idea of the 'Eternal Beauty,' may be compared with, if not attributed to, Christian's first vision in his Interpreter's House, 'the Picture of a very grave Person . . . eyes lifted up to Heaven, the best of Books in his hand, the Law of Truth . . . upon his lips, the World . . . behind his back'—authorized guide of the Pilgrim as the 'Eternal Spirit' is the Soul of the first sympathies of the Poet.

There are also in that early MS JJ some twelve lines resembling a passage in what is called the 'overflow' from the poem *Nutting,* written at Goslar, all three passages dealing with wanton, ungentle behavior tutored by Nature's spirits into reverence and forbearance. This theme may be read in other manuscripts, said by de Selincourt [4] to have been written in 1798. For instance, in the discarded 'beginning' of *Nutting,* addressed to 'Lucy,' such a maiden as we have already met in the *Lines . . . on the Wye,* and MS JJ, there are reminiscences of allegorical influence. The destructive maiden is likened to a 'houseless being in a human shape, an enemy of nature'; 'blessed be,' says Wordsworth,

> the powers
> That teach philosophy and good desires
> In this their still Lyceum.

Behind these beings and powers stand as schoolmasters not only Platonic ideas, but allegorical figures of Bunyan functioning to the same end. In this very fragment the powers who rebuke idleness in the Poet, the powers who 'restore the springs of his exhausted frame,' and the powers who protect him from 'the uneasy world' and 'his own unquiet heart' are such as Fear, Help, and the Shining Ones who assist Christian to lose his burden. Worldly Wiseman and Pliable as villains in Bunyan's allegory are in Wordsworth's simpler presentation natural tendencies to be resisted.

But Pliable and Christian 'being heedless, did both fall suddenly into the bog.' And that brings us to the episode of *Nutting* itself, which, by a little, antedated its 'beginning.'

Nutting represents the adventure of a youngster in 'beggar's weeds,' and 'more ragged than need was,' sallying forth from his 'cottage door' 'with a wallet o'er [his] shoulders slung, a nutting-crook in hand,' a kind of youthful Christian. Christian, too, was 'cloathed with Rags . . . with his face from his own house . . . and a great Burden upon his back,' and the old woodcuts show him, appropriately, with a staff in hand. So far, then, Christian, the 'craz'd-headed coxcomb,' and William in his 'motley accoutre-

[4] Pp. 592–4, 596. Cf. also *Poetical Works,* Vol. 2, pp. 504–6.

ment' are both ready for their pilgrimage; but how different are the 'bog' or Slough of Despond, signifying Christian's 'heedless' sins, from the 'green and mossy bower' in which William works his 'merciless ravage.' This 'dear nook' near Hawkshead, now 'deformed and sullied,' is, I suggest, Wordsworth's equivalent of Bunyan's Slough of Despond, and the word 'sullied' is a possible reflection from the 'grievously bedaubed' of the earlier text.

Working slowly backward—MS V to MS JJ to manuscripts of *Nutting*—we arrive at the *Lines . . . on the Wye.* During their pilgrimage to the banks of that river in July of 1798, did William and Dorothy mention Christian and Christiana on the shores of the last 'Riverside'? His advice to her shows him aware that she must recapitulate his own 'many wanderings' from joy to joy; and his visions are thus both retrospective and prospective. He recalls the lightening of 'the burthen of the mystery . . . the heavy and the weary weight' of this 'unintelligible world' as Christian would have recalled the loss of his burden. The 'beauteous forms' presiding over his deliverance from it are akin to the 'Shining Ones' who assisted at Christian's Deliverance. 'The fretful stir unprofitable and the fever of the world' resemble Christian's Vanity Fair. And William and Dorothy, standing on the banks of this delightful stream together, are in the relation of hierophant and initiate in the worship of Nature, a service demanding ever 'deeper zeal of holier love.'

Not only from the Wye and the Derwent, but also from the 'stream . . . Imagination' to be traced in *The Prelude*, Wordsworth draws 'the feeling of life endless, the great thought by which we live, Infinity and God.' [5] Another pleasant river this, the like of which 'David the King called the River of God, but John the River of the Water of Life. Now their way lay just upon the bank of the River; here therefore Christian and his Companion walked with great delight.' No by-path-meadow of postgraduate errancy, no despairing castle of revolutionary disillusionment could dim this vision in Wordsworth's mind.

[5] *Prelude* XIII, 172–84.

There is in these *Lines . . . on the Wye,* however, more of a prospect for Dorothy than for William. Not until March of 1800 when he wrote 'Home at Grasmere,' Book I of *The Recluse*, does he arrive in his 'Paradise' of poetry with a definite program for himself as poet. The recent publication of the manuscripts behind this Book and its Prospectus [6] makes us aware of a literary relationship hitherto unsuspected. In the images and situations of MSS A and B of *The Recluse* we find reminiscences of Christian's entrance, not into so natural a paradise as Grasmere, but into the archetypal Paradise. For instance, at Hart-leap Well on their pilgrimage to Grasmere, William and his 'Emma' have an 'intimation of the milder day which is to be [come], the fairer world than this.' In Christian's Country of Beulah the pilgrims were 'within sight of the City they were going to, also here met them some of the inhabitants thereof; for in this land the Shining Ones commonly walked, because it was upon the borders of Heaven.' Instance again, in an 'awful trance' William and his 'Emma' see

> The vision of humanity, and of God
> The Mourner, God the Sufferer.

Had not Christian in his 'mind' seen one 'hang bleeding upon the Tree'? Had he not hoped on Mount Zion 'to see him *alive* that did hang *dead* on the Cross'? Was he not fain to be where he should 'die no more, and with the Company that shall continually cry, *Holy, Holy, Holy*'? There he would 'enjoy the perpetual sight and vision of the Holy One.' Third instance, when we read that the paradise of William and 'Emma' would 'be sought by kindred spirits, Sisters of our hearts and Brothers of our love,' we recall the 'happy Arrival' to join Christian and Christiana of their friends Honest, Valiant, Stand-fast, and others. John Wordsworth, whom William calls 'a never-resting Pilgrim of the sea,' was indeed to be a Stand-fast when and where 'the Waters . . . [were] to the Palate bitter and to the Stomach cold, yet the thoughts of . . . the other side [did] lie as a glowing Coal at

[6] In 1949, *Poetical Works,* Vol. 5, pp. 313–39, 3–6.

[his] Heart.' In 1800, however, John's death on the deck of the Abergavenny was not literary history. The reference to him as a Pilgrim of the sea is only one of several instances of parlance more religiously traditional than we are accustomed to associate with the poet in 1800.

'Home in Grasmere' is the end of a pilgrimage, and hence it will not be vertebrate in its purposes nor sharp in the outline of its energies. Shall we say that this frustrum of Wordsworth's great philosophical poem is well-nigh amorphous, and that its lack of plot can be better understood when its relation to the seventeenth-century Heaven is acknowledged? The best Wordsworth as an arrived pilgrim could do was to translate the traditional wingèd ones into Westmoreland birds, whose grace seemed scarcely 'inferior to angelical'; the musical instruments of glory into 'sweet passions like music' (MS B), 'prelusive songs,' and 'the happy Quires of Spring'; and to reflect Bunyan's 'City shining like the Sun, its Streets paved with Gold' from his own 'mountain built of silver light.'

> Behold the universal imagery
> Inverted, all its sun-bright features touched
> As with the varnish, and the gloss of dreams . . .

such dreams as the dream of John Bunyan. Especially indicative is Wordsworth's transformation of the Shining ones about Christian into his own friends and neighbors. He asks: 'Why shine they round me thus whom thus I love?' and he answers in words characteristic of Bunyan's pilgrim to Mount Zion: he has within him, too, something that power and effort may impart, 'immortal in the world which is to come.'

It would be difficult to disentangle the influence of Milton, of Akenside, and of Bunyan in the last passage of Book I of *The Recluse*, 'Home at Grasmere,' now to be read in an early form, MS B. Here there are, however, further hints that, as first conceived, it owed somewhat more to the piety of Bunyan's pilgrim arrived in Heaven than to the theology and verbal splendor of

Bunyan's great contemporary. The common speech of Christian rings within these homelier phrases of MS B: 'Hope for this earth and hope beyond the grave' (later excised), 'virtue' instead of 'moral strength,' 'the one great Life' instead of 'law supreme of that Intelligence that governs all,' 'the darkest Pit of the profoundest Hell' instead 'of lowest Erebus,' 'but a dream' instead of 'a mere fiction,' 'blessed' instead of 'blissful,' 'Soul of Man' (later excised), 'unto me vouchsafe thy guidance' instead of 'upon me bestow a gift of genuine insight,' 'verse as a light hung up in heaven' instead of 'Song with star-like virtue,' 'to cheer mankind' instead of 'shedding benignant influence,' 'little realities of life' (excised), 'great God' instead of 'dread Power,'

> Thou who art breath and being, way and guide
> And power and understanding

instead of

> Whose gracious favour is the primal source
> Of all illumination.

The boy William says that he was 'no Prophet' when he first caught a glimpse of the Vale of Grasmere from his 'aerial' Station; but his memory of Bunyan's Shepherds on the Delectable Mountains and Prophets on Mount Zion helped him to the fifteenth line of his *Recluse* and to the initial, and terminal, Book of that unfinished and unfinishable heavenly poem.

When did these likenesses make themselves evident to Wordsworth for a strength rather than a weakness as he advanced from one manuscript to another and was feeling ahead toward a more significant pattern for those 'boyish pleasures' destined, not without Bunyan's help, to become an autobiographical poem?

The fragmentary jottings of the Preamble in MS JJ tempt us to infer that it had not been written into its present form when the rest of that manuscript and, possibly, *Nutting* were composed. Following his casual reference to the 'burden' in the *Lines . . .*

on the Wye and the institution of his plan to exchange Bunyan's —or at least seventeenth-century—morality for his own cult of Nature, he would transform Bunyan's allegorical figures into natural beings; under their discipline in their school he would make such a pilgrimage as if, two centuries later, he were following in Christian's footsteps through another territory. How well could he fit his own valid experience into the old pilgrim framework? *Nutting* instead of a Slough of Despond; Birding and Woodcock-snaring, and Mimic Hootings to the Silent Owls instead of the Valley of the Shadow; Painting of the Eternal Spirit instead of the Picture of Our Lord in the Interpreter's House; Stolen Boat instead of Mount Sinai: this is MS JJ in its main substance and outline.

And—here my assumption merely—he may, in a manuscript now lost, have sketched the difficulty and humiliation of his effort to write the great poem Coleridge expected from him, a sketch reminiscent of the Hill of Difficulty and Valley of Humiliation of *Pilgrim's Progress.* At some later time this tentative composition would become what is now Book I, lines 55–271; and at that time he would incorporate with this passage Book I, lines 1–54, which had set forth what was analogous to the Loss of the Burden, the projected Work of Glory, the New Garments, and the Three Leaps for Joy?

Although from Goslar Wordsworth could not reach his unhusbanded mate and fatherless child in Orleans, where he had left them in 1792 for England and his own poetical career, he must have borne back to the continent a heavy burden of moral error or obliquity. His travels could not take him again into conjugal or domestic life on the Loire; he must look ahead into professional life for his salvation. Let us assume that again he noted his likeness to Bunyan's Christian, who, when wife and children began to call after him to return, 'put his fingers in his ears, and ran on, crying, *Life! Life! Eternal Life!*'

His prepossessions being heavy upon him, let us assume that like Christian he craved release and unburdening so sorely that in his imagination he left the City's walls and reached his Place of Deliverance, uttering the substance of the first fifty-four lines of *The Prelude*, now spoken of as its Preamble.[7] With its account of his escape, his disemburdening, and his dedication to and progress toward holiness, it is a kind of foreshortening of Christian's initial adventures, more mature than the initiation of pilgrimage in the boyish departure from home as written for *Nutting*.

At this point the idea occurs to him—still my premise—that the pilgrimage in its main adventures lies ahead of him, not behind him as a record of the past, not a retrospect from the banks of the Wye, but a prospect into the Heaven of a permanent home with his sister; in this ordeal of the future, the life of a poet dedicated to the service of poetry, he may compensate for personal, conjugal, and domestic failure.

Then on his return to England, writing in the agricultural surroundings of Sockburn and in the company of Mary Hutchinson, and faced anew by problems of a conjugal nature, under the influence of Thomson's *The Seasons* and Akenside's love story of the Poet and Nature he would rearrange his design to accord rather with a mythic seasonal cycle or human sacrament than a moral journey. He would soon be residing at home, not venturing abroad. Moreover, he specially liked those experiences of his own, alien from all obvious morality—skating, for instance; and the seasonal occupations of his later boyhood would more and more take on the form of a ritual around the emergent figure of Nature Herself, or a love affair with Her. As we have seen, this is the main substance and outline of MS V. These are his 'boyish pleasures.'

But he has grown up swiftly and irrevocably. Arrived at Dove Cottage, early in 1800 he reaches for the tentative sketch of his Hill of Difficulty and Valley of Humiliation, say some 190 lines of it. Now he will consider putting it at the beginning of the first

[7] Dated variously and located variously by scholars and editors who assume *The Prelude* to be biographical fact. Early editors, Bishop Wordsworth, for instance, may have been right in the assumption that he fled from Goslar.

Book of *The Recluse*, where it will be followed by another kind of deliverance, the stable life of the dedicated poet: the 'we will be free' [8] of MS A of 'Home at Grasmere.' The 'boyish pleasures' of MS V are for the time being shelved or held in suspended animation.

Just when MS A of 'Home at Grasmere' lost its first 190 lines could not, I presume, be determined; but I suggest that it was at the same time that MS A of *The Prelude* gained its first 271 lines. And to bridge the gap between 'boyish pleasures' and his professional Prospectus, Wordsworth would need to write new lines for this Book I of his Westmoreland paradise. That *The Recluse*, like the Pilgrim's Heaven, was a blind alley need not surprise us. All along there had been more energetic life in the 'boyish pleasures.'

Thomson's vivid contribution to *The Prelude* as a nature myth, and Akenside's fine gifts of intelligence and imagination to the poem as a creative process need not be disregarded; but whenever Wordsworth began to write 'Residence at Cambridge' as a kind of Autumn or Winter of the ritual year, an episode in a kind of Castle of Indolence, *Pilgrim's Progress* was again reverberating in his thought, this time with a reminder of Christian's Evangelist, kin to his own college saint ('The Evangelist St. John my Patron was'). This would help to explain why at some time between 1800 and 1804 as he composed what is now Book III he reverted to allegorical figures for those 'old Humourists,' the professors of his college life, 'of texture midway betwixt life and books': Labour, Hope, Idleness, Shame, Fear, Pleasure, Honour misplaced and Dignity astray, Feuds, Factions, Flatteries, Enmity, Guile, murmuring Submission, bald Government, Decency, Custom, Truth, blind Authority, Emptiness, Worth. These abstractions are as different from the Shepherd Swains of Hawkshead as *Pilgrim's Progress* is from the 'Book of rudiments' in Nature's 'great school'; but both Bunyan's Interpreter and Nature aim

[8] *Poetical Works,* Vol. 5, p. 475. See within, pp. 318–20, for its Miltonic relationships.

to enter early on [the] tender scheme
Of teaching comprehension with delight,
And mingling playful with pathetic thoughts.

We need not be reminded that Wordsworth thought of college as a Dusty Parlour, nor that as an Interpreter's House it was another

privileg'd world
Within a world, a midway residence
With all its intervenient imagery.

But Book IV, 'Summer Vacation,' despite its dedication faintly recalling Christian at the wicket gate, derives rather from the pattern of nature cycle than the outline of pilgrimage. It is a kind of Thomsonian Spring. At the time he had started upon MS W in the early months of 1804, temporarily Wordsworth set aside his memories of *Pilgrim's Progress;* and when in MSS AB his 'boyish pleasures' came finally into shape as Books I and II, they had been relieved of their gloomier episodes (now distributed into Books V and XI), and he could afford to reinstate lines which described poetic deliverance, literary difficulty, and humiliation as an Introduction to the whole poem (lines 1–271) without too obvious a reminder of any certain tradition or any particular literary ancestor.

Vanity Fair and MS X; the Delectable Mountains and MS Y

Bunyan, however, had not done his utmost for the poem. By the late spring of 1804 when Wordsworth was revising his memories of the continental tour of 1790 for Book VI, and when Coleridge was on pilgrimage in the south of Europe, Malta and Sicily, the author of *The Prelude* again took to the open road, imaginatively speaking. Himself and Robert Jones had been 'two brother Pilgrims' (478) on a 'pilgrimage' (690). In Book X, recalling this 'glad time when first [he] travers'd France, a youthful pilgrim' (451), he uses for Robespierre, leader 'of the atheist crew,' a word never occurring elsewhere in his poetry: we can with propriety refer this *hapax legomenon* to Bunyan's Atheist,[9] as well as to Milton's Satan.

MS X opens with a rough draft of Book VII; Wordsworth is on his way to Vanity Fair. The analogies between London and its Bartholomew Fair and the Town called Vanity with its Fair 'of ancient standing' are so obvious that they need few illustrations. As Vanity has its 'Britain Row,' its 'French Row,' its 'Italian Row,' its 'Spanish Row,' its 'German Row,' so London to Wordsworth displayed a like if not identical national catalogue, not only the Italian, the Jew, the Turk, but

all specimens of Man
Through all the colours which the sun bestows,
And every character of form and face,
The Swede, the Russian; from the genial South,
The Frenchman and the Spaniard; from remote
America, the Hunter Indian; Moors,
Malays, Lascars, the Tartar and Chinese,
And Negro Ladies in white muslin gowns.

A distinguished lesson in poetic transfiguration, this. What was for Bunyan a 'hubbub' was for Wordsworth a 'thickening hubbub.' The 'Truth,' which was the only purchase of Christian and Faithful in Vanity Fair, became the 'truth . . . hated' by the 'froward multitude' when Burke and Fox spoke out, in a much revised passage of MSS A, D, and E. Wordsworth's 'brawls of Lawyers in their Courts before the ermined Judge' re-echo from the Judge and Jury of Vanity Fair, among them Mr. Blind-man whom Wordsworth has mercifully turned into 'a blind Beggar'; and Wordsworth's 'comely Bachelor' ascending the pulpit with his 'seraphic glance' is another Mr. Two-tongues, Bunyan's 'Parson of our Parish.' Most important to the structure of Book VII

[9] Also in Book X, 935–6, the unlikely metaphor of 'dog returning to his vomit' to emphasize the opprobrium of 'a Pope . . . summon'd in to crown an Emperor' recapitulates Bunyan's quote from II Peter 2:22, when Christian and Faithful talk about Pliable the Turncoat, 'not true to his profession': 'The Dog is turned to his own Vomit again, and the Sow, that was washed, to her wallowing in the Mire.'

is the device of listing items, homogeneous or heterogeneous; once observed in Bunyan's composition of Vanity Fair, it cannot be disregarded by the author of Bartholomew Fair. The reader may further investigate for himself these perilous similitudes between these two instances of the 'Parliament of Monsters.'

Let us rather contemplate another city, in that passage of MS X finally placed in Book II of *The Excursion.* It represents

> Glory beyond all glory ever seen
> By waking sense or by the dreaming soul! . . .
> The appearance, instantaneously disclosed,
> Was of a mighty City—boldly say
> A wilderness of building, sinking far
> And self-withdrawn into a wondrous depth,
> Far sinking into splendor—without end!
> Fabric it seemed of diamond and of gold,
> With alabaster domes, and silver spires;
> And blazing terrace upon terrace high
> Uplifted; here, serene pavilions bright
> In avenues disposed; there, towers begirt
> With battlements that on their restless fronts
> Bore stars—illumination of all gems! . . .
> O, 't was an unimaginable sight! . . .
> That which I *saw* was the revealed abode
> Of Spirits in beatitude: my heart
> Swelled in my breast.—"I have been dead," I cried,
> "And now I live!"

The Solitary of *The Excursion,* therefore, was first conceived in MS X as a Pilgrim on the Delectable Mountains coming out of the Valley of the Shadow of Death and Doubting Castle and looking toward the Coelestial City, hoping 'to see Him *alive* that did hang *dead* on the Cross.' Bunyan had written of the Coelestial City:

> It was builded of Pearls and Precious Stones, also the Street thereof was paved with Gold. . . . The reflection of the Sun upon the City (for the City was pure Gold) was so extremely glorious, that they could not as yet with open face behold it, but through an Instrument

made for that purpose. . . . [The Shining Ones] told them that the beauty and glory [of the place] was inexpressible.

—Whose Delectable Mountains are these? And whose be the sheep that feed upon them?

—These mountains are Immanuel's Land. And they are within sight of his City; and the sheep also are his, and he laid down his life for them.

Let us repair at once to these Delectable Mountains and the shepherds who inhabit them in Westmoreland as in Bunyan's equally homely but more schematic country. In *The Prelude* as record of a pilgrimage, Wordsworth went on from the Vanity Fair of MS X to the Delectable Mountains of MS Y.

While yet a very Child,
I saw a sight, and with what joy and love!
It was a day of exhalations, spread
Upon the mountains, mists and steam-like fogs
Redounding everywhere, not vehement,
But calm and mild, gentle and beautiful,
With gleams of sunshine on the eyelet spots
And loop-holes of the hills, wherever seen,
Hidden by quiet process, and as soon
Unfolded, to be huddled up again:
Along a narrow Valley and profound
I journey'd, when, aloft above my head,
Emerging from the silvery vapours, lo!
A Shepherd and his Dog!

Not an unusual sight on his native hills; but the literary use of pastoral life to illustrate the degenerative and redemptive process would come to Wordsworth from Bunyan in a particularly helpful form. *Michael*, and 'the Matron's Tale' carried from MS J into MSS AB, have the same homely and local shepherds to be met with on Christian's Delectable Mountains. Moreover, what Wordsworth learned on his own Delectable Mountains—Hawkshead seen in retrospect—saved him from a literary Enchanted

Ground whither he might otherwise have been seduced: 'Gehol's famous gardens,' other 'resplendent gardens,' 'Arcadian fastnesses . . . of the Golden Age,' Shakespeare's Arden and Bohemia, Spenserian fairyland, and those classical spots on the banks of the Galesus, Adria's shore, Clitumnus' stream, and underneath the brows of 'cool Lucretilis' which the art of Virgil and Horace had charmed for the young English poet. But Wordsworth does not forget that the drowsy dependence against which the Shepherds warned Christian must be resisted; like Christian he turns from the 'smooth life,' the 'sweet life' of pastoral tradition, to honor the shepherd life of his own mountains, 'severe and unadorned.'

We may be grateful that, again like Christian, he gained from his shepherds

> a sure safeguard and defence
> Against the weight of meanness, selfish cares,
> Course manners, vulgar passions, that beat in
> On all sides from the ordinary world
> In which we traffic. Starting from this point,
> I had my face towards the truth.

Did not Bunyan's Knowledge, Experience, Watchful, and Sincere show Christian and Hopeful the Mountain of Error and Mount Caution and finally take them 'to the top of an high Hill, called Clear, and [give] them their Glass to look' toward the Gates of the Coelestial City? For such a moment of vision the chief analogue in *The Prelude* is Wordsworth's experience crossing the Alps, his erroneous assumptions, and, through the imagination, his recognition of ultimate glory. Read in this connection, several phrases of the famous passage gain new meaning and value.

> Imagination! *lifting up itself*
> *Before the eye* and progress of my song . . .

this is the Perspective-Glass.

> I was lost as in a cloud . . .
> And now recovering, to my Soul I say
> I recognize thy glory; in such strength

Of usurpation, *in such visitings*
Of awful promise, when the light of sense
Goes out in flashes that have shewn to us
The invisible world, doth Greatness make abode. . . .
Our destiny, our nature, and *our home*
Is with infinitude, and only there;
With hope it is, hope that can never die,
Effort, and expectation, and desire,
And something evermore about to be.

'By this time,' said Bunyan, 'the Pilgrims [Christian and *Hopeful*] had a *desire* to go forwards, and the Shepherds a *desire* they should.'

Wordsworth is not Christian, and Coleridge is not quite Hopeful, though he shares with Hopeful traits not explicitly mentioned in *The Prelude:* his imprisonment with Christian in the Doubting Castle of Giant Despair, his drowsiness in the Enchanted Ground, and their discourse to prevent it. With Faithful, however, we may profitably compare Michel Beaupuy, who was sacrificed in that vainest of Vanity Fairs, the French Revolution. His *character*, copied into MS Y and later removed to Book IX, has many traits in common with Bunyan's martyr. Meek though enthusiastic, made more gracious by injuries, Beaupuy wandered through the events of his time 'in perfect faith'

As through a Book, an old Romance or Tale
Of Fairy, or some dream of actions wrought
Behind the summer clouds.

At this we remember in Bunyan's prefatory Apology the question

would'st thou see
A man i' th' Clouds, and hear him speak to thee?
Would'st thou be in a Dream, and yet not sleep?

Like Faithful, Beaupuy was a friend speaking in

the voice
Of One devoted, one whom circumstance

Hath call'd upon to embody his deep sense
In action, give it outwardly a shape,
And that of benediction to the world;
Then doubt is not, and truth is more than truth,
A hope it is and a desire, a creed
Of zeal by an authority divine
Sanction'd of danger, difficulty or death;

and it was death for Beaupuy as it had been martyrdom for Faithful. Christian must find a new companion, Hopeful; and in time Wordsworth found his new fellow pilgrim, Coleridge. 'By different roads at length [they] gained the self-same bourne.' [10]

When thus we set the persons of *The Prelude* side by side with the abstractions of *Pilgrim's Progress*, Wordsworth's accomplishment is undeniable; Nature has served him well. When we look closer, however, we detect as a gift from Bunyan to his successor a pattern for the skilful activation of the great human story by agents both humble and exalted.

The most fitting epilogue to this devious literary pilgrimage is a quotation from Dorothy's Journal for January 31, 1802: 'With the encyclopaedias . . . gone . . . there is a nice elbow place for William, and he may sit for the picture of John Bunyan any day.' [11] We may add a passage from a fragment found, so says Knight, among Wordsworth's papers:

The fate and fortune of books is in many respects most remarkable. Some that on their first appearance have been extolled in Courts and by Universities and Academies, have quickly forfeited that kind of favour without ever making their way to the public, or deserving to do so. Others have been eagerly received by the middle and humbler ranks of the community, while they were disregarded by the upper classes, and have continued to be dear to the many, though centuries perhaps may have passed away without their obtaining the sanction, except in rare instances, of those who value themselves upon a culti-

[10] *Prelude* II, 468–9.
[11] *Journals,* Vol. 1, p. 105.

vated taste. Take for example *The Pilgrim's Progress.* Cowper, the poet, being prompted to speak his thought of that beautiful allegory, more than a hundred years after its publication, says in the course of his panegyric:—

> I named thee not, lest so despised a name
> Should move a sneer at thy deserved fame;

and who but must be struck with the clouds that darken for a time the splendour of those productions whose merits were at first unacknowledged in the highest quarters.[12]

[12] *The Poetical Works of William Wordsworth*, ed. by Wm. Knight, Edinburgh, 1889, Vol. 11 (Vol. 3 of *The Life of William Wordsworth*), pp. 356–7.

X

Man of Science

The Pleasures of (the) Imagination and *The Recluse* of 1798

TRUTH, the truth about the mind of man: psychology, as we should say. What part does psychological truth have in *The Prelude?* To make this clear, we must answer several associated questions. First, what are the relations between psychological truth and the geography, economics, and natural science Wordsworth was planning to study for his 'views of Nature, Man and Society,' *The Recluse* as conceived in March, 1798? [1] Second, what relations does psychological truth bear to the domestic truth of which he intended to sing in 'Home at Grasmere,' Book I of *The Recluse* of 1800? Third, in what relation does psychological truth stand to ethical truth, that is, to the truth about goodness or virtue, to the truth about the 'active' life of the poet and his fellows? And to this question in ethics we may add a final question in aesthetics and poetics: what is the relation in Wordsworth's mind between truth and beauty, between all science and all art, and what is his view of the influence of the poet on taste?

[1] *Early Letters,* pp. 188, 190. Cf. also Coleridge's letter to Davy, February, 1801, in *Letters,* ed. by E. H. Coleridge, Vol. 1, pp. 345–7, associating Wordsworth with the study of chemistry.

These are imposing questions, to be satisfied only in part by explicit reference to the Prefaces of 1800 and 1802 and the Essay, Supplementary to the Preface of 1815. There is also an implicit answer, to be heard from his blank verse of 1798–1800 when this is studied by the side of what would be for Wordsworth recent blank verse of the same kind; and to this we shall first direct our attention.

In the Advertisement to *Lyrical Ballads* of 1798 Wordsworth took one certain position: 'It is the honourable characteristic of Poetry that its materials are to be found in every subject which can interest the human mind. The evidence of this fact is to be sought, not in the writings of Critics, but in those of Poets themselves.'

As a man of science in search of poetical truth he went to poetry for his evidence rather than to philosophy, criticism, or dogma for his authority. He read the English poets. Along with the social sciences transfigured for him by our elder writers—ethics, politics, theology—certain new aspects of truth were inciting him to researches of his own. Even before he began his discipleship to Chaucer, Spenser, Shakespeare, and Milton in 1800, in 1796–7 his essay prefatory to *The Borderers* reveals him interested, with Shakespeare, in what our jargon calls abnormal psychology. His *Guilt and Sorrow* and *The Ruined Cottage* are among the earliest documents which illustrate what was then the new sociology, and for these he had been not a little indebted to the homilies of the age of Anne. But nowhere in the poetry of the century was the concomitance of physiology, psychology, ethics, aesthetics, and poetics, and even sociology and theology, more feelingly and compactly set forth than in Dr. Mark Akenside's *The Pleasures of Imagination.*[2]

The poem is valuable in its own right. At its first publication in 1744 it had stirred the reading public somewhat as early novels

[2] Henceforth I refer to *The Poetical Works of Mark Akenside*, edited by the Reverend Alexander Dyce with a Memoir, Little, Brown, and Company, Boston, 1865.

based on psychoanalytical surmises stirred us in our time. Pope judged it when in manuscript to be the work of 'no everyday writer'; [3] Gray, however, thought the first edition, published by Dodsley, anonymously, 'too much infected with the Hutch[e]son jargon'; [4] Warburton assumed that the anonymous author was 'a follower of Ld. S[haftesbury]'; [5] and Dyce himself says that this 'great didactic poem' was founded on Joseph Addison's *Spectator* papers, 'number 411, *et seq.*' [6] Whatever part *The Spectator*, the *Characteristics*, and the *Inquiry into the Original of Our Ideas of Beauty and Virtue* had in Akenside's own thought, his poem remains a distinguished attempt to transfigure for men the truth about the mind of man. Its revised edition was fresh news when William Taylor, who taught Wordsworth to love the poets, himself studied them at Emmanuel College, Cambridge; and it was not old news at the turn of the century when Samuel Taylor Coleridge and William Wordsworth discussed poetic theory and the imagination. Had not Coleridge placed Akenside in his literary pantheon on December 17, 1796? 'Do not let us introduce an Act of Uniformity against Poets. I have room enough in *my* brain to admire, aye, and almost equally, the *head* and fancy of Akenside, and the *heart* and fancy of Bowles, the solemn lordliness of Milton, and the divine chit-chat of Cowper.' [7] Indeed, just fifty years later, in 1846, when at Rogers' request Wordsworth helped Sara Coleridge identify certain quotations in her father's *Biographia Literaria,* he was surprised that Coleridge *fille* had not justified in this regard the training of Coleridge *père:* 'If Mrs. C[oleridge] had been a reader . . . of Akenside, she would not have been ignorant that "The gayest, happiest attitude of things" is the con-

[3] Samuel Johnson, *Life of Akenside.*

[4] For this comment Dyce quotes Gray's letter to Wharton from Cambridge, April 26, 1744, Memoir, *op. cit.*, p. 21.

[5] *Ibid.*, p. 24.

[6] *Ibid.*, p. 105. On August 13, 1791, Wordsworth wrote to William Mathews that 'two or three papers of the *Spectator* half subdued' and 'three volumes of *Tristram Shandy*' summed up his incursions into modern English literature (*Early Letters,* p. 55), by which we may assume he meant prose.

[7] *Letters,* Vol. 1, p. 197. Italics by Coleridge.

cluding line of the first paragraph of the Pleasures of Imagination.' [8]

Wordsworth owned the first edition of Akenside's poem and it was much annotated. In his psychological and poetic researches he was likely to find it more assimilable than the works of Addison, Shaftesbury, and Hutcheson, although these, too, were in his library. When his books were sold in 1856, *The Pleasures of Imagination* was put up with Beattie's *Poems* (the quarto of 1765), Armstrong's *Art of Preserving Health* (the quarto of 1744), and Mason's Odes (1751) as lot number 451, and sold for 18 shillings.[9] Failing or pending further knowledge of the whereabouts of Wordsworth's annotated copy of *The Pleasures of Imagination*, let us turn to remarks about it made by Barron Field in his manuscript 'Memoirs of the Life and Poetry of William Wordsworth,' where he states that Wordsworth possesses 'the earliest editions of Milton, Dryden, Pope, Thomson, Akenside, Collins, Gray, etc., some of them with the subsequent alterations in MS. These comparisons afford the best of all studies of the art of poetry.' [10] If,

[8] *Correspondence of Henry Crabb Robinson with the Wordsworth Circle*, Vol. 3, p. 630. In Akenside's revised edition this line read: 'The fairest, loftiest countenance of things.'

[9] *Transactions of the Wordsworth Society*, No. 6, pp. 233, 236, 237. The price of sale of each item of the library has been inscribed in my copy of the *Transactions* by Mr. Arnold Varty of Ambleside, its former owner.

[10] British Museum MS 41325, Vol. 1, p. 87 *verso*. I quote from Arthur Beatty's transcript notes. A microfilm of part of this manuscript, furnished me by the British Museum through the kindness of Winifred Comstock Bowman, indicates that Field had made a study of similar passages in the poem of Akenside and Wordsworth's *Excursion* and *Recluse* I. Of Akenside's poem Field says (Vol. 1, pp. 305–13):

> I consider, in spite of the cold opinions of Gray and Johnson, that this poem evinces the *mens divinior;* but the Excursion appears to me to be a work of much higher order. The poet of Imagination perpetually cramps himself by didactics: the professor's square cap and gown are constantly obtruded. The subject is mere metaphysics partially treated, and the poem wants not only the divineness but the humanity of the more enlarged Excursion. . . . Highly as it is praised by Dr. Johnson and Mr. Southey, the blank verse of Akenside is, in my humble opinion, inferior to this in grandeur and harmony. Much of Akenside is as prosaic as a metaphysical treatise, which the whole poem too nearly resembles. I consider Mr. Wordsworth's versification to be the most Miltonic since the Paradise Lost, with the Latinity of the great epic

as I hope to show, both editions of Akenside's poem are involved in Wordsworth's blank verse of 1798–1800, we might the more readily assume an early date for Wordsworth's collation of the first edition of *The Pleasures of Imagination*, 1744, with the revised edition, *The Pleasures of the Imagination*, made public in 1772 by Akenside's friend, Jeremiah Dyson. For a young poet of whom his sister had written in 1791 'his pleasures are chiefly of the imagination' such a collation would have been likely at Cambridge or at Montagu's in London; but when Coleridge, Akenside's disciple, arrived at Racedown with Akenside's doctrine on his tongue, discussion of the two versions is more than likely.

And even if Wordsworth's own copy had remained in London with Montagu, there to be catalogued by William Mathews, we know that another text of the first edition, the one with Mrs. Barbauld's Preface, was at hand in the few weeks preceding the domestication of brother and sister at Racedown in September of 1795. It had been presented to Dorothy by her uncle, Mr. Rawson,

poet properly exchanged, by our narrative and interlocutory moralist, for the happy simplicity of the dramatic Shakespeare. The quotations from Wordsworth, which are in everybody's mouth, taste more like Shakespeare than any other poet.

It is therefore not without sensibility to the philosophical poetry of Dr. Akenside—to the awful but too paradoxical sententiousness of the Night Thoughts (Dr. Young was the Pope of blank verse); to the elegant descriptiveness of the Seasons; (I should not have thought worth mentioning a sort of imitation of this poem by Mallet in two cantos, but for its title, *The Excursion*); and to the original eloquency of The Task (a happy union of Young and Thomson, in religious and descriptive poetry, but more natural than either) that I have ventured to pronounce Mr. Wordsworth to be the greatest poet that has risen in England since the star of Milton "dwelt apart," and to have fully redeemed his pledge of recording in verse a work, which, to use his own words,

> The high and tender Muses shall accept,
> With gracious smile, deliberately pleas'd,
> And listening Time reward with sacred praise.

So much for Barron Field on Akenside and Wordsworth. Newton P. Stallknecht in his *Strange Seas of Thought*, Durham, 1945, on pages 170 (footnote) and 198, has discovered the importance of Akenside in any discussion of Wordsworth's thought. See also the work of Charles T. Houpt, *Mark Akenside: A Bibliographical and Critical Study*, Philadelphia, 1944, pp. 77, 79 and footnote; E. W. Gosse in *The Living Age* 311 (1921), 791; George R. Potter in *Modern Philology* 24 (1926), 55–64.

at Halifax on August 18, 1795, elegantly bound with Rogers' *Pleasures of Memory*. This must have gone with its owner from Halifax to Racedown to Alfoxden;[11] and when William and Dorothy left Alfoxden it would be packed and stored with those 'Somersetshire goods' finally unpacked at Dove Cottage, Friday morning, July 24, 1800. That was the day after the Coleridges ended a three-week visit with the Wordsworths, a visit full of talk about the art of poetry and contingent matters. Wordsworth later told Barron Field (MS, Vol. 1, p. 111 *verso*):

I never cared a straw about the Theory, and the Preface was written at the request of Mr. Coleridge out of sheer good nature. I recollect the very spot, a deserted quarry in the Vale of Grasmere, where he pressed the thing upon me and but for that it would never have been thought of.

Nevertheless, on September 13, two months after the departure of the Coleridges, and possibly helped by a review of Akenside's poem so recently unpacked, William was 'writing his Preface'; and on September 30 Dorothy 'wrote the last sheet of Notes and Preface' for *Lyrical Ballads* of 1800. On October 3, Wordsworth 'talked much about the object of his essay for the second volume of "L.B." '; and on October 5, he and Dorothy were employed all morning in writing an addition to the Preface.[12] The 'essay for the second volume' was abandoned on December 23, 1800;[13] was it resumed in 1815 as the Essay, Supplementary?

There seems to be no proof that the revised edition of 1772 was in Wordsworth's personal library; but evidence to follow will indicate that this edition weighs more heavily in the blank verse written at Alfoxden, whence Coleridge's books were accessible at Nether Stowey; and that the first edition prevails in the meditations and metaphors of 1800 at Grasmere.

With Akenside in mind, then, let us review the early manuscript version of that passage of *The Excursion* written, so Wordsworth

[11] *Early Letters*, pp. 52, 155, 142.
[12] *Journals*, Vol. 1, pp. 51–2, 61, 62, 63, 64.
[13] *Early Letters*, p. 257.

told Miss Fenwick, at Racedown or Alfoxden. The outlines of what Coleridge quoted in April, 1798, as a 'philosophical tail-piece' [14] appear to be traced from Akenside's doctrine in *The Pleasures of the Imagination* II on 'Truth' and 'Science' and their relation to 'Virtue' and to duty and sacred law. Next, we should reread the *Lines . . . on the Wye,* Wordsworth's psychological poem, from which, as part of the same fabric, we should go on to consider afresh MSS JJ and V of *The Prelude,* Book I of *The Recluse* of 1800, the Prefaces of 1800 and 1802, and the Essay, Supplementary, of 1815, and finally refer *The Pleasures of Imagination* to *The Prelude* as a whole. With or without benefit of Samuel Taylor Coleridge, the echoes in Wordsworth's verse and prose from Akenside's distinguished blank verse indicate high respect for what was both a philosophical poem on Nature, Man, and Society, and a psychological poem on the mind of man. He studied it as science; he loved it as poetry. Reading it humbly through his eyes, we shall, I believe, discover one powerful literary ancestor of *The Prelude.*

Before he wrote his *Lines . . . on the Wye,* Wordsworth had composed for the project which included his *characters* of the Pedlar, the Cumberland Beggar, the discharged Soldier, the lost Man of the Yew-tree, and Margaret of the Ruined Cottage, a more general passage, as if to correlate these other studies. It represents man communing with the '*forms* of nature' and 'contemplating these *forms*' 'in the relations which they bear to Man.' He is scientifically precise:

> We shall discover what a *power* is theirs
> To stimulate our minds, and multiply
> The spiritual presences of absent things.
> Then weariness shall cease. We shall acquire
> The [ ] habit by which *sense is made*
> *Subservient still to moral purposes*[,]
> *A vital essence, and a saving power.*

[14] *Unpublished Letters of Samuel Taylor Coleridge,* ed. by E. L. Griggs, Vol. 1, p. 76.

Or, as Akenside had declared in his Argument to the revised Book II, 'On the *power* of discerning truth *depends* that of *acting with the view of an end;* a circumstance *essential to virtue.*'

Wordsworth goes on to say:

Science then
Shall be a precious visitant; and then,
And only then, be worthy of her name:
For then her heart shall kindle; her dull eye,
Dull and inanimate, *no more shall hang*
Chained to its object in brute slavery;
But better taught, and mindful of its use
Legitimate and its peculiar power[,]
While with a patient interest it shall watch
The processes of things, and serve the cause
Of order and distinctness; not for this
Shall it forget that *its most noble end*
Its most illustrious province must be found
In ministering to the excursive power
Of intellect and thought. So build we up
The being that we are.

Thus writing of the 'excursive power of intellect and thought,' 'a reader of Akenside' would not have forgotten the following passage in *The Pleasures of the Imagination:*

But from what name, what favourable sign,
What heavenly auspice, rather shall I date
My perilous *excursion*, than from Truth,
That nearest inmate of the human soul? . . .
. . . To the *brutes*
Perception and the transient boons of *sense*
Hath Fate imparted: but to man alone
Of sublunary beings was it given
Each fleeting impulse on the sensual powers
At leisure to review; . . . to conduct
From sense, *the portal* turbulent and loud,
Into the mind's wide palace, one by one,
The frequent, pressing, *fluctuating forms,*
And question and compare them.

From repeated experience men generalize, says Akenside. These generalizations, 'authorized' by 'experience,' are 'Truth . . . the parent . . . of Science.' On Science depend 'the wants and cares of social life,' and Science is

the substitute
Of God's own wisdom in this toilsome world;
The providence of man, . . .
. . . [whose] *duller visual ray*,
The stillness and the *persevering* acts
Of Nature oft elude. . . .
Whence also but from Truth, the light of minds,
Is human fortune gladden'd with the rays
Of Virtue? with the *moral* colours thrown
On every walk of this our social scene,
Adorning for the eye of gods and men
The passions, actions, habitudes of life,
And rendering earth like heaven, a sacred place
Where Love and Praise may take delight to dwell?
. . . Man, whose *eyelids* Truth has fill'd with day,
Discerns how skilfully to bounteous ends
His *wise affections* move; with *free accord*
Adopts their *guidance;* yields himself secure
To *Nature's* prudent impulse; and converts
Instinct to *duty* and to *sacred* law. . . .
So *all things* which have *life aspire* to God,
Exhaustless fount of *intellectual day!* [15]

And in phrases which anticipate his *Lines . . . on the Wye* Wordsworth echoes Akenside:

. . . Was it ever meant
That this majestic imagery, the clouds
The ocean and the firmament of heaven
Should lie *a barren picture on the mind?* . . .
. . . Let us rise
From this oblivious sleep, these fretful dreams

[15] *Pleasures* II, 42–91, 150–7, 185–90, 269–70.

Of feverish nothingness. Thus disciplined
All things shall live in us and we shall live
In all things that surround us. . . .
. . . Thus *the senses and the intellect*
Shall each to each supply a mutual aid,
Invigorate and sharpen and refine
Each other with a power that knows no bound,
And forms and feelings acting thus, and thus
Reacting, they shall each acquire
A *living spirit* and a character
Till then unfelt, and each be multiplied
With a variety that knows no end.
Thus deeply *drinking in* the soul of things
We shall be wise perforce, and we shall move
From strict necessity along the path
Of order and of good. Whate'er we see[,]
Whate'er we feel, by agency direct
Or indirect, shall . . . raise to loftier heights
Our *intellectual soul.*[16]

Another significant echo of Akenside's revised poem, this time from his General Argument, can be heard in the metaphors that prevail throughout the passages of blank verse written at Alfoxden and now to be read in Miss Darbishire's Appendix B. Wordsworth was studying the modes of imagination apparent in painting, sculpture, architecture, and music; and from these arts he was drawing help in his efforts to describe the 'powers . . . that colour, model, and combine the things perceived' [17]—a lesson which would soon be put to good use in the diction of the *Lines . . . on the Wye* and MS JJ of *The Prelude.*

Akenside's revised edition is also a collateral, possibly a lineal, relative of the *Lines . . . on the Wye*, written July 13, 1798. Here, it seems, we have the authentic Wordsworth; but in com-

[16] *Poetical Works*, Vol. 5, pp. 400–3. This passage, an Addendum to MS B of *The Ruined Cottage*, may be read in revised form as *Excursion* IV, 1230–75.
[17] *Poetical Works*, Vol. 5, pp. 340–3.

parable lines of his predecessor we have, also, the authentic Akenside. We observe the same orderly procedure from 'natural objects' to 'moral and intellectual objects,' the same help given the 'fancy' by the 'heart.' In tranquillity, Wordsworth recollected not only his experience on the Wye five years before, but his experience with Akenside's congenial passage:

> *For what are all the forms*
> *Educ'd by fancy from corporeal things? . . .*
> *Not tending to the heart, soon feeble grows . . .*
> *Their impulse on the sense:* while *the pall'd eye*
> Expects in vain its tribute; asks in vain
> Where are the ornaments it once admir'd?
> Not so *the moral species,* nor *the powers*
> *Of Passion and of Thought. The ambitious mind,*
> *With objects boundless as her own desires,*
> *Can there converse; by these unfading forms*
> *Touch'd and awaken'd still, with eager act*
> *She bends each nerve, and meditates well pleas'd*
> *Her gifts, her godlike fortune.*[18]

At this point in his recollection of Akenside he may well have begun his own more famous account of the bond between eye and heart and mind. The banks of the Wye have not been to him 'as is a landscape to a blind man's eye'; sensations from them have been felt along the heart, have passed into the mind.

Meanwhile, his memory would be busy with Akenside's subordination of the mind's earthly stores to its 'nobler dower,' to those '*purer gifts,*' and he would recall those '*forms*' of Akenside

> which *never* deign'd
> In eyes or ears to dwell, *within the sense*
> *Of earthly organs; but sublime* were plac'd
> *In his essential reason,* leading there
> That vast ideal host which all his works

[18] Revised edition, II, 12–26. Cf. Wordsworth's 'godlike faculties' (*Poetical Works,* Vol. 5, p. 343). Akenside's advance on Pope is evident in comparing this passage with similar ones in the *Essay on Man,* e.g., II, 13. Cf. also Young's passage (pp. 199–200).

Through endless ages never will reveal.
Thus then endow'd, the feeble creature man,
The slave of hunger and the prey of death,
Even now, even here, *in earth's dim prison* bound,
The language of intelligence divine
Attains.[19]

To certain 'beauteous *forms*' he, too, has owed not only

In hours of weariness, *sensations* sweet,
Felt in the blood, and *felt along the heart;*
And passing even into my *purer* mind,
With tranquil restoration. . . .
To them I may have owed another *gift*,
Of aspect *more sublime;* that blessed mood,
In which the burthen of the mystery,
In which the heavy and the weary weight
Of all this *unintelligible* world
Is lightened.

But the 'forms' acknowledged by Akenside, the classical scholar, to be 'sovereign dictates,' Platonic ideas heard by Eternity from coëval Truth,

when Chance nor Change,
Nature's loud progeny, nor Nature's self,
Dares intermeddle or approach her throne,[20]

will not satisfy Wordsworth, the lover of Nature. His psychological terms may echo the traditional vocabulary of his predecessor, whose 'forms' were

Sequester'd far from sense and every *spot*
Peculiar in the realms of *space or time;*[21]

but he himself has experiences, later to be called 'spots of time,' deriving from what *is* 'peculiar,' both in space (the banks of the

[19] *Ibid.* II, 101–13. Cf. Wordsworth's 'essential energy' (*Poetical Works,* Vol. 5, p. 343), and, of course, the 'shades of the prison-house' from the *Ode.*

[20] *Ibid.* II, 116–19.

[21] *Ibid.* II, 131–3. Wordsworth adopts the word 'peculiar' for *The Excursion* I, 157, 'the power of a peculiar eye,' and I, 472, 'peculiar nook of earth.'

Wye) and in time (July 13, 1798). His attention comes back to Dorothy and to the green pastoral landscape about them. Associating the idiom of Dr. Akenside with some 'admirable lines' of Dr. Young, and both with the 'holier love' of such as Habington's Holy Man, he sets down his own psychological truth. He concludes his argument in a resolute spirit of natural piety, more as a sturdy theist, even as a cautious pantheist, than as a docile Platonist. Let us say, rather, that he ends his poem in the way of all good poets, as a lover and worshipper of Nature and her peculiar forms.[22] Good scientist that he is, he does not throw away his specimens for a mere abstraction.

Wordsworth Takes Over from Dr. Akenside

Akenside and Wordsworth were both interested in process. Ever since 1744, when Akenside's didactic poem had been closely followed by his doctoral dissertation entitled *De Ortu et Incremento Foetus Humani*,[23] as a physician and as a poet he had studied origin and growth. When death from putrid fever ended his natural cycle, two months after Wordsworth was born, he was still at work upon his growing poem; and, two years after his death, the publication of his final fragment, lines of increased power and sharper intention, revealed that he had been making still another 'cheerful sally,' this last time setting himself a 'different task,' 'the secret paths of early genius to explore.'

Imagine Wordsworth coming upon or now first aware of this fresh and exciting fragment of Book IV at Racedown, when he and Dorothy had daily under their eyes young Basil Montagu, or at Alfoxden in conversation with the Coleridges about Hartley, then an infant of two years. The child about whom Wordsworth knew most, however, was himself; and William, the son of John and Ann Wordsworth, gradually took possession of the literary

[22] Somewhat later he was to pen those lines of *The Prelude* (I, 162–4) in which he still insisted that 'general truths' were 'a sort of Elements and Agents, Under-Powers, Subordinate helpers of the living mind'; they were not the 'vital soul.'

[23] This detail Wordsworth would have known from Dr. Johnson's *Life of Akenside*.

scene, until MSS JJ and V of *The Prelude* had their way, in spite of the philosophical poem to be entitled *The Recluse*, or the excursion of that other tempting figure, the wandering Pedlar.

As Akenside left behind him his theoretical Books I and II on Beauty and Truth and Goodness and his brief narrative of the Recluse, Solon, in Book III, and as he began in the fragment of Book IV to explore the mind of the child and the nature and function of the mature poet, so Wordsworth was to leave behind him those tentative passages for a philosophical poem and that somewhat theoretical treatment of the pleasures of the imagination written near Tintern Abbey—also various ballads of humble life written at Alfoxden—in order to explore his own childhood and the growth of his own mind. Thus viewed, *The Prelude* is a kind of *Pleasures of the Imagination* in reverse; exploration first, theory last. Nor is it only a curious fact that the interest of Akenside in the secret paths of early genius anticipated Wordsworth's description of his 'boyish pleasures,' as Dorothy called MS JJ.[24] That the later poet consciously took over the unfinished task of Akenside is suggested by several echoes in Wordsworth's salutatory from Akenside's valedictory. For Akenside

> A different task remains: the secret paths
> Of early genius to explore; to trace
> Those haunts *where Fancy* her predestin'd sons,
> Like to the demigods of old, *doth nurse*
> Remote from eyes profane. Ye happy souls
> Who now her tender *discipline* obey,
> Where dwell ye? What wild river's brink at eve
> Imprint your steps? What solemn groves at noon
> Use ye to visit, often breaking forth
> In rapture 'mid your dilatory walk,
> Or musing, as in slumber, on the green?
> —Would I again were with you!—O ye dales
> Of Tyne, and ye most ancient *woodlands;* where
> Oft as the giant flood obliquely strides,

[24] *Early Letters,* p. 208.

And his banks open, and his lawns extend,
Stops short the pleased traveller to view,
Presiding o'er the scene, some rustic *tower*
Founded by *Norman* or by Saxon hands:
O ye Northumbrian shades, which overlook
The rocky pavement and the mossy falls
Of solitary Wensbeck's limpid stream;
How gladly I recall your well-known seats
Belov'd of old, and that delightful time
When all *alone*, for many *a summer's day*,
I wander'd through your *calm* recesses, led
In silence by some powerful hand unseen!
Nor will I e'er forget you; nor shall e'er
The graver tasks of manhood, or the advice
Of *vulgar wisdom*, move me to disclaim
Those *studies* which possess'd me in the *dawn*
Of life, and fix'd the colour of my mind
For every future year.[25]

Even as Mark Akenside passed away in June of 1770, William Wordsworth, born in April of 1770, was in his 'dawn of life,' or, as he phrased it, 'dawn of infancy.' A few years later, in sight of 'the towers of Cockermouth,' [26] the 'Derwent' would blend his murmurs with the 'nurse's song' of this other lad, giving him, too,

Amid the fretful dwellings of mankind
A foreknowledge, a dim earnest, of the *calm*
That Nature breathes among the *woodland* [hills?].

When a child, Mark had wandered through calm recesses for many a summer's day; at five, William Wordsworth 'made one long bathing of a summer's day.' By such 'discipline' (both poets use the word) William's soul was built up and his passions were sanctified.

[25] Revised edition, IV, 20–51. Houpt, *op. cit.*, p. 164, says: 'In Book IV there are . . . lines which remind the reader of Wordsworth.'

[26] In a late revision Wordsworth substituted 'these *Norman* towers' for 'the towers' (MS D²; see de Selincourt's edition, p. 16).

Ye visions of the mountains and ye Souls
Of lonely places[,] never may I think
A vulgar hope was yours.

Neither Akenside's 'advice of vulgar wisdom' nor in Wordsworth's phrase a 'vulgar hope' suffices to invalidate this 'discipline' or disclaim these 'studies' (Akenside's word) and the lessons learned in this 'school' (Wordsworth's metaphor). The professional zeal of the poet has so invigorated Book IV of *The Pleasures of the Imagination* and MS JJ of *The Prelude* that both are lifted above the level of sentimental recall, of mere nostalgia for what is gone.

Feeling his way in MS JJ ('while I tread the mazes of this argument') Wordsworth, as I have suggested, also reread or recalled the General Argument of the revised edition of Akenside's poem. If we wish to understand the metaphors of MS JJ, we must do likewise:

The pleasures of the imagination proceed either from natural objects . . . or from works of art, such as a noble *edifice*, a *musical tune*, a *statue*, a *picture*, a poem. . . . In [the latter] we find *interwoven* frequent representations of truth, of virtue and vice, of circumstances proper to move us with laughter, or to excite in us *pity, fear, and the other passions.*

We may now point out that the metaphorical pattern of MS JJ, which explores the imaginative process of Wordsworth's childhood, follows the catalogue of Akenside's 'elegant arts': architecture, music, sculpture, painting.

Oh not in vain ye beings of the hills
And ye that walk the woods or open heaths
By moon and starlight thus from my first *dawn*
Of childhood did ye love to *interweave*
The *passions* that *build up* our human Soul,
Not with the mean and *vulgar* works of Man,
But with *high objects*, with enduring things,
With *life and nature.*

Here the Wordsworthian soul is thought of as the 'noble edifice' of Akenside. Again, also in MS JJ, 'the soul of man is fashioned and built up even as a strain of music.' This is Akenside's 'musical tune.' For Akenside's 'statue' we find an analogy in those 'huge and mighty Forms that do not live like living men,' the haunting shapes of rebuke in William's mind when he had stolen the pinnace by the shores of Patterdale. And, most important, Wordsworth's Eternal Spirit of MS JJ, 'painting what He is in all the visible imagery of all the World,' renewing for the child his naked feelings, his hallowed and pure motions of the sense, is like Akenside's 'great Artificer' working through a 'picture.'

With this difference: the tapestry or building, the melody, the forms, the painted imagery, of MS JJ are not merely instances of the 'elegant arts' of Akenside; they are metaphors for what another doctor turned poet, John Keats, would call the art of 'soul-making.' [27] Although in Akenside's argument both Wordsworth and Keats would find a system to describe process and to distinguish high objects and enduring things from mean and vulgar objects and things, both later poets transcend system and look to the living soul as the prime *objet d'art.* Thanks to Wordsworth's unconquerable selfhood, aesthetics, a science, is becoming a poem.

In this connection, too, we observe that the *Lines* written near Tintern Abbey share with MS JJ the metaphor of the elegant arts. The poet's mind is thought of primarily as a gallery or museum of 'beauteous forms,' a 'picture,' a series of sounds, colors, forms to arouse 'passion' and 'appetite'; it is a sounding board for the 'still, sad music of humanity,' a stage for a disturbing and joyful and impelling presence, a boat of purest thoughts needing anchorage. At the age of twenty-eight Wordsworth still represented the poet as a minor to be nursed, guided, guarded, and animated, and daily life, as the adult knows it, to be a 'dreary intercourse.' Still a bit homesick for aching joys, dizzy raptures, and wild ecstasies, still a young man of escapist 'mood' and 'elevated thoughts,' his wish for Dorothy, too, remains aesthetic rather than

[27] *Letters of John Keats,* ed. by Maurice Buxton Forman, Vol. 2, pp. 362–5.

poetic. Her mind is to be 'a mansion for all lovely forms,' her memory 'a dwelling-place for all sweet sounds and harmonies.' On July 13, 1798, as during the winter of 1798–9 at Goslar while at work on MS JJ, Nature is his homely nurse and schoolmistress, though her possibilities as a beloved are dimly foreseen. Aesthetic delight, whether documented by Akenside or another, will in time lead to the investigation of the creative process, and to full responsibility for his literary progeny.

Witness his account in MS JJ of the reconciliation of '*discordant* elements' in the soul of the child as accomplished by some figurative artisan with his 'dark invisible workmanship.' Similarly, Akenside, comparing the 'various aspects' of the mind with the diverse moods of a landscape now solemn with 'sable woods' and now gay with 'streams of splendour,' had assumed artistry or artful custom:

> Whence is this effect,
> This kindred power of such *discordant* things?
> Or flows their semblance from that mystic tone
> To which the *new-born* mind's harmonious powers
> At first were strung? Or rather from the *links*
> Which artful custom twines around her frame? [28]

Although Wordsworth agrees rather with the former of Akenside's suppositions, he does not abandon the metaphor; in MS JJ there is an artful something which 'fits' something to something else, and the result is aesthetic pleasure,

> that calm delight
> Which, if I err not, surely must belong
> To those *first born* affinities which fit
> Our *new* existence to existing things,
> And, in our dawn of being, constitute
> The *bond of union* betwixt life and joy.

Akenside goes on to speak of the 'eternal tie and sympathy unbroken' which images of things 'by chance combin'd' have gained

[28] First edition, III, 278, 286, 296, 306–11.

under the 'frequent *eye*' of the 'attentive soul.' By these 'mysterious ties, the busy power of Memory' preserves 'her ideal train,'

> thus *collecting all*
> *The various forms* of being to present,
> Before the curious aim of mimic art,
> Their largest choice: like *Spring's unfolded blooms*
> Exhaling sweetness, that *the skilful bee*
> May taste at will, from their selected spoils
> To work her dulcet food. For not *the expanse*
> *Of living lakes* in Summer's noontide calm,
> Reflects the bordering shade, and *sun-bright heavens*
> With fairer semblance . . .
> Than [the poet's] attemper'd bosom must preserve
> The seal of Nature.[29]

As if testing Akenside's theory by his own dissimilar experience, Wordsworth recombines and modifies this honied metaphor as follows:

> The Sands of Westmorland, the Creeks and Bays
> Of Cumbria's rocky limits, they can tell
> How when the Sea . . .
> Did send sweet notice of *the rising moon*,
> How I have stood, to images like this . . .
> A stranger, *linking* with the spectacle
> *No body of associated forms*
> And bearing with me no peculiar sense
> Of quietness or peace, yet have I stood,
> Even while my *eye* has mov'd o'er *three long leagues*
> *Of shining water*, gathering, as it seem'd,
> New pleasure, *like a bee among the flowers*.

Granted that the 'dulcet food' of Akenside's bee and the 'new pleasure' of Wordsworth's bee are different to the taste, the two kinds of honey come from the same hive. When Akenside put the question of questions:

[29] *Ibid.* III, 312–18, 348–67.

By what fine ties hath God connected things
When present in the mind, which in themselves
Have no connection? [30]

he invited a long answer from Wordsworth, *The Prelude* itself.

Artificer or Sire

At this stage the metaphor of vegetative or bodily growth has not yet supplanted the various instances of discipline, tutelage, and artistry in MS JJ, unless we allow the word 'engrafted,' indicating a horticultural artifice, to point the way. Nor has the soul of the author come into its majority; this will be the accomplishment of MS V, where the reactive and creative powers emerge from Wordsworth's adventure in composition as they did in his boyhood from the previously docile soul of the child. MS JJ, as we have seen, considers Nature, the nurse, guide, teacher, as an influence from outside in the form of beings of the hills, woods, and heaths, powers of earth, spirits of the springs, clouds, lakes and pools, visions of the mountains and souls of lonely places, in short 'genii,' says Wordsworth, possibly recalling Akenside's

Genii, who conduct
The wandering footsteps of the youthful bard,
New to your springs and shades; who touch his ear
With finer sounds; who heighten to his eye
The bloom of Nature, and before him turn
The gayest, happiest attitude of things.[31]

The mind is 'peopled' with 'beauteous objects,' but by Nature; the 'feelings' of the infant being are renewed, but by the Eternal Spirit or Soul of things; the faces of the moving year are stamped on the child's mind, by the seasons. Yet, as there is only one metaphor in MS JJ to suggest vegetative growth, there is also one concept to furnish the theme of bodily growth: in the unconscious

[30] *Ibid.* III, 462–4.

[31] *Ibid.* I, 25–30. In the tranquillity of his seventy-sixth year, Wordsworth recollected the last line of this passage and the emotion connected with it (see p. 246).

intercourse between the Child and Nature the pleasure is 'organic.'

Growth in MS V, whether of plant or of body, is allied with the pattern of the nature ritual and seasonal sports learned from Thomson, discussed elsewhere (pp. 101–4). Was there aught in the summer of 1799, spent at Sockburn, to encourage this change from aesthetic to creative imagery? Possibly on the meadows about the Tees, in talk with the Hutchinson sisters and brothers, Wordsworth for the first time looked upon Nature as farmers look upon her, as a husbandman upon a spouse, for generation and comfort.

> We should ill
> Attain our object if from delicate fears
> Of breaking in upon the unity
> Of this my argument I should omit
> To speak of such effects as cannot here
> Be regularly classed, yet tend no less
> To the same point, *the growth of mental powers*
> And love of nature's *works*.[32]

This passage in MS V marks the shift in the conception of what came to be the poem on the growth of a poet's mind. We are chastened for asking the very questions we ask here:

> Who knows the individual hour in which
> His habits were first sown, even as a seed?

But when we read that certain objects and appearances slept

> Until maturer seasons called them forth
> To impregnate and to elevate the mind,

we observe the abandonment, little by little, of the metaphor of the elegant arts, and the figure of the artificer. Wordsworth has accepted the vegetable and animal cycle as supremely important. Botany and physiology have come alive for him in a new and productive relationship with psychology and poetics.

[32] de Selincourt, p. 158.

Furthermore, in his daily association with Mary, he was forgetting those abstract meditations at Goslar on time vs. eternity, sense vs. soul, the city vs. the country, the worldly vs. the holy; and the prospect of a domestic settlement with Dorothy and Mary at the hearth of it were doing much to modify his retrospective and anxious mood. MS V gives more than a hint that he was outgrowing Nature's 'discipline' as he knew it in childhood, even his frolics with Her and cruelty upon Her in youth. To his recently accomplished manhood and his newly awakened interest in husbandry and reproduction we may owe also the part played in MS V by the Babe, who is also a creator, working in alliance with the works which it beholds, according to 'the first poetic spirit of our human life.'

We must, then, reconsider the following regnant passage of MS V:

> Let this . . .
> Be not forgotten, that I still retain'd
> My first creative sensibility,
> That by the regular action of the world
> *My soul was unsubdu'd.* A plastic power
> Abode with me, *a forming hand,* at times
> *Rebellious,* acting in a devious mood.
> A local spirit of its own, at war
> With general tendency, but for the most
> Subservient strictly to the external things
> With which it commun'd. *An auxiliar light*
> *Came from my mind* which on the setting sun
> Bestow'd *new* splendor, the melodious birds,
> The gentle breezes, fountains that ran on,
> Murmuring sweetly in themselves, *obey'd*
> *A like dominion;* and the midnight storm
> Grew darker *in the presence of my eye.*

This is, it seems to me, not only a valid expression of Wordsworth's own experience, but a sensitive and authentic rewriting of Dr.

Akenside's masterful argument in the *character* of the Bard added to his revised edition, Book IV of *The Pleasures of the Imagination:*

> *The bard nor length nor depth,*
> *Nor place nor form controls. To eyes, to ears,*
> *To every organ of the copious mind,*
> *He offereth all its treasures.* Him the hours,
> The seasons him obey; and changeful Time
> Sees him at will keep measure with his flight,
> At will outstrip it. To *enhance* his toil,
> He summoneth from the uttermost extent
> Of things which God hath taught him, every form
> *Auxiliar*, every power; and all beside
> Excludes *imperious*. His *prevailing hand*
> Gives to *corporeal essence* life and sense,
> And every stately function of the soul.

Such an act of creation, the gift to 'corporeal essence' of 'life and sense and every stately function of the soul,' had already in 1798 been substantiated and intensified as an aesthetic if not a poetic experience on the banks of the Wye, when the breath of the 'corporeal frame' and the 'motion of [the] human blood' had been almost suspended in order that the poet might become 'a living soul.' Now, in 1800, the 'imperious' Bard of Akenside makes way for one whose 'plastic power,' at times 'rebellious,' is for the most, says Wordsworth, 'subservient strictly . . . to external things.' For Akenside it has been the forms and powers which are auxiliar; for Wordsworth it will be the light from the mind which is auxiliar. Yet the figure persists. As 'eyes' and 'ears' receive their treasures from 'the copious mind' of Akenside's Poet, and the hours and seasons 'obey' him, Wordsworth's Poet, too, has the deep feeling 'that the mind is lord and master,' that the melodies and lights and sights of nature have for him 'obey'd a like dominion.' This enhancement of poetic 'toil,' as Akenside considers it, is modified by Wordsworth in a later passage of *The Prelude* to refer to 'spots of time' by whose virtue 'pleasure is enhanced.'

Moreover, Dr. Akenside, though Platonist enough to recognize the stately functions of the soul in its vision and love of ideal beauty, is Aristotelian in his insistence that beauty is the result of right function, and companion of the 'health and active use' of the body.

> More lively still
> Is Nature's charm, where to the full consent
> Of complicated members, to the bloom
> Of colour, and *the vital change of growth*,
> Life's holy flame and piercing sense are given,
> And *active* motion speaks the temper'd soul:
> So moves the bird of Juno; so the steed
> With *rival* ardour *beats* the dusty *plain*.

Wordsworth would use that line in this very MS V which he had begun at Sockburn and was even now revising there or at Grasmere:

> When summer came
> It was the pastime of our afternoons
> To *beat* along the *plain* of Windermere
> With *rival* oars.

The sports of the boy William had a ministration of their own, leading from action to health and from health to a quiet independence of the heart. The activity of the man Wordsworth would be as vital: the domestic action, the civic action, the religious action awaited him in their due season; they were all parts of the poetic action.

Now Akenside had veered from the figure of Sire, Father, and Almighty Parent in his first edition toward the more sophisticated figure of the Almighty Legislator and Sovereign Guide in his revised edition. Coming finally to grips with artistic procedure as distinguished from aesthetic experience, he had adapted from Milton for his *character* of the Bard in the frustrum of Book IV the image of 'the great Artificer,' who portrays 'his own immense idea' in 'Nature's frame . . . this outward frame of things.' Contrariwise, Wordsworth, who may have studied the revised edition first, came back to the natural metaphors of the first edition just when he needed to reconsider himself, no longer as an aesthete but as an author: in his personal life as a spouse and parent, and in his professional life as one able to create volitions and passions where he does not find them 'manifested in the goings-on of the Universe.' In *The Pleasures of Imagination* he would note that Akenside had made a love affair of the relation between Nature and the Artist. This theme, 'yet still unsung' in 1744, is the attraction of the '*goodly frame*' of Nature for 'the consenting hearts of mortal men' with the 'pregnant stores' thence derived 'to deck the poet's or the painter's toil.'

To the image of the spousal and creative relation Wordsworth decided to give even ampler and more explicit treatment. The figure that Akenside had abandoned Wordsworth salvaged, as it were; and, in keeping with his own spousal hopes, it furnished the main theme of the ultimate prothalamium of the eighteenth century,[33] to be sung when 'the discerning intellect of man' is 'wedded to this *goodly universe* in love and holy passion.'

> —I, long before the blissful hour arrives,
> Would chant, in lonely peace, the spousal verse
> Of this great consummation: . . .
> . . . while my voice proclaims
> How exquisitely the individual Mind
> . . . to the external World
> Is fitted:—and how exquisitely, too—
> Theme this but little heard of among men—
> The *external World* is fitted to the Mind;
> And the creation (by no lower name
> Can it be called) which they with blended might
> Accomplish.

This it is to transfigure physiology into poetry.

Dr. Akenside, neurologist, physiologist, psychologist, had im-

[33] Following Blake's *Marriage of Heaven and Hell* by some ten years.

agined that the wedding of the mind of man and 'external things' took place in Egypt:

> For as old Memnon's image, long renown'd
> By fabling Nilus, to the quivering touch
> Of Titan's ray, with each repulsive string
> Consenting, sounded through the warbling air
> Unbidden strains; even so did Nature's hand
> To certain species of *external things,*
> Attune the finer organs of *the mind:*
> So the glad impulse of congenial powers . . .
> Thrills through Imagination's tender frame,
> From nerve to nerve; all naked and alive
> They catch the spreading rays; till now the soul
> At length discloses every tuneful spring,
> To that harmonious movement from without
> Responsive.[34]

The altar for such poetic union in *The Recluse* of 1800 is no statue of old Memnon, but the very heart of the poet, a 'metropolitan temple' indeed; and the spousals of Nature and the Mind of Man are solemnized by no mere 'Titan' but by the 'prophetic spirit' of Milton's epic. Nevertheless, in Akenside's figure the glad impulse of congenial powers eventuating in a moment of poetic inspiration with a poetic harvest of love and joy is not unlike the ultimate effect of Wordsworth's spousal verse, to

> arouse the sensual from their sleep
> Of Death, and win the vacant and the vain
> To noble raptures.

As if by poetic parturition both writers create new life. Beauty is, in Akenside's words, '[the] child of Nature and the soul in happiest hour brought forth.' [35]

[34] First edition, I, 109–24. Wordsworth had summed this passage up in a note to the 1793 edition of *Descriptive Sketches* (*Poetical Works*, Vol. 1, p. 44). In his study of *The Excursion*, New Haven, 1950, p. 33, Judson Stanley Lyon says that Wordsworth's knowledge of the passage was first pointed out in *Blackwood's Edinburgh Magazine*, Vol. 26, pp. 774–88.

[35] Revised edition, I, 287–8.

When at line 116 of Book I of *The Prelude* Wordsworth begins to describe the mature poetic life which ensued upon residence in his chosen Vale, he asserts his 'admiration' of and 'love' for 'common things,' and has set himself to 'reading and thinking' rather than to 'music and verse.' He tells us of his hopes

> that with a *frame* of outward life
> I might endue, might fix in a visible home,
> Some portion of those *phantoms* of conceit
> That had been floating loose about so long,
> And to such Beings temperately deal forth
> *The many feelings that oppressed my heart.*

Although this passage is not in MS V, it echoes the very parlance of Akenside, who had said in his first edition:

> The child of Fancy oft in silence bends
> O'er these mixt treasures of his *pregnant* breast
> With conscious pride. From them he oft resolves
> *To frame* he knows not what excelling things,
> And win he knows not what sublime reward
> Of praise and wonder. By degrees, the mind
> Feels her young nerves dilate; the plastic powers
> Labour for action; blind emotions heave
> His bosom; and with loveliest frenzy caught,
> From earth to heaven he rolls his daring eye,
> From heaven to earth. Anon ten thousand shapes,
> Like spectres trooping to the wizard's call,
> Flit swift before him. From the womb of earth,
> From ocean's bed they come; the eternal heavens
> Disclose their splendours, and the dark abyss
> Pours out her births unknown. With fixed gaze
> He marks the rising *phantoms* . . .

Yes, here are Wordsworth's 'phantoms of conceit.'

> Hither now,
> Now thither fluctuates his inconstant aim,
> With endless choice perplex'd. At length his plan
> Begins to open. Lucid order dawns . . .

Wordsworth would say 'gleams of light flash often from the east.'

The Doctor has furnished the apprentice with a valid literary collateral for the uncertainty in which the composition of every poem begins. These initial 'unruly . . . fits,' which trouble the later poet as he tries to amalgamate the pleasures of his childhood in MS V with his philosophic poem, *The Recluse* of 1800, are normal; to acknowledge them is a literary device; an account of them is in the literary tradition. And for the 'philosophic Song of Truth that *cherishes our daily life*,' Wordsworth's 'last and favourite aspiration,' Akenside also gives sustenance:

> But this eternal fabric was not rais'd
> For man's inspection. Though to some be given
> To catch a transient visionary glimpse
> Of that majestic scene which boundless power
> Prepares for perfect goodness, yet in vain
> Would human life her faculties expand
> To embosom such an object. . . .
> *Hence all the little charities of life,*
> *With all their duties.*[36]

'Passion's Fierce Illapse'

Very deftly Akenside distinguishes between the brutes to whom are imparted 'perception and the transient boons of sense,' and man, to whom it is given

> Each fleeting impulse on the sensual powers
> At leisure to review.[37]

'At leisure to review' is a slight premonition of 'emotion recollected in tranquillity,' that important description of poetic process in the Preface to *Lyrical Ballads* of 1800; and Wordsworth's definition of poetry as 'the spontaneous overflow of powerful feelings' is a reminiscence of Akenside's fluent figure:

[36] *Ibid.* II, 278 ff.
[37] *Ibid.*, 48–53.

and let the yielding strains
From his full bosom, like a welcome rill
Spontaneous from its healthy fountain, *flow!* [38]

In the critical process as in poetry, feeling and imagination are important. Wordsworth's Preface carries, as does the Design of Akenside's first edition, an explicit disavowal of merely rational arguments. Wordsworth knew that 'the Reader would look coldly upon [his] arguments' and considered foolish the 'hope of reasoning him into an approbation of these particular Poems'; Akenside's aim 'was not so much to give formal precepts, or enter into the way of direct argumentation, as, by exhibiting the most engaging prospects of nature, to enlarge and harmonize the imagination, and by that means insensibly dispose the minds of men to a similar taste and habit of thinking in religion, morals, and civil life.'

Wordsworth acknowledges the obligation of the author to 'gratify certain known habits of association'; for Akenside 'the foundation of metaphor and wit' had seemed 'in a great measure' to be 'the early association of our ideas,' and this 'habit of associating' was 'the source of many pleasures and pains in life, and on that account [bore] a great share in the influence of poetry and the other arts.'

Wordsworth would make his incidents and situations interesting 'by tracing in them . . . the primary laws of our nature'; Akenside had hoped to deduce 'whatever our imagination feels . . . from one or other of those principles in the constitution of the human mind which are here established and explained,' and he had been 'careful to point out . . . in every principle of the human constitution here insisted upon' the benevolent intention of the Author of nature.

Wordsworth refers to conditions in which 'the essential passions of the heart find a better soil in which they can attain their maturity, are less under restraint and speak a plainer and more emphatic language'; Akenside had called attention to the value

[38] *Ibid.*, 39–41.

of 'circumstances proper to awaken and engage the passions.' And when Akenside spoke of the 'essential pleasure' of our nature as held from 'passion's power alone' and uttered his quaint dictum, 'passion's fierce illapse rouses the mind's whole fabric,' he had again made way through both psychological and poetical theory for Wordsworth's definition of poetry as 'the overflow of powerful feelings.'

Indeed, the marrow of the great Preface is its emphasis on feeling. When Akenside reminded us that what God 'admir'd and lov'd his vital power unfolded into being,' he had validated, even if he did not initiate a theory of poetics now associated with the pioneer work of William Blake and of Wordsworth and Coleridge. The phenomenon of enhancement or intensification, which Wordsworth was to call 'an auxiliar light' (*Prelude* II, 387), Akenside had also set forth as the gift of passion to the object of its rapture. Wordsworth's 'midnight storm' growing 'darker' in the presence of his eye (II, 392–3) had been anticipated in Akenside's 'flame of passion' which shows its object

vast of size,
With fiercer colours and a night of shade.
What? like a storm from their capacious bed
The sounding seas o'erwhelming, when the might
Of these eruptions, working from the depth
Of man's strong apprehension, shakes his frame
Even to the base; from every naked sense
Of pain and pleasure dissipating all
Opinion's feeble coverings, and the veil
Spun from the cobweb fashion of the times
To hide the feeling heart? *Then Nature speaks*
Her genuine language, and the words of men,
Big with the very motion of their souls,
Declare with what accumulated force
The impetuous nerve of passion urges on
The native weight and energy of things.[39]

[39] First edition, II, 139–54.

Moreover, since Akenside's title rings not only in the 'pleasures' of the Preface of 1800, but in the instances of 'pleasure' added to the Preface in the edition of 1802, we have further reason to assume that during that year as well as in 1800 he put *The Pleasures of Imagination* under fresh scrutiny, possibly to document the continuing discussion with Coleridge of their common subject of research. The new phrases that arrest us are: 'the grand elementary principle of pleasure,' 'we have no sympathy but what is propagated by pleasure,' 'whenever we sympathize with pain it will be found that the sympathy is produced and carried on by subtle combinations with pleasure'—an important argument of Akenside, too—'we have no knowledge, that is, no general principles drawn from the contemplation of particular facts, but what has been built up by pleasure and exists in us by pleasure alone.' 'Pleasure' here is both a Sire, to 'propagate' sympathy, and an Artificer, to 'build up' general principles.

That figure of the Artificer, however, was still inconvenient; and as Wordsworth had in MS V outgrown the metaphorical pattern of 'the elegant arts,' so in his Preface he must abandon, avoid, or transcend the poet as Artificer. He must rather use those organic metaphors from bodily growth and function to which also Dr. Akenside had encouraged him.

This was a conflict not so much between two modes of imagination as between two vehicles of poetic expression; but it was settled in a way to give the utmost freedom to Wordsworth's own characteristic way of thought and feeling as well as to his convictions on style. He would insist that the truth for which he was probing into the mind of man and the writings of the poets must be fit for 'flesh and blood.' Poetics and psychology must not deviate too far from physiology. And hence the buried metaphor of the Preface is physiological. Already in the Preface of 1800 he had spoken of metrical and prose compositions as 'bodies . . . clothed . . . [in] the same substance, . . . shedding . . . tears,' bodies with similar 'vital juices' and 'the same human blood' circulating 'through their veins.' The passions of men, said the poet in 1800, are 'incorporated with the beautiful and permanent forms of nature.' And in the revision of 1802 the science of flesh and blood, physiology, which had sustained the spousal passage of *The Recluse* of 1800, is called upon to furnish the character of the Poet as one who transfigures Science. The poetical life is lived in loving intercourse with Truth; Science is, as it were, impregnated by the Poet; and the resulting poem is the child of their union and the inmate of the human household:

If the time should ever come when what is now called Science, thus familiarised to men, shall be ready to put on, as it were, a form of flesh and blood, the Poet will lend his divine spirit to aid the transfiguration, and will welcome the Being thus produced, as a dear and genuine inmate of the household of man.

The Artificer has become the Sire in Wordsworth's poetical theory as in his poetry.

'Stern Daughter of the Voice of God'

Poets . . . dwell on earth
To clothe whate'er the soul admires or loves
With language and with numbers.

These lines from Akenside's *character* of a poet in Book IV of *The Pleasures of the Imagination* stand at the beginning of *Yarrow Revisited and Other Poems*, 1835, the same year in which Dyce published his Aldine edition of Akenside's *Poetical Works*.[40] The presence in Wordsworth's volume of a cento patched together with a stanza from Akenside, a couplet from Thomson, and a stanza from Beattie suggests that Wordsworth was at that time renewing his acquaintance with Akenside's *Odes*. In these as well as in Gray's *Hymn to Adversity* he might well observe the final hexametrical line handled with questionable success in his own early *Ode to Duty*, 1804.[41] Although he gives Gray the credit for

[40] That Akenside was in 1835–7 freshly discussed by Dyce, Rogers, and Wordsworth is indicated in *The Letters of William and Dorothy Wordsworth, The Later Years*, Oxford, 1939, pp. 732, 906.

[41] *Poetical Works,* Vol. 4, p. 418.

the form of this ode, I suggest that its main indebtedness is in imagery and situation, and that these come from the noble traits and redemptive function of that Daughter of the Voice of God, Virtue, in Akenside's allegory, Book II of *The Pleasures of Imagination.*

Wordsworth's Duty has all the distinguishing traits of Akenside's Virtue. The former wears 'The Godhead's most benignant grace'; the latter wears 'the presence of a god, high on the circle of her brow enthron'd.' There is nothing so fair as the smile upon the face of Duty; Virtue's looks are 'benevolent and meek.' And the more important item in the comparison is the image of Duty casting her 'saving arms' around those who fail through misplaced confidence, and Virtue folding 'with a mother's arms the fainting boy' who has been 'allur'd by meaner joys.' Akenside's vision of the erring youth and the terrifying son of Nemesis is most clearly paralleled in the following cancel of the Longman MS of Wordsworth's poem:

> O Power of Duty, *sent from* God
> *To enforce on earth his high behest,*
> *And keep us faithful to the road*
> Which conscience hath pronounc'd the best:
> *Thou, who art Victory and Law*
> *When empty terrors overawe;*
> *From vain temptations dost set free,*
> From Strife, *and from Despair,* a glorious Ministry! [42]

Moreover, behind the reference in the Preface of 1800 to 'the multiplicity and quality of [the] moral relations' of poetry, lies a substantial agreement with Akenside on the association of ethics and poetics; witness, among many other passages, the following:

[42] *Poetical Works,* Vol. 4, p. 85. Akenside revised his vision into a straightforward doctrine of 'godlike function' exerted in this 'humble sphere' through the 'superior functions' of the soul (II, 285 ff.). These phrases may have determined Wordsworth's line 'To humbler functions, awful Power!' Cf. also the *Vernal Ode,* where a vision is the main device, and where (line 118) the vivid phrase 'the imperial front of man' comes from Akenside's revised edition (I, 550), 'man's imperial front,' rather than from the Popian 'man's imperial race' (*Essay on Man* I, 209), to which it is sometimes referred.

where the powers
Of Fancy . . . paint [the images of things] in all
Their genuine hues, the features which they wore
In Nature; there Opinion will be true,
And Action right.[43]

Similarly, when the author of *The Prelude* considers that solitude may be 'more active, even, than "best society," ' he does not forget Akenside's conviction that poetry is one of the 'active labours' of men; and when he states his conviction that the young man should judge between good and evil not as an aesthete, 'for the mind's delight,' but 'for her safety, [as] one who [is] to *act*,' [44] he is again in thorough agreement with Akenside's ethical theory. The poet is not only an undeceived observer and a feeling soul, but an active agent, responsible ultimately for that most difficult of actions, the formation of taste.

In the Essay, Supplementary, published in 1815 but possibly conceived earlier, Wordsworth used again as a kind of hidden metaphor the allegory of the second Book of Akenside. The illusions of the inexperienced reader, his rapture from what the disciplined reader knows to be a vicious passage, remind us of the stripling's immature preference for pleasure, Euphrosyne. 'Magnificence herself' in the Essay is another like Akenside's Virtue. The dilemma of the stripling as between Virtue and Pleasure reappears in Wordsworth's sentence: 'It is in the fine arts as in the affairs of life, no man can *serve* . . . two Masters.' [45] There are in the world 'select Spirits . . . whose fame shall be . . . an existence like that of Virtue, which owes its being to the struggles it makes, and its vigour to the enemies whom it provokes.' Pope in his Eclogues, says Wordsworth, 'wandered from humanity . . . with boyish inexperience.' 'The profound and the exquisite in feeling, the lofty and universal in thought and imagination, or, in ordinary language, the pathetic and the sublime': are these not

[43] First edition, III, 18–23.
[44] *Prelude* II, 313–14; VIII, 667–9. Italics by Wordsworth.
[45] Italics by Wordsworth.

Euphrosyne and Virtue presented in another and more friendly aspect? And progress in poetry as 'an advance, or a conquest, made by the soul of the poet': is this not like the conquest made by the stripling of Akenside's allegory? 'The qualities which dazzle at first sight . . . are essentially different from those by which permanent influence is secured.' Then, at the end of his Essay, from the yet unpublished *Prelude* Wordsworth quotes the phrase 'the great Spirit of human knowledge.' 'The VOICE that issues from this Spirit,' he says, 'is that Vox Populi which the Deity inspires.' So much for the literary progeny of the Voice of God.

'What is so fair as virtuous friendship?' Akenside had asked. Reading this question, did Wordsworth recall, among many other friends, John Milton and Edward King, William Habington and George Talbot, Mark Akenside and Jeremiah Dyson? What more fitting than that his *Prelude* should be dedicated to the friend who had room in *his* brain to admire the head and fancy of Akenside?

And yet, even as we associate *The Pleasures of Imagination* with *The Prelude* in such a literary friendship, we must temper our zeal and chasten our research by a quotation from Wordsworth's own MS V:

> Who shall parcel out
> His intellect, by geometric rules,
> Split, like a province, into round and square?
> Who knows the individual hour in which
> His habits were first sown, even as a seed,
> Who that shall point, as with a wand, and say,
> 'This portion of the river of my mind
> Came from yon fountain?' Thou, my Friend! art one
> More deeply read in thy own thoughts; to thee
> Science appears but, what in truth she is,
> Not as our glory and our absolute boast,
> But as a succedaneum, and a prop
> To our infirmity.

XI

Scholar

WORDSWORTH's literary biography is not established between December 21, 1800, and October 10, 1801, an intermission in Dorothy's Journal for which there appears to be very little other documentary evidence. We are therefore impelled to a more careful scrutiny of her record following this period; her brother's habits of study and composition as she set them down during the winter of 1801–2 presumably continue from earlier months of 1801. In this research we shall ask anew what themes in the books he chose to study were related to his own projects; and where we find his contemporary verse dealing with such themes, we must observe how he combined and modified what he read.

He was in need of a new apprenticeship. For the portrayal of nature and humble life in the *Lyrical Ballads* of 1798 he had disclaimed assistance from books. Those poets of the eighteenth century who had helped him with the early manuscripts of *The Prelude* and certain writers of the seventeenth century whose influence is obvious in *Lyrical Ballads* of 1800 and 'Home at Grasmere' no longer served his scholarly purpose. Now, in 1801, his poem went haltingly; he must have discipline from greater masters.

Certain personal problems also demanded his mature thought. By the exigencies of war he had been for almost a decade parted from his daughter Caroline and her mother, Annette Vallon. Circumstances meanwhile were strengthening the affection between himself and his sister's friend, Mary Hutchinson. What he might learn from Chaucer, Spenser, and Milton, whom he studied during the winter, and by clear inference earlier in 1801, would bear helpfully upon such matters as inconstancy in love, transience, the old and the new in their right relation, and above all, on the profound themes of disillusionment and rededication. As he told Crabb Robinson later: 'When I began to give myself up to the profession of a poet for life, I was impressed with a conviction that there were four English poets whom I must have continually before me as examples—Chaucer, Shakespeare, Spenser, and Milton. These I must study, and equal *if I could;* and I need not think of the rest.' [1] From their ethical and poetical wisdom his autobiographical poem profited in such wise as the following chapters aim to set forth.

'Litel Clergeon,' 'Flour of Bachilrie,' 'Love's Servaunt'

Out of Wordsworth's study of Chaucer came modern versions of *The Prioress's Tale*, published in 1820; of *The Manciple's Tale*, first published in 1947; [2] of *The Cuckoo and the Nightingale*, then supposed to be Chaucerian, and of *Troilus and Criseyde* V, 519–686, both published in 1841. Assuredly he translated the first three in 1801; [3] and presumably the last also dates from this period.[4]

[1] *Prose Works*, ed. by A. B. Grosart, Vol. 3, pp. 459–60. Wordsworth's emphasis appearing in Robinson's italics.

[2] *Poetical Works*, Vol. 4, pp. 358–65.

[3] *Journals*, Vol. 1, pp. 80, 86–8, 95–6, 139, for November 15, December 2, 4–9, 22–3, 26, 1801, and April 28, 1802. In a letter of July 30, 1931, Gordon Wordsworth wrote: 'I have found an 1801 transcript of the Manciple's Tale, partly in the writing of William and partly in that of Mary (cf. entry of Dec. 5, 1801), written on foolscap paper uniform with that of the other Chaucer items, and in not a few lines altered by William. In style it does not vary from the other Chaucer "modernizations," save that he has cut down the 54 lines of Chaucer's final paragraph to 43. . . . I should guess this was a first clean copy founded on still rougher notes.'

[4] Cf. *Modern Language Notes* for April, 1930, p. 216. Wordsworth's letter of

The love of parent for child and the marvel of childhood itself recur as themes in Wordsworth's poetry all through the decade of his separation from his own child; we are not surprised, then, to find him attentively at work on the *Prioress's Tale* of the 'litel clergeon,' the chorister who glorified the Mother of Jesus with his song *Alma Redemptoris Mater.* That 'little scholar,' as Wordsworth translates it, 'scarcely seven years old,' on his way to the 'little school of Christian people,' has somewhat in common with eight-year-old William on his way to Hawkshead. What is more important, and what may have invited closer study and modernization, the scholar's 'holy lay' sung for his 'blissful Lady free' may well have been associated in Wordsworth's mind with those passages in MS V of *The Prelude* in praise of Lady Nature. The mariolatry of the fourteenth century has reappeared in the nature worship of the late eighteenth and early nineteenth century. This literary consonance would be insignificant to Wordsworth, and to us, except that in 1801 the poem on Wordsworth's 'boyish pleasures' was at a standstill. Might there be anything in the Chaucerian analogue to help him on with his own tale?

Knowing that the mind of a poet is particularly sensitive to mythic form, to the outlines of plot, and that *Pilgrim's Progress* and *The Castle of Indolence*, currently in his mind,[5] had inclined him to the study of ordeals, we may suggest that the martyrdom of Chaucer's little scholar had its part, too, in the ordeal of Book III of *The Prelude.*

When Wordsworth set down the lines of the Prioress:

1839 or 1840 to Thomas Powell speaks of these four modernizations together, and of *Troilus and Cresida* 'from a recollection only of many years past.' He discusses the technique of translation in regard to *Troilus and Cresida* and *The Cuckoo and the Nightingale* as if he had wrought both at the same time. In a letter of November 11, 1931, Gordon Wordsworth wrote: 'The only MS. scrap of *Troilus and Cresida* that I possess (lines 47–98) is on a sheet of paper, 9 in. by 5¾. Three sides are machine-cut—the fourth is torn off a larger sheet. The three clean-cut edges do not fit any of the various foolscap sheets used at Dove Cottage at that date, though the quality of the paper is much the same. There is a slight difference in colour, but that may be due to varying exposure to light. . . . I can see no reason to doubt that the scrap of *T. and C.* is contemporary with the other Chaucer MSS.'

[5] *Journals,* Vol. 1, pp. 105 and 145, for January 31, 1802, and for May 9–11, 1802.

'O Martyr 'stablished in virginity!
Now may'st thou sing for aye before the throne,
Following the Lamb celestial,' quoth she,
'Of which the great Evangelist, Saint John,
In Patmos wrote . . . '

the leap of the mind to his own St. John's at Cambridge would be immediate. Nor had he himself been

unprepared,
If high occasion called, to act or suffer
As from the invisible shrine within the breast
Nature might urge, or antient story taught.
Why should he grieve who was a chosen Son[?] [6]

It was at Cambridge that this chosen son had been reading Chaucer's tales. There, too, he had dreamed of (III, 440–3)

a Sanctuary for our Country's Youth,
With such a spirit in it as might be
Protection for itself, a Virgin grove,
Primaeval in its purity and depth;

and thence returning to Hawkshead for his first summer vacation and the renewal of his worship of Nature, he had learned (IV, 156–8)

How the immortal Soul with God-like power
Informs, creates, and thaws the deepest sleep
That time can lay upon her.

'The image . . . of Jesu's Mother' of the fourteenth century has become Nature's 'invisible shrine within the breast'; 'Abbey' and 'altar while the Mass doth last' are now reconceived as 'Sanctuary' with a self-protecting 'spirit'; 'Jesu's Mother sweet,' that 'well of mercy,' may reside within 'the Virgin grove, primaeval in its purity and depth'; and the 'Innocent' little scholar 'upon his bier' singing *Alma Redemptoris Mater* although his throat was 'cut unto the bone' has been first translated from Chaucerian

[6] de Selincourt, p. 74.

language and then transformed into Wordsworthian imagery in the supreme religious discovery of Books III and IV, the 'God-like power' of 'the immortal soul' to 'thaw' the indignities of 'time.' The ordeals of 'litel clergeon' and Cambridge freshman are circumstantially very different, and essentially very much the same. Our Lady and Nature are alike beneficent; and the 'cursèd Jews' of *The Prioress's Tale* as modernized by William Wordsworth lurk behind the 'unscour'd, grotesque . . . old Humourists' of Book III, his tale of a freshman. As a 'wild flower' in the 'garland' upon the 'matron temples' of his Alma Mater the scholar is mysteriously preserved; and when reunited with the Nature to whose prior service he is vowed, he finds 'restoration.' Possibly we have discovered in his Chaucer scholarship one reason for the strain of homesick mother-worship in *The Prelude*.

Again, we know that he had already turned his scholar's eye with sharp challenge upon other of the tales told by the Canterbury pilgrims. Why from all of them did he choose at this time to modernize *The Manciple's Tale* of a white crow turned black because it tattled of marital infidelity?

The story is one of disillusionment and concerns the fortunes of a minstrel and singer, the 'flour of bachilrie,' the most joyous of young men and the best of archers, even the sun-god himself, Phoebus, who came down from heaven to earth and dwelt here with a belovèd wife. Now this Phoebus for many a day fostered in a cage a crow, white as a snow-white swan; and he taught the crow to mimic the speech of every man, and no nightingale could sing so merrily and well.

Birds, however, desire liberty; and human beings are newfangled in their affections: nature will not be gainsaid. And hence it came about that in Phoebus' absence his wife played him false with her leman. 'Cokkow! cokkow! cokkow!' sang the bird when Phoebus returned; with seemingly undeniable evidence in bold words he reported the wife's misdeed. Credulous, intemperate, and enraged, Phoebus set an arrow to his bow and slew his wife;

he broke his harp, his lute, his arrows, and his bow. Then, with swift reversal, on a sudden suspicion that the white bird had deceived him, he upbraided himself for his hasty and inconsiderate judgment and action, and—not less hasty and inconsiderate—he despoiled the crow of its melodious voice, its power of speech, and its radiant plumage. Thenceforward all crows would be black, would croak of tempest and of rain.

It were idle to infer from the mere events of this tale aught of importance in Wordsworth's biography; the fable itself fits many a career. But biographers might be spared many diligent hypotheses if they took to heart the advice our poet translated from Chaucer's shrewd manciple on the authority of Solomon, David, and Seneca:

> My sone, be war, and be non auctour newe
> Of tydinges, whether they ben false or trewe.
> Wher-so thou come, amonges hye or lowe,
> Kepe wel thy tonge, and thenk up-on the crowe.

Or, as Wordsworth wrote to Dora and Mr. Quillinan in 1840: 'How could the mischief of telling truth, merely because it is truth, be more feelingly exemplified?' [7]

So much for reticence; but, the moral aside, Wordsworth must have found something else in agreement with his mood as he translated this vigorous picture of the sun-god's eclipse and the metamorphosis of the white crow with dire results for speech and song. Through earthly adventures celestial radiance grows dim. Is this not the pattern in brief of the *Ode: Intimations of Immortality?* Is this not the 'Imagination Impaired' of *The Prelude?*

> What then remained in such eclipse? What light
> To guide or cheer?

asked Wordsworth near the outset of the three Books constituting his Poet's tale of the impaired imagination. This question does not appear in the edition of 1850, nor that other echo of the tattle-tale crow and the intemperate minstrel (XI, 134–7):

[7] *Later Years*, pp. 1018–19.

> Danger cannot but attend
> Upon a Function rather proud to be
> The enemy of falsehood, than the friend
> Of truth, to sit in judgment than to feel.

The cry 'cokkow' of *The Manciple's Tale*, bringing disillusionment to the minstrel, would associate itself with the disillusioning argument of the Cuckoo of *The Cuckoo and the Nightingale*, also under Wordsworth's eye and pen at this time. Would he agree with the 'unholy' Cuckoo 'right upon a tree fast by' that

> If long time from thy mate thou be, or far,
> Thou'lt be as others that forsaken are?

Or, hearing these churlish words and stung by the tears of the Nightingale 'in the next bush,' did he, like the medieval poet, take stone in hand and hunt the Cuckoo 'from tree to tree till he was far, all out of sight, away?' Or, finally, might he in some new way reconcile the arguments in this debate between bitter Truth and faithful Love?

Surely when he translated the initial stanzas of praise for the God of Love, 'mighty [to] bind . . . and unbind all that he will have bound, or have unbound,' he would note the proper medieval setting for a debate; he might even wonder how this setting could be adapted for a modern lament. At May time the gentle heart feels 'a stirring—whether to joy, or . . . mourning'; in wood and by stream and on green lawn there are budding leaves and fresh flowers, and the small birds sing; 'all kinds of pleasure [are] mix'd with sorrowing'; and in age comes the memory of past heartaches.

Then, too, when he wrote down the skeptical remark of the Cuckoo ('loving is aye an office of despair') he must have bethought him of the tangled situation which next spring was to give rise to Coleridge's *Dejection* and his own regretful but more courageous lament: Coleridge somewhat like the Cuckoo, and Dorothy much like the Nightingale, and Wordsworth between them! And when the Nightingale called upon the God of Love, and offered the Poet the good old medieval remedy for the dejected lover,

> This May-time, every day before thou dine,
> Go look on the fresh daisy,

the upshot of the debate was that the Poet routed the Cuckoo, and the Nightingale sang the valedictory: 'For term of life Love shall have hold of me.'

We need not wonder that in the *Ode: Intimations of Immortality* the Poet has obediently taken his 'medicine':

> Thanks to the human heart by which we live,
> Thanks to its tenderness, its joys, and fears,
> To me the meanest flower that blows can give
> Thoughts that do often lie too deep for tears.

And, surely, we need not question this one origin of the cure of the Poet of *The Prelude* through the operation of intellectual love and the admonitions of that one of Nature's inmates, beloved of birds and flowers, who preserved him 'still a poet,' Nightingale Dorothy.

Thus, for readers of *The Prelude* as well as the *Ode* to which *The Prelude* (Books XI–XIII) stands in relation of débat to lament, the poem now thought Sir Thomas Clanvowe's but assumed by Wordsworth to be Chaucer's own, may still shed light on the nature of intellectual love and its persistent enemies. When Wordsworth enumerated the progeny of medieval 'love':

> All goodness and all worth;
> All gentiless and honour thence come forth;
> Thence worship comes, content and true heart's pleasure,
> And full-assurèd trust, joy without measure,
> And jollity, fresh cheerfulness, and mirth;
>
> And bounty, lowliness, and courtesy,
> And seemliness, and faithful company,
> And dread of shame that will not do amiss;
> For he that faithfully Love's servant is,
> Rather than be disgraced, would chuse to die . . .

he was not only making the old song of the Nightingale audible to his contemporaries, he was preparing himself for a glorification of that sort of modern love which he would call imagination. In so doing he became in a real sense one of Love's true servants. 'Joy to him' (XIII, 197–210, 380–5),

Oh, joy to him who here hath sown, hath laid
Here the foundations of his future years!
For all that friendship, all that love can do, . . .
All shall be his: and he whose soul hath risen
Up to the height of feeling intellect
Shall want no humbler tenderness, his heart
Be tender as a nursing Mother's heart;
Of female softness shall his life be full,
Of little loves and delicate desires,
Mild interest and gentlest sympathies.
. . . And hence this Song
. . . centring all in love, and in the end
All gratulant if rightly understood.

'Sonne of Alle Blisse'

Early in his study of disillusionment Wordsworth turned to Chaucer's famous romance. In its most touching passage, which he modernized under the title *Troilus and Cresida*, the abandoned lover sought once again to behold the 'Palace . . . of Cresida,' although she herself was 'gone.'

But . . . when he saw *her doors fast bolted all*, . . .
How *shut was every window of the place*,
Like *frost* he thought his heart was icy cold; . . .
Then said he thus,—*O Palace desolate!*
O house of houses, *once so richly dight!*
O Palace empty and disconsolate!
Thou lamp of which extinguished is the light;
O Palace whilom day that now art night,
Thou ought'st to fall *and I to die; since she*
Is gone who held us both in sovereignty. . . .
Palace illumined with the sun of bliss; . . .

O cause of *woe,* that cause has been of *bliss:* . . .
Farewell, thou *shrine of which the Saint is out!*

As for Troilus with Cresida, so for Vaudracour with Julia in *The Prelude* (A^2):

The house she dwelt in was a sainted shrine,
Her chamber-window did surpass in glory
The portals of the East, all paradise
Could by the simple opening of a door
Let itself in upon him: . . . overblest to move
Beneath a sun that wakes a weary world
To its dull round of ordinary cares.

Wordsworth uses Chaucer's metaphor again and with deeper significance in the first of the two reversals of the *Ode:*

Earth . . . did seem
Apparelled in celestial light,
But . . . there hath passed away a glory . . .
. . . the radiance which was once so bright
[Is] now for ever taken from my sight.
Shades of the prison-house begin to close. . . .
. . . *custom* lie[s] upon thee with a weight,
Heavy as frost . . .
The Youth . . . still is *Nature's Priest,*
And by the vision splendid
Is on his way attended;
At length the Man perceives it *die away,*
And fade into the light of common day.

Telling Pandarus *both his new sorrow and his joys of old,* Troilus had pointed out scenes of former bliss: 'Lo, yonder saw I . . . and yonder with joy-smitten heart . . . and once . . . I yonder saw . . . and yonder once . . . and in that very place . . . O blissful God of Love! . . . How thou hast wearied me on every side. . . . And here I dwell *an outcast from all joy.*' Then he sang 'a *fitting song* . . . *somewhat his woeful heart to make more light.*'

O Star, of which I lost have all the light,
With a sore heart well ought I to bewail,
That ever dark in torment, night by night,
Toward my death with wind I steer and sail.

Troilus' particular memories of former delight ('yonder . . . yonder . . . and yonder') suggested to the poet who was translating them a pattern of reminiscence for his future *Ode:* meadow, grove, stream, earth, every common sight, Rainbow, Rose, Moon, Waters, sunshine, the one tree, the single field, the Pansy which repeats the same tale of something that is gone. Troilus' *star* would become Wordsworth's *life's star* soon to grow dim for those *in darkness lost, the darkness of the grave;* but for Wordsworth as for Troilus a *timely utterance* would relieve this lonely *thought of grief.*

'Lo! yonder is my own bright Lady free; . . . and certainly this *wind* . . . is of my Lady's sighs *heavy* and sore; . . . it saith, Alas, why *severed* are we twain?' Thus ends the lament of Troilus. Chaucer had written, 'Why twinned be we tweyne.' In substituting the word *sever* Wordsworth recalled *Romeo and Juliet,* from which he quoted for *Vaudracour and Julia* 'the *severing* clouds.' When in his *Ode* he should write, 'Forbode not any *severing* of our loves,' he would scarcely forget the parting of Troilus and Cresida, of Romeo and Juliet, of Vaudracour and Julia, even of William and Annette. Behind his passionate demand in the *Ode* for 'habitual sway' as against transient and random 'delight' in nature lurk memories of human separation and the fading light of romantic love.

To be sure, shades of the prison house and reversals in fortune must be finally referred to their literary source in classical and Biblical tradition: the Myth of the Cave, the devices of pastoral lament, the imagery of the Psalms, and the diction of Virgil. Doubtless all had their influence upon the *Ode.* As we follow Wordsworth's study, however, noting his attention to the lost illusions of Phoebus and his translation of the debate between the truthteller and the love-worshipper, as we read in his own words of the personal disillusionment of Troilus, we can see clearly prefigured in its English origin the universal human disillusionment of the *Ode* which he would begin in March, 1802. The memories of the 'imperial palace' whence man comes to earth are as evanescent as the bliss Troilus once felt in the 'Palace of Cresida' now desolate. From him whom our poet later addressed as 'great Precursor, genuine morning Star,' [8] radiated the archetypal pattern of 'visionary gleam' and 'fond illusion' as we know them in his *Ode* and *Elegiac Stanzas;* and the shadow that creeps over the Poet of *The Prelude* had been earlier cast over Phoebus by his own intemperance and the unsympathetic tattling of his white crow.

'Bright Sunne of Glorie' and 'Triple-coloured Bow'

At the same time that he was translating the tales of Chaucer, Wordsworth studied the wedding songs and hymns of Spenser and memorized the pattern of error, conflict, and costly victory within the 'fierce warres and faithfull loves' of *The Faerie Queene.*[9] Spenser's very phrase, 'spousal verse,' had been adopted in the Prospectus of 1800 to celebrate the poetical task of Wordsworth's mature life: the 'spousal verse' of the 'great consummation' whereby 'the discerning intellect of Man' is 'wedded to this goodly universe in love and holy passion.' More particularly, the *Prothalamion* and *Epithalamion* furnished a large part of the diction, rhyme, properties, and images of the *Ode: Intimations of Immortality.*[10] Witness the 'sullen care' of Spenser's discontented poet, which reappears in Wordsworth's 'Oh evil day! if I were sullen.' And when the poet of the *Epithalamion* has advanced

[8] *Ecclesiastical Sonnets,* Part 2, no. 31, line 12. Wordsworth studied Chaucer's Works in volume 1 of Anderson's *British Poets,* on the title page of which appears a quotation from Denham's verses on the death of Cowley, where Chaucer is called 'morning star.'

[9] *Journals,* Vol. 1, pp. 80, 138, 166 for entries on November 16, 1801, and April 25 and July 1, 1802.

[10] Cf. Abbie F. Potts, 'The Spenserian and Miltonic Influence in Wordsworth's "Ode" and "Rainbow,"' *Studies in Philology* 29 (October, 1932), 607–16.

from 'doleful dreriment' and 'sorrowfull complaints' to the 'holy' day of 'wedlock' he must still anticipate a 'sunne . . . declining daily by degrees.' Spenser's declining sun is reflected upon the sober-colored clouds that gather about Wordsworth's 'setting sun.'

For his luminous Platonism in the *Ode* Wordsworth needed to look no further than to the four *Hymns* of Spenser. The earthly 'sunshine' and the 'celestial light,' 'the radiance which was once so bright' and 'the visionary gleam,' 'the fountain-light of all our day' and the 'master-light of all our seeing' show him contemplating the Platonic idea through the mind and eyes of an Elizabethan. The 'glory' of Spenser's 'infant Love' (*Love*) and the 'pure glory' of his Divine Child (*Heavenly Love*) shine from the Renaissance upon those early nineteenth-century 'clouds of glory' which we come trailing 'from God, who is our home.' And in the Spenserian *Hymn of Heavenly Love*, which traces the life of the Heavenly Child from cratch to cross, we may discover the outline for the adventures of Wordsworth's human child on his way from cradle to grave. Last but not least of the gifts of Spenser to the *Ode*, we must mention the graces of 'Cytherea' (*Beauty*) and the 'imperial' power of 'Sapience' (*Heavenly Beauty*); in their lineaments the young poet caught sight of his own 'homely Nurse' and the heavenly glories of that imperial palace which she was tempting him to forget.

The 'works' of the Spenserian 'great workmaster,' 'fashioned' from 'a goodly pattern' (*Beauty*) and the 'Ideas . . . which Plato admired' (*Heavenly Beauty*) give added meaning and value not only to Wordsworth's 'Earth' on a 'sweet May-morning' and the 'primal sympathy which having been must ever be.' In that MS W of *The Prelude* which Wordsworth would compose while he was finishing the *Ode*, in 1804, the ideal features of 'Cytherea' and 'Sapience' are to be seen emergent on the face of 'Nature.' Further, the ordeal of the Poet begins to resemble the ordeal of the hero in the *Hymn of Heavenly Love*. And the 'higher love' of MS W, later to be called 'intellectual love,' exhibits the traits of 'heavenly love.'

In Wordsworth's spots of time there is no definite theory of the Platonic *anagnorisis;* but the 'primitive hours,' and the 'conformity,' and the 'bond unknown to me' of MS W suggest him newly aware of 'form' in the Platonic sense. If the autobiographical poem were to traverse any important arc of individual life, it needed certain assumptions as to the whence and the whither. These were easily accessible in the doctrines and imagery of the Spenserian *Love* and *Beauty*.

On February 2, 1802, after a week of anxiety and weariness, William and Dorothy had read the eleventh book of *Paradise Lost*. 'We were much impressed,' says Dorothy, 'and also melted into tears.' Spenser's account of the sinful soul which should 'melt into teares, and grone in grieved thought' (*Heavenly Love*) has not been forgotten. But Milton's more profound study of regeneration and his promise of a new covenant must have been timely. To the doctrine of justice and joy the brother and sister would have listened with keenest attention:

> Anon drie ground appeers, and from his Arke
> The ancient Sire [Noah] descends with all his Train;
> Then with *up*lifted hands, and eyes devout,
> Grateful to Heav'n, over his head *beholds*
> A dewie Cloud, and in the Cloud a *Bow*
> Conspicuous with three listed colours gay,
> Betok'ning peace from God, and Cov'nant new.
> Whereat the *heart* of Adam erst so sad
> Greatly *rejoyc'd*, and thus his *joy* broke forth. . . .
> But say, what mean those colourd streaks in Heavn,
> Distended as the Brow of God appeas'd,
> Or serve they as a flourie verge to *binde*
> The fluid skirts of that same watrie Cloud,
> Least it again dissolve and showr the Earth?
> To whom th'Archangel. Dextrously thou aim'st:
> So willingly doth God remit his Ire, . . .
> Such grace shall one just Man find in his sight,
> That he relents, not to blot out mankind,

And makes a Covenant never to destroy
The Earth again by flood, nor let the Sea
Surpass his *bounds*, nor Rain to drown the World
With Man therein or Beast; but when he brings
Over the Earth a Cloud, will therein set
His triple-coloured *Bow*, whereon to look
And call to mind his Cov'nant: *Day and Night,*
Seed time and Harvest, Heat and hoary Frost
Shall hold their course, till fire purge all things new,
Both Heav'n and Earth, wherein the just shall dwell.

When Wordsworth saw his rainbow in the Vale of Grasmere he had every reason to remember Noah's 'bow conspicuous with three listed colours gay' foreseen by Adam on his specular mount. Nor could the author of *The Prelude* forget that the cost of a new covenant is a just life. Although William and Dorothy wept, in the rainbow which Adam, through Noah, recognized as a new covenant, the poet discovered a symbol for his own regenerate purposes. And on March 26 he reached a Miltonic conviction in his *Rainbow:*

My *heart* leaps up when I *behold*
    A rain*bow* in the sky:
So was it when my life began;
So is it now I am a man:
So be it when I shall grow old,
    Or let me die!
The Child is father of the Man;
And I could wish my *days to be*
Bound each to each by natural piety.

Thus the specular adventures of the original spouse, Adam, were added to Wordsworth's memory of the regretful spouse Phoebus and the miserable spouse Troilus, and to the patterns of idea, image, and melody which he had absorbed from Spenser's spousal verses. These would be fused to give resonance to the love story of the Poet and Nature and its wedding song, the *Ode*. But Wordsworth brings the celestial delight under a 'more habitual sway'; his 'natural piety' binds the actual days of all of us more operatively through earthly storm and sunshine than do the romantic and heroic fictions he had been studying in the poetry of his literary masters.

'Fierce Warres and Faithfull Loves'

Except as any poetic idea must be hidden in or peered at through words, *The Prelude* is no Spenserian 'dark conceit,' nor is it 'clowdily enwrapped'; its meaning stands as clear as the vernacular of its time can present it. Yet when Wordsworth read of Spenser's purpose 'to fashion a gentleman or noble person in vertuous and gentle discipline,' he would be encouraged to assume that the mind of a poet must likewise grow through an extensive and elaborate metaphorical discipline. Fashioning a gentleman and consummating a poet have somewhat in common; 'so much more profitable and gratious is doctrine by ensample than by rule,' says Spenser.

Challenged thus, *The Prelude* yields us many glimpses, explicit and implicit, of that other gracious world of 'fierce warres and faithfull loves.' Above all, in his story of the Poet's adventures abroad at the time of the French Revolution, a story begun very soon after he had finished the *Ode*, he would need a richly substantial metaphor. Words of MS Y, and now to be read in Book IX, 304–7, associate the Poet of Wordsworth with a Knight of the 'Chivalry of France,' who wandered through the events of political change

in perfect faith,
As through a Book, an old Romance or Tale
Of Fairy, or some dream of actions wrought
Behind the summer clouds.

The main reference here, of course, is to the knighthood of Spenser's *Faerie Queene*. After the wedding song and the new covenant, the spouse must undergo the vigils and ordeals of chivalry. William Wordsworth became, as it were, the squire of Michel Beaupuy.

Urging his poem on from the shepherds and pastoral scenes of Book VIII toward the patriots and revolutionary conflicts of Books IX and X, Wordsworth changed his 'oaten reeds' for 'trumpets sterne' as surely as did Spenser on his way from *Shepheardes Calender* to *Faerie Queene*. Moreover, of all poets Spenser was the best guide for an inexperienced writer entering the lists of the romance or epic, as Beaupuy had been the best comrade for the young patriot. Within Spenser's cantos there were variously and inexhaustibly arrayed for the service of Gloriana what Wordsworth needed for his amplifying service of Human Nature, 'fair forms' (IX, 206–10).

Spenser had been a constant mentor in the earlier passages of *The Prelude*. When Wordsworth sought 'time, place, and manners' for his 'glorious work,' he first considered some 'British theme, some old romantic tale by Milton left unsung';

> More often resting at some gentle place
> Within the groves of Chivalry, I pipe
> Among the Shepherds, with reposing Knights
> Sit by a Fountain-side, and hear their tales.

The chivalric sympathies between Spenser and Wordsworth had been strengthened at Cambridge:

> That gentle Bard,
> Chosen by the Muses for their Page of State,
> Sweet Spenser, moving through his clouded heaven
> With the moon's beauty and the moon's soft pace,
> I call'd him Brother, Englishman, and Friend.

Standing foot-bound 'beneath a frosty moon,' uplooking at the 'single Tree' of his college years, 'an Ash with sinuous trunk, boughs exquisitely wreath'd,' green with ivy, tipped, tasseled, and festooned with seeds, the younger 'Brother, Englishman, and Friend' defined their relationship as follows (VI, 102–109):

> The hemisphere
> Of magic fiction, verse of mine perhaps

May never tread; but scarcely Spenser's self
Could have more tranquil visions in his youth,
More bright appearances could scarcely see
Of human Forms with superhuman Powers,
Than I beheld, standing on winter nights
Alone, beneath this fairy work of earth.

As a tranquil visionary Wordsworth had not yet learned to watch the 'state arras' of artificial life, 'woven with silk and gold' in a 'wily interchange of snaky hues': a metaphor which, as de Selincourt notes, gains its 'lurking' colors from the 'goodly arras' of Busirane's Castle,

Woven with golde and silke so close and nere,
That the rich metall lurked privily, . . .
Like a discolourd Snake.[11]

Nevertheless he realized that the 'goings on' of the world itself were 'collaterally portray'd' in the 'mock fight,' the 'tournament of blows' to be observed in the college court and hall. He thought of college life somewhat as a 'pageant'—had Britomart not stood aside for Cupid's Masque and the 'jolly' company marching through the House of Busirane? In his heart, of course, the 'artless rustic' knew that St. John's was no 'mimic shew,' that it was 'a living part of a live whole'; but when he described the scholars of his Alma Mater he was enough of a literary courtier to make good use of such a catalogue of allegorical 'Degrees and Shapes' as Spenser's Masque of Cupid had possibly furnished also for the retinue of Dullness in Pope's *Dunciad* IV.

Finally, after 'Residence at Cambridge' had been written, and while the conflict between the imaginative faculty and its many foes was emerging in MS W as the central agony of *The Prelude*, we may be sure that Spenser's six Books of adventurous morality served his successor well. The 'vows' and 'bond' of MS W, its 'dedicated Spirit,' its Dwarf Man whose 'corpse slips from us into powder' when brought forth into 'the air of common sense,' are

[11] *Faerie Queene* III, xi, 28.

so many echoes from Spenser's profoundly ethical fairyland. More than that, a passage added to the episode of the man drowned in Esthwaite when it was carried over from MS V (1799) into MS W (1804) looks like a reminiscence of Spenserian aesthetic (V, 475–81):

> My inner eye had seen
> Such sights before, among the shining streams
> Of Fairy land, the Forests of Romance:
> Hence came a spirit hallowing what I saw
> With decoration and ideal grace;
> A dignity, a smoothness, like the works
> Of Grecian Art, and purest Poesy.

Although *The Prelude* is to be other than a pastoral romance, Wordsworth takes care not to disjoin the shepherds of his native mountains, the men who pleased him first, from the shepherds of the Arcadian and Shakespearean tradition, or 'such as Spenser fabled' in his *Shepheardes Calender*. In that MS Y, which extends the human scope of the poem to its liturgical utmost, there are still Virgilian and Horatian shepherds to link the quiet of nature with the sacraments of man. The lights and shadows of Wordsworth's theme, however, are heightened and deepened in MS Y; and throughout this manuscript there appears more than a hint of sacrificial devotion. The argument will be taken from the sequestered vales and sheltered coves to the uplands or plains on which affairs of knighthood are more significantly conducted.

Back then we shall go to the banks of the Loire 'or in wide Forests of the neighbourhood,' 'a solemn region' where, deep in conversation, Beaupuy and Wordsworth travel the realms of ethical and political theory, but where the poet's mind now and then slips from the patriot's argument to the adventures of Ariosto's Angelica and Tasso's Erminia and Spenser's Una—or Pastorella.

Is Beaupuy a Calidore, Knight of Courtesy, who 'hosies' with the humble Meliboe? It was Beaupuy, 'bent on works of love or freedom,' who (IX, 312–16)

to the mean and the obscure
And all the homely in their homely works
Transferr'd a *courtesy* which had no air
Of condescension, but did rather seem
A passion and a gallantry.

Pastorella, made captive by the Brigants,

Where day and night she nought did but lament
Her wretched life, shut up in deadly shade,
And waste her goodly beauty, which did fade
Like to a flowre, that feeles no heate of sunne,
Which may her feeble leaves with comfort glade. . . .
That who so heares her heavinesse, would rew
And pitty her sad plight, so chang'd from pleasaunt hew;

Pastorella, feigning 'a sodeine sickenesse' 'till Fortune would her captive bonds unbynde,' 'wan and weake,' 'decayd and mard,' left in charge of one who 'scarse yeeld[ed] her due food, or timely rest': [12] is she not the prototype of Wordsworth's 'hunger-bitten Girl,' at the sight of whom Beaupuy, Knight of Courtesy, called out in agitation (IX, 517–18): ''T is against *that* which we are fighting.'

The tragic tale of Vaudracour and Julia, too, following the sketch of the hunger-bitten Girl in Book IX, gains meaning when related to the episode of Bellamour and Claribell which follows the deliverance of Pastorella. Both stories concern an angry sire forbidding wedlock, and a child born of lovers attempting to circumvent parental tyranny.

Book VI of *The Faerie Queene* and Books IX and X of *The Prelude* thus share largely in the antityranny, antislavery purposes of Knights of Courtesy. Nor may we leave this point without indicating to those bent on the biographical interpretation of *Vaudracour and Julia* the analogy between Calidore-Coridon-Pastorella and Beaupuy-Wordsworth-Annette. When Spenser's 'three together went . . . to gather strawberies' and 'a Tigre

[12] *Ibid.* VI: x, 44; xi, 2 and *passim.*

forth out of the wood did rise,' and when Coridon 'fled away as fast, ne durst abide the daunger of the end,' readers of Spenser and Wordsworth are reminded of the latter's flight to England from Orleans and Paris, which he found 'defenceless as a wood where tigers roam.' Tigers in Paris? Rather, tigers in Book VI of *The Faerie Queene*, and a Wordsworth leaving his Annette to her compatriots as Coridon left Pastorella to Calidore 'comming to her ayde.' [13]

Except for dim reminiscence of Sir Guyon's Palmer in Wordsworth's 'grand and simple Reason,' 'Reason which indeed is reason,' and the disasters into which the Poet falls 'when reason . . . is . . . sequestered,' [14] as the Palmer was sequestered from Guyon during his jaunt over Phaedria's Idle Lake to the Cave of Mammon, the Book of Temperance seems less amply related to *The Prelude* than does the Book of Courtesy. Temperance was not Wordsworth's chief business. Yet when he recalls his fairer memories of France (X, 441–2)—'as the desart hath green spots, the sea small islands in the midst of stormy waves'—he may be thinking of himself as a Guyon in the 'desert wilderness' around Mammon's Cave or amid the 'surging waters' on his way past various 'enticing' islands to the Bower of Bliss. In *The Prelude* the 'rocky Island' on the sands of Leven, 'fragrance' from arbors on the shores past which the Poet must sail toward his 'business . . . upon the barren sea,' his errand 'to other coasts,' the 'weary labyrinth' of his moral despair, his 'man to come parted as by a gulph from him who had been' [15] are so many faintly audible marine echoes of Guyon's departure from the House of Alma in a 'well-rigged boat,' his perilous passage between the Gulf of Greedinesse and the Rocke of vile Reproch, the 'sweet and pleasant' temptations of 'the wandring Islands,' and the 'Labyrinth' of the 'Whirlepoole of decay.' The Poet of Wordsworth is an-

[13] *Ibid.* VI: x, 34, line 4; x, 35, lines 3–4; xi, 27–51.

[14] *Prelude* XI, 123–4; XIII, 264–5; X, 392–3.

[15] III, 496–503; X, 519; XI, 50, 55–6; X, 923; XI, 59–60.

other and later 'Childe' [16] of Old England's Land of Faery, subject to deceit, delay, defeat, and the many other antagonists whom a student of Spenser recognizes in every romance or epic since Spenser's time.

It is the enterprises of Spenser's Book of Justice rather than the characters of the Knights Arthur and Artegall which furnish the mythic design for Wordsworth's account of the French Revolution. The tyrant Robespierre is another Geryoneo, 'fell Tyrant' of 'tortious powre,' whose misdeeds in the country of Queen Belge were avenged by Arthur, 'the noble Briton Prince.' That Artegall might not share in this exploit but must return to his earlier task, 'to worke Irenaes franchisement,' reminds us of Wordsworth's hope to join the Brissotins, frustrated by his summons back to his native land. More than that, when the degenerate British statesmen of Wordsworth's day, who refused help to the young French Republic, are contrasted with the magnanimous Briton who slew Geryoneo and encountered the hideous monster lurking under the 'Idole' for which Belge's children and people had been a 'daily sacrifize,' they may well deserve the poet's scorn.

Now, says Spenser, Geryoneo was son of that Geryon slain by Alcides; says Wordsworth in *The Prelude*, 'the Herculean Commonwealth' had throttled the snakes about her cradle. The idolaters subsequently usurping the land of Belge become in *The Prelude* those who 'throned the human Understanding paramount and made of that their God.' And the 'loathly matter' gushing from the monster's womb when finally 'brust' by Arthur's sword

> Like to a great Mill dam forth fiercely gusht
> And powred out of her infernall sinke
> Most ugly filth, and poison therewith rusht:

this 'puddle of contagion' is in the verisimilitude of Wordsworth's

> reservoir of guilt
> And ignorance, fill'd up from age to age,

[16] *Faerie Queene* II, xi and xii *passim.*

> That could no longer hold its loathsome charge,
> But burst and spread in deluge through the Land.[17]

Following the Spenserian account of Arthur's defeat of Geryoneo, Artegall proceeds to the seacoast. And in comparable circumstances the news of Robespierre's death reaches Wordsworth while walking on the sands of Leven. Artegall is accompanied by the old Knight, Sir Sergis; Wordsworth stands by the grave of his schoolmaster, William Taylor.

No one coming to *The Prelude* from Spenser's Giant with the balances and his absurd efforts to reduce all things unto equality can overlook the modifications of this figure in Wordsworth's account of his own experience with justice. His 'scale of love,' his 'Nature' as a 'counterpoise,' his 'scale of Liberty' which grew light and 'mounted up' when Frenchmen changed a war of self-defence for one of conquest are all reminiscent of the sententious judgments of Artegall about scales. When the Giant 'strove extremities to way,' he erred as Wordsworth was to err when he stuck

> More firmly to old tenets, and to prove
> Their temper, strained them more. . . .
> Pleas'd with extremes, and not the least with that
> Which makes the human Reason's naked self
> The object of its fervour.

Like the Giant, Wordsworth, too, was mistakenly resolved to shake off 'the accidents of nature, time, and place'; he would accomplish his end

> by such means
> As did not lie in nature, sacrificed
> The exactness of a comprehensive mind
> To *scrupulous* [cf. scruple] and microscopic views
> That furnish'd out materials for a work
> Of false imagination, placed beyond
> The limits of experience and of truth.[18]

[17] X, 363–5, 318–20, 437–40.
[18] VIII, 867; XI, 31–2; X, 800–49.

This is only one of the hidden metaphors in the anticlimax of the poetic life; but it is an important one. Nature, like 'right,' sits 'in the middest of the beame alone.' [19]

The most fruitful suggestion from Spenser to Wordsworth in these matters of justice is the vision of Britomart at the Temple of Isis, who 'doth the moone portend.' The priests of the Temple 'with long locks comely kemd,' the Goddess herself with her 'long white sclender wand,' may partly account for the Wordsworthian 'bearded Teachers, with white wands uplifted,' seen in the Poet's reverie upon the Plain of Sarum at the end of Book XII. And from the vision itself, vouchsafed Britomart to motivate her deliverance of Artegall from Radigund, 'outragious flames' of the Altar of Isis burn again in the 'dismal flames' of 'the sacrificial Altar' of Wordsworth's reverie at Stonehenge. The relationship between Britomart delivering Artegall from Radigund and Dorothy delivering William from his mistaken surrender in France is also important: the Moon presides over the enterprise of Britomart; and the moonlit scene on Snowdon, betokening imaginative power, introduces the poet's acknowledgment of Dorothy's redemptive influence. The Wordsworthian Sarum and Snowdon, then, are both in the literary domain of the Spenserian Isis; and Dorothy is one of the cousins or daughters of Britomart.

Foremost in Wordsworth's affection, and the climax in our study of his Spenserian affiliations, is that Book of Holiness which he might reasonably have called the Book of Intellectual Love. As the loftiest of love stories of Knights and their Ladies, it had been often read, so he tells us in the Dedication to *The White Doe of Rylstone*, by the spouses William and Mary during their early 'years of wedded life.' Una, like Desdemona, was 'pre-eminently dear.' [20]

Reading of the spousal misadventures of the Redcrosse Knight

[19] *Faerie Queene* V, ii, 30–50 *passim*.

[20] *Personal Talk* 40–2. The Spenserian echoes in *The White Doe of Rylstone* have been noted in Alice Pattee Comparetti's edition of that poem, Cornell University Press, 1940.

and Una, would the recently espoused poet and his bride relive the situations in a romantic fiction very like their own solid fact? Would William compare the discipline and espousals of the Knight of Holiness with the discipline and consummation of a poet's mind? He, too, had been a Trevisan under the spell of the miscreant Despair,[21] to be rescued only by the exhortations of a faithful companion; and Dove Cottage had since then become a House of Holiness, in which the virginal Sara and Dorothy and the matronly Mary, like the Spenserian Fidelia and Speranza and fair Charissa, were 'well upbrought in goodly thewes, and godly exercise.' Indeed, the poet's home was another 'holy hospital' of Spenser's Mercie, as Dorothy's Journal amply illustrates. But it is in painful ascent to the 'sacred chappell' and 'little hermitage' of Contemplation that the Grasmere readers of the Book of Holiness would have discovered their fairest analogy, and we must not neglect to add the Orchard Seat above Dove Cottage to Spenser's 'highest Mount' and those hills rising behind and beyond it. For the poet and his spouse and their sisters, Goldsmith's Alpine peak, Young's Christian hills of the spirit, Bunyan's Delectable Mountains, and Milton's specular mount would be no more significant scenes for dedication, discipline, suffering, and contemplative joy than these mountain ranges nearby.

In the Prologue to *Peter Bell* Wordsworth had renounced the dragon's wing and the magic ring; there are none such in *The Prelude.* Yet the old Dragon was not a denizen of the realms of the *Faerie Queene* alone, and the revolutionary books of the later poem with their 'ephemeral monsters' of massacre, and their 'impious crests' of tyranny, and their 'Giants' of impiety suggest that the imagery of Spenser's 'fierce warres' still resided in the poet's mind as he wrote of his journey 'towards the fierce Metropolis' or recounted the 'bitter truths' of British unwisdom. 'Goaded land,' 'domestic carnage,' 'ghastly visions . . . of despair and tyranny,' and 'rivers of blood' are to be found in *The Prelude* as well as in the Book of Holiness. Many are the grim collaterals of unholi-

[21] *Faerie Queene* I, ix, 28, line 5.

ness which test the nerve of St. George, and the faith of Wordsworth's Poet, whose life and mind are to be rigorously disciplined ere they be consummated. Moreover, since the Poet's own 'errors' are his 'theme,' that saddest of personal mistakes, entanglement with another than the one woman, must be wrought into appropriate form, hidden within the tale of Vaudracour and Julia. Those crises arising in 'the Country of Romance' when 'the prime Enchanter'—Archimage as Reason?—means mischief, must be surmounted. What was to the Redcrosse Knight water of the well of life and balm from the tree of life, came to Wordsworth's Poet from the 'belovèd Woman' whose 'voice . . . like a brook' crossing a lonely road and whose 'charm of sweetness' in 'a kind of gentler spring' served him as equally valuable refreshment.

Despite the betrothals and the banns and the spousals, as William and Mary of Dove Cottage must have realized when they held the Book of Holiness on their knees; despite the 'song of love and jollity,' the 'great joy' and the 'solemne feast' and the 'deare delights,' the Redcrosse Knight must leave his Una and return to the Court of the Faerie Queene. Well, this other dedicated servant of the better life, Wordsworth, must also take up his patriotic and civic duties. 'Old idolatry' and 'servitude,' however, call upon the joint laborers Coleridge and Wordsworth and their successors for a subtler mode of attack than do giants and dragons. 'Redemption' or 'deliverance'—the final paragraph of *The Prelude* plays tentatively with both words—calls for teachers. Spenser would agree:

> The Patron of true Holinesse
> Foule Errour doth defeate.

XII

Patriot

The poet's advance from chivalric jousting and romantic love to heroic conflict and civic loyalty must next concern us. Studying Wordsworth's Poet as patriot, we look for no scheme of black enemy and white hero but rather for those tensions in the soul of man which constantly imperil or save the commonwealth, the fatherland, to which he devotes the main strength of his manhood. Although in MS V of *The Prelude* he had spoken once of feelings analogous 'to patriotic and domestic love,' the word 'patriot' denoting a man in relation to his fatherland did not come into Wordsworth's poetry until he was at work on Book IX of MSS AB. Yet this loftier connotation had been prepared by his study of Milton in 1800, when as a householder he used the epithet 'paternal' of 'home' and 'vale,' and for *The Recluse*, MS B, universalized the relation of father and children in terms recalling *Paradise Lost:*

Society is here
The true community, the noblest frame
Of many into one incorporate.
That [1] must be looked for here: paternal sway,

[1] Wordsworth's italics. 'Temple,' 'recess,' 'cave,' 'society . . . brute . . . human,' are Miltonic echoes (*Paradise Lost* I, 713; II, 254 and XI, 303–4; VI, 4–5; VIII, 383, 391–2). Cf. also Milton's 'One Kingdom, Joy and Union without end' (VII, 161) and 'Our happie state under one Head' (V, 827).

One household, under God, for high and low,
One family, and one mansion; to themselves
Appropriate, and divided from the world
As if it were a cave, a multitude
Human and brute, possessors undisturbed
Of this Recess, their legislative Hall,
Their Temple, and their glorious Dwelling-place.

The problems and errors of such a 'family' he detailed for us during the same year in two short pastorals, *Michael* and *The Farmer of Tilsbury Vale.*

By 1802, thanks partly to his reading of Milton's sonnets in May, the idea of paternal sway received fresh and powerful illustration in the sonnets which introduce the series of poems 'Dedicated to National Independence and Liberty.' The doctrine of Milton had thus helped Wordsworth into a responsible and profoundly thoughtful patriotism. Feeling for his country 'as a lover or a child,' he had been led to consider anew the nature of loyalty, and the poet's part in civic life. 'Sidney, Marvel, Harrington, young Vane'—Milton's friends—and Milton himself, supremely, would teach him 'how genuine glory was put on.' The tongue of Shakespeare, the faith and morals of Milton, investing with nobility all who speak the one and hold the other, would now be his charge; like their true son he in his time would 'pen' and 'utter' wisdom. Meanwhile, contemporary events strongly prompted him to investigate national danger from without and national corruption within. He must more searchingly distinguish between 'a seemly reverence . . . to power' and the feebleness of 'Heads to slavery prone,' between 'true Sway' or 'true Power' and tyranny. To Milton of the starlike soul he cried out for 'inward happiness.' This, then, was the criterion by which in his own mind and writing he would test what to the outer eye might appear disloyal rebellion or servile conformity in national life.

At some time before 1804 his poem of 'boyish pleasures,' MS V of *The Prelude*, shelved since 1800, received an addition describing the exile of the Poet from his patrimonial fields into the dangerous world of the collegian, what is now Book III of *The Prelude*. When, in this and subsequent passages looking toward a story of impairment and rebellion, he would send the hero—himself—to Cambridge, to London, to France, again he must avail himself of the matter, design, and phrase of Milton's epics. Already, for his revision of *Peter Bell*, for his *Ode*, for *The Leech-Gatherer*, and for *The Pedlar*, whose chief agent was rehearsing Miltonic arguments later to be used in 'Despondency' and 'Despondency Corrected' of *The Excursion*, he had been at work on *Paradise Lost*, Books I and XI.[2] How should he in his time portray evil? The title of Books XI and XII of MSS AB of *The Prelude*, 1805–6, 'Imagination, How Impaired and Restored,' is even more obvious an echo of 'Paradise Lost and Regained'; we are, therefore, impelled to set these two actions also side by side. Until Wordsworth should have confronted Milton, matched his project for a philosophical poem with Milton's epics, grasped their design and tested their doctrine, he would be ill provided to edify a 'fit audience' of his own. When with him we reread the *a priori* reasoning, splendid fictions, and magniloquent language of seventeenth-century theology as these were intensified by Milton's genius, we better understand Wordsworth's tentative nonconformity and the reason why *The Recluse*, begun in Grasmere only to fail in that same 'Paradise,' was set aside for its 'prelusive song.' Chiefly, we are moved to sympathize with a young writer describing himself in 1800 as 'Fellow-citizen,' 'Outlaw,' and 'Borderer of his age.' [3]

Restless in a static poesy, tempted out of his reclusive paradise into autobiographical operations of freer scope, Wordsworth must, as Milton did, deal with his own experience of ill-doing and ill done; but in his generation he would interpret evil as a fall not from celestial comity but from imaginative integrity. While he reconsidered the unfilial Lucifer and the credulous and servile

[2] *Journals*, Vol. 1, pp. 103 and 106, for January 29 and February 2, 1802.
[3] *Poetical Works*, Vol. 5, p. 6.

Adam as symbols of poor citizenship and outlawry, he learned that Milton's theology would not serve him as a frame of reference. What poetic treasons might he substitute? How had the eighteenth-century mind, his own, deviated from the ways of poetic health? How could the nineteenth-century mind, also his own, better maintain or successfully restore its proper loyalties? His answers would not be asserted as a doctrine but represented as an action.

Above all he would need new 'machinery.' Observing afresh the universal principles of creation and restoration that validate Milton's myth, especially in Books VII and VIII of *Paradise Lost* and in *Paradise Regained*, he would come upon the Messiah as 'the Omnific Word,' the Poet-extraordinary of English literature. In such operations as His resides, he might well observe, the beauty of scholarship and poetry not less than the truth of theology and the goodness of religion. Jesus' will power and wisdom, the confidence of Milton's 'one greater Man' in ultimate values, made a Poet somewhat like Jesus the fitting agent for Wordsworth's new kind of action.

Finally, we may well discuss the epic traits in *The Prelude* as deriving from and also deviating from the greatest English epic poem; here we shall be at the threshold of that modern idea of exalted narrative which houses Wordsworth with Milton in the home of the spirit, yet invites him over the sill with Byron and later autobiographers into the utmost adventures and revelations of personal experience. Whether he glances backward or forward, however, to furious warfare in heaven or on earth, to costly errors arising from rebellious pride, or equally costly errors arising from an impaired imagination, his conflicts and wanderings are to be represented as the conflicts and wanderings of a man—not of angels and demons, still less of superhuman, subhuman, or ahuman monsters.

Old Adam, and Michael and Luke

About the time when, at Sockburn, Wordsworth's interest had been aroused in the agricultural and domestic activities of his friends, the Hutchinsons, and when, partly for that reason, his metaphors had changed from Nature as a beloved to Nature as a mate and parent, from the Poet as lover to the Poet as husbandman, he wrote an ironical little poem which we may call his 'Paradise Lost,' told by a man speaking to men. *The Farmer of Tilsbury Vale* with its Miltonic action and its Miltonic agent he begins very simply, in anything but a Miltonic vein, as a song 'of old Adam, the pride of old men.' [4]

Reducing the Miltonic story of humankind to the life span of one erring farmer, self-exiled from his native vale to London and what might have been the life of 'a Devil in H—l' (1800), Wordsworth illustrates vividly his power to transform a literary text for his own purposes. During exile, the Adam of Wordsworth, like the Miltonic Adam, still bore on his cheek the unfaded rose set there by the sunshine of morn, 'mid the dews, 'mid the joy of the fields. In Tilsbury Vale had been fashioned the countenance since stained. Set in that 'sweet valley' to dress and keep it, he was as generous as the fields he mastered, but he was indolent—notice the substitution of indolence for disobedience as the human flaw. For thirty years the poor lived upon him, until they had exhausted his means and driven him into debt; then, mismanaging both debts and creditors, he must leave the Vale secretly on borrowed pelf—again notice the simplification of the theme of guilt as debt, introductory in Milton's thought to the act of redemption.

In the big city the exile from Tilsbury Vale plied the various trades by which the laboring soul humbly earns bread in the sweat of the brow: stableboy, errandboy, porter, and groom.

[4] In 1800 this line read 'There's an old man in London, the *prime* of old men'; the phrase recalls Raphael's address to Adam in line 563 of Book V of *Paradise Lost*, 'O prime of men.'

There, like a stranger 'whose own country's far over the sea,' in fancy he re-enacts his earlier and happier life as a farmer;

> And Nature, while through the great city he hies,
> Full ten times a day takes his heart by surprise.

In proud Covent Garden he stops short, looks long, and smiles 'where the apples are heap'd on the barrows in piles'—he has seen better; up the Haymarket he smells 'to the hay'; repairing to Smithfield he 'inhales the breath of the cows'; 'and his heart all the while is in Tilsbury Vale.' Happy Eden, Adam, Devil, apple, false mate—in Wordsworth's poem Eve has become the devouring 'poor'—mistaken motive, creditors, exile, homesickness, labor, redemption: these themes of Milton's epic poem are present in the situations of Wordsworth's tale.

With one notable exception: Nature has taken the place of archangels and redeemer. The assumed rigor of God and His angels has made way for the assumed kindness of Nature. The torments of hell and the agony of redemption are modified into the ordeals of spiritual life.

While in this manner he was scaling down and into simpler outlines the Miltonic design for the fall of man, he transformed, to make humanly valid, that other and prior action of *Paradise Lost*, the conflict between obedient and disobedient angel. In his affecting story of Michael and Luke (query: Lucifer?) there is a dim analogue of the archangelic myth. Although *Michael* bears little external resemblance to the early books of Milton's epic poem, its concern with the love of father for son and the breaking of the covenant between them indicates that in 1800 Wordsworth was prepossessed by Milton's ethical ideas. The filial duty of preserving ancestral fields when a bond is forfeit, the common effort toward a common end interrupted by the slackening loyalty of the son in the dissolute city, his evil courses, his exile, and the unfinished common task: all these figments of Wordsworth's imagination in this, the most resonant of his pastorals, run true to the Miltonic story of the First Father and His Disloyal Son; the action into which these details are organized is another and simpler form of the angelic revolt.

But the building of a Pandemonium and the elaboration of a Hell are for Wordsworth uncongenial matters. Instead of amplifying the defection of his Luke, he sets forth the obedience and fortitude of his Michael, who struggles on alone 'to build the Fold of which the flock has need,' and loves his errant son 'to the last.' The great war against evil which Milton's Michael could not quite win, Wordsworth's Michael cannot quite lose. The operation of love is not less authentic than the operation of justice.

The Cottage which was named the EVENING STAR
Is gone—the ploughshare has been through the ground
On which it stood; great changes have been wrought
In all the neighbourhood; yet the oak is left
That grew beside their door; and the remains
Of the unfinished Sheep-fold may be seen
Beside the boisterous brook of Greenhead Ghyll.

In this homely way paradise was lost according to William Wordsworth in 1800. All the grandeur and the mystifying thought, the elaborate oratory and the sonorous music with which Milton endowed his version have been consciously disregarded. The redemptive action on earth must begin at an 'unfinished Sheep-fold.'

'Fellow-Citizen, . . . Outlaw, and . . . Borderer'

Just at the turn of the century, then, Wordsworth was studying not only the action but the doctrine and art of Milton's epics; he would re-examine the Miltonic Paradise that he might better conceive his own. While *The Prelude* and *The Recluse* were in the making it was important, also, that Wordsworth's Poet, hero of both, should inherit from the agents of *Paradise Lost* and *Paradise Regained* whatever dynamic and theoretic endowment was proper for this new literary task of redemption through intellectual love.

It is not surprising, therefore, that in MS 1 of his poet's Prospectus (the final passage of 'Home at Grasmere' in *The Recluse* of 1800) he spoke of himself in a triple role, 'in part a Fellow-citizen, in part an Outlaw, and a Borderer of his age.' He would make a study of the Poet as if he were an Adam caught between a Raphael and a Satan, or between the Raphaelic and Satanic potencies and tendencies of the universe. In so doing he would return, of course wiser and more assured, to the theme of his drama, *The Borderers.* Thinking of himself as a Borderer of 1800, possibly as another Marmaduke under villainous temptation, he must now more successfully than hitherto in 1795–6 mediate between the prerogatives of cultural sovereignty and revolt. This he was already doing in the domain of literary style—'Poetry sheds no tears "such as Angels weep," ' quoted in his Preface from *Paradise Lost* I, 620. Was he also committed to challenge the substance and doctrine of Milton?

One clear repudiation of Milton's fictions in dealing with universal life can be read in MS 1 of the Prospectus, where Milton's Paradise is far surpassed by Wordsworth's green earth, and the Miltonic 'darkest pit of the profoundest Hell, night, chaos, death' are less fearful and awesome than the Poet's own soul, 'the soul of Man.' Written in a notebook similar to those used for drafts of *The Prelude*,[5] this manuscript seems to emphasize the near-Satanic traits of the Poet: he is subject 'to Conscience only'; he passes 'unalarmed' by

> Jehovah—with his thunder, and the choir
> Of shouting Angels, and the empyreal thrones,

and he insists on the 'inviolate retirement' of the 'individual Mind.' The 'history' or 'dream' of a Paradise he sets aside for the 'growth of common day,' a phrase in tune with the Prologue of *Peter Bell;* his words will 'speak of nothing more than what we are.' And it is the 'human Soul of the wide earth,' no archangelic spirit, whom he invites into its metropolitan temple in the hearts of mighty

[5] *Poetical Works,* Vol. 5, p. 372.

poets. This is to deflate Milton a little, if not to out-satan Satan.[6]

Already MS 1 has appropriated Milton's phrases 'numerous verse,' 'fit audience . . . though few,' and the address to Urania; but Milton's celestial and infernal topography has been renounced for the terrestrial scene, and angelic and diabolic attitudes abandoned for the fellowships and passions of men. Most impressive is Wordsworth's disavowal of Milton's dictatorial God and the principle of archangelic intermediation. In ill sights of ravenous passions, insult, injury, wrong, strife, solitary anguish, or the fierce confederate storm of sorrow, the Poet will himself try to find the meaning these would have for God, and hence he will not be heartless or forlorn. And when finally he offers a prayer, he prays not by way of archangel or even only-begotten Son, but directly: 'O great God, to less than thee I cannot make this prayer.' Thus he comes into his own religious sonship and literary majority, grateful for Milton and Milton's poetry, but not oppressed by Milton's God.

Initial lines in MS B of 'Home at Grasmere' [7] describe the visit of the schoolboy Wordsworth to the 'steep hill' and the 'aerial . . . Station' above the 'paradise' of the beloved vale which later he was to inhabit. Like Satan to that other 'Station bright' he came alone and devious; but Wordsworth's compassion has metamorphosed into a genial and hopeful experience the evil approach of Milton's fallen archangel

> to th' ascent of that steep savage Hill. . . .
> Beneath him with new wonder now he views
> To all delight of human sense expos'd
> In narrow room Natures whole wealth, yea more,
> A Heaven on Earth.[8]

[6] The evidence for emulative study of *Paradise Lost* is clearer in MS 1 than in MS 2 (*Poetical Works*, Vol. 5, pp. 3–6), where Akenside's theme and images have helped to modernize the Wordsworth Prospectus (see within, pp. 268–9).

[7] Revised to constitute lines 1–151 of MS D, now printed in *Poetical Works*, Vol. 5, pp. 313–18.

[8] *Paradise Lost* IV, 172, 205–8.

That Wordsworth consciously reconceived the archangelic enterprise, we may be sure; in MS B of 'Home at Grasmere' he is not 'unmindful . . . of Angels and winged Creatures that are Lords without restraint of all which they behold.'

Furthermore, when finally he came to dwell where earlier he had paused to look, he reconceived also Milton's Adam and Eve, prime man and woman, as the Poet and his 'Emma.' In MS B they are not yet explicitly represented as brother and sister; but he will be at some pains to avoid the conjugal pattern within which Milton's theology had been awkwardly confined, while for his own purpose maintaining the spiritual values of close human association. The companionship of the Poet and 'Emma,' like that of their first parents yet unfallen, is represented not less winsomely:

> Where'er my footsteps turned,
> Her Voice was like a hidden Bird that sang,
> The thought of her was like a flash of light,
> Or an *unseen* [9] companionship, a breath,
> Or fragrance independent of the wind. . . .
> —What Being, therefore, since the birth of Man
> Had ever more abundant cause to speak
> Thanks . . . and in Song resound his joy.
> The boon is absolute; . . . among the bowers
> Of blissful Eden this was neither given,
> Nor could be given, possession of the good
> Which had been sighed for, ancient thought fulfilled
> And dear Imaginations realized
> Up to their highest measure, yea and more.

Along with its Miltonic reminiscence this sounds somewhat like a hymn of gratitude for the fall of man; yet Milton himself had justified an assumption that the first great human nonconformity might be made into a good thing, when he permitted Raphael to speak to Adam of the 'Paradise within thee, happier farr,' and to cheer him 'with meditation on the happie end.' [10]

[9] Italics by Wordsworth.
[10] *Paradise Lost* XII, 587, 605.

In this same MS B there are, however, two tales of Husband and Wife, later transferred to Book VI of *The Excursion*, which do reconstitute the Adam and Eve theme in Wordsworth's Grasmere paradise: first, the story of the 'easy-minded' 'Master of a little plot of ground' and his speciously industrious Housewife, with the 'decay' of their 'worldly substance' and the Husband's resort to 'thoughts of troubled pleasure' and infidelity; second, the compensatory tale of 'conjugal fidelity' wherein a Widower and his six motherless Daughters dress their 'little Spot' with jasmine and rose to illustrate the continuing 'partnership' of Husband and dead Wife despite their separation. 'Unhappy Man!' the former; 'delightful family,' the latter. The Poet and his 'Emma' thus do not stand 'in a solitary world,' although they approach it as did the prime man and woman who 'through Eden took their solitarie way.' [11] Indeed, when he considers the wealth of folk, animals, and flowers in the Vale, Wordsworth is even more emphatic: 'solitude is not where these things are.'

Again, the account of the Poet and 'Emma' passing through 'bursts of sunshine' and 'flying showers' *to* Grasmere, opposed as it were by 'the stern . . . face of Nature,' is the Wordsworthian analogue of the Miltonic expulsion of Adam and Eve *from* Paradise. How similar and how different these two journeys are! For the brother and sister

> All things were mov'd, they round us as we went,
> We in the midst of them. And when the trance
> Came to us, . . .
> The intimation of the milder day
> Which is to be (come), the fairer world than this,
> And rais'd us up, dejected as we were,
> . . . the awful trance
> The vision of humanity, and of God
> The Mourner, God the Sufferer, when the heart
> Of his poor Creatures suffers wrongfully—
> Both in the sadness and the joy we found

[11] Last line of *Paradise Lost.*

A promise and an earnest that we twain,
A pair receding from the common world,
Might in that hallow'd spot . . .
. . . in that individual nook
Might, even thus early, for ourselves secure,
And in the midst of these unhappy times,
A portion of the blessedness which *love*
And knowledge, will, we trust, hereafter give
To all the vales of Earth and all mankind.[12]

Other details of the journey of the Poet and 'Emma' to Grasmere by very contrast recall the less-favored travels of Adam and Eve from their ready-made Paradise to the 'paradise within.' In Grasmere there shall be no

dearth of aught
That keeps in health the insatiable mind;
. . . we shall have *for knowledge and for love*
Abundance. . . .
Possessions have I that are solely mine,
Something within which yet is shared by none, . . .
I would impart it, I would spread it wide,
Immortal in the world which is to come. . . .
And would not wholly perish even in this, . . .
Love, Knowledge, all my manifold delights
All buried with me without monument
Or profit unto any but ourselves.
It must not be; if I, divinely taught,
Be privileged to speak as I have felt
Of what in man is human or divine.

Like other rebellious readers of Milton, Wordsworth longs to restore knowledge to its more honorable place beside love.

Even knowledge of evil does not deter him. To Grasmere he came 'not dreaming of unruffled life, untainted manners'; he did

[12] MSS AB of *The Recluse, Poetical Works,* Vol. 5, pp. 313–39 *passim,* especially 318–20.

not shrink 'from the evil with disgust or with immoderate pain'; he expected selfishness, and envy, and revenge, ill neighbourhood, flattery and double-dealing, strife and wrong; but he would be 'confident,' not 'depressed':

> Truth justifies herself, and as she dwells
> With Hope, who would not follow where she leads?

Throughout MS B he consistently mollifies even if he does not disavow Miltonic rigor: for instance, he transforms into 'a human voice' of Shepherd summoning mountain sheep that 'awful voice' of Grasmere Vale, which reminds the student of the fallen Lucifer, calling 'so loud, that all the hollow Deep of Hell resounded.' [13] Above Grasmere Lake, moreover, fly birds 'scarcely . . . inferior to angelical.'

Although we recognize a kind of ethical, if not theological, independence in the following pronouncement of Wordsworth's Poet, with its echoes of Satanic peril—

> 'T is not to enjoy that we exist,
> For that end only; something must be done. . . .
> Of ill-advised Ambition and of Pride
> I would stand clear, but yet to me I feel
> That an internal brightness is vouchsafed
> That must not die, that must not pass away;

and although Nature and Man will displace God and the Angels as 'machinery' in Wordsworth's philosophical poem of the man and woman whose paradise is within, and its prelusive song of a greater man who brings redemption through poetry, neither *Recluse* nor *Prelude* contravenes the idea of divine justice. Witness the following manuscript reading:

> Nature to this favourite spot of ours
> Yields no exemption but her awful rights
> Enforces to the utmost, and exacts
> Her tribute of inevitable pain,

[13] *Paradise Lost* I, 314–15.

with 'the sting . . . added' that 'man himself' is 'for ever busy to afflict himself.' [14]

In 1800 Wordsworth does not deal with the problem of theoretical evil; but he transforms Miltonic disobedience into a natural trait. As an 'innocent Little-one,' he tells us, he 'loved to stand and read' the forbidding looks of deep pools, tall trees, black chasms, and dizzy crags, 'read and disobey, sometimes in act, and evermore in thought. . . . But me hath Nature tamed.' To such lowest terms has the archangelic episode been reduced.

We are now in a position to ask what became of the initial 190 lines removed from a prior version of 'Home at Grasmere,' MS A, and now lost. Might they have been revised to serve as a Preamble to MS V of *The Prelude?* and thus to Book I of that poem?

Echoes from Satan's rebel slogan in the first Book of *Paradise Lost* ('We shall be free') resound in the corroborative assertion of Milton's God about Adam and Eve at the beginning of the third Book:

> I formed them free, and free they must remain,
> Till they enthrall themselves.

Such can be heard also from the beginning of the decapitated portion of Wordsworth's *Recluse,* MS A,[15] where he says of the Poet and 'Emma':

> We will be free and as we mean to live
> In culture of divinity and truth
> Will chuse the noblest Temple that we know.

Where can this fabric of freedom and consecration be better matched than in the so-called Preamble of *The Prelude* with its sequent lines (1–271)? The fragments thus assumed torn asunder

[14] *Poetical Works,* Vol. 5, p. 334.

[15] Miss Darbishire kindly looked up MS A of *The Recluse* at Dove Cottage. She reports that it 'begins at the top of the page *in medias res* on one large folio sheet folded in four. There must have been a similar sheet or half-sheet on which the first 190 lines of this draft were written, now lost, probably by accident.' She and I agree that this neither supports nor gainsays my conjecture.

early in 1800 appear to be all of a piece, and the piece is Miltonic in its associations.

The two agents of 'Home at Grasmere,' however, the Poet and 'Emma,' have become one agent in the Preamble of *The Prelude;* the weather is different; and the Poet is now alone, but still a 'captive . . . set free.' John Milton had said of Adam and Eve:

> The World was all before them, where to choose
> Thir place of rest, and Providence thir guide:
> They hand in hand with wandring steps and slow,
> Through Eden took thir solitarie way.

The lost Preamble of MS A of 'Home at Grasmere' may have read:

> The earth is all before *us:* . . .
> . . . and should the guide *we* chuse
> Be nothing better than a *wandering* cloud,
> *We* cannot miss *our* way.

Change the presumptive *us, we, we, our* to *me, I, I, my*, and you have lines 17–19 of Book I of *The Prelude.* William Wordsworth will continue where John Milton leaves off; he lends his poetic genius to the rehabilitation of the homeless wanderer.

Like the Poet and 'Emma' of 'Home at Grasmere,' the Poet of *The Prelude* is looking for a 'dwelling,' a 'harbour' in a 'Vale.' 'Enough that [he] is free,' has 'the hope of active days'; he will be 'cloth'd in priestly robe' for his 'holy services' in the 'one sweet Vale'; to it he has journeyed amid 'Aeolian visitations,' a 'banded host of harmony'; he has been enjoying a 'sabbath' on his way to his 'hermitage.' And what ensues? He, too, braces himself for the culture of divinity and truth: 'some philosophic Song of Truth,' 'immortal verse.'

If my suggestion that this was originally the utterance of a Preamble for the Paradise in Grasmere (MS A) be credible, then we have further evidence as to the location of the 'hermitage' in *The Prelude* (I, 115) and the duration of the 'pleasant loitering journey' (I, 114). The Preamble which was a few sketchy phrases in MS JJ and may have been poured out originally in Goslar, would be vested in its next and authentic literary form to celebrate the trip to Grasmere in the fall of 1799.

Why might it be detached from 'Home at Grasmere'? Conceivably to make way for the account (in MS B of *The Recluse*) of a prior, a kind of archangelic, visit of the schoolboy to Paradise to precede the arrival of the Man and Woman. How much later might it have been transferred to *The Prelude* and revised to include stirrings of restlessness and discouragement? Possibly at the very moment when the 'recreant' and interdicted, the 'listless' and perplexed inhabitant of a sterile and tedious heaven decided to shift his energies to an autobiographical poem in which Paradise must be risked before it can be really won.

What lies between the escape of Wordsworth's Poet in the Preamble and the Apocalypse dimly foreseen as he ended *The Prelude?* What, indeed, he seems to say, but the life of a teacher, one who teaches others how to love, 'instruct[s] them how the mind of man becomes a thousand times more beautiful than the earth on which he dwells'—again Milton's 'paradise within.'

This emphasis on teachers recalls what Milton's Michael says of the apostolic mission:

> Thir Ministry perform'd, and *race well run,*
> Thir doctrine and thir story written left,
> They die; but in thir room, as they forewarne,
> Wolves shall succeed for teachers.

One such teacher Wordsworth recognizes in Coleridge:

> Oh! yet a few short years of useful life,
> And all will be complete, *thy race be run,*
> Thy monument of glory will be raised.
> Then, though, too weak to tread the ways of truth,
> This Age fall back to old idolatry . . .

Under the words 'idolatry,' 'servitude,' 'ignominy and shame' the final passage of *The Prelude* sums up Milton's lines 508–39 of Book XII, lines which explicitly describe the effects of bad teaching and the dissolution of Satan's perverted world, lines which strike home in our day of threatening human disaster. Michael's terrible object lesson and stern lecture in the last two books of *Paradise Lost* find a strong ally in Wordsworth's patient record of process: the discipline and consummation of the mind of one teacher, the Poet.

'Atheist Crew'

Not until he started the composition of Book IX of *The Prelude* did Wordsworth set the scene for a conflict with evil such as Milton entered upon in Book I of *Paradise Lost;* nor do we meet the Miltonic 'atheist crew' until Robespierre is represented as wielding 'the sceptre of the atheist crew' of *The Prelude.*[16] Hitherto Wordsworth's argument has avoided any frank statement of inherent evil; as yet he has been another prime Adam

> train'd up in paradise
> Among sweet garlands and delightful sounds,
> Accustom'd in my loneliness to walk
> With Nature magisterially.[17]

Nevertheless there are in Wordsworth's Book III several presentiments of the loss of paradise: 'the truant eyes unruly, [peeping] about for vagrant fruit'; and the rueful descent into a populous plain after those awful 'incumbencies,' 'visitings of the Upholder of the tranquil Soul.' Intimations of 'the one Presence, and the Life of the great whole' as interpreted by the magister, Nature, will avail as little to prevent disaster as did the argument of the magisterial archangel who walked with the prelapsarian Adam.

Although in Book IV the fiction of the Vale of Esthwaite as paradise and the home of 'consummate happiness' is maintained, and although the soul walks 'naked as in the presence of her God' —a point also insisted on in Milton's Book IV—and although the youth of the 'little Vale' has loved 'even as a blessed Spirit or

[16] *Paradise Lost* VI, 370; *Prelude* X, 458.
[17] III, 377–80.

Angel, if he were to dwell on earth,' there is now manifest in him a 'human-heartedness' along with 'thoughts of change, congratulation, and regret.' And in MS W, from which parts of Books IV and V derive, Wordsworth emulates the disquiet and gloom of Milton's Book V. Thus, he darkens the background for that 'magnificent . . . morning' near Hawkshead, which has associations with the Miltonic Morning Hymn loved so dearly by Wordsworth and Dorothy,[18] and itself heart-breakingly shadowed by evil. Moreover, the Wordsworth dream of Arab apprehensively fleeing from the deluge with his stone and his shell (now in Book V, but not previously in MS W) is a simpler, pleasanter literary device than Eve's 'uncouth dream' in *Paradise Lost* V. The main contribution of Milton to MS W, finally, is the *character* of the Dwarf Man, the 'prodigy' of learning who knows everything as if corrupted by Satan Himself, but has forgotten the 'playthings' of old 'Grandame Earth.' He has been 'tam'd to . . . [the] bidding' of those 'mighty workmen of our later age'

> Who with a broad highway have overbridged
> The froward Chaos of futurity.

This undeniable reference to the bridge-building of Milton's Sin and Death [19] suggests to us that the 'wondrous Pontifice' 'at the brink of Chaos' in *Paradise Lost* has challenged Wordsworth to emphasize a new kind of monstrous doing. The immoral work described in the earlier epic will now appear as pedagogical error. Sin and Death are newly conceived as the 'hollow . . . life of lies' which ends 'in lies,' a 'fresh and shewy . . . Corpse.' So much for bad teaching: 'Vanity' its 'soul,' and 'nothing . . . left . . . [to] love.'

Books VI, VII, and VIII of *The Prelude* are primarily concerned with the creative and restorative power of the Poet, and will be considered in the following sections; but in Book IX the

[18] *Middle Years*, p. 406.

[19] *Paradise Lost* X, 235–409, especially 253–61 and 301–4. Cf. R. D. Havens, *The Influence of Milton on English Poetry*, Cambridge, 1922, pp. 607–10, acknowledging the research of Alice M. Dunbar, *Modern Language Notes* 24 (1909), 124.

Miltonic prepossession with evil breaks out afresh into a Wordsworthian action at variance with the easy remedy, the delightful prospect of MSS X and Y, from which Books VII and VIII were to be developed. Milton announced his plan in Book IX of *Paradise Lost:*

> I must now change
> These Notes to Tragic; . . .
> . . . Sad task, yet argument
> Not less but more Heroic [than *Iliad* or *Aeneid*].

Wordsworth acknowledges his new commission in Book IX of *The Prelude:*

> The argument which now
> Awaits us; Oh! how much unlike the past!
> . . . ungenial, hard
> To treat of, and forbidding in itself.

We are promised something of similarly epic proportions; and the 'hubbub wild' of

> Hawkers and Haranguers . . .
> And hissing Factionists with ardent eyes,
> In knots, or pairs, or single, ant-like swarms
> Of Builders and Subverters

comes right from Milton's Pandemonium.[20] To be sure, the 'great theme' of revolution does not enact itself at once in Book IX, although Wordsworth, not entirely unlike Satan, becomes 'a Patriot,' gives his heart and all his love to the noisy 'People.' Instead, we have the new magisterial influence of Michel Beaupuy shifted over from MS Y and a new tragic tale of Vaudracour and Julia. Wordsworth is not yet conducting a revolutionary action; rather, he is debating 'dearest themes.'

The design of Book X of MSS AB of *The Prelude*[21] corresponds with the double disaster of *Paradise Lost:* first, the rebellion

[20] *Paradise Lost* II, 951: 'universal hubbub wilde.'
[21] Originally (in MS Z) and finally (in 1850) divided into Books X and XI.

of the angels under Lucifer, 'the Apostat,' and, second, the fall of man.

In *The Prelude* the analogue of the first action is the French 'apostacy from ancient faith,' which 'seem'd but conversion to a higher creed' until 'tyrants, strong . . . in devilish pleas,' goaded the land, and the 'crimes' of Robespierre's 'atheist crew,' 'foul Tribe of Moloch,' spread into 'madness of the many.'[22] Yet Wordsworth doubts the adequacy of punitive tactics, such as characterize the Miltonic God and his terrible archangels; and, we may add, since the purpose of British statesmen in opposing revolution is less worthy than that of the Messiah and Michael, their means are consequently even more mistaken.

> They who ruled the State
> Though with such awful proof before their eyes
> That he who would sow death, reaps death, or worse,
> And can reap nothing better, child-like long'd
> To imitate . . . leagu'd
> Their strength perfidiously, to undermine
> Justice, and make an end of Liberty.

Indeed, the Satanic presumption in the heart of Wordsworth's Poet begins when he resists such measures on the part of reactionary England, where, amid prayers to the 'great Father,' he alone 'fed on the day of vengeance yet to come.' This parallels Satan's bitter hatred of divine authority and his departure from Pandemonium heavenward to confront the tyranny of God. Satan was 'inflam'd with rage'; Wordsworth is 'inflam'd with hope.'

Wordsworth's treatment of the old issue of God versus Satan, an issue still as acrimonious among scholars as formerly among theologians,[23] may be illustrated by other more specific parallels with the Miltonic myth of war in Heaven. For instance, Milton's Abdiel reappears in the person of Wordsworth's Louvet: Abdiel

[22] Cf. *Paradise Lost* I, 392–6; IV, 393–4; VI, 370: noted by de Selincourt as debts of phrase (pp. 575, 579, 581). *Prelude* X, 87–8, 285–6, 310 ff., 458, 469.

[23] Cf. Professor Bush's summary account of the recent criticism of *Paradise Lost*, in *Philological Quarterly* 28 (January, 1949), 31–43.

> who single [has] maintaind
> Against revolted multitudes the Cause
> Of Truth;

and Louvet, who

> walked singly through the avenue
> And took his station in the Tribune, saying,
> 'I, Robespierre, accuse thee!'

Meditating even on himself as a possible hero in a 'cause so great,' Wordsworth repeats the idea:

> Inly I revolv'd
> How much the destiny of man had still
> Hung upon single persons.[24]

But he is aware that both Milton's Abdiel and his own Louvet are ineffective; reluctantly but wisely he withdraws from conflict and takes himself back to his career of Poet. Therefore, from Book X of *The Prelude* we are spared Milton's martial Book VI, except for the Hymn of Triumph at Robespierre's death sung by Wordsworth on the sands of Leven in the presence of sky, clouds, and mountains like 'burning Seraphs,' recalling Milton's 'Saints . . . in order bright.'

When Robespierre enters the action of *The Prelude* as 'chief Regent' of the 'foul Tribe of Moloch' [25] Wordsworth yields to him the place of Satanic protagonist, and himself becomes the credulous Adam of his own lost Paradise. The assassination of Robespierre in Book X had been no more able to conclude the rebellious action or solve the problem of unimaginative life than had been the victory of the Messiah over the banded powers of Satan in Milton's epic. The mistake made by the Miltonic Messiah himself as to the nature of triumph is made again by Wordsworth's Poet.

> Great was my glee of spirit, great my joy
> In vengeance, and external justice, thus
> Made manifest.

[24] *Paradise Lost* VI, 30–2; *Prelude* X, 98–100, 137–9. [25] X, 469–70.

External justice does not produce final triumph. The means is still inappropriate to the end.

At the beginning of Book VII of *Paradise Lost*, for the 'half' of his poem which yet remains 'unsung,' Milton invokes Urania and returns to his 'Native Element,' singing 'more safe . . . with mortal voice.' Likewise, Wordsworth for the second half of his Book X returns to his 'own History' from the 'bitter truths' of his fatherland's opposition to the French Republic.

The personal struggle yet to come, an episode comparable with Satanic guile exercised on human credulity, appears in Wordsworth's design when, too confident, he surrenders to 'false philosophy.' Like Adam, listening to the instruction of Raphael, the Poet of *The Prelude*

never dreamt
That transmigration could be undergone
A fall of being suffer'd, and of hope
By creature that appear'd to have received
Entire conviction what a great ascent
Had been accomplish'd, what high faculties
It had been call'd to.

The details of this mistake bear a marked resemblance to the Miltonic fall of man. In that blissful dawn when 'the whole earth [wore] the beauty . . . of promise,' the Poet had been led to take 'an eager part in arguments of civil polity . . . before [his] time.' Indeed, like Adam and Eve, he had 'lent a careless ear' to the 'subtleties' of 'wild theories.' Like both rebellious angels and disobedient man and woman he had been convinced that 'self-knowledge and self-rule' were in themselves glorious. He had pursued 'a higher nature,' [26] the folly of Adam and Eve. But his untested feelings were no more 'proof against the injuries of the day' than the untested enthusiasm of Adam under the tute-

[26] X, 590–3, 599–605, 660–2, 702–3, 775–7, 806–49.

lage of Raphael. When British tyranny opposed the liberties of France, and Frenchmen 'changed a war of self-defence for one of conquest,' then Wordsworth's Poet—like Milton's 'Fiend,' who knew 'his mounted scale aloft'—knew the 'scale of Liberty . . . mounted up, openly, in the view of earth and heaven.' With Milton's Satan, he fled out of the Paradise of Faith and Imagination.[27] If he is to be preserved 'still a Poet' and if the 'saving intercourse' with his 'true self' is to be restored, he needs help. Parallel now with the divine 'Mercie collegue with Justice' of Book X of *Paradise Lost* and the redemptive power of the vicegerent Son, in the last half of Book X of *The Prelude* the Poet is assisted by Friend, Sister, and 'Nature's Self.'

When a youth in London, Wordsworth's meditations turned from that awful prospect of human guilt, vice, debasement, 'misery forced upon [his] sight,' which is reminiscent of the vision 'enforc't' upon Adam in Book XI of *Paradise Lost*. Then

> Lo! everything that was indeed divine
> Retain'd its purity inviolate
> And unencroach'd upon, nay, seem'd brighter far
> For this deep shade in counterview, that gloom
> Of opposition, such as shew'd itself
> To the eyes of Adam, yet in Paradise,
> Though fallen from bliss, when in the East he saw
> Darkness ere day's mid course, and morning light
> More orient in the western cloud, that drew
> 'O'er the blue firmament a radiant white,
> Descending slow with something heavenly fraught.'[28]

Now, too, in Book XI of *The Prelude*, which starts with a backward look at Man's unhappiness and guilt as set forth in Books IX and X, we are furnished with a contrast. We return to happier times resembling those in Milton's Paradise before the fall of man.

[27] *Paradise Lost* IV, 996–1015; *Prelude* X, 677, 761–9, 793–7.

[28] *Paradise Lost* XI, 203–7, slightly misquoted by Wordsworth for *Prelude* VIII, 821–2.

'Aires, vernal aires, breathing the smell of field and grove'[29] become Wordsworth's 'motions of delight, that through the fields stir gently, breezes and soft airs that breathe the breath of Paradise'; Milton's 'crisped Brooks' have become in Wordsworth's phrase 'Ye Brooks muttering along the stones'; and Milton's 'Groves whose rich Trees wept odorous Gumms and Balme' are invoked by Wordsworth 'to interpose the covert of [their] shades, even as a sleep, betwixt the heart of man and the uneasy world, 'twixt man himself not seldom, and his own unquiet heart.' In chief, the sketches of unspoiled man and woman at the end of the summary fabric of Book XI are the equivalent of unfallen Adam and Eve.

'Answering His Great Idea'

These words, in which Milton relates the 'new-created' work to the mind of its Creator, lead us to study next the possible relationship between Milton's account of the creative process and Wordsworth's illustration of it in *The Prelude.*

It was under a new compulsion that the latter returned to his poem in the spring of 1804. Revising his Alpine tour into an imaginative apocalypse, he came back to a 'home . . . with infinitude, and only there.' Did he write with Milton's Abdiel in mind?—Abdiel returning home to Him who fills Infinitude,[30] to the sacred hill, the seat supreme of One whose voice comes 'from midst a golden cloud.' The 'I am' of Milton is prototype of Wordsworth's 'Imagination,' the Power that came athwart the Poet when he was 'lost as in a cloud,' the Power to which he owed those 'visitings of awful promise,' those flashes of revelation orienting him in his rightful loyalty. And when he recalled Abdiel on his way back from the 'north' to the sacred hill, he was ready for the message of the 'Quire of Redbreasts . . . that their rough Lord had left the surly North.' In the face of his own less allegorical 'Winter' Wordsworth, too, would choose his part with

[29] *Paradise Lost* IV, 264–5.
[30] *Ibid.* VII, 168–9, 'I am who fill Infinitude.'

hope that can never die,
Effort, and expectation, and desire,
And something evermore about to be.

MSS X and Y, substrata of Books VII and VIII of *The Prelude*, are concerned with the life of the imaginative man in city and country, so viewed as to reveal the difficulties of brotherhood and its hard-won communion, the cost of that long obedience whereby, according to Milton, the earth will be 'changed to heav'n and heav'n to earth, one kingdom, joy and union without end.' Milton's architectonics in creating the earth in Book VII of *Paradise Lost* are exchanged in Book VII of *The Prelude* for an account of 'airy Palaces, and Gardens built by Genii of Romance,' 'Alcairo, Babylon, or Persepolis' or 'golden Cities . . . among Tartarian wilds'; and these make way for 'Vauxhall and Ranelagh,' cosmopolitan London, its edifices, its exhibitions, its theater, its courts, its Church, its festivals. Nevertheless, in his creation of a London for literature Wordsworth has much profited by Milton's elaborate serial account of The First Creation: light, firmament, verdure, constellations, the lower kinds, and man the master work, all 'answering his great *idea*.' [31]

Wordsworth's aesthetic experience in the city is denoted in MS Y and MSS AB by a phrase partly indebted to Milton: 'sensation . . . of union or communion.' In 1850 it becomes even more truly Miltonic: 'a sublime idea . . . vouchsafed for union or communion.' [32] Meanwhile the generous agglomeration of urban appearances in the city has not only impressed him; as with Milton's organization of the various items in the universe, it has evoked the higher poetic power of the author to unify and thus interpret and evaluate them. Whereas Milton's God circumscribes, and conglobes like things to like, Wordsworth deals with the confusion of the mighty city by looking 'in steadiness' and seeing 'the parts as parts, but with a feeling of the whole.' [33]

[31] *Ibid.* VII, 557.
[32] *Ibid.* VIII, 431; *Prelude* VIII, 831–2 [672–5].
[33] MS J, written about 1800.

For the Wordsworthian country, also, Milton's Paradise is the prototype. Yet, as Milton considers any other paradise inferior to his,[34] so Wordsworth believes the paradise where he was reared lovelier far than 'Gehol's famous garden.' Moreover, the Miltonic I AM who fills Infinitude and his son, the Omnific Word, have been humbled into the creative Shepherd and the redemptive son of 'the Matron's Tale' of MS Y; and the Miltonic creation of Eden and, in it, the task of dressing the garden are focused anew as the creative life of the individual mind and the duty of folding Westmoreland flocks and saving lost sheep on Westmoreland hills. The reawakened zeal, in 1804, for creation and redemption as themes bring Milton's Books VII and VIII very close to Wordsworth's Books VII and VIII.

Lastly, for his illustration of the creative process itself, Wordsworth does not forget Milton's analogous passage. In the sensitive operation of the child's mind—an account not carried over from MS Y into MSS AB—the lists of Nature's 'things of . . . rarer workmanship' [35] are almost as ample and varied as those of God's creation in Book VII of *Paradise Lost*. The eyes of the babe in arms catch a prospect of the moon; they discover a little rill of water, a beast, a bird, a flower, peacock's fan, rainbow, glow-worm's fairy lamp. He hears the cuckoo's shout; he feels ice and water and wonders. His mind is fed by 'Nature's unfathomable works, or Man's mysterious as her own'—ship on the seas, arch of stones suspended in air, the cerulean firmament, the river flowing perpetually, the fish and skylark,[36] lightning, thunder, snow, rain, hail. His mind is stretched when he ponders as if it were a miracle 'the world's native produce.' Words take the place of theories and are repeated until faith grows, 'and the name of God stands fixed a keystone of the mighty arch.'

Meantime, a parallel growth in the mind itself brings the child to the point where fable and romance appease him with 'attesta-

[34] Cf. de Selincourt, pp. 550–1.
[35] de Selincourt, pp. 550–8.
[36] Cf. *Paradise Lost* VII, 521, 533.

tions new of growing life, distinct impressions and unbounded thought.' There follows a list of marvels and exotic things which reveal 'another earth, . . . another Nature.' But, as Milton's Adam acknowledged to Raphael, these are 'notions vaine' and 'apte the Mind or Fancie is to roave uncheckt, and of her roaving is no end.'

The third phenomenon in this series of creative episodes is the power of the favored child himself to irradiate all without; his own person, senses, faculties seem to him the soul of all else. Then, fourthly,

> will come
> Another soul, spring, centre of his being,
> And that is Nature,

instead of Milton's Eve, who was the other soul of Adam. The 'converse' of the youthful Poet and his beloved Nature, which may be set side by side with Adam's 'Storie,' in Book VIII of *Paradise Lost*, of his love for Eve and their nuptials, is too curious to invite extended comparison here. But Milton's design for the creation of the Earth, the creation of Man in the Divine Image, the creation of Eve the other self, and the creativity of Adam and Eve, has been accepted and infinitely varied for Wordsworth's account of mental growth, which never found its way into the finished *Prelude*.[37]

'One Greater Man'

In *Paradise Regained* restoration comes 'to all mankind' through 'one man's firm obedience.' Are there any traits common to this 'one greater man' and Wordsworth's Poet?

The situations in the two poems have little superficial likeness; and there is no ubiquitous Arch-fiend in *The Prelude*, no consistent Tempter. Yet both Milton and Wordsworth set forth the discipline of a youthful agent in preparation for a redemptive action. The ordeal in which the 'Son of Joseph deem'd' is fitted

[37] In the de Selincourt edition, pp. 550–8, the whole passage may be read with helpful notes on its indebtedness to Milton's style and phrasing.

to 'begin to save mankind' [38] shares with the subtler propaedeutic of *The Prelude* its statement of purpose, its dedication, its initiation, its training, and its several tests on the several testing-grounds of mundane life.

When we compare the purpose of the protagonists, we find that the Son of God will 'earn Salvation for the Sons of men,' 'work Redemption for mankind.' Coleridge and Wordsworth, also, are 'joint-labourers in a work of [men's] redemption.' [39] Both heroes are dedicated: the Son of God in public baptism; Wordsworth in the presence of the laughing Sea, the bright Mountains, dews, vapors, birds, and laborers, 'the sweetness of a common dawn.' [40] Soon after dedication, both meet by chance an aged man on a deserted way—Miltonic 'dusk with horrid shades,' Wordsworthian 'shades gloomy and dark.' Milton's aged man is the Arch-fiend disguised 'in Rural weeds,' tempting the Son of God to make 'Food' from hard stones. Wordsworth's ghastly old Soldier, in faded military garb, will receive 'food, if food he need.' Instead of the viands with which the Son of God was tempted, the probationer of *The Prelude* was offered as bait the fare in books.

'Get Riches first, get Wealth, and Treasure Heap,' counseled the Arch-fiend; in his second ordeal, Jesus answered patiently that Wealth without Virtue, Valor, Wisdom, is impotent. Wordsworth's Poet agrees: 'Ambition, folly, madness' in the self-elected 'Rulers of the world,' their 'plans without thought, or bottom'd on false thought and false philosophy' when 'brought to test of solid life and true result' reveal 'the utter hollowness of what we name the wealth of Nations.'

Thirdly, instead of Parthia and Rome as temptations toward power and glory, we have London as a challenge to poetic power. When the 'weight of Ages' [41] descended upon the heart of the

[38] *Paradise Regained* I, 23; IV, 635.

[39] *Ibid.* I, 167, 266; *Prelude* XIII, 439–41.

[40] *Paradise Regained* I, 273 ff.; *Prelude* IV, 330–9.

[41] Cf. *Paradise Regained* IV, 282: 'Till time mature thee to a Kingdom's waight.'

boy entering London 'on the roof of an itinerant Vehicle'—poetic diction, that, but most precise—with the weight came power, 'power growing with the weight,' 'a thing divine.' Although he is tempted to subordinate his creative power, his imaginative loyalty, to the burdens and disasters, the ugliness, of city life, the Poet resists. Worldly power as the schismatic Arch-fiend understood and offered it is less powerful than poetic power; the Imagination, chief joy, highest joy of the soul, passes urbanely 'through all Nature'—even through London—to rest 'with God.' [42]

The Miltonic Tempter had saved his subtlest bribes for his ultimate provocation: Arts and Eloquence, Platonic 'Academics,' Aristotelian and Stoic and Epicurean philosophy, epic and dramatic literature, oratory. What kind of temptation might such items suggest for the action of *The Prelude?* Should Imagination be made to subserve these glorious cultural activities or, more daring, must it be made to master and control them? In *Paradise Regained* Wordsworth had read that 'many books . . . are wearisom.' He was not then beset by the 'core curriculum' of our unpoetic campus life; but his own days offered an educational heresy as tempting, a heresy to be followed by a storm as ruinous; and he knew that the deadly doings of the Goddess Reason must be abandoned for the natural processes of intellectual love. Therefore he determined—like Milton's Son of God, discrediting 'Philosophic pride' and subtle shifts—himself to unmask the pretensions of syllogistic words, minute analysis, and all other manifestations of an arrogant reason. He represents his feelings as having stood 'the test of such a trial': another explicit acknowledgment of his literary device.

The last ordeal imposed by the Arch-fiend upon the Son of God was to bear him to the 'highest Pinacle' of the Holy City Herself and there provoke him to exhibit his Divine Sonship. This

[42] Of the many echoes, in Wordsworth's London, of the 'fair edifices' of Milton's Rome, its 'Houses of Gods,' its 'fam'd Artificers' and 'Embassies,' we should mention Wordsworth's line 'And Negro Ladies in white muslin gowns' as a modern writing of Milton's 'Dusk faces with white silken Turbants wreath'd' (*Paradise Regained* IV, 76).

bribe to exhibit is a temptation for the Poet, also; and we are not surprised when Wordsworth betakes himself at the end of his poem to the top of Snowdon amid the glorious fabric of Nature Herself. Here, where 'the universal spectacle throughout was shaped for admiration and delight,' Nature had lodged 'the Soul, the Imagination of the whole'—a Holy City out of doors, as it were. No more than the Son of God on his pinnacle did the Wordsworth Poet on Snowdon lose his balance. He, also, stood. Although the scene held an opportunity for cheap idyllic legerdemain and for personal exhibition, he used it to reveal instead the operations of a Mighty Mind. In this final statement of kinship between the 'Power' of Nature and the 'faculty' of imaginative Man, this final assertion of the filial relation of both Nature and Man to God, lies Wordsworth's real patriotism. As a 'Borderer of his age' he has chosen citizenship, not outlawry, for his part; this is his acknowledgment of Sonship, his pledge of loyalty.

In their comparable restoration after so extended an ordeal Milton's Son of God and Wordsworth's Poet share two advantages. The 'plumy Vans' of the Angels who received the former 'and upbore, as on a floating couch through the blithe Air,' are used again to exalt the latter as 'by an underpresence, the sense of God.' And the table set out for Jesus with

> Celestial Food, Divine,
> Ambrosial, Fruits fetcht from the tree of life,
> And from the fount of life Ambrosial drink,

is spread again for Wordsworth or any other poetic mind that 'feeds upon infinity.' [43]

'Nature' was more than a literary device for Wordsworth, epic 'machinery' to be put in the place of that other literary symbol, the Miltonic 'God'; for each poet his own term betokened substantial experience. Yet the Goodness that was 'God' to Milton and the Beauty that was 'Nature' to Wordsworth, like the Truth that is 'Science' to us, are all too easily abstracted from their col-

[43] *Paradise Regained* IV, 581–94; *Prelude* XIII, 70–2.

lateral substance, only to sound lifeless in the ears of succeeding generations. Aware of this, Milton, as did the Biblical gospellers, had insisted on Fatherhood and Sonship, the paternal and filial relation, to endear his epic action; and in his turn Wordsworth would emphasize the personal tie between the Poet and Nature—a kind of intellectual love affair—to produce an action as emotionally rich and conceptually enduring.

The action proper to this intimate personal tie, and its furtherance of social and political well-being, would succeed or fail as the author succeeded or failed with his 'ordeal.' The Miltonic test of obedience, in which the Son of God was *morally* triumphant must be recreated into an *aesthetic* or *poetic* agony. Thus Wordsworth's 'Imagination . . . Restored' illustrates sensitive and creative power resistlessly exerted over the various levels and diverse content of human life, and also victorious over any partial temptations of it. If *Paradise Regained* be the great moral epic of our literature, 'Imagination . . . Restored' may be considered its aesthetic and poetic sibling.

In a kind of epilogue to his 'ordeal'—did not Milton's hero also go back to his home town, 'his Mother's house'?—Wordsworth disavowed 'private aims.' He has never been 'the dupe of selfish passions'; he has not yielded 'to mean cares and low pursuits'; he has resisted slavery to or oppression by the laws of vulgar sense; he has not substituted a 'Universe of death,' a Miltonic phrase,[44] for that which is 'divine and true.' This reads like an explicit acknowledgment of the similarity between the discipline of the Poet's mind and the ordeal of the Son of God. Whether Paradise be 'Regained' by persistent obedience, or the Imagination be 'Restored' by unfailing intellectual love, there exists between ethics and poetics a fraternal bond.

Choice of 'machinery' will likewise depend on experience and on theory. Supernature? Nature? Wordsworth chose Nature as his spiritual ally, Imagination as his spiritual service; and therefore his epic 'machinery' accords with the inner truth of many

[44] *Paradise Lost* II, 622.

men in many places and in many ages. He did not substitute either Nature or Imagination for God; and hence, long debates on his theology and philosophy are beside the point. Indeed, as a 'Borderer of his Age' he must adopt for his concrete representation of human life a vicegerent unburdened by theological and metaphysical prepossessions. This was his poetic right. There are, to be sure, poets who claim this very privilege for their alliance with powers which disintegrate, mechanize, or pervert Nature, and for their secular worship of unnatural processes. They must run the gauntlet of the critical centuries, too, and with Milton and Wordsworth stand the test of time. We may be sure that Wordsworth's Nature will prove to be not the least powerful of aesthetic allies, nor his Imagination the least fruitful of poetic disciplines.

In conclusion, let us reread Wordsworth's observation made to Southey in 1815:

> Epic poetry . . . of the highest class requires in the first place an action eminently influential, an action with a grand or sublime train of consequences; it next requires the intervention and guidance of beings superior to man, what the critics, I believe, call machinery; and lastly, I think with Dennis that no subject but a religious one can answer the demand of the soul in the highest class of this species of poetry.[45]

The discipline and consummation of a poet's mind, with their consequences in the 'redemption' of men taught 'how . . . to love' is an action influential and sublimely consequential; and its 'machinery,' Nature, satisfies the second requirement. Is its subject religious? A remark of Wordsworth to Henry Alford in 1840 about his 'diffidence in treating subjects of Holy Writ' indicates his fear that he 'might err in points of faith, and I should not deem my mistakes less to be deprecated because they were expressed in metre. Even Milton, in my humble judgment, has erred, and grievously; and what poet could hope to atone for misapprehen-

[45] *Middle Years*, pp. 633.

sions in the way in which that mighty mind has done.'[46] But is there not some other connotation of 'religious' which would include *The Prelude* as an epic poem? Yes, if we consider his letter to Landor in 1824, we learn that

> in poetry it is the imaginative only, viz., that which is conversant with, or turns upon infinity, that powerfully affects me. . . . I mean to say that, unless in those passages where things are lost in each other, and limits vanish, and aspirations are raised, I read with something too much like indifference. But all great poets are in this view powerful religionists.[47]

Seizing upon the implied kinship, almost the identity, of 'imaginative' and 'religious,' as both epithets concern themselves with infinity—or 'infinitude, . . . our heart's being and our home'—we can scarcely deny to *The Prelude* its place among English epics.

[46] *Later Years*, p. 1007.
[47] *Ibid.*, pp. 134–5.

XIII

Poet

THE MAN of arms sung by Virgil, and in our time discredited by Shaw's prosaic Bluntschli, was destined for a long series of cultural revisions. Not only did Jesus supplant Aeneas, but the *nova progenies* foreseen by Virgil and illustrated by Jesus renewed itself in each new age with fresh manifestations of knowledge and power. Disciple, apostle, martyr, monk, servant of the servants of God, scholar and doctor, troubadour and knight, courtier and gentleman: even as these exerted themselves to partake more and more fully of Him whom Milton was to call 'one greater man,' they revealed themselves less and less fitted to live His simple life and do His mighty deed. The intense quality of the one and the deep passion of the other had been lost in the refinement of doctrine and the elaboration of code. Literature, however, is an easier art than life; and poets have lived on to tell the story of saints and heroes dead.

In that eighteenth century which was to the young Wordsworth as momentous as the twentieth century is to us, the Virgilian hero still furnished an outline for Robinson Crusoe and Gulliver and other adventurers in and citizens of this world; but the Christian Hero, too, uncomfortably restricted by his ecclesiastical garments, was restless for new battles in the timeless arena of thought and feeling. Although not of the martyr's seed, nor protagonists for any explicit doctrine or code, Roman Catholic Alexander Pope and Anglican Catholic Edward Young were reviewing the nature and destiny of man. About Pope and himself Dr. Young had said: 'Man, too, he sung: immortal man I sing.' Into this English tradition of Pope and Young came Blake with his 'universal man,' Burns the Scot with his 'man for a' that,' and Wordsworth with his poetic man. Looking back upon these three we must feel more than a slight nostalgia for them. The Shelleyan Prometheus, the Titan and the Latmian shepherd of Keats, and the Byronic rebel were brilliantly extrahuman; but they have left us only the Shavian Superman to oppose Ibsen's men and women of ill will, Hardy's pitiless dynasts, and the sub-men and part-women of many recent plays and novels.

If we are to compare Wordsworth's Poet with these other notable representatives of mankind, we may consider him first as the embodiment of an idea, secondly as agent in an action, thirdly as a man speaking to men, and lastly in his human relationships, that society of men to whom and for whom he will speak.

In the Image; 'Chosen Son'

First, what idea does Wordsworth's Poet embody or illustrate?

In the first 271 lines of *The Prelude*, the lines which describe its genesis, the Poet is revealed as made in the image of his Maker. The Biblical account of the genesis of man, 'And the Lord God formed man of the dust of the ground, and breathed into his nostrils the breath of life; and man became a living soul,' comes alive in Wordsworth's imagination as follows:

> Oh there is blessing in this gentle breeze
> That blows from the green fields and from the clouds
> And from the sky: it beats against my cheek,
> And seems half-conscious of the joy it gives.
> . . . I breathe again;
> Trances of thought and mountings of the mind
> Come fast upon me: . . . this hour

Hath brought a gift that consecrates my joy;
For I, methought, while the sweet breath of Heaven
Was blowing on my body, felt within
A corresponding mild creative breeze,
A vital breeze . . .

Not only do the terms *vital, creative, free, holy, chosen, choice, work . . . begun . . . perform'd, shape out, thoughtfully fitted, sabbath,* ally the poetic creature with the poetic Creator in this process of making; but all the circumstances of the initial passage gain their proper value when considered as a very subtle literary application of the old myth. The Vale in which the enfranchised and consecrated Poet of *The Prelude* is to live his holy life, the grove and sweet stream, the green fields, clouds, and sky, the wild water on shore as he quits the tiresome sea, 'green herbs,' [1] and 'fruits fresh from their native bough,' the vernal promises: these constitute another Eden, in the prime tradition of Hebraic culture.

Noting this, we read more carefully:

Thus long I lay
Chear'd by the genial pillow of the earth
Beneath my head, sooth'd by a sense of touch
From the warm ground, that balanced me, else lost
Entirely, seeing nought, nought hearing, save
When here and there, about the grove of Oaks
Where was my bed, an acorn from the trees
Fell audibly, and with a startling sound.

The Poet of Wordsworth is verily another Biblical Adam, man from the clay. 'The earth is all before' the later as it was all before the earlier man. Here in 'one sweet Vale' his holy life is to be led; here in 'one neighbourhood' ensuing days will bring admiration, love, 'the life in common things,' rare things in endless store; here he will find 'self-congratulation, . . . complete composure, . . . happiness entire.'

Says the Book of Genesis: 'And the Lord God took the man,

[1] Cf. Genesis I, 9–11; and I, 30, 'every green herb.' Milton says (*Paradise Lost* VII, 336–7): 'every herb . . . on the green stemm.'

and put him in the garden of Eden to dress it and keep it.' This and the command to replenish the earth and subdue it reappear in the Genesis of *The Prelude* as 'a longing'

> To brace myself to some determin'd aim,
> Reading or thinking, either to lay up
> New stores, or rescue from decay the old
> By timely interference.

Be fruitful, says the Book of Genesis. Wordsworth's Poet obediently hopes to 'endue,' to 'fix in a visible home' certain 'phantoms of conceit,' to deal forth temperately 'to such Beings' the feelings of his own heart. Taking a hint from the generations of Adam for his list of patriarchal heroes in the initial passage of *The Prelude*, he gives us a 'little Band of yet remembered names' which include old Britons 'left unsung' by Milton, Knight telling of Knight, Shepherd piping of Shepherd, Mithridates becoming Odin, the friends and followers of Sertorius in the Fortunate Isles, the 'unknown man, unheard of in the Chronicles of Kings' but suffering in silence 'for the love of truth,' Dominique de Gourges, Gustavus of Sweden with his miners of Dalecarlia, and Wallace, whose deeds, 'like a family of ghosts,' were left 'to people the steep rocks and river banks . . . with a local soul of independence and stern liberty.'

'And a river went out of Eden to water the garden': an actual Derwent or the symbolic Imagination, again as this poet would conceive it (XIII, 172–84).

> We have traced the stream
> From darkness, and the very place of birth
> In its blind cavern, . . . follow'd it to light
> And open day, accompanied its course
> Among the ways of Nature, afterwards
> Lost sight of it bewilder'd and engulph'd,
> Then given it greeting, as it rose once more
> With strength, reflecting in its solemn breast
> The works of man and face of human life,
> And lastly, from its progress have we drawn

The feeling of life endless, the great thought
By which we live, Infinity and God.

Why, then, in such a paradise and with such a divine commission and in such a lofty company should the Poet prove 'false Steward'? Remembering Adam, who was put into the garden of Eden to dress it and keep it, but did neither, Wordsworth associates his own vague longing, timorous capacity, infinite delay, subtle selfishness, false activity, with the old human error; his mind, too, turns 'recreant' to her poetic task. This is to be another fall of man, we surmise; the joyful 'sabbath' is over; the lofty hopes are to be yielded up 'for present gifts of humbler industry.' His Poet, like Adam, must get to work.

What are the implications of this Wordsworthian Genesis of a Poet for *The Prelude* as a whole? Will the autobiographical record of one 'chosen Son' recapitulate the history of the chosen people? Is this to be another god-spell? Will there be other clear or dim analogies with the Book of books? Are its 'spots of time' comparable with those prophetic visions that assist the chosen people to fulfil its destiny? Is the episode of the Shepherd and his Son, 'the Matron's Tale' of MS Y and Book VIII, and later excised, a humbler writing of the pastoral Psalm? Are the passages bearing witness to the love of Nature a kind of Old Testament, and the passages bearing witness to the love of Man a kind of New Testament? Is 'intellectual love' a modernization of the old Law and the new Love? May there be trouble ahead for the Poet tempted by circumstances to renounce the life of obedient joy for a curious search into the knowledge of good and evil? Is the ordeal of the Poet pinioned on the frame of social revolution another crucifixion? Is his sense

Of treachery and desertion in the place
The holiest that I knew of, my own soul,

related to the cry, 'Eli, Eli, lama sabachthani'? And is his restoration another resurrection? Will this poem like That Poem leave us 'smitten by a sublime *idea*' (1850), furnished with 'the perfect image of a mighty Mind'? Will it bid us farewell with another transcendent revelation?—poet that is holy, let him be holy still.

These are dim analogies; but the main truth about Wordsworth's Poet as about the Biblical Adam is clear beyond question. From the first breath of 'the vital soul' to the last, the power to create will be the distinctly human trait. The mind of the Babe,

> Even as an agent of the one great mind,
> Creates, creator and receiver both.
> . . . Such, verily, is the first
> Poetic spirit of our human life.

When the Youth leaves his beloved Vale to enter the college named for St. John, he is still a 'chosen Son,'

> train'd up in paradise
> Among sweet garlands and delightful sounds.

He has come, like that other Man, under the conduct of that other precursor named John,

> with holy powers
> And faculties, whether to work or feel:
> To apprehend all passions and all moods
> Which time, and place, and season do impress
> Upon the visible universe, and work
> Like changes there by force of my own mind.

Finally, the collegian of 1787–8 abates no jot of his kinship with the Creator and creature of the traditional account of genesis:

> Of Genius, Power,
> Creation and Divinity itself
> I have been speaking, for my theme has been
> What pass'd within me. . . .
> . . . There's not a man
> That lives who hath not had his godlike hours,
> And knows not what majestic sway we have,
> As natural beings in the strength of nature.

. . . I had hopes and peace
And swellings of the spirit, was rapt and soothed,
Convers'd with promises, had glimmering views
How Life pervades the undecaying mind,
How the immortal Soul with God-like power
Informs, creates, and thaws the deepest sleep
That time can lay upon her.

Agent in an Action

In all writing not so avowedly independent of time as are science and philosophy, sequence is important. What logic does for inductive and deductive prose, action must accomplish for poetry. This action may be broadly and deeply mythic, a figment of yesterday-today-and-tomorrow. It may be rigorously dramatic or epic, a Shakespearean play or a Miltonic fable of paradise lost and regained. It may be cosmic, a deed to be done *per saecula saeculorum*, the ordering of the individual soul or of humankind for ever. Or it may be didactic, a process of learning and teaching with compacts, codes, an ordeal, discoveries, and reversals as impelling as those in the action of *The Bacchae*, *King Lear*, or *The Divine Comedy*. Where indeed could we find, or how imagine, a poem without a new loyalty, a new conflict and ordeal, a new vision, and a new life?—even at the cost of an old pattern denied or misinterpreted. In this sense all the didactic poems of Western culture, and among them *The Prelude*, take us home to the action of the Old and New Testament.

Not to insist too curiously on the likeness between Adam's expulsion from Paradise and William's departure from his beloved Vale and later his divorce from his fatherland, nor on the visions by which as a chosen son he is from time to time attended even in exile, let us without further delay acknowledge the main source of the action of *The Prelude*, the restoration of the poet's mind so that he may redeem mankind, by teaching. This action allies *The Prelude* with the tradition founded in the New Testament and relates the Poet of Wordsworth with the Great Teacher, with Christ Himself.

When Coleridge hoped that Wordsworth would write a poem proving 'the whole state of man and society subject to, and illustrative of a redemptive process in operation,' [2] he was thinking of a *Recluse*. But it was no recluse who ended his autobiographical poem with an address to Coleridge, his 'joint-labourer in a work . . . of redemption.' The Poet of Wordsworth, somewhat like the traditional Christ, has been invested with the burden and glory of teaching. As we watch the restorative psychology and pedagogy of *The Prelude* emerge from the redemptive theology with which Coleridge would have had him deal, we are grateful both for the tradition and for his powerful modification of it.

In terms of what action other than Biblical did Wordsworth disentangle himself from the diction and imagery of that supreme artifice, the Universal Church? Of less mighty artificial actions there are plenty in the world of men: there are deeds-to-be-done by merchants of Venice, governors of Cyprus, princes of Denmark, kings of Sicilia or Scotland or Britain, triumvirs of Rome, and their successors in the nowadays. Even the Miltonic Raphael and Michael seem overanxious about the earthly success or failure of their enterprise. Milton's Son of God in *Paradise Regained* has a quiet victory in mind; but among Shakespeare's agents only Belarius, Ulysses, Paulina, and Prospero have on hand business comparable in quietude and real power. Their purpose is education in its more patient sense, the inner form of discipline; and education in this Shakespearean sense is the lay equivalent of the redemptive action which Wordsworth had undertaken.

Much the same kind of training as was given by Belarius to the sons of Cymbeline came to the Wordsworth boys from their mentors at Hawkshead. Beaupuy conversing with Wordsworth

[2] *Table Talk*, London, 1835, Vol. 2, p. 70, quoted in Christopher Wordsworth's *Memoirs*, 1850, Vol. 1, p. 302. Also *Poetical Works*, Vol. 5, p. 364.

on the banks of the Loire had been prefigured in Ulysses standing by the arrogant Achilles and the intemperate Troilus on the plains of Troy. Dorothy, who maintains for her brother a saving intercourse with his 'true self,' is a milder Paulina with a less violent Leontes. Paulina's goddess, too, was the 'good goddess Nature,' and to their co-operation Leontes owed, as did Wordsworth, the rediscovery of himself.

Exile from oneself and ultimate repatriation is, of course, a political statement of this action. Posthumus, who had forgotten 'Britain' and 'himself,' was an alien in a foreign land, as were Marmaduke of *The Borderers,* Vaudracour of *The Prelude*, and Wordsworth himself: Posthumus and Wordsworth in Orleans; Posthumus and Marmaduke on Welsh or Scottish border; Vaudracour in Auvergne. But Shakespeare's supreme exile returned is his consummate schoolmaster, Prospero, 'for the liberal arts without a parallel.' That 'poor isle' in which the exiled Duke of Milan found again his dukedom, 'and all of us ourselves when no man was his own,' where amid Nature's bounty man was so illiberal, such an isle was Britain to Wordsworth during the crisis of his strong disease. And when with Dorothy's help he rediscovered his 'true self' under the 'name' and 'office' of 'Poet,' he illustrated anew and in its more universal form the dramatic ordeal Shakespeare had set for his kings and princes, for his generals and cardinals, and for his lovers and merchants.

'The rarer action is in virtue than in vengeance,' says Prospero. Like Ariel's 'great master' in league with the 'elves of hills, brooks, standing lakes, and groves,' Wordsworth and Coleridge are 'Prophets of Nature,' pledged to win happiness for their fellow men, who need only to be taught how to love. Behind the words 'old idolatry,' 'servitude,' 'ignominy and shame,' with which Wordsworth acknowledges the difficulties of the teacher, lurk Setebos and Caliban and the drunken and dull fools whom the thrice-double ass took for gods. Like the 'baseless *fabric*' of Prospero's vision, his '*insubstantial* pageant,' 'the great globe itself . . . shall dissolve and . . . leave not a rack behind'; but there is a fabric which is not baseless and a pageant which is not insubstantial. Those who have read the final passages of *The Tempest* are ready for the finale of *The Prelude*. 'Above this Frame of things,' says Wordsworth, 'the mind of man' is exalted in beauty, 'as it is itself of *substance* and of *fabric* more divine.'

With this lesson in the pedagogy of love, Wordsworth, like Prospero, required some heavenly music, buried his staff, and drowned his book, fortunately not lost to us. In it, as on Prospero's isle, we find 'all of us ourselves when no man was his own.'

It is figurative speech chosen from natural life, however, and from the life of natural man, that most fruitfully served this 'Prophet of Nature' on an isle not very far from the home of Caliban, Ariel, Prospero, Ferdinand and Miranda. With some assurance we can date the 'natural' action of *The Prelude* as conceived in 1799–1800. It is strange that the metaphor of growth occurs neither in the *Lines . . . on the Wye*, July 13, 1798, nor in the earliest manuscript of *The Prelude*, JJ, 1798–9; only in revision at Sockburn and Grasmere does the mind of the poet grow from 'fair seed time' into harvest. Somewhat like the growth of a plant or tree, the growth of the mind of a poet, that is, the growth of the mind of man, is the prime and ultimate action in the natural world. To reach the right artistic statement of it Wordsworth himself needed the regeneration which came with the culture of the domestic affections.

So-called poet of nature that he is, nevertheless the vales, groves, streams, and clouds of the Preamble had not yet lured him to be 'a Settler on the soil'; the falling acorn of what we have called the 'Genesis' of *The Prelude* tempted him to linger only one day out of seven, the Sabbath; the vision of one sweet Vale and the hermitage where the 'pleasant loitering journey' of his youth was to be ended carried little warning of patience and toil, of growth and discipline; 'the trust that mellower years will bring a riper mind' hints, but merely hints, at cultivation ahead.

It is in MS V and passages later excised from or added to it that the poet is explicit about his argument: 'the growth of mental powers and love of nature's works.' He speaks of himself as 'transplanted' to the Vale of Hawkshead and calls his spots of time 'fructifying.' In one addition to MS V he describes himself and his companions at Hawkshead as a 'race . . . worthy of the ground where they were sown'; and in a summary passage he asks us:

> Who knows the individual hour in which
> His habits were first sown, even as a seed?

Yet he asserts that the habit of observing affinities was 'rooted . . . deeply' in his mind by his seventeenth year. Human life is a matter of 'change of growth or of decay.'

Where MS JJ builds the soul, weaves or paints or composes it, and MS W finds it susceptible of a 'malady' (revised to 'degradation'), only the intervenient MSS V and U predicate of the mind of the poet the traits and growth-cycle of vegetative nature.

Sometime between MSS V and U, on the one hand, and W, on the other, growth as the action of the poet's boyhood and youth was forgotten or set aside, but not until he had written Book III, for which any initial manuscript has been lost. Here, too, his poem grows with its theme of growth: he speaks of 'child-like fruitfulness in passing joy,' of 'steady moods . . . of thoughtfulness, matur'd to inspiration.' The world appears to him as a 'wild field' where young souls are 'sown'; the mind of the youthful poet can suffer from 'a treasonable growth of indecisive judgments'; college students are a 'wide and fair . . . congregation'

> in its budding-time
> Of health, and hope, and beauty; all at once
> So many divers samples of the growth
> Of life's sweet season . . .
> That miscellaneous garland of wild flowers
> Upon the matron temples of a Place
> So famous through the world.

College is a garden of great intellects for 'fruits . . . of truth or virtue.' Lapsed from duty and zeal, the mind of the collegian, like a floating island, produced for a while only

> a fair face of water-weeds
> And pleasant flowers. . . .
> . . . Hush'd, meanwhile,
> Was the undersoul, lock'd up in such a calm,
> That not a leaf of the great nature stirr'd.

The old scholars of St. John's, Cambridge, were

> trick'd out like aged trees
> Which, through the lapse of their infirmity,
> Give ready place to any random seed
> That chuses to be rear'd upon their trunks.

This undeniable knot of metaphors from nature's kind of growth emboldens us to date Book III more nearly with MSS V and U; it also suggests that where metaphors of vegetative growth and decay occur in other passages of still undated origin we may assume, although not prove, the work or reminiscence of the year 1799–1800.

The better to understand this action of natural growth in *The Prelude*, we must remind ourselves that in Wordsworth's imagination space is more vivid than time; witness his memorable phrase 'spots of time,' not moments in space. Witness also several titles of the books of *The Prelude:* 'Residence at Cambridge,' 'Cambridge and the Alps,' 'Residence in London,' 'Retrospect,' 'Residence in France,' 'France.' Furthermore, of the poem's two presiding metaphors from nature, the stream and the moon, it is the moon which prevails. Her slow rhythm, her exalted position, her extending influence were more congenial to the poet, and more fitting for the final myth of *The Prelude* than the stream whose course he would follow in the action of *Duddon*, *Poems . . . to National Independence and Liberty*, and *Ecclesiastical Sonnets.*

Therefore, in his space world, almost as small and stationary as ours, the growth of Wordsworth's mind was upward out of it or downward into it rather than restlessly over it forward, backward, and outward. In the Vale of Grasmere as in the narrow streets of London a man must solve the problem of the interrelations of men by emphasizing not a distinct office for one kind of man but the consummate human nature and function in all men. He gave it the name 'Poet,' an old name for a freshly invoked quality. Whereas earlier epochs would have recognized such a man under the name philosopher, redeemer, saint, holy man, Christian, the nineteenth century craved a lay rather than a learned title. Along with the Founder and disciples of that other prelude whose spot of time is the Kingdom of Heaven always at hand, the Poet accepts choices and an ordeal less obvious than the choices of his lay brothers; but he must patiently recommend to them within their own seven-day week those moments of dedication, communion, penance, rededication, and reconcilement possible to them as they are men within themselves.

'The Man Asserts a Poet's Name'

Characters of the blessed or happy man in literature resemble each other too closely to endear them. Fortunately *The Prelude* was not to be a mere beatitude; its action should proceed toward happiness through costly struggle; and its final books would profit by the review of similar experience in the career of other poets. It was to Wordsworth's advantage that he knew well the poetry of that afflicted man who was happy at such cost, William Cowper.

Wordsworth's regard for Cowper can be detected in his earliest published verse. *An Evening Walk,* written in 1787–9 on the morrow of Cowper's *Task* of 1785, echoed sounds and images from his congenial forerunner, but it had not availed itself of Cowper's new ironic treatment in blank verse of physical and mental perambulation. Thomson's sentiments and Milton's couplets still beat too strongly in Wordsworth's mind. When he should come to reread Books V and VI of *The Task:* 'The Winter

Morning Walk' and 'The Winter Walk at Noon,' these might seem to him fresher than his own *Evening Walk*, or the *Descriptive Sketches* for which in 1792–3 he had borrowed certain phrases and themes from Cowper.[3]

Cowper's diction, of course, was inimitable; but Cowper's images he had always tested on his own vision and in his own heart. During 1799, writing of yellow grunsel, lilies of the valley, and autumnal crocus in his 'boyish pleasures' (MS V of *The Prelude*), he was doing for a wilder countryside what Cowper had done for a more formal garden in his pattern of cypress and yew, laburnum, syringa, rose, lilac, and jasmine. Cowper's cucumber[4] and Wordsworth's actual strawberries and mellow cream and metaphorical wild wood-honey both belong to the permitted menu of late eighteenth-century verse; but Wordsworth would have noticed for future use Cowper's way of ridiculing poetic diction, tongue in cheek, might even have shared Cowper's amused grimace over that 'stercoraceous heap,'[5] which the farm hand calls 'dung.'

He could not have been unaware of the likeness between Cowper's Crazy Kate and his own deserted women, especially Ruth, or between Cowper's Gypsies and his own Beggars. And indoors, while Cowper stirred the fire for his 'Winter Evening,' found 'cards . . . superfluous,' and passed scornful judgment on the world's 'time,'

> tinctur'd black and red
> With spots quadrangular of di'mond form,
> Ensanguin'd hearts, clubs typical of strife
> And spades the emblem of untimely graves,

Wordsworth was listening. In April, 1800, Cowper lay dead; but the author of MS V, Book I of *The Prelude*, had already built

[3] Lienemann, *Die Belesenheit von William Wordsworth*, p. 87; also Legouis, *Early Life*, p. 144.

[4] 'The Garden' 462. My citations refer to *Cowper's Poetical Works*, ed. by H. S. Milford, 3d ed., Oxford University Press, 1926.

[5] 'The Garden' 463. In a letter of April 2, 1781, to the Rev. William Unwin, Cowper enjoys fabricating the phrase 'extra-foraneous occupations.'

up another 'warm peat fire,' for Loo or Whist, where he and his boyhood companions 'precipitated down with scoffs and taunts'

> Ironic Diamonds, Clubs, Hearts, Diamonds, Spades,
> A congregation piteously akin.

Meanwhile, 'the frost raging abroad' for Cowper at Olney during those eighties when 'the frost raged bitterly' at Hawkshead for Wordsworth had endeared to both the warmth within.[6]

Moreover, Cowper's monitory way with institutions, so passionately different from Pope's, had arrested his sympathies. In 'Residence at Cambridge' he would be mindful of Cowper's satires on schools and colleges and those who manage them. Emboldened by Cowper's warning against emulation, that 'gross compound . . . of envy, hatred, jealousy, and pride,' he would make mention, although 'short mention,' of 'excessive hopes, tremblings withal, and commendable fears, small jealousies, and triumphs good and bad' among his fellows at St. John's. Pleased by Cowper's reference to boys as 'pretty buds unblown,'[7] he would amplify Cowper's metaphor, calling the students of his Alma Mater a wide and fair congregation 'in its budding time of health, and hope, and beauty.' Nor for his picture of the Cambridge of yore would he forget Cowper's description of 'colleges and halls in ancient days'

> When learning, virtue, piety, and truth,
> Were precious, and inculcated with care.[8]

And it was Cowper who brought into one medium of easy exchange not only the rural minstrelsy in which Wordsworth delighted, but the 'divine chit-chat' of indoors as Wordsworth and Coleridge knew it, and the country spectator's comment on those distant but ubiquitous institutions the Mart, the School, the Bar, the Court, the Church. This would justify the diverse content of Wordsworth's poem on the growth of his own mind

[6] 'The Winter Evening' 207–19, 308–9; *Prelude* I, 535–70.
[7] *Tyrocinium* 458–94, 446.
[8] 'The Time-piece' 699–702.

as already composed, up to the autumn of 1804; and when, in MSS X and Y, he was gathering his energies for the last stretches of his own task in *The Prelude*, Cowper's poetry reread or recalled would help him disengage 'Residence in London' and 'Residence in France' from the matrix of remembered experience in those places.

That he did reread Cowper we know. In October, 1804, Dorothy so assured Lady Beaumont: 'We have received great pleasure from that poem of Cowper which you mentioned to us. I believe that it did my Brother some good, and set him on to writing after a pause sooner than he would otherwise have done.' [9] Any argument as to the particular poem thus reviewed must be inconclusive; the Wordsworths were already familiar with Cowper's poetry.[10] What would likely take place, however, was the recollection in tranquillity of many passages of Cowper's blank verse earlier memorized and now to be helpful for the interpretation of London, in chief that incisive sketch of the preacher, which Lienemann has already referred to *The Task*,[11] and that tender picture of the Artificer used as 'foil' to ecclesiastical 'foolishness and madness in parade.' Wordsworth had not forgotten the propinquity of 'clerical coxcomb' and 'smutch'd artificer' in 'The Time-piece.'

Above all, it was Cowper who taught Wordsworth to deal with homely and humorous matters in blank verse, and to sharpen and refine the diction of his ironic and critical passages. Cowper's habit of distinguishing this from that and himself from both in his narrow world helped Wordsworth toward poetic assurance in his delineation of a wider scene and mightier affairs. Wordsworth sees London and France as clearly as Cowper saw Olney; Cowper's delicate system of ideas innervates the active revolu-

[9] *Early Letters*, p. 418.

[10] *Journals*, Vol. 1, p. 69: on October 25, 1800, they were reading 'Rogers, Miss Seward, Cowper, etc.' Cowper's *Poems* in two volumes, 8vo, calf, 1794, was numbered lot 509 for the sale of Wordsworth's library (*Transactions of the Wordsworth Society*, No. 6, p. 243).

[11] *Die Belesenheit*, p. 90.

tionary passages of *The Prelude;* and many a Wordsworthian phrase has been more deftly turned because of Cowper's sense of the ridiculous. Nevertheless, Cowper's wrath and love are too circumscribed both within and without for the sustained management of blank verse in the conduct of great affairs. Without the whiplash of rhyme, the burden of expostulation is too great for the attention of a modern reader, better pleased with *Table Talk* than with *The Task.* The two poets exhibit alike caesural variety and bold patterns in their use of *enjambement;* the elongating reach of their clauses toward a climax is often exciting, but with this mighty difference: Wordsworth is going somewhere himself with his blank verse, while Cowper is staying at home. Personally and professionally, Cowper has retreated from the haunts and institutions of men, and Wordsworth will seek them out.

For instance, that costly earthquake and flood which had devastated Sicily in Cowper's time ('Alas for Sicily!') [12] are interpreted by the earlier poet as the result of divine wrath on a sinful people; Cowper retires from the tension of analysis to the comfort of doctrine. On the other hand, although Wordsworth confesses 'a kind of sympathy with power' amid 'the awe of unintelligible chastisement,' and although he shares in the spirit of 'the ancient Prophets,' denouncing (X, 316–18, 402–6)

> On Towns and Cities, wallowing in the abyss
> Of their offences, punishment to come,

he is more concerned with man's responsibility for the right use of affliction. This he accepts as the poet's task and resolutely penetrates the thorny tangle of events in France or in Sicily or wheresoever. His own Sicilian 'catastrophe' will be interpreted as a moral disaster, and thus susceptible of imaginative treatment and cure (X, 947–1020). The irresponsibility of men and the Responsibility of their Maker, as Cowper understood these, have

[12] 'The Time-piece' 75 ff.

been transmuted into the humble working of the human imagination in the moral world.

In spite of reservations of this sort, we must acknowledge Cowper's priority in the literary design common to the finale of *The Task* and *The Prelude:* the advance of the argument from the political to the poetical arena. What was, in the earlier poem, a mere philosophical sequence would be substantiated by Wordsworth as a personal adventure, from revolutionary entanglement to spiritual deliverance as follows:

Book V of *The Task* includes the discursive treatment of freedom and slavery, estimates of English versus French loyalty, with a description of the Bastille, a eulogy of liberty, and sketches of patriot and martyr. The genesis of war, the invention of kingship, and the glowing aspect of freedom as Cowper sets them forth during his 'Winter Morning Walk,' remind us of the conversations of Beaupuy and Wordsworth on the banks of the Loire. It was a 'terrible sagacity' that informed Cowper's heart with its contingent distrust of British statesmanship; [13] and the anger subsequently indulged by Wordsworth at his beloved country for its official hostility to the young French Republic is as honest and even more bitter. But we must remember that the loyalty and fearlessness of neither critic is in question: 'England, with all thy faults I love thee still—my country!' [14]

Toward the end of *The Task* Cowper permitted himself an apocalypse in the vein of Isaiah, replete with metaphors from the Old Testament. This, Wordsworth would naturally discount; but he would not overlook Cowper's brief summary:

> Thus heav'n-ward all things tend. For all were once
> Perfect, and all must be at length restor'd.

Such belief and the word itself, 'restor'd,' undergird and overspan Books XI and XII of *The Prelude*, 'Imagination, How Impaired

[13] *Table Talk*, 494–5; 'The Winter Morning Walk' 491–511.

[14] 'The Time-piece' 206–7.

and Restored.' The happy man with whom Cowper concludes his poem not only bequeathed certain traits to Wordsworth's *Character of the Happy Warrior;* as one whose 'warfare is within' he is progenitor of Wordsworth's Poet. Therefore, when we look forward with him to 'the renovation of a faded world' where all shall 'flush into variety again,' we seem to see that 'gentler spring' of Wordsworth and Dorothy and their new earth 'budding' with the 'gifts of more refined humanity.' This it is to justify a literary inheritance.

Cowper had prefigured a poet of redemptive power,

> A soul exalted above earth, a mind
> Skill'd in the characters that form mankind; . . .
> An eye . . . to catch the distant goal,
> Or ere the wheels of verse begin to roll;
> . . . to shed illuminating rays
> On ev'ry scene and subject it surveys:
> Thus grac'd, the man asserts a poet's name,
> And the world cheerfully admits the claim.

He had even warmed his sketch with traits characteristic of Wordsworth:

> 'T were new indeed to see a bard all fire,
> Touch'd with a coal from heav'n, assume the lyre,
> And tell the world, still kindling as he sung,
> With more than mortal music on his tongue,
> That He, who died below, and reigns above,
> Inspires the song, and that his name is love.[15]

Yet Cowper's connotation of 'love,' as of 'charity,' and the theological preconceptions under which he labored and suffered were of little help in erecting the theory of 'intellectual love' which gives *The Prelude* its propulsive strength. And his 'bard all fire' would not have bethought him to write the autobiography of a poet. Wordsworth's genius, moreover, could ill support the ample expostulation that overburdens the poetry of Cowper. He would

[15] *Table Talk* 704–5, 734–9.

give his strength rather to the dynamic concerns of the poetic life—witness not only his *Happy Warrior* and his *Poems . . . to National Independence and Liberty*, but his *Convention of Cintra*, and some years later those *Ecclesiastical Sonnets*, which set forth in all the vigor of thought and feeling not only the polity but also the action of the Universal Church.

One Society Alone

Before we decide that *The Prelude* is more a universal human *character* than a professional monodrama, we should search out the principle of cohesion that gives social aptitude and responsibility to the poet to be charactered. Without benefit of liturgical communion or civil contract or even professional devotion, is a society possible? Can a natural man among natural men still participate in the one great society alone of the noble living and the noble dead? What assumption underlies Wordsworth's autobiographical poem to give it truth and value as a picture of desirable human life?

In the Alfoxden Notebook, which dates from January of 1798 and reveals Wordsworth a student of Boswell's *Life of Johnson*, the poetic content is a premature series of *characters*, not yet in narrative or dramatic relationship: the Old Cumberland Beggar, the Discharged Soldier, the Wanderer. Already these have taken on a sobriety, or identity, to distinguish them somewhat from those types dear to the eighteenth century, whose views of Man and Society are shadowed in a long series of trueborn Englishmen, careless husbands, recruiting officers, intriguing chambermaids, busybodies, distressed mothers, Spartan dames, gentle shepherds, female Quixotes and fools of quality, travellers and men of the world, to the man of feeling himself.[16] Wordsworth, as we know, had renounced satire, nor did he possess the comic genius to gather his persons into some new Liberty Hall with a

[16] The abortive *Philanthropist* of Wordsworth and Mathews and the short-lived *Watchman* and *Friend* of Samuel Taylor Coleridge further illustrate this inveterate literary cult in England of the eighteenth and early nineteenth century.

more substantial Squire Hardcastle or under the elbow of some less fatuous kinswoman of Mrs. Malaprop. On the other hand, a young poet who had discovered the literary value of balladry would not revive the somber agents of *The Borderers* or the lugubrious victims of *Guilt and Sorrow* for his picture of the folks under his own eyes, the beggars, soldiers, and wanderers, the forlorn maidens and anxious mothers of Somersetshire. Was there still another method of social portraiture?

Such *coups d'oeil* as Thomson's *Liberty* and Goldsmith's *Citizen of the World* or *Deserted Village*—not to mention the poetry and prose radiating from doctrinal assumptions of Rousseau—would serve him only as a point of departure from the literature of a period dealing sentimentally rather than compassionately with the outlines of human endeavor and mistake. Operating still, as did his predecessors, under the shadow of Volney's *Les Ruines*, he had written a poem, of which Coleridge thought well, to deepen and intensify ethical and social themes; but *The Ruined Cottage*, focal picture of Nature, Man, and Society, was too subservient to its artificial plot, too entangled in circumstantial event to do aught but father the maxims of the Pedlar-Wanderer. What, then, was the proper society for a man among men? And what was the proper way to set it forth?

Befitting his personal experience with nature, there was, indeed, a social tradition which had prepossessed him ever since 1793, when he wrote of the 'pastoral Swiss' in his *Descriptive Sketches* (526–9).

> As Man in his primaeval dower array'd
> The image of his glorious sire display'd,
> Ev'n so, by vestal Nature guarded, here
> The traces of primaeval Man appear.[17]

To this very myth of the Golden Age he would now return in *The Prelude*, with encouraging memories of that Michel Beaupuy

[17] Wordsworth relates his interest in the myth of a Golden Age to M. Ramond's account of such a tradition among the Swiss (*Poetical Works*, Vol. 1, p. 70).

who loved 'Man . . . as Man,' and whose dearest theme was (IX, 360–9)

> Man and his noble nature, as it is
> The gift of God and lies in his own power.

'Primaeval Man' guarded by 'vestal Nature': this myth dear to Boethius and Chaucer, and cleared of its absurdities as a historical or sociological statement, became the desired social objective of his autobiographical poem. Although the boy Wordsworth is scarcely doomed, as was 'the pastoral Swiss,' 'to pant slow up the endless Alps of life,' he will be a vertical man with prior and higher relationships; thus he will differ from the horizontal man of history and the central or focal man of philosophy. His scholarship and his art of education, like his art of poetry, will be servile neither to events nor concepts; they will have regard mainly to beloved persons and to intense feelings of worship and kindness. Men and women as sons and daughters of the glorious Sire would be of Earth's best blood; however prodigal, they had prior rights. He would choose one of them, the shepherd, as an index of society; and pastoral life, actual and metaphorical, would substantiate his interpretation of the Poet as a social being.

Next, what mode of composition might best accord with this congenial myth? As an idyllist Wordsworth would not delineate social man by striking a circumstantial average or inducing a nonexistent type; he would not, as does the dramatist, choose a representative hero; rather through his affections he would elicit man from his origin in God and his surroundings in nature, and hence accredit each, man and nature, with the vital powers of their Creator. Trusting to that 'most wise passiveness in which the heart lies open and is well content to feel as nature feels,' [18] he emphasized those traits of his poem which, in spite of its epic passages, would preserve it as a *character* or idyl.

The value of the old myth for his social purposes in the poem on his own early life seems not at first evident to him. In the

[18] Alfoxden Notebook.

Lines . . . on the Wye, though the 'farms' and 'landscape' are 'pastoral,' the 'still, sad music of humanity' has no pattern, suggests no frame of reference. And in MS JJ of *The Prelude* there is no social metaphor, except that his mention of 'the Shepherd's hut,' 'the Churchyard,' 'the Village School,' 'a man' and 'his horse,' 'shepherds' on some 'high promontory,' implies a very simple pastoral or rural scene.

But into MS V literary and cultural reminiscence has to some extent made its way: the 'naked Savage' on 'Indian plains'; 'coward tongues' in the 'haunts of men' and 'the mean and vulgar works of Man' in a neglectful and ungrateful 'world'; the courtly personages in the pack of playing cards, the 'Gibbet-mast' betokening the courts of justice, 'gleams like the flashing' of a chivalric 'shield,' and bereavement at Christmastide demanding the funeral ceremony of the Church; the structures of society from 'lowly cottages' and grotesque and beautiful 'old Hall' to the 'holy scene' of a 'sequester'd ruin'; 'signboard' of 'rustic painter,' 'bowling-green' and boyish pastimes and minstrelsy, 'rustic dinners' and 'festive banquet'; 'Sabine fare' and 'a more than Roman confidence'; 'Science' as a mere 'succedaneum' and 'solitude more active, even, than "best society" '; the 'tragic facts of rural history'; 'hermit' and 'inn-keeper.' As yet, however, in 1800, these are the 'incidental charms' of a poem socially imperceptive, even immature, aggregated in the service of an action which itself scarcely coheres.

In Book III, composed sometime between 1800 and 1804, society is tentatively set forth as an academic dream: 'motley spectacle' and 'novel show,' 'pageant,' 'Cabinet or wide Museum' or 'gaudy Congress.' Its 'companionships, friendships, acquaintances,' served mainly to deepen the collegian's nostalgia for the 'one Presence,' and 'things view'd by . . . earth's first inhabitants.' He pays his loyal tribute to the 'generations of illustrious Men,' and his respects to the 'congregating temper'; but from the follies and false-seeming of the campus he appeals to the 'Shepherd' and his 'Flock' as an example of the right method of teaching, and refers to the 'Virgin grove, primaeval in its purity and depth' as the right 'habitation . . . for ruminating creatures.' The abstemious life of olden Doctors, 'spare diet, patient labour, and plain weeds' are recommended; but the shepherd on the promontory who 'rather makes than finds what he beholds' brings most comfort to the homesick dreamer; and the 'Shepherd Swains' of his native hills confront the grave 'unscour'd' Elders of the campus to the great disadvantage of the latter.

Somewhat later, in MS W (1804), it was again his nostalgia for the Golden Age that helped him with the account of his freshman vacation at Hawkshead:

That summer was not seldom interspersed
With primitive hours when . . .
. . . I recognized within myself
Conformity as just as that of old
To the end and written spirit of God's works,
Whether held forth in Nature or in Man.

Against this 'view' of Society as a 'soul divine which we participate,' Milton's 'conformity divine,' another theme in another myth enters MS W, and even as Wordsworth advances to illustrate 'imagination,' his new name for the 'holy indolence' and 'wise passiveness' of 1798, the primal condition of power and benevolence, he must take stock again of the foes of the imagination as they shine through his own errors and through disasters clouding the career of Coleridge; he must make way in his poem for the Fall of Man.

Noting that he now consciously establishes 'the analogy betwixt the mind of man and nature,' those siblings of the Golden Age, we watch the interaction of the two social myths with renewed interest. Moon over Snowdon and Rainbow over Coniston help him to illustrate the benevolent power; Columbus, Humphrey Gilbert, Mungo Park, William Dampier and his Malayan companion do not help him to illustrate it and are excised; the Lamb and the Lamb's mother suggest it, but imagination is a higher love. It can be warred against, perverted, misemployed; yet Nature protects it. Dorothy, and William at Esthwaite and in the Alps—recall the pastoral Swiss—yes, they illustrate it. They are the primeval woman and man. Dorothy is 'Nature's inmate'; William stands 'in Nature's presence a meditative and creative soul.' Whatever it is that transmutes scenes, men, societies, into something 'more permanent' ('holy indolence' or 'wise passiveness' or 'imagination' or 'intellectual love' or 'higher love,' not yet *caritas* indeed) the poet owes it in large part to the myth of a Golden Age. The Fall of Man will yield in importance to the prior and more significant theme.

MS W, probably intended as a sketch for the final book of a *Prelude* in five books, had to maintain the primacy of its Golden Age in competition also with the ecclesiastical pageantry of MS X and the liturgical communion of MS Y; but primal Man guarded by vestal Nature won out in the poetic economy of the finished MSS AB of 1805–6. Wordsworth never forgot that he had been part of 'the sweetness of a common dawn,' that 'vows' had been made for him, that he and Nature were alike descended and alike endowed. The Shepherds were the men who pleased Wordsworth first and last, and such sweet life as he glimpsed 'from the melancholy Walls of Goslar, once Imperial,' was destined from 1798–9 to 1805–6 to serve as the most fruitful symbol of Society in *The Prelude*. What gives the autobiographical poem its distinctive social quality is its pre-Christian myth.

XIV

The Prelude: What Is It For?

THE WAY in which the mind of Wordsworth dealt with what he called 'the great Nature that exists in works of mighty Poets' (V, 618–19) needs little further illustration or comment to shape it into a theory of poetry that is also a right theory of scholarship, and hence a right theory of education. Moreover, if we grant that intellectual love be indeed general and operative, from our acknowledgment of imagination as a principle will come the right theory of criticism.

Implicit in this book and explicit in the titles of its chapters can be read another old assumption: man's slowly maturing idea of and respect for himself as a creator follows the course of human life in all areas of personal conduct and civic responsibility. His works cannot be judged apart from the way in which he keeps faith. Among poetics, ethics, and politics there is a sisterhood of knowledge for the very reason that all of them record the exercise by sensitive beings, creative souls, of the same kind of power, intellectual, loving, and greatly purposive. It remains for us, then, as our final task of interpretation, to acknowledge such kinship in answer to the question, 'What is *The Prelude* for?'

Even as we elicit from the substance of Wordsworth's poetry what we think to be its inner form, or grow shrewd about the multitudinous associations of its outer form, we must come to grips with the problem of function. What is the 'natural,' 'proper,' or 'characteristic' action of the poem? Its author states conclusively that he will teach men how to love what he has loved. In scores of explicit passages throughout the poem he has set forth the nature of love and the procedure of loving. Love of Nature, all varieties of human love, love intellectual or spiritual or religious, however named, radiate from this discipline of a poet's mind as contagiously as joy and sorrow, laughter and tears, spring from the human heart by which we live. What is avowedly an art of love takes form as a 'Song . . . centring all in love' (XIII, 380–5). What is *The Prelude* for? It is for learning to love and for singing of love.

But *The Prelude* has a further use; it is a testimony and a judgment and a vision (XII, 367–79):

> *The mind is to herself*
> *Witness and judge, and I remember well*
> *That in life's every-day appearances*
> *I seem'd about this period to have sight*
> *Of a new world, a world, too, that was fit*
> *To be transmitted and made visible*
> *To other eyes,* as having for its base
> That whence our dignity originates,
> That which both gives it being and maintains
> A balance, an ennobling interchange
> Of action from within and from without,
> The excellence, pure spirit, and best power
> Both of the object seen, and eye that sees.

The mind as witness of 'every-day appearances' will make many pictures of what it sees, idyls whose candid or obscure photography profits and delights a reader grateful for the chance to recognize what has been or is. And the mind as judge is a critical mind; its vision within what it sees of a new world fit to be transmitted gives rise to the critical action. Such sights might be. Thus scholars and critics are also poets, whose writing, like that of Wordsworth, may become a Spenserian 'faire mirrhour' or a Miltonic justification.

A revision made in MS D at some time between 1828 and 1839 [1] substitutes for the word 'base' in the passage quoted the phrase 'those fixed laws,' and for 'pure spirit' the words 'pure function.' This warrants a final reference to certain critical theories of Plato and Aristotle. The premise of fixed laws in a world fit to be transmitted may well take us to the *Laws* and the interest in function send us to the *Poetics*. We shall also refer briefly to those other three powerful thinkers, students of the late Renaissance, whose imaginative prose is tesselated with quotations from classical theory: not only John Milton, but Francis Bacon and Thomas Browne. Bacon was known to and revered by young William Wordsworth at Hawkshead, and better known to him later when, with Browne, he gave authority to many of the positions taken by the poet ever more consciously in the service of learning and religion. Browne he valued highly 'as a most original author,' and Bacon he considered 'one of the greatest Writers that our Country has produced.' [2] To their prose, as to the writings of Plato and Aristotle before them, his poetry owes somewhat of its wisdom and virtue.

Nevertheless, by our invocation of Bacon's *philosophia prima* we shall not be released from further specific answers to the question asked. Reading in the Preface to *The Excursion* about *The Prelude* as a record in verse of 'the origin and progress of his own powers' as far as he was acquainted with them, we learn that it is also the record of an 'investigation' made by him, 'a review of his own mind.' More particularly he called it a 'preparation' for a 'literary Work that might live.' Thinking of it as a record, an

[1] de Selincourt, p. xix.

[2] *Later Years,* pp. 1203, 1317: letters of April 8, 1844, and May 20, 1848.

investigation, and a review, all of them quasi-scientific modes of research, we might be tempted to say that *The Prelude* is a scientific document, were we not reminded of its propaedeutic relation to something about to live, a work of literature.

What neat term have we for a poem that prepared Wordsworth and prepares us to live the poetic life and to do the poetic deed? 'Didactic' and 'homiletic' are adjectives associated with teaching and preaching of a less delightful kind. 'Propaedeutic,' while precise, is not endearing. Proem? If the English word better translated Plato's term προοίμιον, 'proem' would most closely fit *The Prelude*. Yet we need quibble no further about terms; in Plato's *Laws* we find the best answer to our prior question, What is *The Prelude* for?

Plato's προοίμιον and Wordsworth's Prelude

It was little more than dawn when we began talking about laws, and now it is high noon, and here we are in this entrancing resting-place; all the time we have been talking of nothing but laws, yet it is only recently that we have begun, as it seems, to utter laws, and what went before was all simply preludes to laws. What is my object in saying this? It is to explain that all utterances and vocal expressions have preludes and tunings-up (as one might call them), which provide a kind of artistic preparation which assists towards the further development of the subject. Indeed, we have examples before us of preludes, admirably elaborated, in those prefixed to that class of lyric ode called the 'nome' and to musical compositions of every description. But for the 'nomes' which are real 'nomes'—and which we designate 'political'—no one has ever yet uttered a prelude, or composed or published one, just as though there were no such thing. . . . *To ensure that the person to whom the lawgiver addresses the law should accept the prescription quietly—and, because quietly, in a docile spirit,—that, as I supposed, was the evident object with which the speaker uttered all his persuasive discourse.* Hence, according to my argument, the right term for it would be, not legal 'statement,' but 'prelude,' and no other word.[3]

[3] Plato, *Laws* IV, 722–3, ed. by R. G. Bury, Loeb Classical Library, William Heinemann Ltd., London, G. P. Putnam's Sons, New York, 1926, Vol. 1, pp. 315, 317.

If such a prelude serve to ensure quiet and docile acceptance of the laws of education, Wordsworth's *Prelude* runs true to form.

Had Wordsworth read Plato's *Laws?* Since 1918, when Lane Cooper set forth what had been learned about the poet's knowledge of the works of Plato to date,[4] H. E. Cookson has announced his ownership of Thomas Taylor's translation of the *Cratylus, Phaedo, Parmenides,* and *Timaeus* with Wordsworth's autograph on the title-page, and marginal notes by Samuel Taylor Coleridge.[5] Moreover, Frederick E. Pierce has given evidence for Wordsworth's probable knowledge of Taylor's *Works of Plato,* in five volumes, published in London in 1804.[6] But there is no reference to the *Laws* in Wordsworth's correspondence; nor has Professor Havens been able in his Index for *The Mind of a Poet* to support with particular citations his five allusions to the Platonism of *The Prelude.* Here, then, is one point at which recourse to Coleridge's scholarship should be helpful; but Coleridge himself [7] was seemingly little concerned with Plato's great text on education.

Even were the many instances of agreement between the *Laws* and *The Prelude* fortuitous,[8] or arrived at without benefit of

[4] *Modern Language Notes* 33 (December, 1918), 497–9.

[5] *London Times Literary Supplement* for November 25, 1926. Coleridge read the *Parmenides* and *Timaeus* in the winter of 1801–2 (letter to W. Sotheby in *Letters of Samuel Taylor Coleridge,* Vol. 1, p. 406), and Wordsworth's book with the annotations by Coleridge was put up for sale as lot 408 of Wordsworth's library (*Transactions of the Wordsworth Society,* No. 6, p. 234).

[6] *Philological Quarterly* 7 (1928), 60–4.

[7] The Gutch Notebook, his correspondence, even that treatise in which he attempted to reconcile the positions of Plato and Bacon, and those manuscripts toward a Theory of Method (cf. Alice D. Snyder, *Coleridge on Logic and Learning,* Yale University Press, 1929, and *S. T. Coleridge's Treatise on Method,* Constable & Co. Ltd., 1934) yield no references to the *Laws.*

[8] For Plato's pleasure and pain in the discipline of the young we have Wordsworth's 'fear and love' (XIII, 143), 'beauty and . . . fear' (I, 306). Wordsworth as 'a moral agent . . . one who was to *act,*' was conducted to the truth even by 'dislike and most offensive pain' (VIII, 667–76); he approves his 'early intercourse, in presence of sublime and lovely forms, with the adverse principles of pain and joy' (XIII, 145–9). These passages read like a summary adaptation of Book II of the *Laws.* The deluge of Plato's Book III and his surviving hill shepherds have an analogue in Book V of *The Prelude;* both texts employ for educational theory the metaphor of growth; nor should we neglect to compare both for the part played by gymnastic in education, nor the contribution of the Muses and Apollo

Coleridge or theorists preceding him in the line of Quintilian, the association of songs and laws for good or ill might have been suggested to Wordsworth by his reading of Milton's *Tractate of Education*, and, in it, Milton's reference to the *Laws* of Plato.[9] Also Milton's summary paragraph from *The Reason of Church-Government* should be quoted here as likely help in the growth of the mind of a poet:

> In the publishing of human laws (which for the most part aim not beyond the good of civil society) to set them barely forth to the people, without reason or preface, like a physical prescript, or only with threatenings, as it were a lordly command, in the judgment of Plato was thought to be done neither generously nor wisely. His advice was, seeing that persuasion certainly is a more winning and more manlike way to keep men in obedience than fear, that, to such laws as were of principal moment, there should be used as an induction some well-tempered discourse, showing how good, how gainful, how happy it must needs be to live according to honesty and justice [here Wordsworth would add 'intellectual love']; which, being uttered with those native colors and graces of speech as true eloquence, the daughter of virtue, can best bestow upon her mother's praises, would so incite, and in a manner, charm, the multitude into the love of that which is really good as to embrace it ever after, not of custom and awe (which most men do), but of choice and purpose, with true and constant delight.[10]

Among less searching portrayals of the nature of things and the art of persuasion toward discipline and learning, we should mention the Epicurean 'honey' of Lucretius in a poem early fa-

---

to the young citizen, nor his debt to geometry and astronomy, his experience in hunting, angling, birding, horsemanship. Yet we must allow that Wordsworth has bettered Plato by giving to the poet an equal responsibility for the state to that borne by interpreters, teachers, lawgivers, and guardians, in *Laws* XII, 964.

[9] Oliver Ainsworth, *Milton on Education*, Cornell University Press, 1928, p. 344. How early Wordsworth studied Milton's prose is uncertain; on July 7, 1808, Dorothy asked DeQuincey to obtain Milton's *Prose Works* for her brother (*Middle Years*, pp. 233–4), and on June 11, [1816], William quoted the *Tractate* to John Scott (*ibid.*, p. 748).

[10] Quoted also by Ainsworth, p. 262, from *Prose Works*, ed. by J. A. St. John, Vol. 2, pp. 439–40. Cf. Irene Samuel's 'Table of Milton's References to Socrates and Plato,' in *Plato and Milton*, Cornell University Press, 1947, pp. 22–5.

miliar to Wordsworth: 'sed veluti pueris absinthia taetra medentes cum dare conantur, prius oras poculum circum contingunt mellis dulci flavoque liquore, ut puerorum aetas inprovida ludificetur labrorum tenus, interea perpotet amarum absinthi laticem deceptaque non capiatur, sed potius tali pacto recreata valescat.' [11] This is a signal instance of the Lucretian 'power of illustration,' which Wordsworth valued highly, more highly than the Lucretian 'system, which is nothing.' [12] He employed Lucretius' simile for the same purpose in *The Prelude*, in his address to Theocritus, whom he hears tell (X, 1022–8)

> how bees with honey fed
> Divine Comates, by his tyrant lord
> Within a chest imprison'd impiously[,]
> How with their honey from the fields they came
> And fed him there, alive, from month to month,
> Because the Goatherd, blessed Man! had lips
> Wet with the Muses' Nectar.

A revision of MS A goes on to relate these 'fancied images' and cheering 'thoughts' to the educational process,

> Teaching our souls to flow, though by a rough
> And bitter world surrounded, as, unting'd
> With aught injurious to her native freshness,
> Flowed Arethusa under briny waves
> Of the Sicilian sea.

Such comfort he prays for Coleridge in Sicily,

> A Conqueror wresting from the dwindled earth
> And from the invaded heavens, capacious thoughts

[11] *De rerum natura* I, 936–42, in the Loeb Classical Library, translated by W. H. D. Rouse as follows: 'but as with children, when physicians try to administer rank wormwood, they first touch the rims about the cups with the sweet yellow fluid of honey, that unthinking childhood be deluded as far as the lips, and meanwhile that they may drink up the bitter juice of wormwood, and though beguiled be not betrayed, but rather by such means be restored and regain health.' Quoted with the permission of G. P. Putnam's Sons, New York, agents for William Heinemann Ltd., London.

[12] Lienemann, *Die Belesenheit von William Wordsworth*, p. 224.

Far-stretching views, magnificent designs
Worthy of Poets, who attuned their Harps
. . . for discipline
Of Heroes, and in reverence to the Gods.[13]

Granted the likelihood that the young classical student who quoted Lucretius readily at the front of his *Descriptive Sketches* of 1793 knew the poem *De rerum natura* and the eclogues of Theocritus better than Plato's prose, and may not have read the *Laws*, we shall here go on to ask whether there would in time come to be a Wordsworthian system of learning, 'capacious thoughts, far-stretching views, magnificent designs,' to accompany the 'honey' of poetic life, Wordsworthian laws to follow upon the 'tunings-up' of the harp in *The Prelude?* The answer is found in those 'views of Nature, Man, and Society' which in 1798 were to constitute his *Recluse*, and which in 1814 he knew better than to announce formally as 'a system.' When the views of *The Recluse* had been abandoned or postponed for the quasi-Platonic dialogue of *The Excursion*, he wrote for Books V–IX of that poem something comparable with the arguments of Plato's Lacedemonian, Cretan, and Athenian in the *Laws*. The mature discussion of different ages, dispositions, callings, and responsibilities of men and women in 'a large and populous vale' not unlike Plato's Cretan colony, and the long passage, not used in its entirety for Book V, retracing human life 'from morn to eve,' do not prove literary inheritance from Plato. Nevertheless, there is literary analogy in Wordsworth's development of his old Pedlar into a sententious Wanderer who engages his auditors, the Solitary and the Poet, and his friend, the Pastor, in the discussion of many doctrines earlier set forth in Plato's dialogue. They are convinced of 'the hollowness of all national grandeur if unsupported by moral worth'; they assert that 'an active principle pervades the Universe'; they wish earnestly 'for a System of National Education established universally by Government.' This is not more tedious in *The Excursion* than in the *Laws*. The poem Keats so much admired has affiliations of a sort little enjoyed by readers without

[13] de Selincourt, p. 420.

Wordsworth's knowledge of classical literature or Keats's interest in it.

What is often loosely spoken of as Wordsworth's Platonism—an influence as yet studied in a very small group of his poems, the great *Ode* in chief—has something in common with the meditations of Sir Thomas Browne. In the *Religio Medici* let us consider a few passages likely to catch the eye of an autobiographer setting forth a kind of Religio Poetae: 'I am . . . of the same belief our Saviour taught, . . . but . . . so decayed, *impaired*, and fallen from its native beauty, that it required the careful and charitable hand of these times to *restore* it to its primitive integrity.' [14] The 'times,' it would seem, must always face a task of restoring what has been impaired. And when, in one of his references to Plato and the 'Hermetical Philosophers' Browne insists that 'the severe schools shall never laugh me out of the philosophy of Hermes, that this visible world is but a picture of the invisible, wherein as in a portrait, things are not truly, but in equivocal shapes, and as they counterfeit some more real substance in that invisible fabrick,' [15] we recognize him as another contributor to the last paragraph of *The Prelude*. Underlying Wordsworth's passage, which represents the mind of man exalted 'above this frame of things, . . . of quality and fabric more divine,' there is reminiscence of Browne as well as of Plato.

Indeed, when the author of the *Religio Medici* quotes the Socratic Γνῶθι σεαυτόν as 'the greatest knowledge in man,' Wordsworth would find added reassurance for his autobiographical poem. Browne's 'cosmography of myself,' his conviction that 'the soul of man may be in heaven anywhere, even within the limits of his own proper body,' point him out as one of the forerunners of the author of *The Prelude*. 'For my life,' he says in phrases which his readers know by heart, 'it is a miracle of thirty years, which to relate, were not a history but a piece of poetry, and would sound to common ears like a fable. . . . The world

[14] *Religio Medici*, ed. by John Peace, London, 1844, p. 2.
[15] *Ibid.*, p. 20.

that I regard is myself, it is the microcosm of my own frame that I cast my eye on' [16]—harmony of a distinguished sort between the *Religio Medici* and Wordsworth's Religio Poetae. Browne's metaphors serve not only for the Prospectus of 'Home at Grasmere,' where 'the Mind of Man' will be the 'main region' of Wordsworth's song, but also for the initial conception of a poem located in the mind of one man, William Wordsworth. *The Prelude*, we may say in Browne's words, is for living 'in heaven anywhere,' a way of worship.

Bacon and Wordsworth; 'Georgics of the Mind'

We have already answered our question about *The Prelude* by noting its functions as an art of loving, a testimony for critics, the delightfully persuasive introduction to an educational discipline, even as a form of worship. Next let us consider it as an invitation to learning and a revelation of truth.

Writing to Southey on July 29, 1802, after many months of association with Wordsworth, Coleridge approved of the new additions to the Preface to *Lyrical Ballads* as follows: 'There is . . . one on the dignity and nature of the office and character of a Poet, that is very grand, and of a sort of Verulamian power and majesty.' [17] Has Bacon, then, a substantial part in the famous passage beginning 'What is a Poet?' Or is Coleridge referring to style alone?

We may assume that the qualified approval Coleridge expressed to Southey he had previously given as counsel to Wordsworth when the Preface was undergoing revision. And we may allow that for the powerful and majestic passage in the revised Preface, Wordsworth had the best of models in the 'Verulamian' flights of the *Advancement of Learning*. Where Bacon exemplifies his own *philosophia prima*, or refers to the Pauline *caritas* in words foreshadowing the 'intellectual love' or the 'esemplastic power' of his

[16] *Ibid.*, pp. 21, 26, 89, 137.
[17] *Letters*, Vol. 1, p. 387.

students in Grasmere, his prose approximates their most inspired verse.

Moreover, both Wordsworth and Coleridge, like the great instaurator, were engaged in 'an experiment': Bacon to raise or rebuild the sciences, art, and all human knowledge from a firm and solid basis; Coleridge toward an encyclopedia; Wordsworth, more humbly in his Preface and *Lyrical Ballads*, to ascertain the true relation between the real language of men in a state of vivid sensation, and poetic pleasure. Although he modestly disclaims the 'systematic' defense of a theory, with Bacon he shares a disapproval of the first distemper of learning, Bacon's 'vain affectations,' or 'luxuriance of style,' 'when men study words and not matter.' In his own art he objects to 'poetic diction' or 'falsehood of description.' Again, as one intending in future years to make verse deal boldly with substantial things, in 1800 he has deprecated, with italics, 'contemptible' '*matter*'; witness his reference in the Preface to Dr. Johnson's parody, 'I put my hat upon my head,' etc. 'This wants sense,' he says; and thus he agrees with Bacon that 'vanity in matter is worse than vanity in words,' the second distemper of learning. Bacon's third distemper as it gives rise to 'credulity in arts and opinions,' whether this be 'too much belief to arts themselves, or to certain authors in any arts,' has been dealt with by Wordsworth in 1800 as a warning against complete acceptance of 'the present state of the public taste.' He would approve Bacon's rebuke to writers who are averse 'to treat of trite and vulgar matters'; and he would agree with Bacon's counsel to dwell longer upon discovering 'the roots and fibres of good and evil.' Has he not himself advised, in 1800, the unostentatious tracing of 'the primary laws of our nature,' and hoped for 'a class of Poetry . . . not unimportant in the quality, and in the multiplicity of its moral relations'? This substantial agreement of two great writers with two centuries between them underlines the fundamentals of all good writing, of all good thinking.

As if he would profit by Bacon's insistence on 'the pleasure and delight of knowledge and learning,' he calls the pleasure produced by the poet's art 'an acknowledgment of the beauty of the universe'; and his flight, called by Coleridge 'Verulamian,' continues as follows:

> We have no knowledge, that is no general principles drawn from the contemplation of particular facts, but what has been built up by pleasure, and exists in us by pleasure alone. . . . Prompted by this feeling of pleasure, which accompanies him through the whole course of his studies, the Poet . . . converses with general nature, with affections akin to those, which, through labour and length of time, the Man of Science has raised up in himself, by conversing with those particular parts of nature which are the objects of his studies. . . . The knowledge both of the Poet and the Man of Science is pleasure.

Then he writes the well-known differential; but even in contrasting these two knowledges, the scientific and the poetic, Wordsworth has been paced by his aphoristic predecessor. Says Bacon in Book III, 'Poetry is, as it were, the stream of knowledge'; says Wordsworth, with a change in metaphor, 'Poetry is the breath and finer spirit of all knowledge; it is the impassioned expression which is in the countenance of all Science.' 'To conclude,' says Bacon, 'the dignity of knowledge and learning are what human nature most aspires to for the securing of immortality.' Says Wordsworth, 'Poetry . . . is as immortal as the heart of man.' Contemporary with the Shakespearean mirror held up to Nature, Bacon's mind of a prudent man is like 'water, or a mirror, which receives the forms and images of things.' Somewhat like, but also somewhat unlike, both of these in the long line of literary mirrors, Wordsworth's 'mind of man [is] naturally the mirror *of the fairest and most interesting qualities of nature*': 'Poetry is the image of man and nature.'

And what is the function of poetry in the view of Francis of Verulam? As to its nature, it is no more than 'feigned history or fable'; as to its effect, 'it gives that to mankind which history denies, and in some measure satisfies the mind with shadows when it cannot enjoy the substance.' Bacon's 'shadows' instead of 'substance' become in Wordsworth's Preface 'certain shadows' of the passions of real life, shadows 'which the Poet . . . produces, or feels to be produced, in himself.'

And, in chief, Wordsworth's concern throughout his description of the Poet as following the steps of the Man of Science, 'at his side' and 'carrying sensation into the midst of the objects of the science itself,' may be profitably compared with Bacon's concern to divide those objects of science into their proper fields, Natural History, Natural Philosophy, and the knowledge of 'man himself.' The subdivisions of Natural History (including the History of the Heavens, the History of Meteors, the History of the Earth and Sea, the History of Massive or Collective Bodies, and the History of Species), Physics and Metaphysics as the Speculative Branch of Natural Philosophy, and 'The Great Appendix of Natural Philosophy' (Mathematics), reappear in Wordsworth's phrases as 'astronomer,' 'mineralogist,' 'mariner,' 'chemist,' 'physician,' 'botanist,' 'natural philosopher,' and 'mathematician,' with 'lawyer,' 'biographer,' 'historian,' to represent Bacon's Civil History, and 'Poet' to represent Bacon's Poetry, and a reference to Aristotle (poetry as 'the most philosophical of all writing') to pay honor to Metaphysics. Metaphysics itself Bacon subordinates to *Philosophia prima*, 'the Mother of all the Sciences'; and he unifies his knowledges under the figure of growth, 'rather like the branches of trees that join in one trunk.' Wordsworth's Nature in her fostering relation to the growth of the poet's mind is a collateral Mother of all the Arts, dimly visible in the passage 'What is a Poet?' but clearly announced in the contemporary MS V of *The Prelude.*

Assuming the 'Verulamian' passage, 'What is a Poet?' to be one main articulation between MS V and later manuscripts of the autobiographical poem, we may next watch Wordsworth advancing to his doctrine of 'intellectual love' in the affairs of men much as Bacon advanced from Natural History and Natural Philosophy to Civil History and Civil Philosophy with the recognition at the end of his great Seventh Book that charity 'ties up and fastens all the virtues together'—the most likely source next to I Corinthians

13 for Wordsworth's delineation of the Poet: carrying 'everywhere with him relationship and love'; binding 'together by passion and knowledge the vast empire of human society, as it is spread over the whole earth, and over all time.' [18]

When, in Book VIII of *The Prelude*, Wordsworth went on from 'Love of Nature' to 'Love of Mankind' in a 'Retrospect' made from the high point of his own loyal devotion to Nature, he may well have recalled the advance of Bacon's argument and its ultimate concern with the study of Man, chiefly the fruitful discussion of 'the Georgics of the Mind.' As a boy of fourteen years, the poet had been aware of the might of 'Bacon's name'; [19] at the age of thirty-four, while he was enlarging his MS V, 'boyish pleasures,' into an account of the growth and discipline of a poet's mind, his thought would be amply profited and his images richly colored by a review of Bacon's Georgics. That such influence had its due part in *The Prelude* we may infer from a letter written by Dorothy to Mrs. Clarkson at Christmas, 1805. In it she sends William's recommendation of Bacon's *Essays* and *Advancement of Learning*.[20] During or directly following the months when *The Prelude* underwent its final organization, Bacon was freshly in the mind of the autobiographer, Wordsworth.

Internal evidence for this assumption comes not only from the importance of that outline of action, Nature to Mankind, shared by Bacon and Wordsworth, but from the fact that Wordsworth's *Prelude* is an answer to Bacon's prayer. 'At present,' says Bacon, 'few have any great regard to *the cultivation and discipline of the mind* and a regular course of life.' Speaking of those 'characters [i.e., character-sketches] of natures [i.e., dispositions] commonly drawn with excess by 'poets of all kinds,' 'and exceeding the limits of nature,' he asks for

[18] Wordsworth owned a 1623 quarto of the *Two Books of the Proficience and Advancement of Learning* (*Transactions of the Wordsworth Society*, No. 6, p. 228), and the edition of his friend Basil Montagu (*Later Years*, pp. 248, 266).

[19] *Poetical Works*, Vol. 1, p. 260.

[20] *Early Letters*, p. 559.

> an accurate and full treatise . . . upon this fertile and copious subject, . . . outlines, and first draughts, . . . so that artificial and accurate dissection may be made of men's minds and natures, and the secret disposition of each particular laid open, that, from a knowledge of the whole, the precepts concerning the cures of the mind may be more rightly formed.[21]

Such, then, was the commission from Francis of Verulam to William Wordsworth. As Bacon's 'Posterity' in the advancement of learning, Wordsworth has his own place on 'the Coast of the Intellectual World.'

Moreover, many of the primary philosophical assumptions of Bacon's work reappear in Wordsworth's poem. The determination of the earlier writer 'to employ his utmost endeavors towards restoring or cultivating a just and legitimate familiarity betwixt the mind and things' is a scientific aim comparable with Wordsworth's establishment of intellectual love between the Poet and Nature. The 'peccant humors' of the *Advancement of Learning* receive poetical life in the mistakes of the Poet of *The Prelude*. For instance, like Wordsworth, Bacon rebukes 'too great a reverence and a kind of adoration paid to the human understanding,' and the withdrawal 'from the contemplation of nature and experience' to sport 'with their own reason and the fictions of fancy'; and he would repair the 'mistaking the ultimate end of knowledge' by 'the more intimate and strict conjunction of contemplation and action.' Again, in the Proemium to *The Great Instauration*, Bacon 'thought all trial should be made, whether [the] commerce between the mind of man and the nature of things . . . might by any means be restored to its perfect and original condition, or if that may not be, yet reduced to a better condition than that in which it now is.' This is a substantial prototype for Wordsworth's thesis in his Books on impairment and restoration.

In the *Advancement of Learning*, Wordsworth would have found also the formal equivalent of his own advance from *The Prelude* to *The Excursion*. Had Bacon not distinguished between

[21] *Advancement of Learning* VIII, chap. iii.

individual or 'self-good,' divided into active and passive, and 'the good of communion,' which regards society? Bacon's 'conservative' or 'passive' good and Wordsworth's 'holy indolence' of the Alfoxden Notebook are comparable; and Bacon's 'active' good reappears in Wordsworth's 'solitude, more active, even, than "best society" ' of Book II of *The Prelude.*

The story of the Wanderer's familiarity with Bacon's prose, however, is yet to be told, and elsewhere. Here we may hint that the Baconian 'good of communion,' which regards society, 'and usually goes by the name of duty,' finds illustration not only in the *Ode to Duty* but also in much of what impatient critics find burdensome in *The Excursion.* Bacon's insistence that the term 'the good of communion' be properly used, that is, of a mind well disposed toward others, helps somewhat to explain the predominantly social themes of Wordsworth's later poetry; and the titles of Wordsworth's poems in their series illustrate Bacon's 'respective duties.' *The Excursion* and *Ecclesiastical Sonnets* with their effort to reveal the characteristic goodness of Wanderer, Pastor, Disciple, Monk, Bishop, Pontiff, Schoolman, Crusader, Martyr, Teacher, Saint, Reformer, or Priest, remind us of Bacon's interest in the wide fabric of man as functioning for the commonwealth. 'Mutual duties between husband and wife, parent and child, master and servant, as also the laws of friendship, gratitude, and the civil obligations of fraternities, colleges, neighborhoods, and the like' are to be treated, 'not as parts of civil society, in which view they belong to politics, but so far as the minds of particulars ought to be instructed and disposed to preserve these bonds of society': tedious task, indeed, for any except a great writer, and not always successfully performed by the greatest.

If, in the following passage, for Bacon's word 'charity' we substitute Wordsworth's phrase 'intellectual love,' we see even more clearly the kinship between the philosophy of the *Advancement of Learning* and the 'Growth of a Poet's Mind.'

The Christian religion comes to the point by impressing charity upon the minds of men; which is most appositely called the bond of perfection, because it ties up and fastens all the virtues together. . . . So without doubt, if the mind be possessed with the fervor of true charity, he will rise to a higher degree of perfection than by all the doctrine of ethics, which is but a sophist compared to charity.

Truth General and Operative: Aristotle's οἷα ἂν γένοιτο

Behind *The Prelude* as a song, a vision, and a mode of culture—its lyric, idyllic, and georgic functions—there resides in its optative beauty a strong command, a call to action. A life like this, lived with such purpose by a man among men, and shaped so significantly, so valuably, among the common circumstances of the day, might happen to many. With a clearer view of what constitutes happiness, and the ensuing release of feelings and energies, these sensitive beings and creative souls, these proper selves, might well restore the commonweal to its rightful dignity, its proper civic self, and 'fit to be transmitted.'

Were it not that one poet has brought the fact and the truth so close together, any other honest autobiographer might be discouraged by Aristotle's distinction between what has been and what might be. Yet, out of a personal career, it seems, there can be elicited something serious rather than pompously dull or foolishly scandalous, something complete rather than inconclusive, something of a magnitude to satisfy the great-souled reader of any age or country. However short of tragic effect we must allow the operation of *The Prelude* to be, it presents us with that sort of *catharsis* most welcome to the world-weary in days when violent emotions threaten to disintegrate life as they have already corrupted its arts.

More than that, the growth and discipline of a poet's mind, artistically imitated, satisfies the Aristotelian, the timeless, principle of artistic imitation in a triple way: the means, the object, and the manner are all poetic: poetic language, the means; poetic life, the object; the autobiography of a poet, the manner. When Aristotle further divides the three objects of artistic imitation into 'things as they once were, or are now,' 'things as they are said or thought to be,' and 'things as they ought to be,' he is again illustrated by Wordsworth's fusion of all three in one poem: Wordsworth as he was; Wordsworth as he is said or thought to be in the tradition of English letters; and Wordsworth's Poet in his functional or ideal nature.

'To imitate,' says Aristotle, 'is natural in us as men'; and the reader of *The Prelude* may assist the poem to perform its function if by a *mimesis* of his own he shares in Wordsworth's action as it was and as it might be. Whatever similar disturbing emotions he has suffered, however dim his understanding of himself may have been, and however uncertain he may still be about the course of his life, such a vicarious or empathetic exercise will help him. The reader's feelings of compassion and reverence, Aristotle's pity and fear at their deepest and highest, are often balked and thwarted by untoward circumstances within and without him, old hurts and new confusions. Let him travel humbly with Wordsworth through the operative sequence of *The Prelude*, and in so doing find relief and enlightenment. The adventures and misadventures of creation in his own soul will then be seen in their right proportions, his energies will be set free for his work as a man and a citizen. He, too, will grow under discipline.

Furthermore, whatever his respective duty, as a creator, father or founder, inventor or prophet, he must undergo the same kind of discipline: when he chooses a line of action, when he generalizes, proves, or persuades, magnifies or minimizes, *The Prelude* offers him a rigorous ethical and logical pattern, Aristotle's *ethos* and *dianoia*.[22]

It is also likely that under the natural process of growth which Wordsworth predicates of his own mind, and which in this book is assumed to be his characteristic mode of composition, the reader will detect a plot, and if he be familiar with the *Poetics* of Aristotle

[22] For those interested in the devices of the poet, as set down by Aristotle, or inferred from the Aristotelian *Tractatus Coislinianus* (accessible in Lane Cooper's *An Aristotelian Theory of Comedy*, 1922, pp. 269–81), there is ample illustration to be found in *The Prelude*.

will recognize in it many of the constituents of the Aristotelian *mythos*. *The Prelude* has a beginning, a middle, and an end, he will say. The beginning, however, is not the first 271 lines, but those primal hours, 'spots of time,' in which the poet's conformity is absolute. *The Prelude* has a middle in which the dedicated Poet struggles,

> with . . . dismal sights beset
> For the outward view, and inwardly oppress'd
> With sorrow, disappointment, vexing thoughts,
> Confusion of opinion, zeal decay'd,
> And lastly, utter loss of hope itself,
> And things to hope for. *Not with these began*
> *Our Song, and not with these our Song must end.*

And *The Prelude* has an end: the praise of 'men as they are men within themselves.'

> Thus haply shall I teach,
> Inspire, through unadulterated ears
> Pour rapture, tenderness, and hope.

In the Aristotelian view, omissions or deviations from a strict chronology are not to be blamed; the reader will not expect from this poem what too often the nearsighted commentator demands, factual veracity. Nor will he assume that unity of the hero in itself gives unity of the plot. On the contrary, he will notice that the plot has been most carefully organized. It is involved, and the change in fortune from worse to better is accompanied by an intelligible reversal of situation bringing restoration and happiness in the natural and reasonable way; the change in fortune is also accompanied by a discovery, the Poet's recognition that he himself and every other human being is by nature a poet, an intellectual lover, however long or woefully the fulfilment of his destiny may be delayed.

This is the main discovery. It is reflected in all the particulars of the Poet's experience, whether from Nature's forms or the human form, that 'index of delight, of grace and honour, power and worthiness' (VIII, 413–15). The other five kinds of discovery, according to Aristotle, are again and again illustrated in *The Prelude*. Not only is the identity of the Poet hinted to him in his 'spots of time'; but through books and the counsel and help of sister and friends his high descent and wide kinship are explicitly declared. The testimony of his own feelings remembered at the instance of circumstances originally associated with them is another revelatory device, as is the use of inferential powers exerted upon Nature and Man to prove the creative principle. Even in his mistakes, whether through unintentional fallacy or sophistical deception (as in the revolutionary crisis and his surrender to a false philosophy), what he discovers to be wrong assists by its very sterility in his re-establishment as Poet. Within this fabric of tokens, declarations, memories, true and false inferences, there is of course no conscious obedience to Aristotle's poetical scheme; but as Aristotle analyzed the effective plots of his own time to discover function in form, and method in structure, so Wordsworth's practice appears to substantiate and certify an age-old theory.

Finally, Wordsworth's 'spots of time' are not only revelations of his creative destiny. With their 'fructifying,' 'vivifying,' 'renovating virtue' [23]—Wordsworth tried again and again for the right word here—they serve the emotionally relieving purpose of the Aristotelian work of art. Theirs is 'a virtue by which pleasure is enhanced.' What they do for Wordsworth, his *Prelude* does for us: it vivifies, renovates, fructifies. As much of its wisdom and beauty as we receive, we may transmit; like a symposium or communion the poem is to be shared. Not what has happened, but what might happen: οὐ τὰ γενόμενα . . . ἀλλ' οἷα ἂν γένοιτο. Against this poetic day, meanwhile, *The Prelude* will accomplish its harmony wherever its readers are shaped anew to obey the laws and do their proper deed.

[23] de Selincourt, p. 436.

Index

[This Index lists authors and, under the name of the author, works important in Wordsworth's literary biography, 1785–1805. Scholars significantly advancing our knowledge of *The Prelude* as a poem, or otherwise helpful in this study, are also named. Titles of Wordsworth's own poetical and prose works appear without mention of his authorship, and literary terms used by him or familiar to him are included. Under the entry 'Manuscripts,' the MSS of his autobiographical poem and related poems are alphabetically arranged; but the necessarily frequent references to William Wordsworth, to his sister Dorothy, to his sister's Journals, to their Letters, and to *The Prelude*, entire or in part, have been omitted from the Index.]